Praise for *Lincoln's Ladder to the Presidency*

"Packed full of fascinating history, this book is for those interested in Illinois, in Lincoln or in the art of making friends and influencing people, all the way to the Presidency of the United States of America."

—**LARRY DUNPHY,** owner of Books on First

"Guy C. Fraker's fine, detailed study of Lincoln's legal career in *Lincoln's Ladder to the Presidency: The Eighth Judicial Circuit* reveals that Lincoln, a highly respected trial lawyer, actively assumed the role of peacemaker, mediator, and settlor of lawsuits as the vagaries of his caseload demanded."

—**DENNIS J. CURRAN,** associate justice of the Massachusetts Superior Court; and **EMMA KINGDON,** Massachusetts Dispute Resolution Services

"Guy Fraker's superb book about Abraham Lincoln and the Illinois Eighth Judicial Circuit provides an effective lesson on the importance of political networking. For more than twenty years, Mr. Lincoln rode the circuit with other lawyers and judges. These were smart, influential and ambitious men. Lincoln made them his friends and, in time, they would help Mr. Lincoln climb the ladder to the presidency. Fraker's book is great history but it is also an excellent primer for aspiring politicians."

—**JIM EDGAR,** Illinois governor, 1991–1999

"It is obvious that attorney Guy Fraker has spent a lifetime examining Abraham Lincoln's extensive legal practice on the Eighth Judicial Circuit. The results are an edifying, microscopic view of Lincoln the man, politician, and lawyer. If you want to understand why and how President Lincoln became the 'lawyer in the White House,' read this book. If you want to know how Lincoln was able to maintain the support of the people, read this book. And if you wish to see and feel Lincoln's evolution to greatness, enjoy this book. No one has described the tedium of the Lincoln law practice as well as the author; his friends, enemies, and associates; as well as the people they represented are all here."

—**FRANK J. WILLIAMS,** retired chief justice of the Rhode Island Supreme Court and founding chair of The Lincoln Forum

"Guy Fraker's *Lincoln's Ladder to the Presidency* is a refreshing and revisioning portrait of Lincoln the Illinois lawyer. As a central Illinois lawyer himself, Fraker knows the Eighth Judicial Circuit better than anyone. As a Lincoln scholar, he has an eye for the revealing legal story and an ear for the interplay of Lincoln's legal and political ideas and language."
—**RONALD C. WHITE JR.**, author of *A. Lincoln: A Biography*

"Guy Fraker traverses the 'Lincoln Country' of central Illinois in this richly detailed account of Abraham Lincoln's life on the Eighth Judicial Circuit. Here he introduces the lawyers with whom Lincoln traveled or met on the circuit for over twenty years during his ever-growing practice of law, a pursuit that simultaneously gave him a network of friends who supported his political career. Drawing together both contemporary and reminiscent sources, and bringing a sense of place to each locale on the circuit, Fraker provides a comprehensive view of Lincoln's life in law and politics on the Illinois prairie."
—**JOHN HOFFMANN**, Illinois History and Lincoln Collections, University of Illinois Library at Urbana-Champaign

Lincoln's

Ladder

to the

Presidency

Lincoln's Ladder to the Presidency

The Eighth Judicial Circuit

Guy C. Fraker

With a Foreword by Michael Burlingame

Southern Illinois University Press
Carbondale

Southern Illinois University Press
www.siupress.com

Copyright © 2012, 2023 by the Board of Trustees,
Southern Illinois University
All rights reserved.
Cloth edition 2012.
Paperback edition 2023.
Printed in the United States of America

26 25 24 23   4 3 2 1

Cover illustrations: Ambrotype of Abraham Lincoln taken
by Samuel G. Alschuler, April 25, 1858 (Champaign County
Historical Archives, The Urbana Free Library, Urbana, Illinois); and *Eighth Judicial Circuit, 1847* (painting by Don
Pollack; courtesy of Perimeter Gallery, Chicago). *Frontis-
piece*: Alschuler ambrotype.

ISBN 978-0-8093-3921-1

Library of Congress Cataloging-in-Publication Data
ISBN 978-0-8093-3921-1 (paperback)
ISBN 978-0-8093-3201-4 (cloth)
ISBN 978-0-8093-3202-1 (ebook)

This book has been cataloged with the Library of Congress.

Library of Congress Control Number: 2023941970

Printed on recycled paper ♻

SIU
Southern Illinois University System

To Aunt Lola

Every man is said to have his peculiar ambition. Whether it be true or not, I can say for one that I have no other so great as that of being truly esteemed of my fellow men, by rendering myself worthy of their esteem.

—Abraham Lincoln to the people of
Sangamon County, March 9, 1832

CONTENTS

ILLUSTRATIONS

FOREWORD

Michael Burlingame

A ttorney Guy C. Fraker's entertaining, informative study of Abraham Lincoln and the Eighth Judicial Circuit is a welcome addition to the growing literature on Lincoln's career at the bar. Here readers will find not only colorful accounts of life on the circuit and sketches of his fellow circuit riders but also an insightful analysis of the ways in which the circuit experience enhanced Lincoln's political career. Writing with the insight of a veteran central Illinois attorney, the Bloomington-based author makes good use of the latest in Lincoln scholarship.

In addition, this book is also a handy travel guide for Lincolnians. Attorney Fraker conveniently arranges chapters, taking the reader along the trail that Lincoln and his colleagues traversed. *Lincoln's Ladder to the Presidency: The Eighth Judicial Circuit* thus constitutes a user-friendly Baedeker for all who are seeking Lincoln sites in central Illinois. They may want to take along a copy of the author's valuable article "The Real Lincoln Highway: The Forgotten Lincoln Circuit Markers," which appeared in the *Journal of the Abraham Lincoln Association*.[1]

Lincoln's career at the bar consisted of two distinct stages, separated by his single term in the U.S. House of Representatives. In the first phase (1837–47), he handled minor cases of debt collection, property damage, land titles, negligence, trespassing livestock, divorce, and slander, both in Springfield and on the circuit. In the 1830s and 1840s, Lincoln and other Springfield attorneys did not earn enough money by simply appearing before the Illinois State Supreme Court, the Sangamon County Circuit Court, and the Federal District Court and as justices of the peace at the state capital; economic necessity forced them to supplement their local practice by going out on the circuit during the spring and fall, when rural counties held court.

Lincoln thrived on the circuit. In an unpublished essay, Lincoln's astute friend and fellow attorney Judge John M. Scott (like Fraker, he lived in

Bloomington) observed that Lincoln "had many elements essential to the successful circuit lawyer," for he "knew much of the law as written in the books, and had that knowledge ready for use at all times. That was a valuable possession in the absence of law books, where none were obtainable on the circuit." In addition, he "knew right and justice and knew how to make their application to the affairs of every day life. That was an element in his character that gave him power to prevail with the jury when arguing a case before them. Few lawyers ever had the influence with a jury, Mr. Lincoln had." Judge Scott praised Lincoln's exceptional "talent for examining witnesses—with him it was a rare gift," a "power to compel a witness to disclose the whole truth." Even one "at first unfriendly" would "under his kindly treatment" eventually "become friendly" and "wish to tell nothing he could honestly avoid against him, if he could state nothing for him."[2]

Lincoln's lack of egotism endeared him to jurors. According to Judge Scott, "No lawyer on the circuit was more unassuming than was Mr. Lincoln. He arrogated to himself no superiority over any one—not even the most obscure member of the bar. He treated every one with that simplicity and kindness that friendly neighbors manifest in their relations with each other."[3]

Scott maintained that "before a jury or before a court Mr. Lincoln was always logical and usually seemingly candid. Much of the force of his argument lay in his logical and concise statement of the facts of a case. When he had in that way secured a clear understanding of the facts, the jury and the court would seem naturally to follow him in his conclusions as to the law of the case. His simple and natural presentation of the facts seemed to give the impression, the jury were themselves making that statement. He had the happy and unusual faculty of making the jury believe *they*—and not *he*—were trying the case. In that mode of presenting a case he had few if any equals. An attorney makes a grave mistake if he puts too much of *himself* into his argument before the jury or before the court. Mr. Lincoln kept himself in the background and apparently assumed nothing more than to be an assistant counsel to the court or the jury on whom the primary responsibility for the final decision of the case in fact rested. That mode of arguing a case is most satisfactory—especially with a jury who dislike to be ignored as though they constituted no part of the court."[4]

Also useful in winning over juries was Lincoln's legendary talent as a storyteller. "Not infrequently Mr. Lincoln would illustrate his legal arguments with an appropriate story or anecdote," Judge Scott recalled. "That line of legal argument with many lawyers would be a most dangerous experiment but it never failed with Mr. Lincoln. When he chose to do so he could place the opposite party and his counsel too for that matter in a most ridiculous attitude by relating in his inimitable way a pertinent story. That often gave him a great advantage with the jury." To illustrate his point, Scott recalled the case of a young lawyer who "had brought an action in trespass to recover damages done to his client's growing crops by defendant's hogs. The right of action under the law of Illinois as it was then depended on . . . whether the plaintiff's fence was sufficient to turn ordinary stock. There was some little conflict in the evidence on that question but the weight of the testimony was decidedly in favor of plaintiff and sustained beyond all doubt his cause of action. Mr. Lincoln appeared for a defendant. There was no controversy as to the damage by defendant's stock. The only thing in the case that could possibly admit of any discussion was the condition of plaintiff's fence and as the testimony on that question seemed to be in favor of plaintiff and as the sum involved was little in amount, Mr. Lincoln did not deem it necessary to argue the case seriously but by way of saying something in behalf of his client he told a little story about a *fence* that was so *crooked* that when a hog went through an opening in it, invariably it came out on the same side from whence it started. His description of the confused look of the hog after several times going through the fence and still finding itself on the side from where it had started was a humorous specimen of the best story telling. The effect was to make plaintiff's case appear ridiculous and while Mr. Lincoln did not attempt to apply the story to the case, the jury seemed to think it had some kind of application to the fence in controversy—otherwise he would not have told it and shortly returned a verdict for defendant. Few men could have made so much out of so little a story. His manner of telling a story was most generally better than the story itself. He always seemed to have an apt story on hand for use on all occasions. If he had no story in stock he could formulate one instantly so pertinent it would seem he had brought it into service on many previous occasions. It is believed he had never heard before, many of the mirth provoking stories he told at the bar, on the rostrum and elsewhere but formulated them for immediate use. That is a talent akin to the power to construct a parable—a talent that few men possess."[5]

One day Lincoln told a story while defending a client charged with assault and battery. The plaintiff had insulted and attacked the defendant, who trounced the plaintiff after the plaintiff had started the fight. Lincoln "told the jury that his client was in the fix of a man who, in going along the highway with a pitchfork on his shoulder, was attacked by a fierce dog that ran out at him from a farmer's door-yard. In parrying off the brute with the fork its prongs stuck into the brute and killed him.

> "What made you kill my dog?" said the farmer.
> "What made him try to bite me?"
> "But why did you not go at him with the other end of your pitchfork?"
> "Why did he not come after me with his other end?"

At this Mr. Lincoln whirled about in his long arms an imaginary dog and pushed its tail end toward the jury. Thus was the defensive plea of "son assault demesne"—loosely, that "the other fellow brought on the fight," quickly told, and in a way that the dullest mind would grasp and retain.[6]

(This story comes from *Joe Miller's Jests*, a 1739 compilation that Lincoln had obtained from Judge Samuel Treat, who presided over the Eighth Circuit from the time Lincoln began riding it until 1848. Judge Treat noted that the Springfield attorney "evidently learned its entire contents, for he found Lincoln narrating the stories contained therein around the circuit, but very much embellished and changed, evidently by Lincoln himself.")[7]

In the 1850s, as the frontier stage of the state's history ended, life for Illinois lawyers changed significantly. The swift expansion of railroad lines (from 111 miles in 1850 to 2,790 in 1860) and the population increase (from 851,470 in 1850 to 1,711,951 in 1860) helped propel the state into a new era. Railroads reduced travel time between Chicago and Springfield from three days to twelve hours. As lawyers found ever more business in their own towns, they no longer traveled about in search of clients. Judge Scott recalled that after 1854, "there was no such thing in central Illinois as 'traveling the circuit' as was done in earlier days. Mr. Lincoln was probably the last one to give it up in the 'old 8th Circuit.'"[8]

Lincoln stayed on because he loved life on the circuit. Most of his colleagues complained about the hardships of circuit practice; Lincoln, however, did not. As Leonard Swett noted, "I rode the Eighth judicial circuit with him [Lincoln] for eleven years, and . . . I never heard Mr. Lincoln complain of anything."[9] Gibson W. Harris, who studied in Lincoln's law office, similarly observed that "Lincoln was not given to complaining. As I look back over it, the equanimity with which he accepted the rougher features of traveling the circuit seems astonishing."[10] Lincoln's law partner from 1844 to 1861, William H. Herndon, echoed Swett and Harris: "As to what Mr Lincoln ate—it made no difference to him—he sat down and ate as it were involuntarily, saying nothing: he did not abuse the meal ie what he ate—did not praise it—did not compliment the cook nor abuse her: he sat down and ate and asked no questions, and made no complaints. I have seen him do this . . . on the circuit for years. . . . Mr Lincoln was the *most perfect gentleman* that I ever saw to his host—wife and servants—and to all around and about him *on the Circuit:* he never complained—was never captious as to how he was served or treated. Others would growl—complain—become distressed, and distress others—with the complaints and whine about what they had to eat—how they slept—and on what and how long—and how disturbed by fleas, bed bugs or what not. Remember to travel on the circuit from 1837 to 1856 was a soul's sore trial. . . . I have slept with 20 men in the same room—some on bed ropes—some on quilts—some on sheets—a straw or two under them; and oh such victuals—Good God! excuse me from a detail of our meals."[11]

On rare occasions, Lincoln voiced displeasure with the fare at primitive inns. He once said with wry humor, "Well—in the absence of anything to Eat I will jump into this Cabbage."[12] One day he reportedly asked a host, "If this is coffee, then please bring me some tea, but if this is tea, please bring me some coffee."[13]

Lincoln's dear friend Judge David Davis, who presided over the Eighth Circuit from 1848 to 1862 (when Lincoln named him to the U.S. Supreme Court), recalled that Lincoln explained his reluctance to join a law firm in Chicago, saying that "if he went to Chicago that he would have to sit down and Study hard—That it would Kill him—That he would rather go around the Circuit . . . than to sit down & die in Chicago." Davis (like Fraker, a resident of Bloomington) insisted that "Mr Lincoln was happy—as happy as *he* could be, when on this Circuit—and happy no other place. This was his place of Enjoyment." The judge added that for Lincoln, the circuit was a refuge from his unhappy home: "As a general rule when all the lawyers of a Saturday Evening would go home and see their families & friends at home Lincoln would refuse to go home."[14] Usually he remained in the tiny county seats, even though, as one colleague on the circuit explained, "nothing could be duller than remaining on the Sabbath in a country inn of that time after adjournment of court. Good cheer had expended its force during court week, and blank dullness succeeded; but Lincoln would entertain the few lingering roustabouts of the barroom with as great zest, apparently, as he had previously entertained the court and bar, and then would hitch up his horse . . . and, solitary and alone, ride off to the next term in course."[15]

David Davis and the other attorneys "soon learned to account for his strange disinclination to go home." Lincoln "never had much to say about home, and," Davis recalled, "we never felt free to comment on it. Most of us had pleasant, inviting homes, and as we struck out for them I'm sure each one of us down in our hearts had a mingled feeling of pity and sympathy for him."[16] To Davis and others, it seemed clear that Lincoln "was not domestically happy."[17] Herndon remembered that "while all other lawyers, every Saturday night after court hours, would start for home to see wife & babies," Lincoln "would see us start home and know that we were bound to see good wife and the children. Lincoln, poor soul, would grow terribly sad at the sight, as much as to say—'I have no wife and no home.' None of us on starting home would say to Lincoln—'Come, Lincoln, let's go home,' for we knew the terrors of home to him."[18]

Just as Lincoln was unique in spending weekends in county seats rather than going home, he was among the very few to travel the whole circuit. Most of his colleagues remained close to home, practicing only in nearby circuit courts. Lincoln, Swett, Ward Hill Lamon, and Judge Davis—the only ones to make the complete circuit—"constituted substantially one family," Swett recalled. "We journeyed together along the road, slept in the same cabin or small hotel at night, breakfasted, dined, and supped together every day, and lived as intimately and in a manner as friendly as it is possible for men to live."[19] Even after railroads connecting Springfield with most county seats were built, Lincoln rarely went home on weekends.

For bringing the Eighth Circuit vividly to life and for explaining how and why it shaped Lincoln significantly, Fraker deserves the gratitude of all who seek to understand the life and times of America's greatest statesman.

ACKNOWLEDGMENTS

This book would not have been written without the early encouragement of Minor Myers jr., then president of Illinois Wesleyan; Michael Burlingame; and Cullom Davis, then coeditor of the monumental *The Law Practice of Abraham Lincoln, Complete Documentary Edition*. This book could not have been written without *The Law Practice of Abraham Lincoln*. This major achievement of Lincoln scholarship has already made and will certainly have a major impact on knowledge of Lincoln. This edition is the foundation upon which all of the research that went into this book is based. In addition to Cullom Davis, I thank the present editor of the Papers of Abraham Lincoln, Daniel Stowell, and his associate editors, John Lupton, Stacy Pratt McDermott, and Christopher Schnell. Their patient responses to my many inquiries are much appreciated.

I am particularly grateful for the steady, constant advice and assistance of John Hoffmann, curator of the Illinois History and Lincoln Collections at University Library, University of Illinois at Urbana-Champaign. James Cornelius, who was working with John when the work started and is now curator of the Collection of the Abraham Lincoln Presidential Library Museum, was especially helpful. Thanks also to former curator Kim Bauer. I've had the encouragement and support of Frank Williams from the beginning. I'm grateful for the early encouragement of Doug Wilson, Ronald C. White, and Larry Ratner. No recent book on Abraham Lincoln has been written that does not acknowledge the contribution of the eminent past Illinois State Historian Tom Schwartz, and I do the same. The staff of the Abraham Lincoln Presidential Library was always helpful, including Kathryn Harris, Cheryl Schnirring, Gwen Podeschi, and Dennis Suttles.

Each of the Eighth Judicial Circuit towns has its own core of Lincoln supporters, almost as was the case during Lincoln's twenty-three years on the circuit. These people keep the Lincoln traditions in their towns alive.

Remarkably, they know and appreciate Lincoln as one of their own and with a pride born of the knowledge that their predecessors helped shape him. The time and effort they spend in perpetuating the Lincoln story are for no purpose other than serving the legend, with no expectancy of compensation or recognition. The passion and generosity of these people are responsible, in no small part, for the completion of this book. They are, by county:

Champaign—Steve Beckett, Vicki Rowe, Cliff Shipley, Barbara Garvey, Anke Voss, French Fraker Sr., Anita Hodge, Iris Swanson, Allison Davis Wood, and Tim Hartin.

Christian—Judge Ronald D. Spears.

DeWitt—Charlotte O'Dea, Joey Woolridge, Helen Stites, Tom Rudisill, Larry Buss, Joyce Neuman, and Jenny Freed.

Edgar—Chuck Hand, Ned Jenison, Kay Grabow, Patsy Berry, Bruce Baber, and Tim Saiter.

Livingston—Congressman Tom Ewing, Barbara Sancken, Collins Miller, Steve Walters, and Donovan Gardner.

Logan—Paul Beaver, Phil Bertoni, Ron Keller, Shirley Bartlemay, Phil Bartaloni, Betty Hickey, Paul Gleason, Paul Adams, John Gehlbach, and Wally Kautz.

Macon—Pat McDaniel and Brent Wieldt.

Mason—Jim Sarff.

McLean—Marcia Young, Pat Schley, Greg Koos, John Krueger, Bill Kemp, Fred Wollrab, Bob Lenz, Toni Tucker, Maureen Brunsdale, Vanette Schwartz, Robert Eckley, Fred Dolan, Stuart Winger, Robert Neuleib, and Gretchen Knapp.

Menard—Al Grosboll, Ray Montgomery, and John Eden.

Moultrie—Janet Roney and Paul Stone.

Piatt—Thelma Tuggle, Lucia Wilken, Irene Lindell, and Pat Heykorysak.

Sangamon—Nicky Stratton, Curtis Mann, Richard Hart, Wayne Temple, Tim Townsend, James Patton, Bob Crosby, and Hal Smith.

Shelby—Whitney Hardy, Glen Wright, June McCain, and Donna Lupton.

Tazewell—Carol Dorward, Mark Bailey, Steve Monday, Lori Walsh, Mark Walsh, Carl M. Adams, and Don Nieukirk.

Vermillion—Sue Richter, Don Richter, Judge John O'Rourke, and Donna Kenney.

Woodford—Shirley Adams, Rhea Edge, Mary Selk, Paige Proctor, Charlene Proctor, Murlene Kramer, James Stoller, Allen Schwab, and Jean Myers.

And in Terre Haute, Indiana—Barbara Carney, Mike McCormick, and Susan Hahn; Lincoln's boyhood home, William Bertelt.

I also thank the descendants of Lincoln's contemporaries who are listed separately in the bibliography for their assistance. Their guidance in pursuing the Lincoln story in central Illinois was invaluable. Their continued residence in central Illinois maintains Lincoln's continued presence there.

I thank the readers of my initial draft: my brother Bill, longtime copyeditor of *Barrons*; Nancy Steele Brokaw, a talented author in her own right; Illinois State University scholar, Mark Plummer; and Frank Williams.

Thanks to Sara Gabbard for her valuable suggestions.

I thank Henry Bird, publisher of Bloomington's *Pantagraph*, and his editor, Bill Wills, for taking a chance on my public writing for the first time with the four series in their newspaper, each about Lincoln in a different county, McLean, Logan, Woodford, and DeWitt.

Likewise, I thank Tom Kasich of the *Champaign News Gazette* for allowing me to publish three series, Lincoln in Champaign, Vermillion, and Piatt Counties.

I also thank Bill Furry, director of the Illinois Historical Society, for the publication of a series on Lincoln in Macon County and an article on Lincoln in Bloomington in *Illinois Heritage*.

My thanks to Bryon Andreasen for his assistance in publication of "The Real Lincoln Highway: The Forgotten Lincoln Circuit Markers" in the *Journal of the Abraham Lincoln Association*. Portions of these ten articles appear in this book with the permission of the publishers.

My thanks to Frank Paluch, director of Perimeter Gallery, for arranging and Don Pollack for the use of Pollack's painting that adorns the dust jacket. Pollack's painting was discovered for me years ago by longtime friend and renowned papermaker Marilyn Sward of Columbia College.

I'm aware of the risk of missing some of the many who helped, for which omission I ask understanding in advance. I thank Matt Cassidy and Lisa Petrovich, Illinois Wesleyan University students who served ably as research assistants. I am very grateful to my assistants Angela Walters, Tamara Donovan, Karen Cook, and Charmaine Eickhorst, who did the endless transcription of the manuscript. Thank you to Mary Lou Kowaleski for her skillful copyediting and Julie Derden for her assistance with copyediting and the index. My thanks to Diane Liesman, longtime aide to congressmen and cabinet secretaries Ed Madigan and Ray LaHood, for her encouragement and support.

The guidance of my editor, Sylvia Frank Rodrigue of Southern Illinois University Press, with her gentle but quite firm hand, has been indispensable. Her kindness and intelligence have been gifts gratefully received.

Finally, I have noticed over the years that authors' spouses frequently get thanks, which I now fully understand. Ruth Ann's patience and support have been beyond reasonable expectation. Thank you, Ruth Ann.

Counties and County Seats of the Eighth Judicial Circuit, 1839–61

County	County Seat	1839–41	1841–42	1843–45	1845–47	1847–53	1853–57	1857–61
Christian (originally Dane County)	Taylorville							
DeWitt	Clinton							
Livingston	Pontiac							
Logan	Postville (1839–47) Mt. Pulaski (1847–54) Lincoln (1854–present)							
Macon	Decatur							
McLean	Bloomington							
Menard	Petersburg							
Sangamon	Springfield							
Tazewell	Tremont (1839–51) Pekin (1851–present)							
Champaign	Urbana							
Mason	Havana							
Moultrie	Sullivan							
Piatt	Monticello							
Shelby	Shelbyville							
Woodford	Versailles (1841–43) Metamora (1843–96) Eureka (1896–present)							
Edgar	Paris							
Vermilion	Danville							

Source: Compiled from Martha L. Banner, Cullom Davis, eds., *The Law Practice of Abraham Lincoln, Complete Documentary Edition*, DVD (Champaign: University of Illinois Press, 2000); Jesse White, *Origins and Evolution of Illinois Counties* (Springfield: Secretary of State, State of Illinois, 2006).

LINCOLN'S LADDER TO THE PRESIDENCY

INTRODUCTION

A braham Lincoln and Eighth Judicial Circuit Judge David Davis rode their
horses from Sullivan, the seat of Moultrie County, where they had just
completed one circuit court session, toward the hamlet of Decatur in Macon County, where they needed to be in the morning for the next session.
In-between the towns runs the Sangamon River, which Lincoln and Davis
had to cross without benefit of bridge or boat and which was swollen with
rain. The two friends had traveled between the two towns before, but on
this occasion, night had fallen by the time they reached the river. Lincoln
hesitated to cross the river in the dark, but Davis, without a word, plunged
his horse into the two-hundred-foot-wide river. Unable to find a landing
place on the other side, he returned and rode downstream, where he urged
his horse into the water and this time found a place to climb out on the other
side. He built a fire to signal where Lincoln should cross. The next morning,
the judge and the lawyer were in court on schedule.[1]

As the two men practiced law in the familiar circuit courtroom, having
recovered from their dangerous horseback swim, neither of them could
have dreamed what their shared future held. Within a decade, the contacts
Lincoln and Davis made in central Illinois would be of vital importance
to their later careers: the judge would be the architect of one of the great
upsets in American political history, and the winner in that upset would
be the man the judge had guided across the river. Nor could they anticipate
that Decatur would transform into a booming city, the host of the 1860
state convention of the Illinois Republican Party, not yet even founded. The

Decatur Convention's unanimous support of Lincoln's candidacy would put him in a solid position in the national convention, held in Chicago a week later. Judge Davis and a group of lawyers from the Eighth Judicial Circuit would go to Chicago to engineer the Republican Party nomination of their colleague Lincoln for president. Two years later and under intense pressure from the same group of lawyers, Lincoln appointed his former circuit judge to the Supreme Court of the United States.

Twice a year from 1848 to 1860, Lincoln and Davis rode together as part of a cavalcade of lawyers who traveled through dynamic central Illinois from county seat to county seat of the Eighth Judicial Circuit to hold court. The Eighth was one of the nine circuits the Illinois state legislature formed in 1839 to hold consecutive court sessions within groups of contiguous counties each spring and fall. By 1860, the number grew to twenty-six due to the growth of the state's population.[2] At its largest, the Eighth Judicial Circuit encompassed as many as fifteen counties, including Lincoln's home county, Sangamon. Lincoln spent almost as much time every year on the trip around the circuit as he did in Springfield. During this period, the population and influence of the Eighth Judicial Circuit exceeded that of the late-blooming Chicago.

Lincoln's nomination as the Republican presidential candidate and his election six months later culminated his rise. How did this man of such humble beginnings reach this pinnacle? The answer lies in a combination of the remarkable gifts with which he was endowed and the place where he chose to use those gifts. As Don E. Fehrenbacher states, the answer can "begin simply enough with Lincoln's good fortune in his place of residence. The same man living in Wisconsin or Iowa, for example, would have been unlikely to rise so high but Illinois was a pivotal state in the national politics of the 1850s, and its leaders were objects of unusual interest as a consequence." He quotes Joshua Giddings, a delegate: "Lincoln was selected on account of his *location*."[3]

Lincoln's growth and rise are viewed in the context of the forces of great change in central Illinois and his capacity to adapt to change. The population of the frontier exploded during his twenty-three years as a lawyer. The arrival of railroads to the circuit in the early 1850s transformed it seemingly overnight. That transformation coincided with Lincoln's reentry into politics and his arrival at the pinnacle of his profession. The economy boomed, driven also by the immigration of talented, daring, and resourceful people—suitable allies and rivals for the ambitious, highly motivated Lincoln. The locale was a vital element in his advancement and ultimate success.

Decatur, part of the circuit from 1839 to 1853, is a metaphor for the transformation of Lincoln. In 1830 in the village of Decatur, the seat of the county the legislature had created in 1829, about one hundred people lived in a handful of cabins scattered on streets that, although platted, were ill-defined paths; Lincoln was a rough, uneducated, rawboned field hand dressed in homemade clothes dyed with walnut. Thirty-one years later, Decatur boasted an imposing depot with a three-story octagonal tower, constructed five years earlier at the junction with the Illinois Central Railroad; the city's population had grown forty times to approximately four thousand. When Lincoln passed through Decatur on a Great Western Railroad train, he occasionally wore Brooks Brothers suits, had a son attending Harvard University, was one of the most successful lawyers in the state of Illinois, and most important, was going to Washington as the president-elect chosen to steer the nation through what would be its greatest crisis.

A key element of Lincoln's transformation was his law practice. As a general practitioner, Lincoln handled all types of cases representing many types of people. Fehrenbacher notes, "He moved facilely from one kind of case to another and came to know government, business, and society in a wide variety of aspects." Lincoln came in contact with the leading citizens of the area as well as the less fortunate, such as smalltime criminals, unmarried mothers, people of doubtful honesty, and people of dubious morals. His cases ranged from dry real-estate-title disputes to racy divorce cases arising from adulterous behavior to defending a county's move of its seat and taxation of railroads to paternity actions to defamation over charges of bestiality and most frequently to mundane collection cases for both creditors and debtors. The lawyers on the circuit were capable and challenging opponents for Lincoln as well as valuable and talented associates. "Practically all the Illinois men prominently associated with Lincoln's rise to the Presidency," Fehrenbacher comments, "were either leaders of the bar or lords of the press."[4] Lincoln actively sought to learn from all those he worked with and represented. His lengthy travels on the circuit and time with its residents from all walks of life enhanced his understanding of human nature, and he developed an extraordinary ability to listen and understand, without rancor, opposing viewpoints.

Lincoln's networking ability was a valuable tool in the development of his legal and political careers, and throughout his time on the circuit, he proceeded intentionally to advance himself. His life is a classic example of the so-called self-made man of his generation, engaged in a constant quest of self-improvement as the primary end whatever form that took. One school of thought pictures Lincoln as a passive player who was pulled by events, but an examination of Lincoln's life and work on the circuit leads to a different conclusion. In each county, Lincoln's clients included the most influential and often the wealthiest residents. He associated with the leading lawyers of each county. His relationships with the local lawyers resulted in referrals of the law business of many important residents. He created a presence in the county seats that attracted the attention of both the other attorneys and potential clients. He possessed a remarkable ability to identify and connect with the key players, often representing them and associating with them politically as well as professionally. These masterful networking skills have been largely overlooked, but a study of his relationships on the circuit clearly displays them.

He created a broad base of friends and contacts in each county who ultimately provided the structure for him to stand upon politically as he began his rise to the presidency. From the beginning of his career, Lincoln carefully chose the law partner who best served his needs at each stage of his development as an attorney. Lincoln made alliances with leaders and politicians in each town and county, whether they were Democrats or Whigs or, later, Republicans. Regular travel on the circuit provided him with a reason to be in its towns to develop and nurture these contacts without the appearance of politicking.

While Lincoln made good use of the circuit, he also affected its development, frequently aiding the creation of its institutions. His law practice included some of the area's most important litigation, and some of its most prestigious citizens were his clients. The major class of industrial clients was the railroads, and Lincoln was deeply involved in important railroad litigation, both for and against the railroads. His cases involving the taxation of the railroads arguably saved them from being taxed out of existence. Lincoln's representation of the railroads made a significant contribution to the state's development. Fortunately, Lincoln was able to separate himself from the resentment the railroads generated in the communities through which they passed, partly because he took cases against railroads. His railroad litigation placed him at the center of the battle for transportation supremacy between the rivers and the railroads. His ability to deal with these broad and complex issues prepared him for far more difficult issues on a national scale later.

Lincoln abhorred slavery from early on, but because he learned to deal with the mix of attitudes in central Illinois towards slavery, he was perceived as a moderate. His moderation was in his public approach to the explosive issue, not in his private hatred of the institution. The residents of the circuit reflected the festering national schism over race and slavery: racism was rampant, but the circuit also had strong antislavery opponents. The stronger antislavery views of the easterners and immigrants, particularly the Germans, who came to the area in the second half of Lincoln's circuit career, diluted the influence of the racial views of the southerners who had dominated the early settlement of the area. While this division weakened the circuit electoral support of Lincoln's party, it honed and moderated his public statements on the issue. Because he was exposed to diverse points of view, Lincoln learned restraint in his public statements. This contributed to his image as a moderate, which was a major factor in his successful nomination by the Republican Party and ultimately his election to the presidency.

A number of events in the circuit each formed a rung on Lincoln's ladder. The relatively large population and central location of the circuit enhanced its influence. So did the talent and moderation of the antislavery advocates, including Lincoln. These factors, in addition to the presence of the state capital, made the Eighth Judicial Circuit the center of the formation of the Republican Party in Illinois. The organizers, leaders, and core strength of the new party came from the area of the circuit, although the region's division on the issue of slavery created an even split of the population as a whole. In the early fall of 1854, the more extreme antislavery forces met in Springfield to form the State's Republican Party. Lincoln was not yet ready to leave the Whig party, so he left for the circuit to avoid participation in this initial effort. While out on the circuit in Pekin, he crossed the Illinois River to deliver his first nationally noted antislavery speech in Peoria on October 16.

In February of 1856, partisan newspapermen from all over the state met in Decatur to renew the effort to organize these forces. Lincoln, the only non-newspaperman invited, played a key role, drafting the platform that opposed the extension of slavery. The Decatur meeting led to the founding convention of the Illinois Republican Party in Bloomington, also in the circuit. There, in May of 1856, Lincoln delivered his important "Lost Speech." Two years later, he made his famed "House Divided" speech to the nominating convention in Springfield that placed him against Stephen A. Douglas in the senatorial campaign. The final event in the circuit elevating the Eighth Circuit lawyer to the presidency was the Republican State Convention in May of 1860 held in Decatur, where the rail-splitter image was created, and Lincoln gained the unanimous support of the somewhat-fractious Illinois Republican Party. A week later, Lincoln's team, mostly lawyers from the circuit and led by David Davis, captured the nomination in Chicago. Shortly after the nomination, the Democrat Party split, so there were two Democrat nominees, which greatly increased the chances of success of the Republican nominee. At the Chicago convention, the men of the Eighth Judicial Circuit had placed Lincoln in a position to take advantage of that split for his election in November 1860.

Ironically, Lincoln never gained the strong support of the voters in the circuit because of its division over slavery. Rather, the new party's members, whose long-time experience, personal loyalty, and support Lincoln had developed on the circuit, were key to his rise. The Eighth Judicial Circuit—with its explosive, evolving growth, dynamic leaders, talented lawyers and entrepreneurs, racial struggles, and political prominence, along with the dedication of its Republican lawyers to his nomination—truly was Abraham Lincoln's ladder to the presidency.

PART ONE

LINCOLN AND THE CIRCUIT

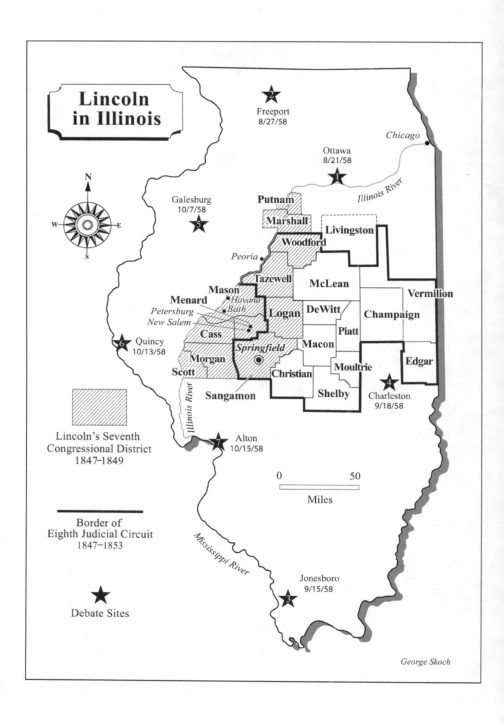

Lincoln
in Illinois

Freeport
8/27/58

Chicago

Ottawa
8/21/58

Illinois River

Galesburg
10/7/58

Putnam

Marshall

Livingston

Woodford

Peoria

Tazewell

McLean

Vermilion

Mason
Havana
Bath

Menard

Petersburg
New Salem

Logan

DeWitt

Champaign

Quincy
10/13/58

Cass

Springfield

Piatt

Macon

Morgan

Edgar

Scott

Christian

Moultrie

Sangamon

Shelby

Charleston
9/18/58

Lincoln's Seventh
Congressional District
1847–1849

Alton
10/15/58

0   50

Miles

Illinois River

Border of
Eighth Judicial Circuit
1847–1853

Mississippi River

Jonesboro
9/15/58

★

Debate Sites

George Skoch

1. A NEW COUNTRY

A braham Lincoln and the Illinois Eighth Judicial Circuit experienced parallel transformations. Between March 1830, when he arrived in Macon County, soon to be part of the circuit, and February 1861, when he departed for Washington, Lincoln spent virtually his entire adult life in the Eighth Circuit. The crude, untrained politician and attorney surfaced in the mid-1830s on the primitive frontier. It would have been far more difficult for him to advance himself and he would have had far less opportunity to do so in a more developed social and political structure. By the same token, it would have been more difficult for him to grow personally and expand his talents and intellect in a less-dynamic and less-changing environment.[1] His exceptional capacity for self-improvement and adaptation to change was perfectly suited to the explosive growth and taming of this time. As central Illinois evolved, so did Lincoln.

The Illinois legislature organized the courts into circuits, each a combination of counties united by a common presiding judge and state's attorney and by consecutive circuit court sessions in each of its counties twice a year. From its creation in 1839 until 1860, the Eighth Judicial Circuit was the center of Lincoln's law practice. There he became one of the leading lawyers in Illinois. There he learned the art of politics that transformed him from a merely clever politician to one of the greatest statesmen democracy has ever produced. He was a product of the place and its people.

An understanding of Lincoln's growth and development requires an understanding of the dynamic vitality of the area of the Eighth Judicial Circuit during his years in it. The Eighth, at its geographic largest, from 1845 to 1853, covered fifteen, then fourteen, counties. The population of these counties in 1840 was 69,100 (Cook County, which includes the City of Chicago, had a population of only 10,200); in 1850, it was 107,000 (Cook, 43,400); and in 1860, 232,700 (Cook, 145,000). Because reapportionment historically trails population shifts, the disparity of influence was even greater in the Illinois legislature. Under the 1848 apportionment, seventeen members in the legislature served from the counties of the circuit; three served from Cook County. That same disparity remained even after the reapportionment of 1854.[2] The Eighth Judicial Circuit included many of the finest legal minds in the state, talented and aggressive entrepreneurs and developers, and most of its influential politicians. All the institutions of state government—the governor, the legislature, and the supreme court—were (and still are) in Springfield; the only federal court in the state was in Springfield until the establishment of another in Chicago in 1849.

The circuit's land, over ten thousand square miles, more than twice the size of Connecticut, was almost entirely prairie, a vast sea of tall grass stretching as far as the eye could see. This grass consisted mostly of Big Blue Stem and Indian Grass, growing as high as a horse's shoulder and full of an incredible variety of wildflowers that came and went through the seasons. The Eighth, which stretched from the Illinois River to the Indiana state line, cradled a substantial portion of Illinois' two million, two hundred thousand acres of prairie, which glaciers had flattened and filled relatively level but for the striking ridges, or moraines. A crystalline network of streams and rivers flowed through this vast ocean of grass, broken only by prairie groves, large islands of hardwoods, oaks and hickories that provided occasional shelter from the elements. The ride around the fourteen counties covered four hundred to five hundred miles.

Illinois became the twenty-first state in 1818 with the smallest population of any state ever admitted into the Union, just 34,620. That population had settled primarily in a triangle formed in the bottom fifth of the state, the tip of the state at the southern corner, Kaskaskia on the Mississippi River as the northwest corner, and Shawneetown on the Ohio River as the northeast corner. Little was known, by the early settlers, of the interior of the state north of this triangle. At the time of statehood, no settlement had occurred in most of the area that would be the Eighth Circuit. Only three future counties had even one settler at that time.

Illinois' population grew to 157,000 by 1830. Southerners made up most of that population, the majority coming from Kentucky, Virginia, and Tennessee. Its politics were pro-Jackson, and it was the only state in the Old Northwest Territory to vote for the Democrat Martin Van Buren in 1836. As settlement proceeded, settlers continued to come from the south, many of whom eased north to central from southern Illinois. Easterners moved into northern and central Illinois in substantial numbers. Thus, three political sections divided Illinois: southern Illinois with a definite leaning toward the south on many issues, including slavery; northern Illinois with its definite Yankee flavor; and central Illinois being a mix of both.[3]

Central Illinois, where Lincoln chose to invest his life, was a place of opportunity and possibility. Lincoln's younger contemporary, Robert Ingersoll of Peoria, who also practiced in the circuit, said of him, "He had the advantage of living in a new country."[4] Central Illinois residents had little wealth, and a controlling establishment with fixed social classes had not yet evolved, although there was clearly an occupational hierarchy. Lincoln would become a prime example of how fluid that hierarchy could be. Though still practically frontier, central Illinois was in the twilight of that phase, on the threshold of change. Its essential parts were in place: its counties, its hamlets, and its location in the path of western migration. Miles of fairly level virgin prairies waited, ripe for exploitation and development, accessible to the civilization of the east. The area sat poised to leap forward in a rush of change, progress, and advancement.

Decatur, the crude village in Macon County, Lincoln's first Illinois home, exemplifies the characteristics of central Illinois then. The first settlers migrated in the early 1820s from Tennessee and Kentucky. In 1828, John Hanks and his brothers, relatives of Lincoln's mother, Nancy Hanks Lincoln, arrived at an early settlement. John's glowing reports of the opportunity in this new country induced Lincoln's father, Thomas Lincoln, to undertake the trip west with his second wife, Sarah; his son, Abraham; her son, John D. Johnston; and two of her daughters and their husbands and families. Her daughter Elizabeth was married to Lincoln's childhood friend and cousin Dennis Hanks, ten years older than Lincoln, whose family had moved to southern Indiana with the Lincolns in 1817.[5]

Dennis was sent to check out John's stories about the potential of the area. On his favorable report, the family moved to Illinois. Around March

1, 1830, the party of thirteen left in three oxen-drawn wagons, one of which Lincoln drove. After five days, they crossed the Wabash River near Vincennes, Indiana, and headed north and west toward Decatur, which was newly platted on July 1, 1829, as the seat of the just-formed Macon County. The trip was arduous with the muddy roads freezing at night and thawing during the warming of the day and swollen rivers to cross, including the Embarras, and the Okaw, and finally the Sangamon, immediately south of the village. The family arrived in Decatur on March 14 and camped near the newly constructed log courthouse in the center of the primitive village.[6]

Early Life in Illinois

The next day, the caravan drove southwest to the home site John Hanks had picked out on the north bank of the Sangamon. He gave them logs that he had harvested, and they immediately went to work building a cabin, smokehouse, and barn. The Lincolns began breaking the sod for a corn crop, and Lincoln split walnut, hickory, and black locust trees to fence off about ten acres. The family homestead sat at the junction of the timberline and prairie about ten miles west of Decatur.[7]

That summer, Lincoln hired out as a farmhand for several neighbors (he split rails for some in exchange for homespun clothes and money), including William Warnick, the young county's first elected sheriff and a leader in the community. Lincoln broke sod for Warnick and with John Hanks split several thousand rails. Lincoln reaped Warnick's wheat in the fall with a scythe. Warnick's farm, across the river and several miles southeast of the Lincoln homestead, sat on the north side of the Paris-to-Springfield Road, one day to be part of Lincoln's Eighth Judicial Circuit ride. While working for Warnick, Lincoln threw a fellow field hand, known to be a good wrestler, in a friendly match Warnick sanctioned. The following day, it is said, Lincoln made a political speech to the resting field hands on a break from work.[8]

Lincoln became close to the entire Warnick family, including their daughter Mary Polly, who married that summer. Family lore has it that Mary Polly rejected any romantic interest from Lincoln because she said she could not sit daily across the table from anyone that homely. Two other Warnick daughters married into the Austin family, another of the founding families of the county. The Austins were also close to Lincoln, and for many years, the family had passed down an early biography of Napoleon that they loaned to Lincoln. During the winter while crossing the frozen Sangamon to visit the family, Lincoln fell through the ice and got frostbite. He spent a week at the Warnick's home being nursed back to health by William's wife, who applied a mixture of bear grease, skunk oil, and rabbit fat to his injury. In 1833, the Warnicks moved to a larger cabin that would become a well-known tavern variously called the Huddleston House and the Thirty-Three-Mile Inn, where Lincoln may have stayed as a circuit rider.[9]

Lincoln soon became part of the young community, attending socials and a wedding. In May 1830, he was one of a number of signatories on a petition to change the voting place from a private home to the courthouse in Decatur. In December in a request suggesting confidence in the young new arrival, the county clerk asked Lincoln to appraise an "Estray Mare."[10] The following summer, Lincoln was breaking sod for his cousin William Hanks, on the Hanks farm near the town square, when he heard a crowd gathering to listen to two Democrat candidates: a legislator Joseph Posey and William L. D. Ewing, one of the state's leading Democrats. According to Hanks, Lincoln wandered over to hear their speeches. He could not yet vote because he hadn't lived there long enough; nevertheless, he stood on a stump and responded with a speech of his own, addressing improvement of the Sangamon River for navigation, a subject important to Whig voters.[11] Lincoln and Ewing would clash bitterly after Lincoln became a member of the legislature several years later.

The Lincoln family suffered during 1830, like the other residents, from the late-summer swarms of mosquitoes hatched in the numerous bogs and swampy, wet prairie. Most settlers were stricken by alternating chills and fevers into the fall from the "Illinois Shakes," or ague, a form of malaria. The most common treatment was a Peruvian bark and whiskey tonic, which the Lincoln family purchased twice in August from the Renshaw store.[12]

The malaria subsided as winter killed off the insects, but then hit "the Deep Snow" of 1830–31, a brutal winter that the era's pioneers all remembered and loved to describe even years later. The Lincolns had a rough time in that winter of snow; the first of December to the middle of February saw nineteen separate snowfalls, snow piling on snow to three or four feet deep with drifting twice or three times that depth and day after day without sunshine. The harsh conditions substantially obliterated wild game, and as the temperature fell below zero for extended periods, food became even scarcer.

Lincoln and John Hanks struggled across the Sangamon and traveled four miles east to a grist mill. When they told the proprietor, Robert Smith, they were there because they had run out of corn, he took his oxen into his field to move the deep snow and expose the grain on the ground to sell to them.[13]

When spring came, as soon as the terrain was passable, Thomas Lincoln and his family immediately began planning their exodus and as soon as feasible abandoned Macon County and headed southeast to Coles County, where Thomas and Sarah lived the rest of their lives. In the meantime, John Hanks negotiated an agreement with Dennis Offutt of Springfield for Offutt to hire Hanks and his relatives Abraham Lincoln and John D. Johnston to float a flatboat to New Orleans. So, in early March, they left as well. The snow melt had flooded the countryside to the point that travel over land was too difficult, so they bought a large canoe and floated down the Sangamon to Sangamo Town, now a part of Springfield, to build the flatboat.

Thus ended Lincoln's year in Macon County. The crew that John Hanks had assembled for Offutt built the flatboat and then floated it first down the Sangamon to Beardstown on the Illinois River.[14] On April 19, during that first leg of the journey to New Orleans, the loaded flatboat hung up on the mill dam at the tiny village of New Salem. After unloading its full cargo and with considerable ingenuity, Lincoln tilted the boat over the dam, saving the cargo and preventing the boat from being swamped. Impressed by the skill of his young boater, Offutt offered him a job at his store in New Salem, once Lincoln completed the trip to New Orleans. He accepted and arrived at his new home in July 1831.

New Salem provided an arena for Lincoln to make the transition from farmhand to lawyer. Founded in late 1829, the village, which never had more than perhaps twenty-five families, reached its zenith in 1832 and disappeared by 1840. Its ephemeral existence coincident with Lincoln's arrival and departure is almost mystic. Many of its residents seemed to have specific roles in mentoring Lincoln through this formative period. Mentor Graham, the school teacher, taught him grammar and the mathematics necessary to perform land surveys. Bowling Green, the justice of the peace, allowed him to appear in his court in rudimentary cases. Jack Kelso, a dreamer and avid reader, nurtured Lincoln's love of literature. Dartmouth-educated Dr. John Allen was a strong temperance advocate and abolitionist. James Rutledge, whose family embraced Lincoln, had a modest library of twenty-five volumes and started a debating society in which Lincoln participated with increasing confidence. It is claimed that Lincoln fell in love with Rutledge's daughter, Ann, whose premature death caused Lincoln severe grief. Several members of the small community, including James's son David, William Berry, and Billy Greene, attended college at Illinois College in Jacksonville. Storekeeper Dennis Offutt and then Abner Ellis hired Lincoln and taught him the rudiments of business. It was Lincoln's consistent, uncanny intuition and ability to capitalize on opportunity, hints of which were first seen in Decatur, and the characteristics of New Salem that combined to transform him from an itinerant, uneducated youth to a grounded, confident, relatively educated community leader during his formative six years in the village.

Lincoln tried three successive occupations—storekeeper, postmaster, and surveyor—each of which provided a fertile source of acquaintances and contacts. Although Lincoln was a Whig, John Calhoun, a prominent Sangamon County Democrat, appointed him assistant county surveyor, and the Democrat Andrew Jackson's administration appointed him postmaster. He performed numerous surveys, including the road through Athens, a resurvey of portions of nearby Petersburg, and two for the town of Bath in fall 1836, including his last recorded survey.[15]

While in New Salem, Lincoln's pursuit of a career took a life-changing turn. His contemporaries remember that as early as 1832 or 1833, he obtained a copy of Blackstone's *Commentaries*, the most influential law text of the day, and he studied it avidly. John T. Stuart, the leading Whig in the state legislature in 1834, encouraged him to pursue the law. Lincoln provided rudimentary legal services for New Salem residents, including drafting of documents and appearing in amiable Bowling Green's court. Two aspects to Lincoln's training separated him from most of the lawyers of his day. He became a politician first. The more common, less-formal route to the law was to clerk for an established law firm, which Lincoln never did. He himself said in 1860, "He studied with nobody."[16] Usually on foot, Lincoln regularly traveled twenty miles to the office of Stuart and his partner, Henry Dummer, in Springfield to borrow books from their modest library. Their encouragement and selection of essential texts, which included Chitty's *Pleadings*, Greenleaf's *Evidence*, and Story's *Equity Jurisprudence*, were enough support for the highly motivated Lincoln.[17] He directed his own education with focus and persistence. William H. Herndon, later his law partner and biographer, described the process: "His determination to master any subject he undertook and his application to study were of the most intense order."[18]

About the same time he began his study and practice of law, he decided to run for the legislature. In March 1832, he published a platform that included a forthright statement of his lifetime goal: "Every man is said to have his peculiar ambition. Whether it be true or not, I can say for one that I have no other so great as that of being truly esteemed of my fellow men, by rendering myself worthy of their esteem."[19] In the middle of the campaign, he volunteered to serve in the Black Hawk War, the brief hostilities provoked by the return from Iowa of the restless Black Hawk, a chief of his Sauk tribe. Lincoln's three terms of enlistment (during the first one, his company elected him captain) provided another source of contacts. With his 1832 campaign interrupted by service in the war, Lincoln lost the election. He ran again and won in 1834. Lincoln was the youngest member of that legislature except for Jesse DuBois of Lawrence County, who later recalled that by the end of the session, Lincoln was already a "prominent man."[20] Two-thirds of the members of that first legislature in which he was eventually to serve were veterans of the Black Hawk War.[21] He won reelection in 1836, 1838, and 1840.

Lincoln's service in the legislature established lifelong contacts, acquaintances, and allies. That body included a future president, a future candidate for president, six future U.S. Senators, eight future members of the House, a future cabinet secretary, and three future governors.[22] Because the north-moving tide of settlement required another shift of the state capital to the north, Lincoln in 1837 was the successful floor leader who accomplished the move from Vandalia to Springfield, Sangamon County's seat, with the assistance of the other members of the large Sangamon County delegation—two senators and seven legislators, known as the Long Nine because they were all at least six feet tall.[23]

Lincoln gained admission to the practice of law on March 1, 1837. It required little more than certification by a practicing lawyer that this rudimentary training was complete and that the applicant was of good moral character. After returning to New Salem to bid his friends farewell, he moved to Springfield on April 15 to begin his legal career in partnership with his mentor, Stuart. Residing and practicing law in the state capital were critical to Lincoln's development both professionally and politically.[24]

Springfield, part of Sangamon County, settled in 1817, was the earliest settlement in the future Eighth Judicial Circuit. Four years later, a small settlement on the state's most important road, the Edwards Trace, arose a few miles to the north on Spring Creek. The arrival of entrepreneurial merchant Elijah Iles and the town's designation as the permanent county seat after the county's initial formation assured Springfield's future. By 1830, the city of Springfield had grown and matured, and within a few years, the town had brick commercial buildings, a variety of retail shops, and four hotels.[25] Simeon Francis and Josiah Francis founded its first real newspaper, the *Sangamo Journal*, which began publication in 1831. Simeon, who became a particularly close friend of Lincoln, later renamed his newspaper the *Illinois State Journal*, which became one of the state's most influential publications and one that always staunchly supported the Whigs and Lincoln. Over the years, Lincoln loved the excitement of the newspaper's office and spent a great deal of time there, spinning yarns and talking politics. During the late 1830s and early 1840s, Lincoln wrote a number of anonymous, highly partisan editorials for the paper attacking the Democrats and Stephen A. Douglas, in particular.[26] Vandalia's principal Democratic newspaper, the *State Register and People's Advocate*, moved its entire operation to Springfield in August 1839. The paper's founder was William Walders; its staff included Walders's younger brother-in-law Charles H. Lanphier, who took over upon Walders's death in 1846. The *State Register* became the Democrat's principal organ in the state, and Lanphier became a central figure in the Democratic Party of Illinois.[27]

Lincoln took full advantage of the opportunity Springfield offered to meet and gain friendship with influential visitors throughout his career. Lawyers from around the state gathered in Springfield for the entire terms of the Illinois Supreme Court and the Federal Court, where Lincoln met many of them. These contacts later became a substantial source of referrals of legal business for Lincoln. In the 1830s and 1840s, Springfield men dominated the central committees of both the Whig and Democratic Parties because residence there made for easy contacts with men from all over the state. Because of the difficulty of travel, legislators and often their wives stayed throughout the legislative session.[28]

Lincoln assimilated easily into the fabric of the new state capital. He first looked up Ellis, formerly of New Salem, who owned a store with Joshua

Speed. Lincoln and Speed immediately became friends, and Lincoln moved
in with him in the room above Speed's store. Lincoln lived there for the next
four years. Speed, a native of Louisville, Kentucky, was a well-bred, college-
educated member of a prominent family. Despite Speed's return to Louisville
in 1842, he became perhaps the closest friend Lincoln ever had, a friendship
that lasted Lincoln's entire life. Although Lincoln roomed with Speed, he
took his meals at the home of William Butler and his family, who became
like Lincoln's family during those early years. Butler, a veteran of the War
of 1812 and twelve years older than Lincoln, had emigrated from Kentucky,
where he had known Stephen T. Logan. Butler, who had followed Logan
to Springfield in 1828, was the circuit clerk and influential in Whig politics. Lincoln owed a great deal to Butler's friendship and support, although
their friendship was sometimes rocky and difficult over the years.[29] Other
young community leaders congregated at Speed's store, including James
Matheny, a Springfield lawyer and the son of one of the town's founders,
Charles Matheny. Attorney James C. Conkling, Springfield's mayor in 1845
and a legislator in 1851, joined this close circle. A native of New York, he
read law in New Jersey after graduating from Princeton. Although a Whig,
he partnered for a time with Democrat James Shields. Conkling and his
bride, Mercy Levering, were part of the social scene in which Lincoln and
the others participated.[30]

    This circle also included Edward D. Baker, another lawyer/politician
with whom Lincoln became close almost immediately. The English-born
Baker gained admission to the Illinois bar in 1832 at the age of twenty-one.
He served in the Black Hawk War, after which he came to Springfield to
practice law. He partnered briefly with Logan, who terminated their partnership due to Baker's questionable handling of clients' funds. Although
of shallow character, Baker was an eloquent and persuasive speaker, who
enjoyed quick political success as a Whig in the General Assembly from 1837
to 1840, followed by service in the Illinois Senate until 1844. Like several
others to whom Lincoln was drawn into close friendships over the years,
Baker was not a model citizen. Nevertheless, Lincoln's affection for him was
described as like that of a brother. When his second son was born in March
1846, Lincoln named him for Baker.[31]

    Being designated the state capital changed everything for the already
promising town. The first legislative session convened in Springfield on

December 9, 1839, a little more than two years after the decision to move the state capital. In the absence of an adequate meeting space, Second Presbyterian Church hosted the senate, the Methodist Church the house, and Saint Paul's Episcopal the supreme court. The county donated the courthouse square to the state on which the state capitol was built of stone quarried from Sugar Creek. Dr. Anson Henry, a Lincoln ally, served as the superintendent of construction. The grand, massive building rose above the modest buildings of the young town and its surrounding prairie. A Greek Revival building of brick and wood pillars, across Sixth Street, eventually replaced the county courthouse, demolished for the capitol. Because the county faced financial difficulty due to the money committed to the capitol, court was held in rented space in Hoffman's Row until a replacement courthouse was completed in 1846.[32] Hoffman's Row, erected in 1835, consisted of six, two-story buildings east of the capitol and where Lincoln entered the law practice with Stuart when he arrived in Springfield in 1837.

In 1840, Springfield was not only the center of government for the almost-twenty-year-old state but also its social and cultural center. Springfield's cultural institutions included the Young Men's Lyceum, founded there in 1833. Part of the national movement for self-education and improvement, the Lyceum provided an early forum for Lincoln to mature intellectually with its free exchange of ideas. His speech "The Perpetuation of Our Political Institutions" to the group on January 27, 1838, a somewhat pretentious lecture, demonstrates the extent of Lincoln's efforts toward self-improvement and reflects his lifelong respect for law and his deep admiration for the founding fathers.[33]

By this time, Springfield's leading citizens had firmly established a social hierarchy and turned their frontier town into the state's most fashionable city. The same group, which included the Edwardses and the Todds, held political and economic power statewide as well. The Edwards family and its circle of friends from the Bluegrass Region of Kentucky dominated this scene. Ninian W. Edwards, born in 1809, was the son of Kentuckian Ninian Edwards, territorial governor of Illinois, then a senator, and then governor of the state. The son, a law graduate of the University of Pennsylvania, married Elizabeth Todd, daughter of Robert S. Todd of Lexington, Kentucky, a wealthy lawyer, banker, slaveholder, and prominent Whig. The first Todd in Sangamon County was Robert Todd's brother, John, a University of

Pennsylvania graduate and a physician. John Stuart was the son of Robert Todd's sister Hannah. Elizabeth's sister Frances Todd married Dr. William Wallace, also a graduate of the University of Pennsylvania Medical School, who moved to Springfield in 1836. Mary, the third of the Todd girls to come to Springfield, arrived in 1839; she was twenty-one. Benjamin Edwards, brother of Ninian and born in 1818, came to Springfield a newly admitted attorney in 1839 after studying under Logan, who, with his Kentucky ties, was part of this tight-knit circle.[34]

The tortuous course of Lincoln's courtship with the vivacious, charming, but high-strung Mary is well documented. Their engagement broke off on what Lincoln referred to as "the fatal first" of January 1841. A reconciliation took place, and they were married in the home of Elizabeth and Ninian Edwards on November 4, 1842. Matheny served as best man. During her life with Lincoln, Mary required care and attention, neither of which Lincoln showed himself able to provide to those close to him. Other women testified to Lincoln's lack of attention and customary courtesy toward women. The outspoken, highly ambitious Mary saw Lincoln in light of his newfound eminence. Her age of twenty-three put her almost four years past the average marrying age. The true nature of the relationship is clouded and controversial with all sides and facets still being debated. Although the contentment and compatibility of Abraham and Mary Lincoln will always be debated, the convenience of the match for both cannot be.[35]

Lincoln's Partnerships

Lincoln's aptitude for identifying relationships, including perhaps even marriage, that would be advantageous for his twin careers can also be observed in his careful selection of law partners. Each of his three partnerships clearly contained the attributes needed by him at that time in his career: Stuart from 1837 to 1841, Logan from 1841 to 1844, and Herndon from 1844 until Lincoln's death. All three were born in Kentucky, Stuart in 1807, Logan in 1800, and Herndon in 1816. Stuart and Logan were admitted to the practice of law in Kentucky before coming to Springfield. All three were active Whigs.

Stuart, an 1826 graduate of Centre College in Danville, Kentucky, practiced in Kentucky for a year before settling in Springfield in 1828, the sixth attorney in that community of three hundred people. Six feet tall, he was a dignified, courtly gentleman, likable and well respected. He quickly built a law practice in Springfield and neighboring counties. An early supporter of Henry Clay, Stuart played an instrumental role in the organization of the Whig Party in central Illinois. First elected to the legislature in 1832, Stuart, a member of the Long Nine, served with Lincoln in 1834. William May defeated Stuart for Congress in 1836, but Stuart defeated Douglas for that seat in 1838 after a heated campaign that saw Douglas and Stuart come to blows three days before the election. Stuart, reelected to Congress in 1840, declined to run in 1842. He served in the Illinois Senate from 1848 to 1852.

Stuart's partnership with Dummer dissolved when Dummer moved his practice to Beardstown. Stuart's political involvement left him in need of a junior partner. He had observed Lincoln's intellect and ability to deal with people while they worked together closely in the legislature. They had also become close friends. Stuart's circuit-wide practice required an associate who was willing to go out on the circuit, and Lincoln suited this need perfectly. Stuart's voluminous practice was thrust on young Lincoln, who had limited clientele.[36] Now often on his own, Lincoln learned the complexities of pleadings, the rules of evidence, and other intricacies of the law. Even though Lincoln was often left alone, he benefited from his association with Stuart with an abundance of work, immediate credibility and professional standing, and a wide range of clients and acquaintances.

One highly visible, early case Lincoln tried alongside Stuart was *People v. Truett*, involving Henry Truett and Jacob Early, two of the state's prominent Democrats. On March 7, 1838, Truett confronted Early in Springfield's Globe Tavern about the latter's authorship of an article critical of Truett's performance operating the Land Registration Office in Galena, Illinois. Early did not respond; Truett pulled a pistol and shot Early, who died three days later. For the trial seven months later, fellow Democrat Douglas was the state's attorney, and Lincoln and Stuart represented the defendant. Lincoln, though second chair, delivered the closing argument of self-defense; Truett was acquitted. Nine years later, the victim's widow, Catherine Early, engaged Lincoln to represent her in a dispute over her widow's dower interest, which was settled.[37]

Another highly charged case, a civil one with significant political overtones, is the slander case of *Logan v. Adams*. Mary Anderson, Joseph Anderson's widow, sued James Adams and claimed he had fraudulently acquired land from her; Joseph Anderson's estate filed a separate suit to recover the

John T. Stuart was Lincoln's early mentor in the Illinois legislature and guided him to the law. Lincoln was his law partner from 1837 to 1841. Notwithstanding their ultimate political split over the slavery issue, they remained good friends throughout Lincoln's life. Abraham Lincoln Presidential Library and Museum.

Lincoln became a much-improved lawyer at the hands of his second partner, Stephen T. Logan, during their partnership from 1841 to 1844. Logan, a meticulous, highly respected lawyer, remained a staunch political supporter of Lincoln. Abraham Lincoln Presidential Library and Museum.

William H. Herndon was a good lawyer in his own right. Herndon was Lincoln's partner from 1842 until Lincoln's death. Content to be in the background, Herndon served Lincoln loyally in both the law and politics. Abraham Lincoln Presidential Library and Museum.

land. Adams's defense was that Stephen T. Logan had forged the assignment that was the basis of Adams's claim to Anderson's land, and Adams claimed Logan forged the document in order to destroy Adams's character, the two being enemies. Logan sued Adams for libel. Logan himself and Stuart joined Lincoln, a witness as well as one of the attorneys. Douglas was one of the attorneys defending Adams. Twenty-two witnesses testified, but the case was settled. One of the terms was that Adams state he had never intended to accuse Logan of forgery.[38]

Through Stuart, Lincoln gained access to high-profile cases around the circuit. For example, he joined Stuart in the successful defense of *People v. Cordell*, an attempted-murder case in Macon County in 1838. The charge alleged their client had struck his victim with a scythe to kill him.[39] The victim, Josiah Abrams, also sued David Cordell for assault and battery, which resulted in a hung jury in Macon County. In the retrial, held in McLean County after a change of venue, Abrams recovered a $100 verdict. Another significant case was in Tazewell County with Benjamin F. Kellogg Jr., a major figure in the county's early history. An attorney and the city's first city clerk, he partnered with Lewis Crain in 1829 in a dry-goods store known as Crain and Kellogg. The firm ended when Crain died in 1838, and Kellogg engaged Stuart and Lincoln to assist him administering the decedent's estate. Ultimately, Kellogg himself had to sue the estate because of substantial debts Crain owed him. In 1841, Lincoln and Stuart recovered $16,000 for Kellogg, the largest verdict they were ever to recover as partners. Things did not always go so well for Lincoln. In 1838, he made his first appearance in McLean County when Stuart sent him to represent a man named John W. Baddeley, who, apparently appalled upon meeting Lincoln by his appearance and lack of finesse, discharged him at once.[40]

Close friendship characterized Stuart and Lincoln's partnership. "Socially, and politically, in Vandalia they seemed inseparable," observed Jesse Fell of Bloomington, himself one day to become a close friend of Lincoln. "It took no Solomon to find out they were boon companions." Two letters from Lincoln to Stuart reflect their closeness, one about Lincoln's depression after breaking off his relationship with Mary Todd; these letters are among Lincoln's most unguarded personal communications.[41] In 1841, Lincoln and Stuart dissolved their legal practice for several reasons. Their practice lacked management, organization, and discipline, Stuart was a U.S. representative, elected in 1840, not able to devote enough time to the firm. Stuart offered Lincoln little real learning experience from which Lincoln could improve himself as an attorney. For the remainder of his life, Stuart partnered with Benjamin Edwards. Stuart and Lincoln remained friends, and they continued to associate on cases around the circuit.

Lincoln was deeply opposed to slavery, but Stuart had no objection to it. Stuart refused to join the Republican Party upon the demise of the Whigs in the mid-1850s. He supported Know-Nothing candidate Millard Fillmore in the 1856 presidential race and was one of a number of former Whigs who declared for Douglas against Lincoln in 1858. He actively supported the National Constitutional Union Party, not Lincoln, and ran for governor on that party's ticket in 1860. He became involved in the Sangamon County Colonization Society, advocating the voluntary colonization of African Americans, and he was opposed to the Emancipation Proclamation. In 1862, riding the anti-Lincoln backlash following the Emancipation Proclamation and running as a Democrat for Congress, Stuart defeated Lincoln's close friend and associate Bloomington's Leonard Swett. Stuart lost his seat to Republican Shelby Cullom in the Lincoln groundswell of 1864, after which he retired from politics.[42] The familiarity of their correspondence after Lincoln's election to the White House suggests that their longtime friendship survived their political division; in fact, Lincoln gave a reference for Stuart as late as March 6, 1865.[43] Usually Lincoln did not allow friendship to color his legal agenda or political agenda. In this instance, his political agenda did not affect a close friendship.

Lincoln's partnership with Logan remedied any deficiencies in Lincoln's training and experience from the partnership with Stuart. Logan was a brilliant attorney of meticulous habits, Springfield's leading attorney, and perhaps the best lawyer in Illinois. Admitted to practice at the age of twenty in Kentucky, he moved to Springfield in 1832 and served as a circuit judge from 1835 to 1837. About the time that Stuart and Lincoln separated, Logan's partnership with Baker likewise dissolved, leaving the busy Logan looking for a younger partner. He had adequate opportunity to observe Lincoln during Lincoln's three years of practice, including their joint effort in the *Truett* case. After Logan's unpleasant experience with Baker's loose ethical standards, Lincoln's integrity offered a welcome change. Following Logan's short partnership with Baker, Logan and Lincoln became partners in 1841.

Herndon said, "Yet his mind and makeup so impressed Logan that he was invited into the partnership with him."[44]

That year, they became involved in a notorious murder case, *People v. Trailor and Trailor*. Archibald Fischer disappeared, last seen in the company of the three Trailor brothers. After Fischer had been missing for a week, Illinois Attorney General Josiah Lamborn and Springfield's mayor took Henry Trailor into custody and held him incommunicado for two days. After two days of being "plied in every conceivable way, . . . protesting his own innocence, he stated that his brothers William and Archibald had murdered Fischer" and described in great detail the hiding of the body in a mill pond. "Hundreds and hundreds" of people tried to find the body; the dam was destroyed to drain the mill pond. Fischer's body remained undiscovered. A substantial amount of circumstantial evidence accumulated against the Trailors, who were charged with murder, upon which a preliminary hearing was held. Once the prosecution closed its case, the defense, Logan, Lincoln, and Baker, called one witness, Dr. Robert Gilmore of Warren County, who stated that the addled and decrepit Fischer was, in fact, alive at Gilmore's home. The defendants were discharged without a formal trial, and a week later, Fischer appeared in Springfield. Prior to these events, Lincoln had represented Archibald Trailor, a local and respected builder, in two other cases. He died a broken man two years after the bizarre case.[45]

The dominance of Logan and Lincoln is illustrated by a review of the spring 1842 session of the Sangamon County Circuit Court. Lincoln and Logan handled one-third of the cases, representing seventy clients, evenly divided between the city of Springfield and the county, and the two men appeared about a hundred times, averaging seven appearances a day from a low of two to a high of seventeen. They tried ten jury cases, including two in one day on days 10 and 12 of the fourteen-day session that Samuel Treat presided over. Besides trials, the actions taken included motions of all types, dismissals, default and agreed judgments, continuances, the filing and amending of pleadings, changes of venue, filing appeals, opening of depositions, and criminal pleas. The type of cases handled involved collections, injunctions, divorce, slander, foreclosure, contract, fraud, possession of personal and real property, partition, and estates.[46]

Two years later, Lincoln and Logan became involved in a bond-collection case that arose out of the move of the state capital from Vandalia to

Springfield. Baker and Matheny opposed them on this case. The residents of Springfield pledged $50,000 to the state as a condition for moving the state capital to the city. Fifty individuals signed a bond to secure this pledge of payment in three installments of $16,666.00 each. When the bondholders defaulted on the third installment, the state treasurer sued the plaintiff Mather for the entire balance on the bond, which he paid. When the other signers of the bond failed to reimburse him for their shares, he retained Logan and Lincoln to recover from the other forty-nine signers. Eighteen of them had become insolvent; the others claimed they were liable only for their proportion, not for the total amount. The case went from the circuit court to the Illinois Supreme Court, which rejected the proportionate defense and ruled that the obligations of co-sureties entitle one to recover fully from the other sureties.[47]

Lincoln became a much-improved lawyer under Logan's tutelage. Logan's excellence as a lawyer was based on thorough and careful preparation. Although not charming, particularly attractive, or eloquent, he became one of the leading trial lawyers of his time. Years later, Judge David Davis, who presided over the courts of the Eighth Judicial Circuit during this era, said that he had never known Logan's equal: "I cannot but admire every day in court Judge Logan's great skill as a lawyer."[48] Logan taught Lincoln that the law required hard work and careful preparation. He made Lincoln more methodical and more dedicated in his preparation. He taught Lincoln not to be discouraged by his lack of training, which could be overcome by hard work and preparation, and to analyze both sides of a case to anticipate the opponent's strategy. This ability served Lincoln throughout his life, not only in law but also in politics.[49]

This partnership dissolved in 1844 for a variety of reasons. Logan wanted his son to join him in the practice, and Lincoln had tired of serving as a junior partner and desired a junior partner to assist him in the more tedious areas of the law. Lincoln now wanted to be independent and to rely on his own skills and growing practice. Logan and Lincoln were on friendly terms, reflecting mutual respect for each other's professional acumen, as they associated on many cases around the circuit throughout their careers. There is little evidence that Lincoln was ever as close to Logan as he was to Stuart and Herndon, although in March 1862, Lincoln said, "The writer of this [Logan] is almost a father to me." Lincoln himself is quoted as describing Logan as "the best *nisi prius* lawyer he ever saw."[50]

Following the Logan split, Lincoln invited Herndon to join him as a junior partner, at about the time that Herndon was admitted to the bar, which he had earned clerking in the Logan and Lincoln office for three years. His father, Archer Herndon, had come from Kentucky to Illinois in 1820, first to Madison County on the Mississippi near St. Louis, then to rural Sangamon County. After a brush with Indians, in which his wife was nearly scalped, Herndon moved his family into the village of Springfield in 1823. There he established the town's first decent hotel, the Indian Queen. That venture generated enough money to allow him to retire to a farm and lead a fairly prosperous existence. A Democrat, he was elected to the legislature and was another of the Long Nine. William, nicknamed Billy, was his oldest child, a frontier youth, daring, and a bit wild. He attended Illinois College in Jacksonville in 1836, where he became involved in the antislavery movement, which caused his father to remove him from school after only one year. He became active in the Whig Party. As a young man, he worked in Speed's store and roomed there with Speed and Lincoln for several years. In 1840, he married Mary Maxcy of Springfield. They had a happy home and eventually raised six children. Lincoln's invitation to join his law firm surprised and touched Herndon because Lincoln probably could have found a more established and prestigious attorney for a new partnership.[51]

Several explanations have been offered as to why Lincoln chose Herndon. First, he knew and trusted Herndon and respected his work. Second, he wanted to be a senior partner with a junior partner to perform the time-consuming and mundane office-management tasks. Third, politics also had a part in the decision. Because of the demands of politics, there was not room in one small law firm for two active politicians. Herndon was content to support Lincoln to promote him politically throughout their years together. He was Lincoln's political ears during Lincoln's near-disastrous congressional term. He constantly and consistently worked to advance Lincoln politically. The Whig Party in central Illinois was divided between the "establishment" Whigs, with whom Lincoln was associated because of his marital connection to the Edwards-Stuart-Todd clique, and Herndon's dissident group of Whigs, young firebrands who wanted to wrest control from the older leadership. The partnership helped Lincoln bridge this gap.

In his personal life, Lincoln was caught in the middle between Herndon and his sometimes raucous, radical behavior and opinions, on the one hand,

and Mary Lincoln and her hostility to his partner and friend, on the other. Though politically involved, Herndon never had any ambition to hold office himself, which, of course, allowed Lincoln more latitude to do so. Herndon's one-year term as Springfield's mayor from 1854 to 1855 was an exception. He ran as a reform candidate with bipartisan support and strongly advocated numerous causes, including prohibition. His adversarial approach to accomplishing his reforms wearied even his supporters, however, and they asked him not to run for a second term.[52]

Over the years, the role of each partner benefited the other. The quid pro quo of this relationship is more equal than might appear at first glance. Their individual skills and goals complemented each other. Both were accomplished and diligent lawyers, but their differing styles and approaches to the practice, politics, and life in general contrasted sharply. Lincoln performed as the primary "rainmaker" and enjoyed the circuit-traveling lifestyle more than Herndon, who was content to man the office and endure its drudgery. He did not wish to travel. Although he was perhaps not as able as Lincoln, he was a fine lawyer with exceptional courtroom skills in his own right. Herndon did more of the research necessary to support the trial and appellate practice of the firm. His notebook of citations of notable case law, maintained throughout the firm's existence, was valuable to both partners.[53]

One of the firm's most significant cases was the 1857 Logan County case of St. Louis, Alton, & Chicago Railroad Company v. Dalby, which established the far-reaching principle that a private corporation could be liable for an employee's assault and battery. Three railroad employees assaulted the firm's client, Joseph Dalby, and threw him off the train as a result of a dispute over the ticket price. The suit resulted in a thousand-dollar verdict, which the Illinois Supreme Court sustained. Herndon, who handled the case in both the circuit court and supreme court and wrote the appeal brief, did consult with Lincoln on the case, who had brought it to the firm in the first place. Three years later, the grateful Dalby named his newborn son Abraham Lincoln Dalby.[54]

After Menard County was removed from the circuit in 1847, Herndon handled most of the firm's business there. This illustrates his stature in his own right. The county hired him to recover a debt in 1848; he successfully represented the county in a suit over construction of the county's graceful courthouse in the case of *Lesure and Bliss v. Menard County* in 1850. Lincoln and Logan had likewise succeeded in defending a similar case with the same parties in 1842, which lasted until 1844 and ended up in the Illinois Supreme Court. Over the years, Herndon represented the town of Petersburg in a series of cases for various ordinance violations. In 1854, he represented prominent Democrat and Lincoln antagonist James Shields in a suit to recover a note for him there.[55]

Lincoln and Herndon tolerated each other's idiosyncrasies. Herndon had to contend with Lincoln coming in daily, throwing himself across the couch of the one-room office and reading the newspapers out loud. He also had to contend with Lincoln's moodiness and frequent distraction and with Lincoln's children wreaking havoc on the office when they accompanied him to work. On the other hand, Lincoln had to contend with Billy's sheer orneriness, rabid crusading, and his occasional drinking and carousing. Their mutual trust and reliance on each other were principal assets of this partnership. They never argued over money, splitting fees evenly from the beginning. Each was totally loyal to the other. Given the high profile and visible nature of Lincoln's public life and prominence as an attorney, he needed a law partner who would always be there unselfishly willing to put Lincoln's career first.[56]

Billy willingly did this. He said, "He was my senior by nine years, and I looked up to him, naturally enough, as my superior in everything—a thing I continued to do till the end of his days."[57] After the tough and discouraging 1858 loss to Douglas, Lincoln said, "I expect everyone to desert me now, except Billy."[58]

Other Significant Lawyers

Three other attorneys from the circuit whose relationships with Lincoln are particularly noteworthy are Ward Hill Lamon of Danville, later Bloomington, Usher Linder of Charleston, and Swett first of Clinton, then Bloomington.

Lamon is the only attorney with whom Lincoln ever entered into any formal association other than his three partners. One of Lincoln's most colorful circuit associates, Lamon, like Baker, seems unlikely as a Lincoln intimate. Their association, not a true partnership, announced in two newspaper notices in 1852, ran until Lamon became state's attorney for the entire circuit in

1856, replacing David Campbell. Lincoln and Lamon maintained an office in Danville. Limited primarily to Vermilion County, the association provided a steady stream of business for Lincoln there, more than any other county other than Sangamon and its neighbors Menard and Tazewell. Lamon and Lincoln collaborated on 123 cases from 1852 through 1856. During the same period, Lincoln had only eight Vermilion County cases without Lamon. The Lamon family itself generated business for them with ten cases involving various family members, with Hill, as he was known, a party to several of these lawsuits.[59] Lamon and Lincoln were especially close. Lincoln referred to him as his "particular friend."[60]

Born in Bunker Hill in western Virginia in 1828, Lamon arrived in Danville in 1847. He studied law in the office of prominent Danville lawyer Oliver Davis, attended law school in Louisville in 1849 and 1850, and was admitted to the practice in Kentucky in March 1850. Upon his return to Danville, he and early settler John W. Vance organized the first county fair. Lamon returned to Virginia and eloped with Angelina Turner, who brought her slave, Topsy, to Danville. Topsy remained a servant to the family for many years, which caused considerable controversy that Lincoln apparently overlooked, as he did with much about Lamon. In January 1851, Lamon was admitted to practice in Illinois and partnered with Joseph Peters for about a year, until Lamon formed his association with Lincoln. Lamon brought a great deal of business to their association.

Lamon was handsome and blue eyed, stood six-foot-two, and had hair to his shoulders. A man of considerable strength, he loved to wrestle and box. He fought, drank, gambled, and liked the ladies. He had an endless inventory of jokes and loved to sing, often choosing minstrel songs. His dress and demeanor made him a dandy. He was loud, boisterous, and prone to exaggeration and drink, and his charming and convivial nature made him immensely popular. Emotionally intemperate, indiscreet, and impulsive, he displayed the opposite values for which Lincoln was known. The *Danville Independent* implored delegates not to support Lamon for state's attorney because of his "pro-slavery tendencies" and his "reckless dissipation."[61]

Always politically active, his 1856 election as state's attorney prompted his move to Bloomington as a more central location within the circuit. His popularity continued there. He supported the women of the Bloomington Aid Society by staging a fundraiser called the "Lamon Minstrels"

Ward Hill Lamon first practiced in Danville, where he entered into a loose (and mutually beneficial) association with Lincoln. In 1856, he was elected state's attorney for the circuit, so he moved to Bloomington, a more central location. He served as Lincoln's bodyguard on occasion, including the trip through Baltimore when Lincoln entered Washington in February 1860. He was fiercely loyal to Lincoln. This picture shows him in 1859. Abraham Lincoln Presidential Library and Museum.

Leonard Swett, one of the circuit's best trial lawyers, was perhaps Lincoln's closest friend on the circuit. He steadfastly served Lincoln throughout his political rise and during his presidency. This picture was taken in Bloomington in April 1858. Because of his height and facial features, he was occasionally mistaken for Lincoln.
From the private collection of George A. Buss.

in Phoenix Hall. Lamon's wife, Angelina, died tragically on April 13, 1859, and was buried in Evergreen Cemetery in Bloomington in the same plot as two infant daughters and Lamon's sister Virginia, who died while visiting. Court adjourned for Angelina's funeral, and Judge David Davis led the procession, of which Lincoln was a part, to the cemetery for the burial.[62] The correspondence between Lincoln and Lamon reflects their close friendship. For example, Lamon sent Lincoln a letter in 1860 about political matters but enclosed a scatological poem; in the post script, he joked, "Being a candidate for a little office like that which you are running for has not blunted your appreciation for the ridiculous."[63]

According to contemporary accounts, Linder was a trial lawyer as good as, if not better than, Lincoln. Lincoln and Linder both opposed each other and associated with each other in the southeast corner of the circuit in Edgar, Champaign, Vermilion, and Shelby Counties, as well as Linder's home county of Coles.[64] They referred business to each other. Born about ten miles from Lincoln's birthplace two months after Lincoln, Linder was acquainted with Lincoln's Uncle Mordecai Lincoln. Linder's family moved to Indiana six years after the Lincolns. Linder came to Coles County in 1835 and was admitted to the bar shortly thereafter. Elected to the state legislature as a Democrat, he did not finish his term because of his elevation to attorney general. In the legislature, he and Lincoln clashed on a number of issues, including the move of the state capital to Springfield. He converted from a Democrat to a Whig in 1838, and they became political allies.[65] In 1848, Lincoln advised him to support Zachary Taylor and oppose James K. Polk on the war: "In law it is good policy to never *plead* what you *need* not lest you oblige yourself to *prove* what you *can not*." In a long, thoughtful letter to Linder, Lincoln later defended his criticism on the Mexican War, explaining that to be against the war was not necessarily to be an abolitionist.[66]

Renowned for his eloquence and repartee, Linder had a problem with alcohol like many of his day. After two terms when Linder had been compelled to continue his cases due to inebriation, Judge Davis criticized him for his drinking, to which the offended Linder replied to the rotund Davis, "You must eat less and shit more or you will bust." Linder's drinking was probably the cause of an incident in April 1859 in Charleston when he assaulted a fellow attorney in open court during presentation of arguments. A year later, he moved to Chicago.[67]

Also as good as, if not better than, Lincoln, was Swett, an unusually talented trial lawyer whom contemporaries considered one of the nineteenth
century's outstanding lawyers in Illinois. He also played a significant role in
Lincoln's political career. A Mexican War veteran from Maine, Swett found
his way to Bloomington in the late 1840s. With the encouragement of Davis,
he took up the law and was admitted to the practice in 1849. After a brief
period of practice in Bloomington, he opened his office in 1849 in Clinton,
where he practiced until 1854. He returned to Bloomington with a bride
from Maine named Laura. Although younger than Davis and Lincoln, he
became a close confidant of both men in the years of traveling the circuit
roads together. He and Lincoln were among the few lawyers who rode the
entire circuit.[68] They opposed each other on many cases and associated
on many others in at least six counties of the circuit. Champaign County
attorney Henry Clay Whitney referred to Davis, Lincoln, and Swett as the
"great triumvirate" of the circuit.[69]

Whig Legislative Leader

Lincoln's political career continued to flourish after his move to Springfield.
In recognition of his leadership in the Illinois house, he won the nomination
as the Whig candidate for speaker following the 1838 election. His opponent
was longtime political adversary Ewing, a former governor and U.S. Senator. Lincoln was influential in the defeat of Ewing's effort to keep the state
capital in his hometown of Vandalia. Ewing won the speaker's seat by just
a bare majority on the fourth ballot; the two faced off again after the 1840
election, and Ewing won again, though it was not as close. In February 1839,
Lincoln, with uncharacteristic rancor, wrote to Stuart, "Ewing wont do any
thing. He is not worth a damn."[70] The third term was Lincoln's most successful of the four he served, and his influence was at its peak. Clearly one
of the state's top legislators, during the course of the session he served on
fourteen different committees, including the important finance committee
and the Committee on Counties.[71]

Lincoln's close relationship with, and influence over, the area that would
be the Eighth Judicial Circuit grew during the session. He played the major
role in the division of Sangamon County, which had remained quite large,
raising a delicate issue for Lincoln. The voters of Springfield wanted the
county's large boundaries left in place, and Lincoln resisted the breakup.

However, population growth in its outlying areas created substantial pressure favoring the creation of new counties. Proponents of such change included Lincoln's old friends from New Salem days, most of whom who had resettled in Petersburg, as well as residents of northern and southeastern Sangamon County. Lincoln, as chairman of the Committee on Counties, had to deal with this issue. Attempting to obscure his influence in the process, he referred it to a three-man subcommittee. Lincoln drafted the legislation that defined the boundaries of the three new counties, their territory coming primarily from portions of Sangamon County—Logan County, on the northeast corner of Sangamon County; Menard County, on the northwest; and Dane, on the southeast. He chose to present the bill as a committee recommendation rather than his own bill. The final bill passed both houses in February 1839.[72]

Lincoln named Logan County for his friend Dr. John Logan, an Irish-born Democratic colleague in the legislature from Jackson County in southern Illinois. Like Lincoln, Logan was a strong supporter of internal-improvement legislation. In the preceding legislative session, Logan's amendment on this issue received votes from five of the seven house members of the Long Nine. Logan, in turn, voted for Springfield on all four ballots in the selection of the new capital. He was the father of John A. Logan, who was to become a prominent Civil War general and a U.S. Senator, one of the giants of nineteenth-century Illinois.[73]

Dane County was named for Nathan Dane of Massachusetts, a congressman who supported the Northwest Ordinance that barred slavery in that territory, ultimately a critical measure in the battle to limit slavery's spread. The residents of the newly formed county, mainly Kentuckians who had no quarrel with slavery, petitioned to change the name of the county for Christian County in Kentucky from which many of the settlers had come. Lincoln facilitated passage of the legislation to change the name in 1840, the only county in Illinois to ever change its name.[74]

A letter from Lincoln's close friend Butler reflects the controversy over this division. Butler wrote a searing letter to Lincoln and fellow legislator Baker, hinting of possible corruption in drawing the boundaries. The responses of the two recipients of the letter say a great deal about their differing approach to people. Baker responded that if Butler believed the charges, he was a fool. Lincoln, however, said he was going to ignore the charges and not be upset by them and signed this long letter "your friend, in spite of your ill nature."[75]

Lincoln could look back on the 1830s with great satisfaction. The farm-hand traveling with his father's entourage had become a leader in the legislature, one of his party's most influential members, and had successfully launched his career as a lawyer in the state's most important city.

2. AS HAPPY AS HE COULD BE

When Lincoln began his practice in 1837, the county seats to which the judge and lawyers traveled were frontier hamlets. The streets were alternately mud or dust, depending on the season. Because the merchandising of food was still in its earliest stages, town dwellers generally took care of their own food needs. They kept gardens in their yards, and their hogs and chickens, even cows, frequently ran loose in the streets. The houses were small and fairly crude, the commercial buildings not much better. Both were generally clapboard, having recently replaced the initial log structures. Many more people resided in the surrounding countryside than in the towns.[1]

The character of the towns changed little in the 1840s. Populations grew with migrants arriving from the east rather than the south. Commerce became only slightly more sophisticated, and the quality of the buildings began to improve, more often of brick construction. More-elaborate brick courthouses, all on public squares and two stories high, replaced the original log structures. If the town had a hill or just a rise, it built the courthouse on the elevation. The offices were on the first floor, and the courtroom was located on the second floor, which had better light and ventilation. Candles, usually set in brass sconces, lighted the courtrooms, as court days often extended into the evening. Spittoons were common, the floors often filthy from the poor aim of the chewers. A rail, or bar, divided the courtroom between the public area and the official area, the latter holding the judge's bench, usually a large table on a platform, the jury box, the witness stand (often just a chair), and the attorneys' tables.

The courthouses also became the venue for public meetings, social gatherings, and entertainments.[2]

Circuit Riders

Each spring and fall, one judge for the entire circuit and assorted members of the itinerate bar made the rounds from county to county for consecutive sessions of the circuit courts. Samuel Treat, a native of Plainfield, New Jersey, was the Eighth Judicial Circuit's first presiding judge. Born in 1811, he moved to Springfield in 1834. First appointed as judge for the Eighth Circuit in 1839, Treat was elected to the Illinois Supreme Court in 1841. That year, the legislature abolished the position of circuit judge, replacing it with the assignment of each supreme-court justice to preside over a specific circuit. Treat served the Eighth until the 1848 constitution recreated the position of elected circuit judge, to which David Davis was elected for the Eighth Judicial Circuit that year. Treat stayed on the Illinois Supreme Court until 1855, when President Franklin Pierce appointed him as judge for the U.S. District Court in Springfield, a position he held until his death in 1887. He served continuously on the courts in central Illinois for forty-eight years, and Lincoln frequently appeared before him in all the venues in which he sat. Treat served as a pallbearer for Lincoln.[3]

Davis presided from 1848 until 1862, when President Abraham Lincoln appointed him to the U.S. Supreme Court. Manor-born in Maryland, Davis matriculated at Kenyon College and New Haven Law School and then studied law in an office in Lenox, Massachusetts. He moved to Pekin, Illinois, in 1835, and then to Bloomington the next year. Davis's practice flourished, though like many other lawyers of his day, he pursued other avenues to enhance his income. He made his fortune in land, much of which he purchased when few others would or could; he bought at $1.25 an acre and saw the value reach $100 an acre at the time of his death. Davis had been elected to the legislature in 1844 only to be defeated in a race for the state senate two years later. He was elected to the Illinois Constitutional Convention of 1847.[4]

Once established in Illinois by October of 1838, Davis returned to Massachusetts to marry Sarah Walker, to whom he had become engaged three years earlier. They enjoyed a loving relationship, as evidenced in their frequent correspondence over the years when Davis rode the circuit. Sarah played an integral part in her husband's career.[5]

David Davis (seen here in 1848) was as close to Lincoln as anyone on the circuit. He became circuit judge in 1848 and served until 1862, when Lincoln appointed him to the U.S. Supreme Court. He was Lincoln's campaign manager and the principal architect of Lincoln's nomination victory in 1860 in Chicago. Abraham Lincoln Presidential Library and Museum.

Sarah Davis was the loving wife of David Davis and a good friend of Lincoln. Her husband's frequent letters to her from the circuit show a loving relationship and are an excellent source of information about life on the circuit. The child is their daughter Sally born in 1852, shortly after the death of their daughter Lucy and ten years after the birth of their son, George. McLean County Historical Society.

Clover Lawn was the gracious home of David and Sarah Davis, where Lincoln stayed on occasion and where Sarah occasionally held court parties to entertain the lawyers when court was in session in Bloomington. In 1872, it was replaced by the current mansion, a state historic site. Abraham Lincoln Presidential Library and Museum.

They named their gracious home in Bloomington Clover Lawn, which was the scene of "court parties" they held for the lawyers during court week. Lincoln stayed at their home on occasion, and he and Sarah enjoyed a warm friendship. In December 1850, Sarah wrote to Davis, "Remember me to Mr. Lincoln. I esteem him highly."[6] Several months earlier, the Davis's eight-month-old daughter Lucy died of dysentery, and Davis returned home to grieve for several weeks. When he resumed the circuit, he took Sarah and his son with him for the remaining two months of the court sessions. Lincoln joined the Davis family in Bloomington and set off in his buggy with them, taking the Davises' eight-year-old son, George.[7] Although Lincoln and the Davises were close, Davis once wrote to Sarah, "Mrs. Lincoln is not agreeable."[8]

Davis ruled the Eighth Circuit as a benevolent monarch, firm in running his courtroom but pragmatic and expeditious. His size, eventually reaching as much as three hundred pounds, may have enhanced his authoritarian demeanor. The *Urbana Union*, reporting on the spring 1857 court session, noted that the judge was "undiminished in corporal value." A year later, the paper commented, "Judge Davis was as usual the personification of courtly dignity and impartiality."[9] He was amiable, aristocratic in nature, epicurean in taste, and fastidious about his attire. His rule extended beyond the courtroom to the social hierarchy of the circuit, with its countless evenings in relatively primitive taverns and hotels. He invited not only lawyers but also other townspeople to join in the discussions, entertainment, and humor of the occasions. For example, he invented the "orgamathorial court," over which he presided and tried members of the traveling entourage for real and imagined offenses and breaches of decorum during their travels and trials.[10]

Davis, who wielded considerable influence throughout the circuit, probably knowing more people than anyone else in the region, played a central role in the professional and political growth of Lincoln. They first met in Vandalia, in 1836, during Lincoln's service in the legislature. Before Davis became a judge, they opposed each other occasionally in litigation in McLean and other counties. After Davis's election to the judiciary, Lincoln became perhaps the lawyer closest to him. They traveled around the circuit together from 1848 to 1860. They generally shared a room, often with other lawyers, a benefit of being the judge's friend because he generally got the best room in these rough quarters. When Davis could not be in court, he appointed Lincoln to preside; Lincoln, on over three hundred occasions, heard minor matters and entered orders in several counties, most frequently Champaign. Davis also used Clinton's Clifton H. Moore and Danville's Oliver Davis in that capacity, though not as frequently as Lincoln. The other lawyers apparently did not resent the affinity of David Davis and Lincoln.[11] Davis, like Lincoln, became a Republican, though he was more moderate in his antislavery views.

During that prerailroad era, the lawyers generally traveled the circuit together; the traveling group varied in size (some joining for just parts of the circuit) and makeup. In addition to Davis, it almost always included Lincoln, State's Attorney David Campbell of Springfield, and Leonard Swett. In 1839, the legislature chose the Democrat Campbell as state's attorney over the Whig Davis. Occasionally, because of the volume of work, Campbell engaged outside counsel to assist with complicated cases. His untimely death in 1855 saddened the legal community of the circuit. During the McLean County circuit session of April 1855, Davis appointed a committee consisting of Lincoln, Asahel Gridley of Bloomington, Moore, and A. H. Saltonstall of Tremont to prepare a eulogy of Campbell, which Lincoln presented to the assembled lawyers.[12]

As the lawyers rode across the miles of prairie, they sang, told stories, argued politics, and discussed business. They strung out along the route, breaking into groups of several riders traveling at different paces. They often stopped at remote homesteads where the residents welcomed them with better meals than they might expect at inns and occasionally spending the night at such stops. The attorneys rode on their own horses or in their own buggies, depending on the condition of the roads.[13]

In 1840, a Springfield blacksmith made Lincoln his first buggy. His equipment was typical, saddlebags when on his horse or a carpetbag when in his buggy or later the train. Into either suitcase, Lincoln crammed a change of underwear, a fresh shirt, a long, yellow nightshirt, and a few books. He also carried a large, compartmentalized, leather portfolio wallet, which contained necessary legal papers in paper wrappers. When traveling by rail or buggy, he carried a ragged, green umbrella. Lincoln wore a long duster in the dry season to keep the dust off and a large shawl across his shoulders for warmth in the cooler seasons. He carried documents in the deep pockets of his coat and in his legendary stovepipe hat of beaver felt, seven inches high with a two-inch brim. His traveling equipment also included a fold-up lap desk for writing and a folding shaving mirror. Contemporaries said he was fastidious about being clean shaven.[14]

The arrival of this itinerant band was much anticipated by the locals, their numbers bolstered by many rural residents drawn to town by the festival atmosphere of court week and the chance for a respite from their work to socialize, visit, and gossip. And, of course, the people came to watch the court proceedings, a popular spectator sport. The lawyers became celebrities, some developing a large following. The lawyers wandered around the small towns, making friends with the residents, meeting around the stoves and on the porches of the general stores, on the streets and under trees to get caught up on the local news, weather, politics, and crops. Newspapers were scarce, so the traveling lawyers carried the latest news and issues.[15] Occasionally, the lawyers were entertained in local homes, eventually forming close enough friendships that they would stay with that family on future visits. The lawyers attended social events, entertainments, and shows. During a campaign, political rallies and speeches took up a great deal of their time. The lawyers played cards, chess, and billiards, and some drank whiskey. Some engaged in informal athletic contests including wrestling, foot races, and ball playing.[16]

Lincoln's renowned athletic prowess is confirmed by accounts of his winning a foot race in Urbana, long jumping in Clinton, winning a broad-ax-throwing contest in Monticello, playing a form of handball in Springfield, and playing town ball, a predecessor of baseball, and throwing the maul in Postville.[17] In the Ottawa debate, Stephen A. Douglas recalled, "He could beat any of the boys wrestling, or running a foot race, pitching quoits, or tossing a copper."[18] Lincoln played marbles in Postville, Pekin, Paris, and Monticello.[19]

Upon arrival at a county seat, a circuit-riding lawyer, who acquired business both from direct contact with clients and from referrals from nonlitigating local lawyers, met with clients and local referring attorneys. Occasionally, a client contacted the lawyer by mail, and the attorney could prepare the pleadings ahead of time. If it was a referred case, he could meet in the local lawyer's office. If not, he could borrow space from a local attorney or huddle in a corner of the courthouse. Often, he prepared outside on the sidewalk or on the courthouse lawn. The attorney also had to meet with the witnesses and prepare them and the clients as well as possible for the imminent hearing. Most of the legal proceedings were relatively insignificant in subject matter and amount. Though trivial by today's standards, these cases mattered to the litigants of the day because of community focus on events in court, and the litigious nature of the era. As central Illinois evolved, the subject matter of the case work became more complex and significant.

The work itself was intense, difficult, and demanding because of the rushed nature of the proceedings and the limited opportunity to prepare. Each day brought new cases involving a wide range of subject matter and people. The hurried drafting of pleadings, interviewing of witnesses, and development of trial strategy were challenges. The work required flexibility under fire, sharp wits, and innovative, quick thinking. There was no pretrial discovery as there is today, so generally the lawyers had little advance knowledge of the opponent's case. The hearing, with its spontaneous presentation of evidence and cross-examination, demanded focus and concentration. Competition for business and the desire and need to have a satisfied client and referring attorney put a premium on success and substantial pressure on the attorneys.

The difficult living conditions of the circuit added to the stress. The inns varied from mediocre to terrible and lacked amenities. The lawyers slept two or three to a bed as a norm. Sometimes, up to eight men shared a room, some sleeping on a bed, some on the floor, on straw under sheets, or on quilts. The primitive rooms had no furniture other than a bed and sometimes a chair or two. The roofs leaked, and the inns often swarmed with flies, mosquitoes, fleas, and bedbugs. Few towels or washcloths were to be had, either in the room or on the back porch or in the backyard; the sole method of washing was with cold, sometimes even icy water. None of the travelers ever claimed the food to be good. It was often greasy, insufficient in amount, and most would agree just plain horrible. Swett described the coffee as "pretty tough—pretty mean." Whatever the fare was, it was generally served at a long table at which everyone—the judges, lawyers, parties, witnesses, even bailed defendants—all sat together and swapped tales long into the night. The only redeeming feature was the cost. For example, one inn charged seventy-five cents to a dollar for supper, lodging, breakfast, and feed and stable for a horse ($14 today).[20] Lincoln recorded some of these costs in the fee book John T. Stuart and he kept. He erroneously totaled one trip in 1838 to Tazewell County at $21.28½ (about $405 today): road expenses, $2.82½; tavern bill, $9.00; horse hire, $10.00. The firm absorbed these costs rather than being passed directly on to the clients. At this time, fees were nominal, averaging perhaps $10 a case, which in today's dollars, is about $190.[21]

The beauty and solitude of the vast prairies lessened the drudgery of the long treks. Swett recalled "with the vividness of yesterday how the quail whistled to his mate as we passed along, how the grouse with his peculiar whir arose from its hiding place in the grasses, how the wolf fled, and the red deer was startled from the grassy dell. Who that has enjoyed them, can ever forget those good old Indian Summer days, when the atmosphere was filled with the hazy smokiness by day, and it was often so light at night, that one could read a paper by the fire of the burning prairie." Swett's nostalgia for the high drama of prairie fires obscures the danger to life and property the fires represented. In 1854, Lincoln drafted an indictment in Vermilion County against two men charged with setting fire to the prairie.[22]

The circuit experience had the ambiance of men of a later time on a long fishing trip. The camaraderie and fellowship played a large part in what was simply a good time away from the cares and worries of home. Though court often ran late, the lawyers had a great deal of time on their hands to resume the conversations, arguments, storytelling, and music. The time after court took on a holiday atmosphere. Campbell and his fiddle filled many hours as did Ward Hill Lamon and his minstrel songs. Lincoln and his seemingly endless inventory of jokes and anecdotes dominated these evenings as well as other times on the circuit. Whether out on the road, around the meal table, or in the shared room, a grocery, or the court room, Lincoln excelled at his mimicry and storytelling.[23] In 1847, J. H. Buckingham, a reporter for the *Boston Courier*, rode on a stage coach between Peoria and Springfield with Lincoln, a stranger whom he knew only as "a Whig from the state of Illinois. . . . We started in a grumbling humor, but our Whig congressman was determined to be good natured, and to keep all the rest so if he could. He told stories, and badgered his opponent, [a Democratic Congressman traveling with them] who it appeared was an old personal friend, until we all laughed, in spite of the dismal circumstances in which we were placed."[24]

On occasion, Lincoln used his spare time on the circuit to have his picture taken. Lincoln and Thomas J. Hilyard, a deputy sheriff from Ridge Farm, were walking down Main Street in Danville, in May 1857 when they passed the second-floor studio of photographer Amon T. Joslin, the first in Danville. Lincoln suggested that they have their pictures taken, and they exchanged the photographs. This ambrotype of Lincoln was in Hilyard's family for many years.[25] In April 1858, Lincoln went to the Urbana studio of photographer Samuel Alschuler to pose for ambrotype. This picture is unusual because he is suppressing a smile as the picture is taken. Joseph O. Cunningham, who witnessed the sitting, told of Lincoln appearing in a white linen duster, which Alschuler said would not photograph well, so the photographer offered Lincoln his dark jacket. Both men had the same breadth of body, but Alschuler was much shorter, so the sleeves reached only to Lincoln's elbows. Alschuler shot the pictures so that Lincoln's arms would not show. It took Lincoln a while to regain his composure for the picture because of his ludicrous appearance in the jacket.[26]

Accompanied by Deputy Sheriff Thomas J. Hilyard, Lincoln had this ambrotype taken by Amon T. Joslin on May 27, 1857, while on the circuit in Danville. Abraham Lincoln Presidential Library and Museum.

Women on the Circuit

In the man's world of the circuit, there were no women lawyers nor did women hold positions of authority in the court system nor were they allowed on juries. This is not to suggest that the court system itself was opposed to women—their rights of that time were protected in numerous areas of law as can be seen from Lincoln's practice. The antebellum courts were paternalistic in their protection of women.[27] The social life described on the circuit was geared entirely toward men. The difficult travel and rough accommodations discouraged wives from accompanying their husbands around the circuit, and there is little evidence that they did so. One known exception was that of Swett, who took his new bride with him early in their marriage, probably to help her adjust to life in this strange new country so different than her native Maine.[28] Another exception was Sarah joining Davis as they grieved the loss of their little Lucy. On rare occasions when wives did join their husbands on the circuit, they generally stayed in private homes as guests of residents of the circuit towns or in those few taverns that had adequate accommodations. On occasion, Davis affectionately urged Sarah to meet him for a few days on his rounds. Usually, she would decline, stating that such a short visit was "indelicate" and "the lawyers would talk."[29] While Lincoln's cases of divorce and slander included many that involved sexual misconduct, there is very little evidence of sexual wandering by the traveling lawyers. The lack of reference to such activity by the traveling lawyers could be explained by the courtesy and decorum characteristic of the era.

Because of reports of Lincoln's early awkwardness with women, a popular notion holds that he did not like women. While there is absolutely no evidence of infidelity, it is clear that as he attended legislative sessions and traveled the circuit, he enjoyed the company and the friendship of women. Such a friendship is shown by Lincoln's letter to Eliza Caldwell Browning, wife of Orville Browning, about his failed courtship with the Springfield visitor from Kentucky Mary Owens.[30] Springfield's John W. Bunn, Lincoln's friend and client, recalled that Lincoln liked being with women and that he was popular among women at social gatherings: "He was nearly always surrounded by ladies, who took special delight in talking to him."[31] Reporter Buckingham noted that "he [Lincoln] was evidently much disposed to play the amiable to several rather pretty girls that we fall in with at one of our stopping places."[32] Davis stated, "Lincoln was a Man of strong passion for women—his Conscience Kept him from seduction—this saved many—many a woman."[33] In 1847, a Livingston County farmer, attempting to blackmail Davis via letter, alleged that Davis and Gridley had tried to seduce the man's wife. There is no known response to the letter. Given the character of Davis and his strong love of his wife, which is reflected in their correspondence, it seems unlikely that this would have happened. Further, given the relationship of Gridley and Davis, it is not likely they would have trusted each other to share such a transaction.[34]

Lincoln Loved the Life

Riding the circuit placed physical demands and professional challenges on the lawyers. Several reasons explain why Lincoln chose to do it. First, one venue did not supply enough work for a comfortable living. Many lawyers of the day had additional sources of income, such as land speculation or newspaper publishing. Lincoln did not and chose not to speculate in land to any extent. In 1856, Bloomington's wealthy attorney Gridley offered to invest Lincoln's money in McLean County farmland, an offer Lincoln declined. His additional income came from his circuit work.[35] Lincoln was practicing law in some of these counties well before they had a resident lawyer, including Logan, DeWitt, Champaign, Livingston, and Piatt. He became an integral part of bar activity in the counties of the circuit. As in the Campbell resolution, Lincoln was selected to draft a similar resolution during the spring 1845 circuit session in Tazewell County, for the death of William H. Wilmot, a lawyer with whom Lincoln had practiced. Lawyers from Peoria and McLean, Sangamon, and Tazewell Counties attended the memorial. In April 1860, during Lincoln's last visit to Logan County as an attorney, the county bar passed a resolution mourning the death of Governor William H. Bissell, which passed on a motion Lincoln made.[36]

Second, he loved the life out on the circuit. Although Lincoln never reminisced about life on the circuit, Davis recalled, "In my opinion I think Mr. Lincoln was happy—as happy as *he* could be, when on this Circuit—and happy no other place. This was his place of Enjoyment. As a general rule when all the lawyers of a Saturday Evening would go home and see their families & friends at home Lincoln would refuse to go home."[37] He thrived under the affection and respect he enjoyed throughout the circuit. He liked the people of the circuit and showed a personal interest in all of those he met, greeting them with his easy manner and good will, which was returned in kind.

However, Lincoln's remarkably warm, public persona and his conduct among those closer to him contrast sharply. The personal warmth he displayed to the people of the circuit differs from his treatment of his close friends, who recalled that he remained aloof and distant. Davis said, "Mr. Lincoln was not a social man by any means," and that Lincoln never confided in him or sought his advice. He describes Lincoln as a peculiar man with no emotional feeling for others.[38] Herndon describes Lincoln as "a man of many moods who never revealed himself entirely to any one man," as a man who worked to hide his "identity." "His life was cold and indifferent," Herndon comments. "He did not have an intense care of any one man."[39] He was friendly with many, but he had no confidant other than perhaps Joshua Speed in those early days in Springfield. Springfield's John Bunn echoes this: "He had his personal ambitions, but he never told any man his deeper plans, and few, if any, knew his inner thoughts. What was strictly private and personal to himself, he never confided to any man on earth." This reserve included "political or family affairs of a very sacred and secret character."[40] Elizabeth Todd Edwards, one of Mary Lincoln's sisters, said, "He was a cold man—had no affection. . . . Lincoln's habits were like himself odd & wholly irregular. . . . He was a peculiar man."[41] In the opinion of Elizabeth's husband, Ninian W. Edwards, "Lincoln was not a warm hearted man."[42] John Littlefield, who clerked with Lincoln and Herndon in 1859 and 1860, referred to him "as an odd singular man who spent much time in study and thought."[43] James Matheny, who described him as a "curious man," commented, "Lincoln got more and more abstracted" as he got older.[44] This detachment of Lincoln's was frustrating and sometimes disappointing, even hurtful to his friends. On the other hand, perhaps because of this same detachment, he never took umbrage or carried a grudge. As Swett said, "He was certainly a very poor hater."[45]

Third, Lincoln's time in the towns and farms of the circuit created a major political asset and resource.[46] *Boston Courier* reporter Buckingham notes that when riding through Tazewell County, "We were now in the district represented by our Whig Congressman, and he knew, or appeared to know, every body we met, the name of the tenant of every farm-house, and the owner of every plat of ground. Such a shaking of hands—such a how-d'ye-do—such a greeting of different kinds, as we saw, was never seen before; it seemed as though he knew every thing, and he had a kind word, a smile and a bow for everybody on the road, even to the horses, and the cattle, and the swine."[47] As each town fostered its own newspaper, Lincoln had the time and took the time to befriend and cultivate the editors across the circuit. These relationships created respect and appreciation for Lincoln's views, and he developed the stature to influence the editor's views and editorial positions.

Fourth, Lincoln's exceptional physical strength made him well suited to the rigors and apparently indifferent to the discomforts of the circuit-riding life. He never complained about the lodging, the food, weather, or distances across open prairie or about the pressure of the circuit.

Fifth, being on the circuit allowed a certain amount of solitude, notwithstanding the companionship that was always readily available. His contemporaries recalled his occasional withdrawal from the company as he became silent and contemplative. Henry Clay Whitney said, "[N]or was Lincoln, of necessity, physically alone, when in a state of complete mental seclusion. I have frequently seen him, in the midst of a court in session, with his mind completely withdrawn from the busy scene before his eyes, as completely abstracted as if he were in absolute and unbroken solitude." All the time traversing the prairie expanses allowed him time to think and to meditate about the legal and political issues.[48]

Sixth, traveling kept him away from home and his uneven relationship with his volatile wife. Unlike most of the lawyers, he seldom returned home, instead remaining on the circuit, lounging and visiting with the locals through the weekends. There is no evidence that Mary ever visited any of the circuit's other towns.

Finally, this lifestyle also allowed Lincoln time to read and study. He theorized that one could strengthen one's mental faculties by rigorous mental exercise, and he put his theory to the test while on the circuit. He studied Latin and German and read Shakespeare over and over. He read Poe, Byron, and Burns.[49] His traveling companions tell of him reading as he rode—one time the book was Euclid's *Geometry*—and of putting a candle on a chair and pulling it to the bed to read at night. Others recall waking early in the morning only to find him reading before the fire. Lincoln was driven to improve himself. He advised Herndon, "The way for a young man to rise is to improve himself every way he can." Lincoln's days on the circuit with men who accepted this quality allowed him to do so. To present a case competently, a lawyer must know and understand the subject matter of that case. Lincoln's case load itself provided a broad range of increasingly complex legal, social, and economic issues, a substantial resource for learning.[50] Stuart later said, "By 1860, he was a well educated man."[51]

Lincoln leaned heavily on the relations he created and nurtured during the years on the circuit in the three phases of his political career. The first culminated in his hard-earned election to Congress, which depended, in large part, on his circuit connections. The second was the period of partial withdrawal from politics when his circuit travels allowed him to maintain political connections without being overtly involved in politics. The third phase began with his response to the Kansas-Nebraska Act in 1854, and that was built in large part on alliances and opportunities the circuit presented to him.

3. PURELY AND ENTIRELY A CASE LAWYER

I n terms of time, energy, and preoccupation, Lincoln's law practice dominated his life. He was a hard-working lawyer, handling a wide variety of
cases. Lincoln's practice reflects no agenda, causes, or philosophy. As Herndon put it, "he was purely and entirely, a case lawyer."[1] Generally, he took
a case simply to earn a living and represent his client's side. Lincoln would
take whatever side hired him, without regard to the nature of the cause.
In this sense, Lincoln answered the lawyer's highest calling, to honestly
represent the client and let the court concern itself with the morality of the
parties' positions. This admirable tendency is best exemplified by his cases
involving the two principal social issues of the day, slavery and alcohol. In
his casework, he displayed the moral detachment and objectivity required
by the conscientious lawyer's duty to his profession even though he had
strong personal feelings against both slavery and alcohol.

Race

In 1864, Lincoln said, "I am naturally anti-slavery. If slavery is not wrong,
nothing is wrong. And I can not remember when I did not so think, and
feel."[2] This testimony is supported by that of his contemporaries over his
entire adult life and also by his private correspondence. Cousin John Hanks
claimed that Lincoln was deeply offended by the New Orleans slave markets when they visited that city in 1831.[3] New Salem's Caleb Carman wrote,
"Lincoln regarded slavery as an enormous curse on the land." Attorney
and political ally Joseph Gillespie noted that Lincoln viewed slavery as

an "enormous national crime." Circuit associate Samuel Parks, a lawyer from Logan County, recalled Lincoln's intense hatred of the institution. John T. Stuart cited the political parting of the ways over slavery while the two rode the circuit. Democrat attorney and circuit adversary Orlando Ficklin described Lincoln as "conscientiously opposed to slavery all his life."[4]

In 1842, Lincoln visited the slaveholding family of his friend Joshua Speed near Louisville, Kentucky. During this trip, he encountered the transport of twelve slaves chained together on his river boat on the Ohio River. Upon his return, in his thank-you note to Speed's sister Mary, he wrote of the incident, describing the slaves as "strung together precisely like so many fish upon a trot line."[5] A decade later, still haunted by the scene, he wrote Speed, "[T]hat sight was a continual torment to me."[6]

In the case of *In Re Bryant*, this deep hatred of slavery clashed with the moral neutrality reflected in his practice throughout his career. Known as the Matson slave case, it is perhaps his least understood and most controversial case.[7] It is the only case involving the issue of slavery in which Lincoln represented a slave owner. Lincoln's client was Robert Matson, a debt-ridden, slaveholding farmer from Kentucky, who lived with his mistress and their four children on his farm in Coles County, Illinois, while his wife and her children lived on his Kentucky farm. In 1845, he brought five slaves, Jane Bryant and her four children, and her freedman husband, Anthony, to Matson's farm in Illinois. Although Illinois prohibited slavery, bringing slaves into the state in transit or temporarily did not free them. They had to be domiciled in the state to be freed by their presence in Illinois. Upon learning that she and her children were about to be returned to Kentucky, perhaps to be divided as a family by sale, Jane and her children escaped with Anthony's help. They were captured under the Fugitive Slave Law and held in custody on a petition by Matson in fall 1847.

Two abolitionists hired attorneys Ficklin and Charles Constable, both known to be proslavery, to file a writ of habeas corpus to free the mother and her children. Usher Linder, as attorney for Matson, engaged Lincoln to assist him to legally force the slaves back into bondage in Kentucky. Matson had annually announced his intention to return these slaves to Kentucky to maintain their slave status. Lincoln relied on these self-serving statements to prove Jane's and her children's in transitu status to sustain Matson's rights to retain his human property. Lincoln lost the case when the judges freed Jane and her children.[8]

Historians have been critical of Lincoln's role in this case, some going so far as to assert that it casts doubt on the sincerity of his later antislavery politics on which he built his career in the 1850s. Others question his handling of this case, in part, because he made the two-day trek to Charleston to try this case less than ten days before his October 25 departure for Congress. The political expediency of being identified with a proslavery position is a reason offered for his handling of the case. Another is that he made a weak presentation, encouraging the results against his client's interest.[9] These criticisms and questions ignore his role in the case and his duty as a lawyer. Linder was a valued associate and source of business for Lincoln on the circuit, and Lincoln's duty as a lawyer was to present his client's case in an honest and forthright manner and let the court determine the justice of the client's position. Lincoln's practice reflects his understanding of the role of the lawyer.

On the other hand, Lincoln defended men charged with harboring fugitive slaves. State's Attorney David Campbell brought all three prosecutions in 1845. The defendants in *People v. Kern* in Tazewell County on a change of venue from Woodford and *People v. Pond* in Menard County were found not guilty. In the third, *People v. Scott*, defended by Lincoln in Tazewell County, Campbell dropped the charges. These are the last known cases of harboring slaves in which Lincoln was involved.[10]

Racism ran deep in central Illinois. Slavery had existed in Illinois in the mid-eighteenth century under French rule when black slaves constituted over 32 percent of the Illinois population, which strengthened ties to the slaveholding south. The numbers of black persons in Illinois, more than either Indiana or Ohio, aggravated the racist attitude. In the 1820s, a serious effort to restore slavery in Illinois led to a statewide referendum to do so that was narrowly defeated.[11] Illinois' harsh Black Laws prohibited the black population from voting, suing, testifying, or serving in the militia and prohibited the races from marrying. The law did not provide for the education of black people, and it made it difficult for them to own property. In 1847, the Constitutional Convention adopted an article that instructed the legislature to prohibit the immigration of free black residents into the state. It was separately submitted to the voters and ratified by a vote of 50,261 to 21,297.[12] In 1853, the legislature responded to this racist referendum with legislation shocking in its harshness. These laws prohibiting immigration provided that any black person who came into the state in violation of the law could be arrested and heavily fined. If the accused was unable to pay the fine, he or she would be sold to the person who bid the least amount of time of servitude for the $50 fine. The indentured individual had to work off the bid time. Such transactions did occur on occasion and continued to as late as 1863 in Hancock and Edgar Counties. It was not until two years later that the notorious Black Laws were repealed.[13]

The undercurrent of this racism ran through a number of Lincoln's cases around the circuit. *Bailey v. Cromwell and McNaughton* in Tazewell County is such a case, although it is frequently misinterpreted. This simple contract action has been proclaimed as a case where Lincoln's role was to "free a slave," which is simply not accurate. Lincoln's client signed a promissory note in payment for "Nance," a black female indentured servant or "slave." He refused to pay the note because Nance's seller had not provided the promised documentation of her status. Lincoln's defense was failure of consideration. He lost the case in the trial court but won it in the Illinois Supreme Court, asserting that in Illinois, a person was presumed free unless there was proof to the contrary. Lincoln's client did not have to pay the note.[14] Nance's gallant efforts to assert her free status, not Lincoln, resulted in her freedom.

Lincoln also litigated slander cases with allegations of color. In DeWitt County, he represented William Dungey, a dark-skinned man who sued his brother-in-law for slander for saying Dungey was black and calling him a Negro. This allegation cast the shadow of the Black Laws across Lincoln's client. Rather than question the injustice of the Black Laws, Lincoln proved to the satisfaction of the jury that the plaintiff was not black, and they returned a verdict for $600. With his reputation restored and to avoid an appeal, Dungey remitted $400 for a net recovery of $200 and paid Lincoln $50.[15] (Remittitur, a reduction in the verdict by the court to eliminate further post-trial proceedings, was common in these cases then, the goal often being the recovery of reputation rather than money.)

In *Patterson v. Edwards* in Mason County, the defendants alleged that Lincoln's clients had "raised a family of children by a Negro." The supreme court ruled that these words did not constitute slander. In the Christian County case of *Sanders et al. v. Dunham*, the plaintiffs charged that Lincoln's client slandered the plaintiff "Old Black Kate" by saying that she had given birth to a child fathered by a black man and that the child had been sold by her father for two horses. The case was settled. In Edgar County, Lincoln and Linder brought a suit for breach of promise in *Benson v. Mayo*. The defense was that the plaintiff had declined to marry the defendant "because he was a half brother of a Negro." The jury rejected this defense, and Lincoln's client recovered $400.[16]

Alcohol

Lincoln's impartial morality can be observed in his cases surrounding alcohol. Alcohol abuse was a serious problem in this era. Many of Lincoln's fellow lawyers fought alcohol addiction. The popular state's attorney Campbell had difficulty controlling his own drinking, which may account for his premature death in 1855. "My friend Campbell is drinking very hard," David Davis wrote to his wife in 1851. "I'm afraid there is no hope for him." Abraham Smith, a temperance and abolition zealot from Ridge Farm on the south edge of Vermilion County, constantly and openly accused Campbell of not only abusing alcohol but also being soft on the prosecution of liquor cases and colluding with liquor purveyors. Campbell finally tired of the defamation. Knowing the full array of legal talent in the circuit, he chose Lincoln to sue Smith for slander in the Vermilion County Circuit Court. The trial resulted in a $600 verdict, which Lincoln sustained in the Illinois Supreme Court. Oliver Davis of Danville opposed him.[17] Lincoln, himself a temperance advocate who never drank, condemned the substance, not the user, in his empathetic and sensitive speech to the Springfield Washington Temperance Society on Washington's birthday in 1842.[18] The temperance issue heated up in the early 1850s as some cities adopted prohibition ordinances, and otherwise law-abiding citizens took the law into their own hands by attacking lawful liquor establishments. Lincoln defended such vigilantes in cases arising out of seven incidents across the circuit.

In one such incident, the death of a customer allegedly from bad booze consumed in a tavern in Washington, Illinois, provoked three cases in 1854 in Tazewell County. Lincoln, aided by Bloomington's Asahel Gridley, represented over twenty defendants who had stormed the bar. He defended a civil case for damage to the establishment by its owners and a criminal case brought by State's Attorney Campbell, arising out of the incident. A few defendants were held liable, and several were found guilty in each case, but most were found not guilty in both. In the third case, Lincoln assisted Campbell in prosecuting the proprietor of the bar for "keeping a disorderly house."[19] That same year in McLean County, Lincoln defended Blooming-ton's mayor and several policemen in a suit, known as the Whiskey-Zootic case, brought through attorney Gridley by the proprietors of a grocery store. Lincoln's clients had destroyed $2,000 worth of liquor. The jury returned a verdict for $400. In 1853, Lincoln defended a civil suit brought by an Urbana distillery's owners against a who's who of Urbana businessmen and com-munity leaders in *McClatchey v. Sits and Roney et al.* to recover for extensive damage to the distillery and destruction of its product. The case was tried on a change of venue in Vermilion County with Lincoln assisted by Danville's Oliver Davis. A jury returned a verdict for the defendants.[20] The most color-ful of these cases was in DeWitt County, *People v. Shurtleff*, in which nine women in Marion, Illinois, now the town of DeWitt, were prosecuted in 1854 for busting up Tanner's Grocery and destroying large amounts of whiskey. The defendants included the wives of the leading businessmen in town, a physician, and William H. Herndon's brother. In closing, Lincoln strongly condemned whiskey, dubbing the case "The State against Mr. Whiskey." A witness said, "Before he closed his speech many were bathed in tears, the judge not excepted. . . . He moved the jury to tears as he defended the noble act of civil disobedience." The jury returned a verdict of guilty, nevertheless, and Judge Davis levied a fine of $2 each.[21]

On the other side of the temperance issue, Lincoln defended men charged with illegal sales of liquor in thirty-two cases, including some in the same counties as the temperance causes: DeWitt, Champaign, and Vermilion. He defended similar cases in Macon and Christian Counties as well. In Tazewell County, he sued successfully to recover one hundred barrels of whiskey illegally detained from his clients.[22]

The Nature of the Practice

Lincoln's practice consisted primarily of litigation of a mundane and routine nature, overwhelmingly civil, not criminal. The work ranged from debt col-lection to lobbying to murder trials to wills and beyond. The boundaries of the Eighth Judicial Circuit defined his practice in no small part, illustrated by the limited number of cases he handled in Macon, Christian, Edgar,

Tazewell, and Woodford counties after they were removed from the circuit.[23] Lincoln also handled cases in state courts outside the circuit and in the federal courts, first in Springfield and then also in Chicago after that court was established in 1849. Usually, this other work was done when it did not conflict with the circuit. For example, federal court sessions in Springfield were in the winter, between circuit court sessions.

Because Lincoln charged low fees, other members of the bar occasionally criticized him for that. Davis's "orgamathorial court" prosecuted Lincoln for charging too low a fee. Lincoln and Ward Hill Lamon handled a case for Dr. John Scott, conservator for his mentally challenged sister. A scoundrel after her money persuaded her to marry him and filed a petition to remove the conservator, Scott. Lamon arranged a retainer of $250. Lincoln presented his argument so forcefully that he won in a mere twenty minutes. He directed Lamon to return half the fee. After protesting, Lamon did so, astonishing the client. That night as judge of the orgamathorial court, Davis chastised Lincoln, "You are impoverishing the Bar by your picayune charge of fees."[24] In notes Lincoln left for a lecture on the practice of law, estimated to have been written around 1850, he cautions, "An exorbitant fee should never be claimed." He advised that a lawyer should never take his full fee in advance. "When fully paid beforehand, you are more than a common mortal if you can feel the same interest in the case, as if something was still in prospect for you, as well as for your client. And when you lack interest in the case the job will likely lack skill and diligence in the performance. Settle the amount of fee and take a note in advance. Then you will feel that you are working for something, and you are sure to do your work faithfully and well."[25]

Lincoln's mediation skills enabled him to frequently settle cases, not only before trial but also after trial when his client, vindicated by the verdict, would accept less than the verdict to avoid an appeal. In the same notes, he said, "Discourage litigation. Persuade your neighbors to compromise whenever you can. Point out to them how the nominal winner is often a real loser—in fees, expenses, and waste of time. As a peacemaker, the lawyer has a superior opportunity of being a good man. There will still be business enough."[26]

Lincoln's professional detachment allowed him to take both sides of less-significant issues. The detachment also extended to his selection of clients. Throughout his career, Lincoln took business without concern for the identity of the other party, sometimes former clients, sometimes former adversaries, political allies, or political opponents with whom he would occasionally associate or represent, although these did not constitute direct conflict of interest. The legal profession at that time did not have the complex codes of today's ethics—a lawyer's conscience was his guide when it came to such matters.

A client one day might be sued by Lincoln the next. Lincoln did work on behalf of Jesse Fell, a long-standing, ardent political supporter. Jesse had a brother, attorney Kersey Fell, whose office across the street from the courthouse has been characterized as Lincoln's headquarters in Bloomington. Notwithstanding, Lincoln recovered a judgment against Kersey on a note he had given to Lincoln's client Orville Browning, the attorney from Quincy, also a political ally of Lincoln of many years' standing.[27] Over the years, he represented Bloomington's James Allin Jr., son of the town's founder, on several cases but still sued Allin on behalf of Alex Campbell.[28] In April 1851, Lincoln and Benjamin F. James of Tremont brought two cases against the City of Pekin on notes the city had issued to purchase land on each side of the Illinois River for a ferry. Pekin's Benjamin S. Prettyman and Halsey Merriman of Peoria defended both cases. Both were settled and dismissed two years later. Curiously, that same month, Lincoln and Edward Jones represented Pekin in a suit against H. Meyers and Company. In the 1850 Tazewell County case of *Daven v. Armington*, Lincoln successfully sued Hezekiah Armington, whom William Briggs and Prettyman represented. In 1852, Lincoln joined Samuel Fuller on behalf of Armington as he unsuccessfully sued one John Skates.[29]

Range of Cases

Collection cases constituted almost half of Lincoln's practice, fairly even divided between debtor and creditor.[30] In Lincoln's era, because of a lack of currency, people used negotiated notes in lieu of currency, which caused debt-collection cases to dominate the courts. Lincoln's practice was no exception. The collection work led to numerous mortgage foreclosures. In 1839, Lincoln brought a mortgage foreclosure action against Stephen A. Douglas on behalf of James Allin Jr. Douglas didn't come to court and so defaulted, and the court sold the mortgaged lots.[31] Little is known of this case or its impact on the relationship of the two longtime rivals. Douglas was known to have invested in lots in the newly formed towns of central Illinois, only to walk away from the less-promising investments.

Breach of contract, which included these collection cases, was the dominant cause of action in his practice, with over twenty-three hundred such cases.[32] The law of contracts had evolved in the nineteenth century so that the will of the parties governed the contractual relationship rather than the mutual fairness for each party. Accordingly, the legal profession, Lincoln included, considered the sanctity of contracts as a fundamental element in the social order of the day.[33] Author John Frank said, "He was conditioned to the theory of contract as a moral matter."[34] The fact that Lincoln took cases both attacking and defending contracts is another example of the moral detachment characteristic of a well-grounded lawyer.

Next in total volume were 1,750 real-estate cases. Some of these involved partition, a suit to divide real-estate among multiple owners; most involved title disputes. Lincoln handled more than eight hundred inheritance cases. In one of these, Lincoln represented the Toussant DuBois' heirs, including Lincoln's long-time political ally Jesse DuBois, who, born in 1811 and a University of Indiana graduate, served in the legislature from 1834 to 1844. He strongly supported Lincoln's leadership in the house, including support of the move of the capital to Springfield. DuBois remained a strong supporter throughout Lincoln's career in Illinois, even naming his son Lincoln in 1847. The DuBois heirs were asserting inheritance rights to the DuBois family home and land in Lawrenceville, Illinois. The cases, moved to the Edgar County Circuit Court on a change of venue from Lawrence County, resolved with the heirs recovering a portion of the lots.[35]

Lincoln represented over eighty-five persons in slander cases, defamation litigation being much more common than today. Slander cases involving men focused on their honesty and integrity; for women, the contention was over their reputations for chastity.[36] The 1840 Livingston County case of *Popejoy v. Wilson* was a typical men's case. Lincoln and Stuart's client, William Popejoy, was accused by the defendant, Isaac Wilson, of stealing meat from a third party, so Popejoy sued to cleanse his reputation. Wilson withdrew his initial denial confirming the slander, and a judgment was entered for $2,000. Thus vindicated, Popejoy remitted the judgment.[37] Typical of a woman's suit was the 1851 slander case of *Jacobus v. Kitchell* in Tazewell County. Lincoln's clients were Mildon and Elizabeth Kitchell, who accused the plaintiff, Mary Ann Jacobus, client of Tremont attorney Jones, of being a "whore." They embellished the accusation by asserting that she "gets her fine clothes by whoring." Jacobus sued the Kitchells. Twelve witnessed testified before the case was settled when Lincoln's clients agreed to make no further statements against Jacobus's chastity, and she dismissed the case.[38]

Divorce, representing both husbands and wives, plaintiffs and defendants, amounted to 145 cases for Lincoln. Grounds for divorce were more pejorative and more often contested than in today's divorce litigation. In *Dobbs v. Dobbs*, an 1845 Tazewell County case, Lincoln represented a wife seeking a divorce from her husband on the grounds of adultery. Attorneys with Lincoln representing Jane Dobbs included Edward Jones and Prettyman. Twenty-four witnesses testified. The first trial resulted in a hung jury, but the second jury found the defendant guilty of adultery and awarded the divorce. In Vermilion County, George Helmick sued his wife, Eliza, Lincoln's client, in 1853, alleging she had committed adultery with several men. Lincoln filed a denial that charged the husband had "induced different men to make attempts upon her chastity." The case was dismissed.[39]

Lincoln represented clients in nine seduction cases, often by fathers seeking to recover for the loss of services of their pregnant daughters. Lincoln's client Nancy Jane Dunn was the centerpiece of an unusual series of three cases in 1850 arising from her relationship with Albert G. Carle, one of Urbana's pioneers. Carle was represented in all three cases by the talented team of Kirby Benedict, then of Paris, and Gridley. First, Nancy sued Carle for breach of marriage contract but lost because, the court ruled, she had failed to prove her case. Second, on behalf of Nancy's father, Zephaniah, Lincoln went after recovery, which ended up being $180.41, for the father's loss of his daughter's services during the pregnancy. Zephaniah remitted the verdict in exchange for Carle's agreement not to seek custody of the child. In the third suit, in which Lincoln participated, Nancy won a paternity charge and was awarded $50.00 per year in support.[40]

Lincoln handled a smattering of personal injury and negligence cases, much less common then.[41] Two of these created significant precedent. In addition to the firm's *Dalby* case, which established liability of a corporation for the intentional torts of its employees, there is the case of *Browning v. Springfield, Illinois*, which established the liability of municipalities for failure to keep the streets in good repair. Browning fell in a poorly maintained street and broke his leg. Lincoln sued the city, whose attorneys were Stuart and Benjamin Edwards. The city won because the law then provided no such grounds of recovery against a city. The Illinois Supreme Court reversed, adopting Lincoln's theory of liability on the city since its charter imposed the duty to maintain the streets and the means to carry out that duty through taxes. The opinion stated that the duty was "based on sound sense in accordance with strict morality, and keeping pace with the progress of the age." The case was remanded to the circuit court where the retrial resulted in a $700 verdict for Lincoln's client.[42]

Malpractice suits were rare. Lincoln represented Dr. Eli Crothers of Bloomington in a case brought by Samuel Fleming, a middle-aged man who had been an onlooker at a fire that destroyed the block south of the courthouse in Bloomington in 1855. Both of his legs broke when a chimney from a burning livery stable fell on him. The doctor had set Fleming's legs, one of which healed crooked and shorter than the other. Fleming engaged Gridley and Leonard Swett to bring suit the following year. Lincoln and Stuart defended the doctor. Because of the number of witnesses, the trial took a week. Lincoln called the twelve doctors in town whom Swett had not called. In closing argument of the suit that became the "chicken bone case," Lincoln used bones from a young and an old chicken to illustrate the brittle bones of an older man. The jury failed to reach a verdict after eighteen hours of deliberation, so the venue was transferred to Logan County for retrial, but the case was ultimately settled.[43]

County officials of a number of the counties of the circuit engaged Lincoln in the litigation arising out of the performance of their duties—a measure of Lincoln's stature around the circuit. Three sheriffs of Tazewell County, the sheriffs of Macon and Vermilion Counties, and constables in Christian and Menard Counties all hired Lincoln in cases arising out of their official duties.[44] Likewise, Lincoln represented Woodford County in a dispute over damages for land taken for a road between Metamora and Walnut Grove. The circuit court increased the county court's $25 award to $296.85. Lincoln represented Jonathan Mayo, longtime circuit clerk of Edgar County and one of the county's most influential Whigs. Mayo had become the county's first circuit clerk in 1823, serving for twenty-five years. In 1846, as clerk, Mayo issued writs of scire facias, a writ used in enforcement of previous judgment and executed judgment. Since the execution recovered no money, the county refused to pay the clerk's fee of $7.93. Judge Samuel Treat entered judgment for Mayo seeking payment from the county, and the county appealed, motivated by the precedent involved, and won. Mayo engaged Lincoln to appeal to the supreme court, which Lincoln lost.[45]

Christian County contracted to construct a new courthouse in 1856. Circuit clerk and prominent attorney Horatio M. Vandeveer was charged with oversight of the construction. When the builders, Jacob Overholt and Jesse Squier, demanded payment for partial completion of the building pursuant to the contract, the county refused, contending noncompliance with the specifications. The contractors quit the job for nonpayment and sued the county for the lost profits. Venue was moved to Macon County, and Logan and Lincoln as well as Vandeveer and Shelbyville's Anthony Thornton represented Christian County. The builders, represented by Benjamin Edwards, won, and the county appealed. The Illinois Supreme Court agreed with Lincoln that the builders could not recover profits unless they had been prevented from completing construction.[46]

The construction of the Christian County Courthouse in Taylorville in 1854 led to litigation. The county engaged Lincoln to defend the case of *Overholt & Squire v. Christian County, Illinois*, a case Lincoln won in the Illinois Supreme Court. The original courthouse, a white, frame building, was moved to the east side of the square and can be seen across the street to the right of the new building. Abraham Lincoln Presidential Library and Museum.

His criminal cases constituted only about 5 percent of his practice, including cases in which he assisted the prosecution. He participated in twenty-seven murder trials over the course of his career.[47] Other areas in which Lincoln worked were injunctions (233 cases), taxation (44 cases), wills, will contests, patent infringement, partnership settlements, and habeas corpus.

Lobbying also constituted a part of Lincoln's practice because of his location in Springfield and extensive legislative connections and experience.[48] David Davis tired of the marathon journey around the circuit, writing to Sarah at the end of the Spring 1852 session, "My Circuit must be altered next winter or I will resign." He turned for relief to Lincoln, who drafted a bill the following January. He saw to its passage that month. The bill reduced the Eighth Judicial Circuit to eight counties from fourteen, which reduced the trip around the circuit by over 150 miles and two weeks and specified times in each spring and fall session.[49] It is difficult to assess the volume of lobbying because most of it was performed outside the public record. The same can be said of measuring Lincoln's extensive office practice.

An Honest Lawyer

Lincoln was a highly respected and trusted lawyer, his reputation based "on the universal belief in his absolute honesty."[50] He was honest in his dealings with clients, other lawyers, and the court alike and intellectually honest in his arguments to the courts. Hiram Beckwith of Danville, son of the town's founder, who trained under Lincoln and eventually also opposed him, said that Lincoln never knowingly misstated the law or the evidence. In his law lecture notes, Lincoln said, "Resolve to be honest at all events; and if in your own judgment you cannot be an honest lawyer, resolve to be honest without being a lawyer."[51] Parks recalled, "The great feature in Mr. Lincoln's character was his *integrity*. . . . I've often said that for a man who was for a quarter of a century *both a lawyer & a politician* he was the most honest man I ever knew." His characteristic detachment was a valuable tool in the contentious world of the trial lawyer. His demeanor was exemplary. Even-tempered, calm, and imperturbable in the courtroom, he never let his personal feelings show in dealing with other lawyers. He seemingly had no enemies, which is unusual considering the highly charged atmosphere in the courtrooms of the day. James Ewing of Bloomington said, "Courteous to the court, fair to his opponent, and modest in his assertions, he was certainly the model lawyer." Beckwith said Lincoln would never belittle the opponent's side of the case. Davis shared with Sarah his admiration for Lincoln's "exceeding honesty and fairness."[52]

Lincoln had an exceptional ability to be selective and discriminating as to which points he chose to pursue. Attorney Ezra Prince of Bloomington said, "The truth is, Mr. Lincoln had a genius for seeing the real point in a case at once, and aiming steadily at it from the beginning of a trial to the end." Beckwith cited Lincoln's strategy of emphasizing only the most vital points in a case. In June 1860, Jacob Harding of the Paris *Prairie Beacon* describes Lincoln the lawyer whose arguments were as "clearing the brush out of the way as he proceeded. . . . Instead of disputing every inch of ground, as was too common at the bar, he made every concession the opposite side was entitled to, and seemed more like an able and impartial judge stating the case to the jury, fairly and fully, than a lawyer who was paid to attend to one side of the case only."[53] Leonard Swett observed, "By giving away 6 points and carrying the 7th, he carried his case and the whole case hanging on the 7th, he traded away everything which would give him the least and in carrying that." Also noted, by John Littlefield, were Lincoln's abilities to concentrate and focus on a case.[54]

Beckwith noted that Lincoln took no notes during a trial and asked him about this. Lincoln responded it was a bother to take notes and it was distracting in concentrating on the case. He said he relied on his own well-trained memory to recall what had occurred during the trial and that lawyers who used notes ended up confusing the jury. He once described his mind as similar to a piece of steel: It was hard to scratch anything on it, but once there, it was there for good.[55]

Contemporary observations are virtually unanimous in their praise of Lincoln's effectiveness in the courtroom. The Danville *Illinois Citizen*, Beckwith, and Jacob Harding all agreed that Lincoln had no superior before a jury. Lincoln, a skilled cross-examiner, also created excellent rapport with juries because he understood them and spoke their language, once telling Herndon not to aim too high when arguing to a jury.[56] His vast store of anecdotes served him well with juries to illustrate essential points. He had a good sense of what aspects of his case would most arouse the sentiments of a jury. Harding observed that as Lincoln argued he would unconsciously draw near to the jury until he was almost touching it.[57] In May 1850, the

Danville *Illinois Citizen* commented, "That in his examination of witnesses he displays a masterly ingenuity and a legal tact that baffles and defies deceit." The paper describes his arguments as "bold, forcible, and convincing," his summations known for their wit, simplicity, and insight.[58]

Lincoln was not a student of the law reading or studying law in the abstract but a student of the specific areas his cases involved. Both Stephen T. Logan and Herndon said that he never studied or read the law in general.[59] Logan noted that he never tracked the decisions of the Illinois Supreme Court, something most litigators of Lincoln's stature do. Logan concluded, "His general knowledge of law was not formidable." Given his continuous drive to learn in so many areas, it is curious that he did not pursue knowledge of law in the same manner. Logan stated, "He would work hard to learn all there was in a case," terming Lincoln's approach "tenacious." Thus, his reading and study directed to the particular case, Lincoln accumulated knowledge from his specific cases rather than general study.[60] Lincoln scholar Benjamin Thomas wrote that "observation and experience remained his chief instructors."[61] Some of Lincoln's contemporaries said that if he didn't believe in a case, he didn't do a good job.[62] This seems inconsistent with his characteristic objectivity and shows an unlikely lack of commitment to his client's cause. Others suggest a lack of ability in situations where time to prepare was inadequate. This seems contrary to the nature of the circuit practice, which demanded presentation of a case with limited time for preparation and in which he excelled. However, he was at his best when he had time to fully prepare, as exemplified by the quality and volume of his work before the Illinois Supreme Court.[63]

His win-loss record on the circuit is no real indication of his ability. It is not possible to judge the difficulty of each case, and a victory in many instances would be verdict against his client but in a much lesser amount than that sought. The most persuasive evidence of his ability is the sheer volume of work. The remarkable *Law Practice of Abraham Lincoln* has uncovered over five thousand cases Lincoln and his partners handled. This is necessarily an incomplete computation because of the destruction of the federal court records in the Great Chicago Fire in 1871 and the destruction by fire of several county courthouses, including Logan and McLean, the latter thought to be one Lincoln's busier counties. Before the Illinois Supreme Court, he and his partners handled over four hundred cases, in nearly half of which they were not involved in the trial court. These referrals came from all over the state, many from outside the circuit.[64]

Perhaps his most noteworthy quality was his capacity for growth. As he matured from small-time politician to statesman, he matured from a small-time lawyer to a leading lawyer in Illinois. Logan said, "Lincoln was growing all the time, from the time I first saw him."[65] The circuit experience helped ready Lincoln for the demands of the presidency. Dealing with the variety of people and problems of the circuit taught him to listen and schooled him as a quick study, able to assimilate a wide range of information, opinions, and advice from a variety of sources and then to respond quickly and correctly. Facing new issues with minimal time to digest and resolve them shaped him into a persuader and cajoler of people in different and somewhat unfamiliar venues and improved his ability to improvise and create. The bar of the Eighth Judicial Circuit included some of the best lawyers in the state. Constantly matching wits with these capable lawyers likewise prepared him for the challenging relationships of the White House.[66]

Lincoln practiced law until his nomination to the presidency. He was able to separate his two careers, law and politics, so that the demands and partisanship of the latter did not affect the nature of the former. Many of the diverse types of clients and lawyers worked with him in the law but against him politically. He was the leading lawyer in central Illinois, arguably the dominant section of the state.[67] On November 3, 1854, the *Chicago Journal* characterized Lincoln as "the most powerful speaker and one of the ablest lawyers in the West."[68] Citing Lincoln's contemporaries, historian John J. Duff concludes from his in-depth study of Lincoln's career, "No Illinois lawyer could do so many things so well."[69] Lincoln as lawyer provided the foundation of support upon which Lincoln as politician was constructed.

PART TWO

COUNTIES OF THE EIGHTH JUDICIAL CIRCUIT

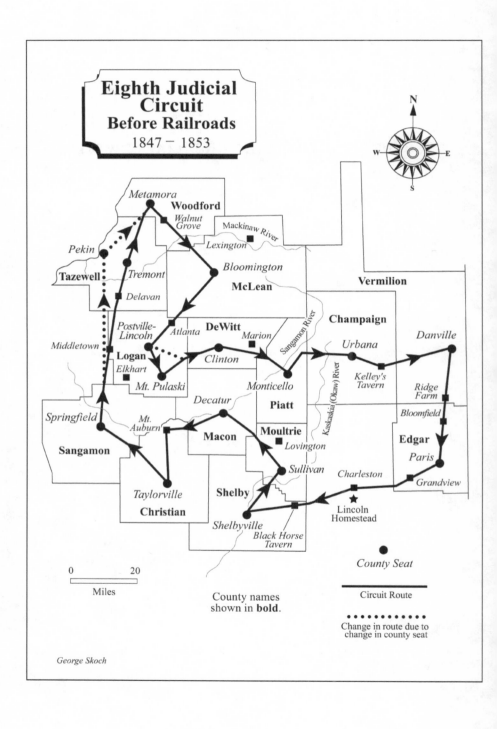

Eighth Judicial Circuit
Before Railroads
1847 – 1853

N
W — E
S

Metamora

Woodford
Walnut Grove

Mackinaw River

Lexington

Pekin

Tazewell

Tremont

Bloomington

McLean

Delavan

Vermilion

Postville-Lincoln

Atlanta

DeWitt

Marion

Sangamon River

Champaign

Urbana

Danville

Middletown

Logan

Clinton

Kelley's Tavern

Elkhart

Monticello

Mt. Pulaski

Kaskaskia (Okaw) River

Ridge Farm

Decatur

Piatt

Bloomfield

Springfield

Mt. Auburn

Macon

Moultrie

Edgar

Sangamon

Lovington

Paris

Sullivan

Charleston

Grandview

Taylorville

Shelby

Lincoln Homestead

Christian

Shelbyville

Black Horse Tavern

● County Seat

0   20
Miles

County names shown in **bold**.

——————— Circuit Route

• • • • • • • • • • • •
Change in route due to change in county seat

George Skoch

4. SANGAMON, TAZEWELL, WOODFORD

T he heyday of the circuit coincides with what Lincoln described as his "as-
siduous" return to the law, 1849 to 1853, when the Eighth Judicial Circuit
attained its largest size and its most colorful ambiance. A "trip" around the
circuit to examine its geography, its towns, and its people shows how they
played a significant role in Lincoln's life.

Sangamon

The semi-annual circuit tours started in Sangamon County, Lincoln's home,
with a two-week session, the longest of any of the counties. Springfield
generated the bulk of Lincoln's law business. He and his partners handled
over two thousand cases there.

Lincoln represented a number of attorneys in Sangamon County, including Edward D. Baker, Mason Brayman, James Matheny, and William
L. May, one-time Democratic Congressman, and Logan County's Samuel
Parks. He associated with other attorneys less in his home county than he
did out on the circuit, no doubt because much of the business on the rest
of the circuit was referred. The lawyers with whom he associated most frequently in Sangamon County included Baker, Albert T. Bledsoe, James C.
Conkling, Henry Dummer, Benjamin Edwards, Silas Robbins, Matheny,
and his former partners John T. Stuart and Stephen T. Logan. He also
frequently opposed Baker, Bledsoe, Conkling, Edwards, and Matheny.
He associated with Stephen A. Douglas on two cases and opposed him
on seventeen.[1]

His clients included many of Springfield's most important people, including Virgil Hickox and John Calhoun, both staunch Democrats and Douglas supporters. Hickox, a director of the Alton and Sangamon Railroad and chairman of the Democratic State Central Committee during most of the 1850s, worked closely with Lincoln to promote the railroad in the 1840s and 1850s. Other prominent clients included Elijah Iles, Charles Matheny, Seth Tinsley, owner of the large building in which Lincoln's office and the courts were located, William Butler, Joshua Speed, Archer Herndon, and Anson Henry. James F. Reed, co-leader and survivor of the ill-fated Donner party, which departed from the capitol square in 1846, was also a client.[2]

Jacob Bunn, a New Jersey native who arrived in 1840 and a key member of Springfield's commercial community, started a grocery business that expanded to include mercantile business. As his wealth grew, he became a significant lender. The breadth of these activities made him a good source of work for Lincoln. Between 1848 and 1856, Lincoln had twenty-nine collection cases for Bunn, either on accounts or on promissory notes. Until 1851, some of the larger, more prosperous storekeepers held money for customers who were accumulating cash to pay taxes. That year, Bunn and John Williams started Springfield's first bank, the Springfield Marine and Fire Insurance Company, but Bunn and Williams soon discontinued the insurance business and changed solely to banking; Springfield Marine Bank, where Lincoln banked, was for many years the largest bank in the state outside of Chicago. Bunn's younger brother John, who worked hard for Lincoln, described himself as "one of his junior political agents. . . . Lincoln was the leading lawyer in central Illinois before his election to the Presidency."[3]

Lincoln also represented less-prominent members of the community. In 1845, Rebecca Thomas sought Lincoln's help for an exorbitant lawyer's fee in a case arising out of her pension rights as the widow of a Revolutionary War soldier, John Thomas, fifteen to twenty years her senior. The Thomases had once lived in New Salem. The suit was against prominent Springfield resident Erastus Wright, a pension agent who had assisted Rebecca when she obtained her pension and for which he had charged what Rebecca claimed was an excessive fee. She lost when she tried to get the amount paid on her own behalf in the Justice of Peace Court so she came to Lincoln, who asked the circuit court for a new trial. William H. Herndon recalled Lincoln's ire being raised by Wright's behavior toward the widow of this Revolutionary

War soldier. He told Herndon before the trial that he was going to "skin the defendant." With impassioned reminders to the jury of Valley Forge and the other sacrifices in the Revolutionary War, he attacked with "fierce and invective" the defendant for his behavior, according to Herndon. Lincoln obtained a judgment for the widow and did not charge her. David Davis also recalled this incident. Lincoln's uncharacteristic anger is, in fact, hard to understand. A review of Wright's efforts on the widow's behalf suggests he had earned a fair fee. Lincoln represented Wright in twenty-nine cases, both before and after the Thomas case.[4]

Tazewell

After Sangamon, the first leg of the journey around the circuit was to the county seat of Tazewell County, settled in 1823 and established four years later. Much larger to begin with, it was reduced by 75 percent when the state made other counties from it. On the Illinois River, Pekin, the county's principal town, enjoyed the spot as a center for commerce and the transport of goods to the east until the coming of the railroads. Lincoln first visited Pekin on his return from the Black Hawk War in 1832 as he canoed from Peoria to Havana, Illinois.[5]

Tazewell, the circuit's third largest county in population and one of its original counties, had two seats during the Lincoln era, Tremont and Pekin. The fifty-mile trip from Springfield to either of those county seats was longer than nearly any other circuit trip. It was a tough two-day circuit ride, whether on horseback in wet weather or in a carriage in the dryer season; Lincoln and his comrades headed north on a road, portions of which Lincoln had surveyed as an assistant county surveyor. The road took them to Middletown, the oldest town in Logan County, where he occasionally stayed. They crossed Salt Creek, Logan County's largest stream. In 1834, Lincoln introduced a bill to permit the construction of a toll bridge there, known as Musick's Bridge. In the next two sessions, he introduced legislation relative to the location of this road.[6]

In this leg lay a prairie, one of the largest in the state, which Boston's J. H. Buckingham describes: "For miles and miles we saw nothing but a vast expanse of what I can compare to nothing else but the ocean itself . . . The tall grass . . . looked like the deep sea; it seemed as if we were out of sight of land for no house, no barn, no tree was visible, and the horizon presented the rolling of the waves in the far off distance. There were all sorts of flowers in the neighborhood of the road which by the way, did not appear to be a road, and all the colors of the rainbow were exhibited on all sides,—before, behind, east, west, north and south—as if the sun were shining upon the gay and dancing waters. . . . [N]umerous yellow, pink, and crimson flowers, and almost everything else that is beautiful, that we have ever heard of. . . . [I]n the distance we saw at intervals, groves of trees which looked like islands in the ocean."[7] From Salt Creek, the road headed north to Delavan, founded as a cooperative colony in 1837. Occasionally, Lincoln stayed at the inn the Delavan House, owned by Ira B. Hall, a client of Lincoln.[8]

The road gradually descends into town coming from the south. Continuing north from Delavan, the road rises slightly out of the town, only to fall more dramatically to traverse the picturesque valley of the tree-lined Mackinaw River, its clear waters filtered by thousands of acres of prairie wetlands. The road climbed from the graveled ford to Tremont, the county seat from 1835 to 1849. Once, when Lincoln stayed at Tremont's Franklin House, on the courthouse square, he left his coat there. In a note, he asked the proprietor, William Doughty, to purchase heavy cloth, wrap the coat in it, and return it to his house via the Springfield stagecoach.[9]

Tremont and the larger city of Pekin fought for many years over the location for the county seat. Lincoln became involved in this acrimonious, eighteen-year dispute. The first county seat was Mackinaw, on the east edge of the county, but when the formation of McLean County in 1830 took away the eastern portion of Tazewell, the county seat moved to Pekin. Three years later, a group of entrepreneurs that included future Lincoln client John Harris of Bedford, Westchester County, New York, organized a colony founding the town of Tremont. When Asiatic cholera devastated Pekin in 1834, Harris offered the county twenty acres and $2,000 to move the county seat to Tremont, a more central location and less disease prone than Pekin on the Illinois River. Tremont became the county seat the following year, and William Flagg of Bloomington built a striking courthouse in 1836 for the then-large sum of $14,450.[10] Four large columns supported the front portico of the two-story, red-brick building. For the view of the vast prairie surrounding the town, sightseers climbed the circular stairway to the cupola, whose copper-covered dome topped the building. Almost immediately, the citizens of Pekin began plotting for the recovery of the county seat, but in

Citizens of Tremont, an early county seat of Tazewell County, climbed into the cupola to view vast prairie vistas. The building served as the courthouse from its construction in 1836 until the county seat was moved to Pekin in 1850. Abraham Lincoln Presidential Library and Museum.

1843, another devastating epidemic, this time scarlet fever, stalled the effort. Voters defeated several referenda to move the county seat.[11] In anticipation of the county seat's move, the county spent over $8,000 on a Grecian-style, two-story, rectangular courthouse with six columns (where the current courthouse stands). The legislature authorized yet another referendum on the issue, Pekin prevailed, and the county seat moved again.[12]

In April 1851, the John A. Jones family in Tremont held a large dinner to commemorate the last session of the circuit court. In the spacious yard of his federal house, known as the Red Brick, Jones, attorney and circuit clerk from 1837 to 1857, welcomed the family's guests, one of whom was

Lincoln, who, the family recalled, had treated a "stone bruise" of the Joneses' small son and had sometimes stayed at the home. Other guests included Judge Davis and the town's residents, including Pierre Menard, son of the prominent leader of the Illinois Territory for whom the county is named. The bittersweet occasion ended with a rendition of *Auld Lang Syne.* Jones's daughter Eugenia Jones Hunt remembered that "the removal of the county seat to Pekin almost tore my native town asunder."[13] Correspondence from Tremont to Lincoln during this period makes reference to the devastating effect of this move on the town.

The legislation moving the county seat provided that the former courthouse would now be used for a school. Harris had already consulted Lincoln and Logan about whether the title to the twenty acres and the courthouse would revert to him if the county seat went back to Pekin. In 1843, Lincoln had written an opinion that although the deed included no such condition, it would indeed revert to Harris since the conveyance was clearly for only the courthouse.[14] In 1851, Harris at last asked Lincoln to get his property back. Lincoln, with his former partners Logan and Stuart, sued the county, represented by the renowned Norman Purple of Peoria and Benjamin Prettyman of Pekin. Judge Davis ruled for the county, and the Illinois Supreme Court affirmed because the deed contained no such condition for reverter.[15]

At 250 cases, Tazewell County listed third of Lincoln's busiest venues, after Sangamon and Menard. The usual variety included a number of replevin cases, a remedy for the recovery of personal property, seeking such disparate items as a hundred barrels of whiskey, livestock, seven thousand bushels of corn shelled and unshelled, a canal boat, and two thousand gunny sacks.[16] The lawyers associated with Lincoln in Tazewell County included not only resident attorneys but also several from Peoria and from around the circuit. The most active trial lawyer in the county was Edward Jones, brother of John A. Jones, whom he had preceded for one year as circuit clerk. Edward Jones associated with Lincoln in more cases and opposed him in more cases in Tazewell County than any other attorney. Born in Georgetown in 1811, he was a veteran of both the Black Hawk and Mexican Wars.[17] In 1851, Jones hired Lincoln to bring in an assault case against Joseph S. Maus, a Tremont doctor, whose claim of graduation from medical school Jones disputed. Maus assaulted him, putting out Jones's eye; Maus claimed he was defending himself. The case was settled the next year.[18] In a letter of September 22, 1852,

Judge Davis said, "I had a hard week in court last week. Edward Jones gave me a great deal of trouble and this place is the hardest place to hold court on the Circuit." In 1851, Davis commented to Sarah, "Edward Jones' drinking as bad as ever." He died six years later, at age forty-six.[19]

Tazewell County was not Davis's favorite stop; he was not fond of Pekin, whose principal hotel was the Tazewell House, at Court and Front Streets near the Illinois River. Lincoln and Davis also stayed at "Mrs. Wilson's" boardinghouse, west of the courthouse. Davis reported it "fine and comfortable" because each lawyer had his own bed. In 1851, he described the hot, humid weather as making the prospect of court in Pekin "anything but agreeable" and reported the sand to be a foot deep "and the place horribly dirty." For relief on one visit, he and Lincoln rode out to Tremont for the night, although Davis described both Tremont and Pekin as "unimproving and dull." He advised Sarah, "I should not like to live in Pekin and I don't think you would."[20]

Other lawyers Lincoln worked with and against include Benjamin Prettyman, Benjamin James, James Harriott, Norman Purple, and Henry Grove. Prettyman, probably Tazewell County's leading attorney, frequently opposed Lincoln and less frequently associated with him. A native of Delaware, he moved with his parents to Pekin in 1831, studied law in the office of Logan and Lincoln, and began practice in 1845 in Pekin. He rode the circuit to Decatur, Clinton, Bloomington, and Metamora. A staunch Democrat, Prettyman became a major land speculator in Pekin; Lincoln, as an attorney, opposed Prettyman in five cases arising out of these transactions. James, who had numerous cases with and against Lincoln, was an aggressive ally in Lincoln's run for Congress in the 1840s. He moved to Chicago a decade later. Harriott, who was to become a circuit judge and preside over Lincoln's famed Armstrong Moonlight trial, was associated with and opposed Lincoln several times before becoming a judge.[21]

Several lawyers from the larger river town of Peoria, across the Illinois River and ten miles upstream from Pekin, traveled to the courts of Tazewell. Purple, born in New York in 1803, moved to Peoria in 1837 and became the most prominent of these lawyers with whom Lincoln frequently associated and also opposed. Purple, a Democrat, suffered a narrow loss in a race for the General Assembly. The contested matter went to the floor of the legislature, where Lincoln took a party position opposed to seating Purple, whose opponent ultimately won the seat. Purple, state's attorney for the Ninth Judicial Circuit from 1840 to 1842, then was appointed to the Democrat-controlled Supreme Court in 1845, presiding over the Fifth Judicial Circuit and sitting on the court until the new constitution of 1848. He then resigned and resumed his practice in Peoria. In 1849, he wrote *The Real Estate Statutes of Illinois* and in 1856 *A Compilation of the Statutes of the State of Illinois*, a standard treatise used by Illinois lawyers for many years. In October 1858, Lincoln wrote an opinion on election laws extensively citing and relying on "Purple's Statutes" and referred a client to "Judge Purple." Purple died in Chicago in 1863.[22] Another Peoria lawyer active in the Eighth Judicial Circuit was Grove, whom a Peoria County history refers to as "a very eccentric and atheistic lawyer."[23] Grove, an active Republican, became a valuable political ally during Lincoln's rise in the 1850s.

Some of Lincoln's clients were also his friends. In addition to Edward Jones, he represented close friend and Tremont attorney Alexander H. Saltonstall and his brother, Dr. Samuel Saltonstall.[24] Lincoln enjoyed a friendship with George W. Minier, another influential early leader of the county, at whose farm, in the eastern part of the county, Lincoln would sometimes stay. Minier, an ordained minister of the Disciples of Christ, an abolitionist, and strong temperance advocate, nursed an ill Leonard Swett when he returned to central Illinois from the Mexican War, and they became friends. In the spring of 1847, Minier observed Lincoln attempting to enforce a contract executed by two minors whose lawyer raised the defense that their being underage invalidated the contract. Lincoln, quoting *Othello*, in a mere five-minute closing argument, convinced the jury that to allow the young men to get off on this technicality would rob them of their good name forever and pleaded for the defendants not to be spoiled by a favorable verdict.[25]

Lincoln's criminal practice in Tazewell County was minimal. He sat at the prosecution's table in about one-third of his twenty criminal cases. Most noteworthy is *People v. Thomas Delny*. State's Attorney David Campbell was absent, so Judge Davis appointed Lincoln, who drafted the indictment for the rape of a seven-year-old girl. The statutes of the day made sex with a female under age ten with or without consent a crime punishable by imprisonment for one year to life. The defendant, an Irish-born immigrant who arrived in 1851, was convicted in a trial on May 10, 1853, with the medical witness being Maus. The anger of the town's residents rose to such a pitch against Delny that one witness claimed, "A mob came near getting the base wretch and nearly hanging him." Seven years later, though, Governor William H. Bissell pardoned Delny. Lincoln received a $5 fee for his work. In one of his Tazewell cases as lawyer for the defense, Lincoln successfully defended Lewis Beal on two separate charges of rape in 1855 two years after the *Delny* case.[26]

The colorful anecdotes of practice in the circuit court rooms include Lincoln versus a bat in the Pekin courtroom. During one court session, a bat began circling the courtroom. Lincoln's height made him the logical one to get rid of the bat, and after a failed attempt with a coat, he swept the bat out a window with a broom.[27]

The county was removed from the circuit in 1857. Accordingly, in July, Lincoln advised a client, "The Circuits are so divided now that I cannot attend the Tazewell Court regularly if at all anymore." He referred his Tazewell clients to Prettyman.[28]

Woodford

After a week in Tazewell County, the court moved to Woodford County, whose seat, Metamora, was thirty miles to the north. From Pekin, the road climbed out of the Illinois River Valley to Washington and then northeasterly on a road that is still in use to Metamora. Woodford, carved out of Tazewell and McLean Counties in 1841, was settled primarily by Kentucky Democrats. It was part of the circuit for the next sixteen years. The act creating the county called for Versailles to be the county seat for two years, where Lincoln attended court. After that time, an election would select a permanent county seat, and the town of Hanover won. When it was determined that name already belonged to a town in Illinois, Hanover became Metamora, a name that the wife of Peter Willard, a prominent merchant and supporter of Lincoln, selected.[29] Metamora was one of the smallest towns in the circuit, and its court session typically lasted just two or three days.

One condition of the move was that the new county seat have a suitable building to house the courts. Apparently, no existing structure met the standard in Metamora. The schoolhouse in which court had been held in Versailles was put on runners and dragged the ten miles to Metamora. Four years later, the county erected a $4,500 brick courthouse, its style classic revival, Greek temple and its front sporting four Ionic columns.[30]

The stately Woodford County Courthouse in Metamora, then the county seat, still stands as one of only two circuit courthouses in their original locations. It served as the courthouse from its construction in 1845 until the county seat was moved by referendum to Eureka in 1896. Abraham Lincoln Presidential Library and Museum.

After-court sessions at the local inn, the Metamora House, went long into the night as the attorneys and locals swapped yarns, gossiped, and talked politics. Like so many circuit inns, the Metamora House was better known for its hospitality than its food. Davis commented, "The tavern at Woodford is miserable, but it may be that Mr. Cross may take compassion and take us to his house," a reference to Samuel Cross, the circuit clerk with whom Lincoln, Davis, and Campbell occasionally stayed. When Robert Ingersoll of Peoria, who practiced in Woodford County and stayed at the Metamora House, saw a centuries-old tapestry in Windsor Castle years later, he said it reminded him of the tablecloth of the Metamora House by the end of court week.[31]

The county could boast only a few local lawyers—Adlai Stevenson, future U.S. vice president, opened his law office in Metamora in 1858—and most of the men in court were from other towns, such as Springfield, Bloomington, and Peoria.[32] Purple appeared against Lincoln most frequently in Woodford

County. Asahel Gridley of Bloomington frequently appeared both in association with and opposed to Lincoln. Others were Springfield's James C. Conkling and Stephen T. Logan.[33]

In a large prairie grove south and east of Metamora is Walnut Grove, a more liberal community, whose leaders included Ben Major, the founder of Walnut Grove Academy in 1847, and his brother-in-law William Davenport, a client and political supporter of Lincoln. Major sought to organize and open Eureka College, but he died of cholera before he could finish the task. Three years after the untimely death, Davenport took up the cause, went to the state legislature, and obtained incorporation, and the college opened. Its board included Davenport, Ben's brother William Major of Bloomington, Logan, and Henry Grove.[34] Davenport unsuccessfully tried to force the county to organize itself into townships as required by law five years earlier. His attorney was Lincoln; the county's attorney was Gridley.[35]

When the Woodford session ended, the traveling retinue left Metamora heading for Bloomington. Once, somewhere along the way, recalled Bloomington attorney John Wickizer, Lincoln heard the squeals of a little pig about to be devoured by an old sow: "Lincoln leaped out of the buggy, seized a club, pounced upon the old sow, and beat her lustily . . . thus he saved the pig."[36]

The lawyers traveled on a ridge to the southeast, along timbered Walnut Creek wending its way through Walnut Grove, on to Versailles, and then descended to the still-existing ford with a now-long-gone grist mill and across the principal tributary of the Mackinaw River, Panther Creek. The road climbed up the bluff through the savannah to the town of Bowling Green, a thriving hamlet of homes, a mercantile establishment, and an inn. Legend has it that Lincoln and his fellows roomed once in a while at the inn and that Lincoln and Democrat Peter Cartwright made a joint appearance during their congressional campaign of 1846. The inn's limestone-lined well and the pioneer graveyard, hidden in the woods that have reclaimed it, are all that remains of the hamlet today.[37]

From Bowling Green, the road traverses a wide basin down to Wyatt's Ford to recross the Mackinaw. In the dryer seasons, the river was benign and gently flowing, but when flooded most springs, it could be treacherous and difficult to cross. Occasionally, the travelers would have to go downstream several miles to Slab Town to a ferry to get across. From Wyatt's Ford, the road gradually scales the bluff, the Eureka Moraine, and past the home of

Abraham Carlock, known as "the Old Democrat," whom Lincoln would often stop to visit.[38] Once the road gains the ridge, it reveals a sweeping view of miles of prairie to the west horizon. From there, the road passed the tiny hamlet of Oak Grove, then southeast across more miles of unbroken tall grass prairie and on to Bloomington, seat of McLean County.

5. MCLEAN, LIVINGSTON, LOGAN, DEWITT

———◦———

McLean

As the road approached Bloomington, it crossed another Sugar Creek and ascended the gradual incline into the town itself. Bloomington was the county seat of McLean County from the county's initial organization in 1830. The town sat on the north edge of Blooming Grove, where the first pioneers in the area settled in 1822 and where remnant large oaks still stand. The three-thousand-acre hardwood grove was mostly oaks and hickories with open understory. Bloomington existed on paper only at the time of its selection as county seat. Founder James Allin donated the courthouse square on the top of a gentle rise, part of the original twenty-acre town site. Early settler Asahel Gridley donated the $338 to build the original log courthouse, which was replaced in 1836 by an $8,500, two-story, forty-two-foot by forty-two-foot building in the coffee-mill design. This building served as the courthouse throughout Lincoln's career.[1]

McLean was one of only three counties to be part of the Eighth Judicial Circuit from its formation until Lincoln became president.[2] Lincoln attended court for almost all its sessions throughout his twenty-three years on the circuit. Bloomington was a major source of law business for Lincoln. More important, it was the home of more significant members of his political team of the 1850s than any other venue: David Davis, Jesse Fell, Isaac Funk, Asahel Gridley, Harvey Hogg, William Orme, John M. Scott, Leonard Swett, and, in the second half of the decade, Ward Hill Lamon, who had moved there from Danville, Illinois.

Davis, Gridley, and Fell, Bloomington's leading citizens, were also the men from that city most instrumental in Lincoln's twin political and legal careers. Davis knew Lincoln from the circuit, of course, and Gridley and Fell knew Lincoln before he came to Bloomington from their attendance at the legislature in Vandalia and were close friends of his. Lincoln did legal work for all of them, particularly Gridley, and all three actively promoted him professionally and politically. Davis, like Lincoln, played a small role in local affairs, probably because of the extended absences required by circuit travel.

Asahel Gridley of Bloomington was an irascible, unpleasant lawyer, then entrepreneur and client of Lincoln whose strong support of Lincoln, including financial, was important to his rise to the presidency. McLean County Historical Society.

Jesse Fell of Bloomington was one of Lincoln's earliest and most liberal supporters. Lincoln's acceptance of Fell's invitation to compose an autobiography in December 1859 was a significant indication of Lincoln's decision to run for the presidency. Douglas Hartley, drawing, private collection of Davis U. Merwin.

All three made their fortunes in land. Gridley involved himself in a broad range of business interests and acquired thousands of acres of farmland. He was probably Bloomington's wealthiest and least popular citizen, known for his profane, arrogant, and hateful manner. Davis hated Gridley, often declaring that Gridley could not have gotten so rich honestly. Urbana attorney Henry Clay Whitney referred to Gridley as Davis's "bête noir" and described heated courtroom exchanges between the two. Whitney observed about Davis's feelings toward Gridley, "Oh! my: but he did hate him." Local lore has it that a fight between the two in Davis's office ended when Davis pinned the smaller Gridley, who bit Davis's finger until he let him up. Davis purchased the site of his home, Clover Lawn, from Jesse Fell, because, Davis said, "The hurry in the decision was that Gridley wanted to buy it; I could not stand to see Gridley get the place."[3]

Gridley and Fell, close friends throughout their lifetimes and both active in politics, had the greatest impact on the growth and development of Bloomington. Gridley came to town in 1831 and opened a store for which he returned east annually to purchase goods.[4] Fell, Bloomington's first lawyer, arrived in 1833. They joined with Allin to start the first newspaper, the *Bloomington Observer*, in 1836. Gridley purchased the equipment on his annual trip east, though Fell, who gave up the law that year when he sold his practice to the newly arrived Davis, was the one who was actually involved in its publication. The community was not ready to support a paper, so Fell discontinued the *Observer* after three years.[5] Fell and Gridley both declared bankruptcy in the early 1840s, Gridley in part because he had cosigned so many of Fell's notes, and both rebounded financially to become quite wealthy. After their bankruptcies, Gridley, at Fell's urging, became a lawyer, a profession at which he was very successful.

Gridley traveled the circuit, appearing in at least eight counties. In McLean County, Gridley associated with Lincoln in more cases and also opposed him on more cases than any other local attorney. Politically active as a Whig, he served with Lincoln in the legislature from 1840 to 1842. In the mid-1850s, Gridley also gave up the law to pursue his more lucrative myriad business interests. In 1861, Lincoln wrote, "Colonel Gridley who writes the accompanying letter, is my intimate political & personal friend."[6]

Gridley won election to the legislature, from which he wielded considerable influence for the progress of Bloomington. Fell actively supported and advised him. The diminutive Gridley seemed to be driven by greed. Attorney Major Packard, in his eulogy of Gridley before the McLean County Bar in 1881, referred to Gridley as the "acknowledged master of invective." Manufacturer William Flagg, whom Gridley had earlier represented in several suits defended by Lincoln, finally tired of Gridley's insults and verbal abuse and sued him for slander. Gridley hired Lincoln to defend him; on January 16, 1860, he wrote Lincoln, "I cannot think of trying the suit of *Flagg v. Gridley* without your assistance." Lincoln's defense was that it was common knowledge that Gridley habitually made untrue pejorative statements about everybody so it was not slander. With this approach, the case was settled for a relatively nominal sum.[7] Gridley can be added to the list of characters close to Lincoln yet so different from him, and his contributions to Lincoln's rise were substantial.

Almost opposite to Gridley in character, Fell declined numerous overtures to run for office. Driven by causes, he was known for his good works, community spirit, and kindly nature. A native of Pennsylvania and a Quaker, he moved to Bloomington on the advice of John T. Stuart. The breadth and extent of his land-speculating activities was a factor in his decision to sell his law practice. He founded numerous communities in central Illinois, sometimes working with Gridley, and purchased land all over the Midwest. Throughout his life, he promoted Bloomington and then Normal, carved out of north Bloomington, where his residence was. Like Lincoln, he was a temperance advocate; he was responsible for Normal being dry for more than its first one hundred years.[8] Fell was more liberal in thought than many of Lincoln's contemporaries, which was a steady and consistent influence on Lincoln.

Other lawyers and residents of Bloomington also played important roles in Lincoln's life. Orme, admitted to the practice of law in 1852 at the age of twenty, appeared with Lincoln in cases in Logan, DeWitt, and Champaign Counties as well as McLean. He served as a deputy under Circuit Clerk William McCullough, whose daughter he eventually married. Lincoln later described him as "one of the most active, competent, and best men in the world."[9] After freeing his slaves in his native Tennessee, Hogg came to Bloomington to practice law. Lincoln befriended the young lawyer, who became an active supporter of Lincoln and the Republicans in 1856, 1858, and 1860 when he won election to the legislature.[10] Another supporter was Scott, a significant associate of Lincoln at the bar, appearing with and against him in McLean County and at least three other counties of the circuit: Champaign, Piatt, and Vermilion. Scott also gave Lincoln steady, firm support throughout his political rise. A native of Belleville, Illinois, Scott came to Bloomington in 1848, already having been admitted to the practice of law.

He also held several public positions, including the commissioner of schools, city clerk, city attorney, and in 1854 county judge.[11] As he did all around the circuit, Lincoln tested and certified a young lawyer, future judge, and dean of Illinois Wesleyan University Law School, Reuben Benjamin, as worthy of practicing law.[12]

Another character who played an important political role in Lincoln's time in Bloomington was Sheriff William McCullough. Born in 1812, he moved in 1826 with his father to Dry Grove, west of Bloomington, where his father is said to have run a "house of entertainment." McCullough served with courage in the Black Hawk War. When he was twenty-eight, his arm was caught in a thresher and had to be amputated. As the doctor was nervously beginning his surgery, McCullough smoked his cigar and cautioned him to stay calm. He was an immensely popular politician, elected circuit clerk for four terms and sheriff for three.[13]

In the 1840s, Lincoln and other traveling lawyers usually stayed at the National Hotel, one of several hotels Lincoln used. It was owned and operated by John Ewing, whose son, James, recalled Lincoln visiting at the hotel and in the Ewings' home.[14] Lincoln frequently was a guest at the homes of Davis or Fell and also visited numerous other friends in Bloomington, including Ewing, Orme, Hogg, Cyrenius Wakefield, McCullough, Reuben Benjamin, and Abraham Brokaw. Judith Ann Bradner, the daughter of James Allin, recalled that Lincoln visited in her home frequently and that she attended social functions in Bloomington with him, dancing the Virginia Reel and other square dances with the future president.[15] Lincoln even made a rare real-estate investment in Bloomington, purchasing two lots in 1852 for $325 from a cousin of David Davis, Levi Davis, and selling them four years later for $400.[16]

Lincoln's wont to help the underdog is also demonstrated in the McLean County case of Springfield's William Florville, "Billy the Barber," a Haitian whom Lincoln had first met when Florville traveled through New Salem. A Bloomington subdivider conveyed four lots to Florville in exchange for his agreement to shave him all his life. Billy lost the deed before recording it, and the developers refused to replace it. Lincoln sued the developers, who did not appear, and the court ordered the defendants to reconvey the lots to Florville. Lincoln charged no fee and paid the court costs. Lincoln continued to pay the taxes on the lot over the years until he left for Washington. In February of 1860, before leaving for Cooper Union in New York, Lincoln asked Bloomington lawyer Packard to collect a fee owed to Lincoln and pay the taxes due. Lincoln had forgotten to do so when in Bloomington. During his presidency, Lincoln stayed in contact with Florville, who wrote him a warm letter of condolence after Willie's death, thanking the president for the Emancipation Proclamation and reporting on the condition of the Eighth Street house and the Lincoln's family dog.[17]

For the brief time that the town of Pontiac was in the circuit, the judge and lawyers headed northeast crossing Money Creek, recrossing the Mackinaw, then Rook's Creek, and finally the Vermilion River into the tiny Livingston County seat on its banks, Pontiac. On the way, the lawyers stayed in Lexington on McLean County's north edge at the double log house of Jacob Spawr, the town's only resident after it was first platted by Gridley in 1835. The home served as the post office, family residence, and a tavern where alcohol was prohibited; Spawr was known as "a first class tavern keeper." His visitors included Lincoln, Davis, Stephen A. Douglas, David Campbell, and Judge Samuel Treat, who presided over the circuit during Livingston's entire time as part of it.[18] Three of his six daughters fondly remembered Lincoln entertaining them with stories and games and telling jokes with his fellow lawyers. Family lore has it that Sarah, the prettiest of the daughters, was assigned to wash the dishes after meals. Lincoln enjoyed her company enough to stay around the kitchen to dry the dishes. Once he arrived just ahead of an impending storm and helped the girls gather the family geese and poultry to move them to shelter. Sarah married Noah Franklin, whose family Lincoln formally advised about a will contest over farmland in 1858.[19]

Livingston

Livingston County, immediately north of McLean County, was included in the Eighth Judicial Circuit from its founding in 1839 until 1847. The brief court sessions there followed McLean's. Livingston County was the somewhat-isolated northern outpost of the circuit, its area not having been settled until 1829. The Mackinaw River seems to have formed an informal northern boundary for settlement. The apprehension caused by the strong presence of Native Americans in the area, aggravated by the Black Hawk invasion, caused a handful of early Livingston settlers to abandon their primitive settlements until the Indians were driven out. Fell was instrumental in the development of the county, which was carved out of portions of LaSalle,

McLean, and Vermilion Counties in 1839. At the same time, the new town was surveyed and chosen to be the county seat. Its founders, from Pontiac, Michigan, named it after their hometown. That year, only three lawyers attended the first court session—two of whom were David Davis and David Campbell. It lasted only one day. Newcomer John Foster from New York built the first, rather primitive hotel. The county's population was 759 in 1840 and only twice that by 1850.[20]

During the period that the circuit included Livingston County, Lincoln occasionally visited. In Pontiac's second court session in 1840, Lincoln tried the first jury case in the county, opposed by Davis and Douglas. Their client, Isaac Wilson, accused Lincoln's client, William Popejoy, of neglect of the horse Wilson had loaned him, resulting in the animal's death. The jury returned a verdict of $70.25 against Lincoln's client.[21]

Livingston was removed from the circuit in 1847. About its county seat, it was said, "At the end of its first decade, 1847 the town of Pontiac was little more than a name. . . . Only half a dozen cabins besides the courthouse and those so scattered and hidden among the clumps of bushes that they were thereby rendered almost invisible."[22]

Except for those eight years of travel to Pontiac, the lawyers headed from Bloomington to Logan County. They left Bloomington and headed southwest through portions of Blooming Grove, traversing several large rolling hills of timber before entering an eight-mile stretch of prairie and then the quiet of Funk's Grove, whose towering oaks rose spire-like, so closely packed that they grew up instead of out as did oaks in a more open prairie. The lawyers crossed gentle Timber Creek in the grove.

Isaac Funk's extensive real-estate holdings centered on this tall oak grove. Funk, a close friend and supporter of Lincoln, arrived in McLean County in 1824, eventually amassing over twenty-five-thousand acres that included considerable acreage purchased from the Illinois Central Railroad. Lincoln the lawyer dealt with Funk on at least two cases. In 1839, he unsuccessfully sued Funk on behalf of Elijah Iles of Springfield. A year later, he successfully obtained a judgment for Funk in a case in Sangamon County. Funk became an active Whig, winning election to the Illinois House in 1840 as the other representative from McLean County with Gridley. In 1854, he joined the Republican Party. Lincoln visited frequently in the home of Funk, his wife, Cassandra, and their ten children.[23]

Logan

After leaving Funk's Grove, the road continued southwesterly into Logan County a short distance north of the Halfway House, a two-story framed inn maintained by Ohio native Samuel Hoblit, where Lincoln frequently overnighted. Stuart remembered fishing with Lincoln on a nearby creek in the evening while staying there. Once, Lincoln arrived and only Samuel's sixteen-year-old son, John, was home. He prepared a meal for Lincoln, which established a friendship that endured as John became an adult.[24] John settled farther south in a scenic spot on top of the Shelbyville moraine east of present-day Atlanta, Illinois, where Lincoln stayed once in a while. Lincoln stopped in 1858 to find that the Hoblits' home had been burned, and they were living in a shed on the property during construction of the replacement house. John and his pregnant wife offered to find Lincoln better accommodations in the neighborhood, but he stayed in the shed with them. When the son was born, they named him Abraham Lincoln Hoblit.[25]

From the moraine, the traveling lawyers viewed a magnificent panorama of thousands of acres of tall grass. They could see Elkhart Hill, twenty miles to the southwest, a glacial kame that rises 170 feet above the surrounding prairie. The hill was owned in its entirety by Lincoln's client John Shockey. The road's descent from the edge of the moraine was so steep so that when the rails came through in 1853, they had to be angled so the trains could ascend the grade. The trip from Bloomington to Postville, Logan's county seat, was about thirty-five miles, with Mt. Pulaski twelve miles to the southeast of Postville.

Abraham Lincoln was instrumental in the early days of Logan County. He performed surveys there and represented the county in his four terms in the Illinois legislature and in his one term in Congress. Not only did Lincoln play a principal role in the formation of the county but he also served as the county's lawyer in the litigation arising from each of the two moves of the county seat in its first fifteen years. Throughout his legal career, he had an active practice in the county and was its leading lawyer, representing some of its most prominent citizens. In 1853, he played a major role in the founding of the city of Lincoln, the first city named for him.

The sons of the first settler, James Latham, who settled at the base of Elkhart Hill in 1819, figure prominently in the Lincoln story. Robert was one of the founders of the town of Lincoln. Richard, elected to the legislature

This building, photographed in the 1870s, served as Logan County's first courthouse in Postville, the first county seat from 1839 until removal to Mt. Pulaski in 1846. A replica in 1952 replaced the first building, which Henry Ford had moved to Greenfield Village in 1928. Abraham Lincoln Presidential Library and Museum.

in 1848, built and operated the Kentucky House along the historic Edwards Trace on the west side of the hill. Many of the circuit-riding lawyers stayed there, including Lincoln, Davis, Stuart, Logan, Douglas, and Treat.[26]

Lincoln's legislation creating the county provided for the appointment of three named commissioners who were to select the county seat. The new county could boast only three towns: Mt. Pulaski in the southeast corner, Middletown in the southwest corner, and Postville in the center. Because settlement was advancing from the south, Postville was the smallest, its population then under a hundred. Its location in the center of the county was a significant factor, as was the offer of its three promoters, Lucien Adams, Seth Tinsley, Lincoln's landlord and Springfield merchant, and Dr. Moses L. Knapp, to donate the land for a public square and to construct a courthouse. The commissioners chose the tiny hamlet of three stores, several families, and a decent tavern. On April 1, 1839, voters elected James Primm, who ran Tinsley's store in Postville, circuit clerk; Dr. John Deskins, proprietor of the Deskins' Tavern, sheriff; and Jabez Capps of Mt. Pulaski recorder.[27] Miles of prairie, including the land that would become the town of Lincoln fourteen years later and whose growth swallowed up Postville, surrounded the town. The legislation creating the county placed Logan County in the First Judicial Circuit, but it became part of the Eighth two years later and remained so throughout Lincoln's career. The circuit included nine counties when Logan was added.

The first session of the circuit court for Logan County was actually held in Deskins' Tavern because the courthouse was still under construction. The tavern was also where the visitors to Postville stayed. Among them were the judge, the lawyers, including Lincoln, the litigants, and witnesses. They frequently shared the same table, and each room held multiple guests, usually sleeping more than one to a bed. A colorful crowd met at the tavern during the court sessions. Lincoln frequently told of an incident there, sometimes to his generals during the Civil War to encourage them to be more innovative when they complained about lack of ordnance. A traveler who arrived late at night at the tavern was anxious for a hard-earned whiskey. He was advised that the tavern had none. His inquiry as to other possible sources in town was greeted with the same negative answer. To this bad news, he responded, "Give me an ear of corn and a tin cup and I'll make it myself."[28] The two-story, twenty-eight-foot-by-thirty-eight-foot, frame courthouse, constructed for $1,176, faced south toward the tavern and was also used as a church, meeting room, and lecture hall.[29]

Samuel Treat, presiding judge at Postville, recalled a trip he and Lincoln made after dark from Postville to Springfield. Near Elkhart, a polecat crossed the road in front of them, causing potential problems with the horse. The frontier-raised Lincoln took the reins from Treat to guide the horse and carriage around the delicate confrontation with the skunk.[30]

Notwithstanding Lincoln's influence in early Logan County, little is known of his legal career in Postville. A fire in 1857 destroyed the Logan County Courthouse, then in Lincoln, and all court records from the three county seats. Lincoln regularly attended the semi-annual court sessions and was a fixture in Postville, both in and out of the courtroom. Locals recalled the judge having to hold up proceedings while Lincoln was summoned from a game of town ball in the square with the town's youngsters. No attorneys lived in the county during those early days, but a number of Logan County residents who had migrated north from the capital knew the circuit's Springfield lawyers who came to Logan County. David Davis and Asahel Gridley attended from Bloomington.[31]

Lincoln played a role in the transfer of the county seat from Postville to Mt. Pulaski, representing the county in the litigation the move provoked. Mt. Pulaski began in 1836, when Jabez Capps, a Springfield merchant of English birth, learned of a beautiful stretch of high prairie on a mound between Salt Creek and Lake Fork and its large, shallow lake in northern Sangamon County. Upon inspection, he decided he would move there and with Dr. Barton Robinson of Springfield and George W. Turley, an early settler in that area, founded the town of Mt. Pulaski, named for Kasimierz Pulaski, the Polish hero of the American Revolutionary War. The site was surveyed and dedicated in July 1836. Capps was the first resident and put up a building on the north side of the square that served as a store with his residence on the upper floor. He lived in Mt. Pulaski until his death sixty years after the town's founding and three months short of his hundredth birthday. He was a friend and political ally of Lincoln.[32]

In 1847, Mt. Pulaski's promoters pushed through a bill in the General Assembly calling for a county referendum to move the county seat to the booming Mt. Pulaski, which, because of its more southern location, had grown quicker than Postville. By the mid-1840s, Mt. Pulaski's population was over three hundred, more than twice that of Postville, and its commercial activity far outpaced that of the smaller town. Mt. Pulaski won the referendum, one factor in the vote the promise of a new courthouse. Its citizens contributed $2,700 for its construction with another $300 coming from the county. The courthouse, a solid, two-story, brick, Greek Revival building, sits on the very top of the "Mount," a kame like Elkhart Hill, that rises about sixty-five feet higher than the edge of town. Spreading stairs lead up to the broad double door, and five double-hung windows grace the front, with six on each side of the building. Each of the six offices on the first floor—recorder, county clerk and circuit clerk, sheriff, surveyor, treasurer, and school commissioner—has a chimney. The second floor holds the utilitarian courtroom, which "the bar" divides, a jury room, and the judge's chambers.[33] The only judge who ever presided in this courthouse was Davis. The comparison between the simple, frame Postville courthouse and this stately, brick building bears testimony to the evolving civilization of central Illinois during this period.

Lincoln's busy practice there dealt with a broad range of subject matter, typical of his practice elsewhere. The three donors of the Postville courthouse brought an early case. After the relocation of the county seat, the county sold the property for $300 and kept the money. The donors, whom Stuart and Logan, Lincoln's former partners, represented, sued to recover the money from the county, which Lincoln, Lionel Lacey of Mt. Pulaski, and Gridley represented. Judge Davis and the Illinois Supreme Court on the appeal ruled that the county could keep the money.[34]

Another case was known as the "Horological Cradle case." Lincoln's clients had purchased the patent rights to a cradle that self-rocks with a series of pulleys and weights. The patent was not for the mechanics of this unique cradle, as represented, but only for the ornamental design on the machine. Lincoln sought to recover for the land his clients had traded for the patent transfer. Judge Davis ruled for Lincoln's clients and set aside the transaction because of the misrepresentation. On appeal, the Illinois Supreme Court reversed that decision, saying the plaintiff should have known that a cradle could not be patented so that the representation could have only related to the ornamental aspects of the cradle and that Lincoln's clients had no standing to sue because they had not dealt directly with the defendants. Lincoln took a model of the cradle to his office and was showing it to John Bunn of Springfield, who asked how one stopped it, because it kept on rocking. Lincoln replied, "It's like some of the glib talkers you and I have known, John; when it gets going it doesn't know when to stop."[35]

Reaching Mt. Pulaski from Bloomington required crossing the sometimes flooded waters of Salt Creek. The Logan County seat continued as an outpost for the Springfield and Bloomington bars. Visiting lawyers from Springfield also included Benjamin Edwards, Josiah Lamborn, and Douglas; from Bloomington, Orme and Swett.[36] Logan County finally had a resident bar in the late 1840s when William Young changed professions from a Postville teacher to a Mt. Pulaski attorney. Then Lionel Lacey came there to practice law. A native of Belleville and an active Democrat, he was an ardent supporter of Stephen A. Douglas, which had no known effect on his professional relationship with Lincoln. He was an active litigator, opposing Lincoln in the county more frequently than any other lawyer. He also associated with Lincoln on many cases.

The leading local lawyer on the Mt. Pulaski scene was Samuel C. Parks. Born in Vermont, the son of an educator, he matriculated at Indiana University before coming to Springfield as a schoolteacher. Soon he was admitted to the bar and began a successful career in Mt. Pulaski. He associated with

Lincoln more frequently than any other Logan County attorney, including on *St. Louis, Alton, and Chicago Railroad v. Dalby*. On occasion, he also opposed Lincoln. Lincoln used Parks's office in Mt. Pulaski as his base there. Likewise, when the county seat moved to the new town of Lincoln, Parks moved with it; his new office on the west side of the square in Lincoln again provided Lincoln's Logan County base. A Whig, then loyal Republican, Parks was a major supporter of Lincoln from the 1840s through his presidency and became a key member of the David Davis team in 1860.[37]

The team's hotel was the Mt. Pulaski House, a two-story, brick building on the northwest corner of the square. Swett and Orme recalled Davis introducing them to Lincoln there in the fall of 1849. Two years later, Davis described the hotel as "perhaps the hardest place you ever saw . . . everything dirty, and the eating horrible." The old woman who waited tables "looked as we would suppose the Witch of Endor looked."[38] Lincoln generally stayed in private homes there, first at the Capps residence and then at Thomas Lushbaugh's. The Lushbaughs had been neighbors of the Lincolns on Eighth Street in Springfield until they moved to Mt. Pulaski. Elizabeth Lushbaugh Capps

The Mt. Pulaski House, where the lawyers stayed, was across the street from the courthouse, which still stands. The accommodations and food were so bad that Lincoln usually stayed with friends. Abraham Lincoln Presidential Library and Museum.

recalled, "As the accommodations at the hotel were miserable," Lincoln stayed with her family on all of his trips to the town for the last five years that it was the county seat. She remembered Lincoln in the front yard of her family's home, sitting under the trees talking to Davis, Stuart, and Swett, among others. When he slept there, Lincoln shared a room with her brother and talked the Lushbaughs into allowing Swett to stay there, as well. Elizabeth said that in this era before window screens, her job at meal time was to wave a large fan to keep the flies off the food and the guests.[39] The typical court session in Logan County was approximately three days, and then the lawyers moved on to Clinton, the county seat of DeWitt County.

DeWitt

The town of Clinton is about twenty-three miles from the Logan County seat. From Postville, the road ran due east through open prairie after crossing Deer Creek just east of Lincoln. As the road approached Clinton, it ascended the Shelbyville moraine. The twenty-one miles of road from Mt. Pulaski were more picturesque, running northeast toward Clinton, paralleling Salt Creek and its timber until crossing the creek and then ascending the moraine. DeWitt County was in the Eighth Judicial Circuit from its founding in 1839 until after Lincoln left for the White House. His practice there brought him into contact with both men who would oppose him in his presidential elections, Stephen A. Douglas in 1860 and George B. McClellan in 1864. DeWitt County would one day contribute two important members to the Lincoln nomination team, attorneys Clifton H. Moore and Lawrence Weldon. It is also where legend has it that Lincoln said, "You can fool all the people some of the time and some of the people all the time but you cannot fool all the people all the time."[40]

The area that was to become DeWitt County was first settled in 1824; the first settlers in the area of Clinton came six years later and five years before the town's founding by Lincoln's Bloomington friends Allin and Fell. Founding towns was an important form of real-estate speculation in that era. In the founding of Clinton, which Allin named for New York Governor DeWitt Clinton, Fell made a "handsome profit."[41] Joshua Speed once said Lincoln's highest ambition was to become the DeWitt Clinton of Illinois because of Lincoln's strong advocacy of internal improvements.[42]

Clinton developed slowly until Allin, in his role as state senator from McLean County, successfully petitioned the legislature for the formation of DeWitt County in February 1839 and actively participated in obtaining passage of the legislation.[43] Although Lincoln was then active on the Committee on Counties, there is no evidence of what Lincoln's role might have been in the formation of the county that took portions of McLean and Macon Counties. The act creating the county called for a referendum to elect officers and select the county seat, in which Clinton prevailed over its neighbor to the east, Marion.

Shortly thereafter, the board contracted for the construction of a twenty-foot-by-thirty-six-foot, frame courthouse for $1,600 to be completed by September, in time for the first session of the Circuit Court of DeWitt County, over which Treat presided. In 1849, a new courthouse, solid, simple, two storied, and brick, went up in the center of the square. The citizens of Clinton donated $1,000 of the $3,500 cost of the thirty-two-foot-by-forty-four-foot building that needed no step up to enter because the first floor was so low to the ground.[44]

The first circuit clerk was Fell's brother attorney Kersey Fell. The act creating the county also specified that DeWitt would be in the Eighth Judicial Circuit, making it one of nine counties in the circuit at that time. The first session of the Circuit Court of DeWitt County in October 1839 lasted but one day.[45] Lincoln appeared, as he would for most of its sessions during his career. Clinton had no resident lawyers until 1841. As in several other counties of the circuit, until Lincoln went to the White House, there was no lawyer who practiced in the county over a longer period of time. Whatever business came before the court during these early years the circuit's traveling lawyers handled, which also included Stuart and Logan; Thomas Harris of Petersburg; Gridley, Orme, Davis, and John Wickizer of Bloomington; and Kirby Benedict of Decatur.

In addition to Swett, two Clinton lawyers stand out among those who practiced with Lincoln—Moore and Weldon. Clinton's first lawyer, Moore would become the town's wealthiest citizen. Born in central Ohio in 1817, he came to Pekin at age twenty, first as a schoolteacher and then a deputy in the offices of the county and circuit clerks. He read law in a Pekin law firm, was admitted to the practice in February 1841, and in August moved to Clinton and began his practice. He had an extensive commercial practice as well as a successful trial practice. The records of Lincoln's cases in the county show that Moore was associated with Lincoln on more cases than any other lawyer and also show him to have opposed Lincoln more than any other lawyer.[46] He made a considerable amount of money purchasing debts from creditors at a discount and then collecting the proceeds for himself. He also acted as a real-estate broker whose activities included selling land for the Illinois Central Railroad. His main source of wealth was land. He eventually acquired as much as thirty-five thousand acres all over the Midwest, much in partnership with David Davis, a relationship that began in 1848. When the federal land office in Danville opened the railroad lands for sale, Davis sent Moore and McCullough, the sheriff of McLean County, to purchase eighty-five hundred acres at $2.50 an acre. Davis and Moore trusted each other, and the partnership was very successful. Moore's real-estate speculations included co-ownership with Douglas in several blocks in the north end of Clinton. In January 1855, Davis conveyed eighty acres to Moore, who built a stately home there where Lincoln on occasion stayed.[47]

Moore's passion was books. His library ultimately numbered seven thousand to eight thousand books. His law library, which Lincoln frequently used, along with his office, was one of the most extensive public or private in the circuit. He constructed a large building south of the square that housed his law practice. Like Lincoln, Moore would occasionally sit as substitute judge during Davis's brief absences, never in DeWitt County but rather in Logan and Champaign counties. Lincoln did this in DeWitt County frequently in 1858 and 1859.[48]

Moore had no political aspirations. He rode the circuit in four counties. He was a humorless man and is never mentioned in the accounts of the colorful gatherings of lawyers around the circuit. Community opinion was of little concern to him. He wrote to his brother-in-law in 1856, "I love to have the hounds after me; it shows at once that I am in the lead." The demands of his business enterprises left him with little time for or interest in politics until the political scene became heated in 1858. The year before, Henry S. Green began studying law in Moore's office. Three years later, Lincoln examined Green for admission to the bar.[49]

Another attorney in the county was Weldon, born in Zanesville, Ohio, in 1829, and a graduate of Wittenberg College. He came to Clinton in 1854, the

Clifton H. Moore was the first resident lawyer in DeWitt County, arriving several years after Lincoln began practicing there. Noted for his arrogance, he was a staunch advocate of Lincoln and associated with him on many cases, including as co-counsel on the Illinois Central Railroad cases. Moore became wealthy by investing in real estate. His two homes still stand. Abraham Lincoln Presidential Library and Museum.

year he was admitted to the practice of law in Ohio. His practice quickly became successful. A frequent litigator, he opposed Lincoln in DeWitt County in over thirty cases and also occasionally associated with him. He also rode the circuit. Weldon, described as charming and brilliant, was an avid supporter of Lincoln and even named his son born in 1857 Lincoln Weldon. He is the source of many reminiscences about Lincoln on the circuit.[50]

Although the bulk of his work in the county was civil, the first important case that Lincoln handled in DeWitt County was the defense in 1840 in *People v. Spencer Turner*, the first murder trial in the county's history. Spencer Turner, who had settled in the area in 1834 on land in northern DeWitt County, married Nancy Hoblit (whose brother Samuel was the innkeeper of the Halfway House in neighboring Logan County). Turner allegedly struck Matthew K. Martin with a club on April 15 of that year; Martin died that day. The coroner's jury's verdict, rendered three days later, found that the blow was the cause of death, "[t]ogether with his [Martin's] own imprudence in keeping himself in a state of intoxication and exposure in rain and inclemency on the night previous to his death." Turner was arrested that same day, his bond was set at $10,000, and he bonded out the next day. An indictment followed at the May term of the circuit court, only its second session. Not only Lincoln but also Douglas and Benedict represented Turner. The prosecutor was David B. Campbell.[51] The trial was set for May 23, 1840. The lawyers used so many challenges in selecting a jury that the panel was exhausted, and bystanders were used to complete the jury. The prosecution subpoenaed nineteen witnesses, though it is hard to believe they all testified because the trial itself was only one day. Lincoln delivered the closing argument. There was no record of the proceedings, but one can imagine that the details in the coroner's verdict provided plenty of material for the defense. Turner was found not guilty. Turner paid Lincoln and Douglas each with a $200 promissory note. Douglas apparently got paid on his note. Lincoln did not, so he sued Turner on the note in the DeWitt County Circuit Court in October 1841 and won a $213 judgment.[52] There is a story that Lincoln accepted a horse from Turner in payment, but the horse was blind so Lincoln renewed his efforts to collect, joining Turner's brother William in the proceedings in 1846.[53]

Lincoln defended another capital case in 1852 from Sangamon County in *People v. Moses Loe*. Lincoln, as he sometimes did in high-profile criminal cases, obtained a change of venue to DeWitt County. The prosecutor again was Campbell. The defendant and the deceased, James Gray, had met on the street. Loe pulled out a knife, and when Gray fled, he chased him and stabbed him in the neck. Lincoln attempted to establish self-defense as a motive since Gray had told several people that he intended to have a fight with Loe that morning. The jury found Loe guilty of the lesser charge of manslaughter, the first conviction for a killing in the history of DeWitt County. It was victory for the defense, given the facts of the crime. The sentence was eight years in the state penitentiary at Alton. Four years after the conviction, Loe asked for a pardon. Lincoln endorsed that petition with an August 18, 1857, letter, citing the defendant's youth as a reason for pardon. The pardon was granted.[54]

As in other communities, Lincoln's practice in Clinton brought him in contact with many of the prominent men of the area, including John Warner, born in Virginia in 1818. He became a doctor in Indiana and moved to Mount Pleasant, now Farmer City, to practice medicine. He moved to Clinton in 1843 and became the DeWitt County Circuit Clerk five years later.

When his daughter died in 1852, he quit medicine. He also served in the Illinois legislature as a Whig; later, he was leader of the Republican party in DeWitt County. In the early 1850s, he started to purchase farmland.[55] In 1852, Lincoln defended Warner in a case of ejectment in which one Bazilla Campbell sued Warner to dispossess him of land Campbell owned. Three years later, Lincoln opposed Moore and Warner in a suit over title to land in *Warner and Moore v. Slatten et al.*, a case that was ultimately settled.[56] Thomas Snell, another prominent citizen of Clinton in this era, sued Jeremiah Kelly, whom Lincoln and Moore defended, over six $50 promissory notes Kelly gave to cover wagers lost in the 1852 presidential election. The court, rejecting Lincoln's claim that the notes were illegal, entered judgment for Snell for $154.98.[57]

The population in 1840 for the entire county was three thousand people. Clinton continued to grow slowly through the 1840s and into the 1850s. In May 1852, Swett wrote his sister in Maine, "The town in which I live is improving rapidly. From the summit of the courthouse the other day, I counted 123 dwelling houses that had been built since I came here [1849]."[58]

The DeWitt County session lasted several days. The next court session was in Monticello, county seat of Piatt County.

6. PIATT, CHAMPAIGN, VERMILION

Piatt

From Clinton, the lawyers headed slightly northeast approximately nine miles to Marion, now called DeWitt, then southeast, crossing another fork of Salt Creek through open prairie. The open road wound through rolling timbered country, crossing another fork of Salt Creek, which had no bridge until 1850. Leonard Swett described the road a year later, "I walked my horse, sunk at least six inches every step for more than half the way and often a foot."[1] The lawyers frequently stayed at Richter's Inn on the square in Marion. It was one of Judge David Davis's favorite haunts because of the good food and "a neat, clean bed—a great luxury."[2]

The lawyers crossed the Sangamon River at Monticello. On May 7, 1852, Davis relates his entrance into Monticello with David Campbell: "Started next morning in the rain to the Sangamon River which is a mile from Monticello. Could not cross for 1 hour, staid in rain waiting for Ferryman = swam the horses—took the buggy over straddle a canoe—we went over ourselves very comfortably in the Canoe." Another time, Davis described, "Gridley & Scott, & Mr. Moore came over to Monticello on Sunday and 6 miles into the prairie (away from any house) & eight miles from their home they found 3 children, two little girls & a little boy who were wandering around about entirely lost. They brought the children home & their parents they said, did not seem to think anything very strange of it."[3]

Piatt County was in the circuit from its creation in 1841 for twelve years, when Lincoln's circuit reduction bill excised it from the Eighth. One of the smallest counties of the circuit in area, its population was the smallest. By 1830, still only about thirty settlers lived in the future county. Monticello, platted in 1837, became the county seat. Its potential for growth was permanently curtailed when the railroad located eight miles south, passing through Bement. In 1858, the *Urbana Union* described Piatt County as "famous as a cattle growing county."[4] Lincoln's practice there had the color of the Wild West.

Although Lincoln had few cases in Piatt County after it left the circuit, he did defend fellow attorney David Longnecker of Monticello on murder charges in 1854. On April 19 of that year, Longnecker killed a local ne'er-do-well, Jacob Ater, in an altercation in Jacob Piatt's store. During the violent argument, Ater raised a chair to strike Longnecker, who then fatally stabbed him in the neck. Longnecker was indicted for murder. Lincoln and Decatur's Joel Post and Richard J. Oglesby defended him, asserting self-defense. After a change of venue to Decatur, the case was tried twice to hung juries in May and June 1856. Lincoln wrote a petition that fourteen attorneys signed that asked the state's attorney to dismiss the case, which was done, and Longnecker resumed his practice in Monticello until his death in 1864.[5] The Maryland native had started his Illinois practice in Edgar County, opposing Lincoln in a case there in 1851. In the late 1850s, he and Lincoln handled ten cases for James Hollingsworth of Monticello.[6]

Piatt County's first courthouse, a simple, one-story building, sat on the square. When court was not in session, a tailor used it. Henry Clay Whitney commented, "The suits the tailor made were more important than many suits tried by the courts." In 1857, a two-story, brick courthouse replaced the old one.[7]

Attorneys stayed at the Tenbrook Hotel on the south side of the square. It is said Lincoln encouraged some children playing with a cured, inflated pig bladder to throw it into the fire. They did, with the not surprising result that it exploded, creating a mess that Lincoln attempted to clean up with a broom that also caught fire. On another occasion, Lincoln and attorney John McDougal entered into a contest to see who could throw an ax the farthest. After showing some restraint early in the contest, Lincoln finally threw the ax with full strength causing his opponent to exclaim that if he had have known upfront that Lincoln could do that, they would have saved a lot of time and effort.[8]

Because of the lack of litigation in the small county, the court sessions only lasted two days, and Lincoln's practice here was light. Thomas Milligan and Hamilton McComas were the most active lawyers during this period. Others who traveled to Monticello included Asahel Gridley, John M. Scott, and Swett from Bloomington; Anthony Thornton of Shelbyville; and Kirby Benedict, Sheridan Waite, Charles Emerson, and Joel Post from Decatur. Post opposed Lincoln in *Ford v. Thorpe*. The owner of a bull had hired Lincoln's client to castrate it, but the surgery resulted in the bull's death and the lawsuit. In contesting damages, Lincoln disputed the value of the animal as a bull due to "his change in condition by which he ceased to be a bull." The jury reduced the justice of the peace's $25 judgment to $20.[9]

Lincoln occasionally helped prosecute criminal cases. The personal reminiscence of Jane N. Johns, wife of Dr. Hiriam C. Johns, who owned a large amount of land in Piatt County, details one. When Dr. and Mrs. Johns moved from Cincinnati in 1849, they brought a fifteen-year-old girl, Alice, to care for their children. She was in the habit of keeping company with some neighbor boys by the last name of See. When she stayed out all night, Dr. Johns went to retrieve her, and she refused to return. Confronted by the men of the See family, he retreated, only to later attempt to seize her at gunpoint when the father of the See boys was taking Alice to town. A fight ensued; Johns was hit over the head. Alice and the father escaped to town, where they filed charges against Johns for assault with intent to kill. Six months later, Lincoln was appointed to prosecute the case. By then, the See family had moved on, and Alice had returned to her mother in Cincinnati. Johns was convicted but freed with a one-cent fine plus costs. Johns invited Lincoln and Davis to his country home for dinner.[10] Lincoln had very little legal business in the county after its removal from the circuit.

Champaign

After Monticello, the lawyers traveled twenty-five miles across open prairie to Urbana, seat of Champaign County. Lincoln rarely missed a court session there from the time it became part of the circuit in 1841 until October 1859 when he made his last trip there. Champaign's ranks of Lincoln supporters who aided the Chicago effort for the presidential nomination include Whitney and Henry Russell.

Just inside the Champaign County line was the home of cattleman and entrepreneur Benjamin F. Harris, an influential friend and ally of Lincoln. A native of Virginia, he moved from Ohio in 1835 and purchased land in western Champaign County. He raised cattle, which he drove annually across the Appalachians to eastern Pennsylvania, where he sold them for a substantial profit. He returned to Champaign and bought more and more land. In 1853, he purchased a sawmill in Peoria and moved it to his farm to cut lumber for a grand home to replace the log cabins in which he and his family were living. His stately home on the Sangamon River was a frequent stop between Monticello and Urbana for Lincoln, who enjoyed the sweeping view from the home's broad porch.[11]

The county's first settlers arrived in 1822, taking up residence in its magnificent groves, the largest of which was Big Grove, several thousand acres just north of what would become Urbana.[12] Settlement was still sparse in the county when it was formed in 1833 by slicing off what was known as the "attached part of Vermilion County." Lincoln's friend, legislative associate, and future client, Senator John W. Vance from west of Danville, authored the bill creating the county. Although between five hundred and a thousand people lived in the county, it had no organized town. After the commissioners selected to organize the county spent the night at the home of Isaac Busey, they chose that area as the county seat, even though no town was there. The owners who influenced the decision, Isaac Busey, Matthew Busey, William Webber, and his son Thomson R. Webber, donated land for the public buildings. The town was platted and lots sold in 1834, but lot sales were so small they had to have a second one a year later.[13]

Lincoln's first visit to Urbana was for its three-day court session commencing on May 10, 1841.[14] The town that Lincoln first saw was fairly primitive—mud streets, livestock roaming through the town, and a population of fewer than five hundred. It had no resident lawyers until 1846 when William D. Somers, under the mentoring of David Davis, gave up his medical practice to become Urbana's first lawyer.[15] Somers became a strong Republican and was elected circuit clerk in 1856. Lincoln occasionally used Somers's decent law library, of which there were few on the circuit.

The Urbana courthouse evolved from an 1836 log structure to the second building on the square in 1840 of frame construction built by Moses D. Harvey, a friend of Lincoln, who built many of Urbana's early buildings.

Only eight years later, Edward O. Smith of Decatur, a friend of Lincoln, constructed a more imposing brick structure with two stories and a bell tower for $2,744.[16] This building figured prominently in Lincoln's political and legal career. Asahel Bruer moved the first courthouse a block east to the northeast corner of Walnut and Main, added clapboard, and opened the Urbana House, where Lincoln and the other lawyers often stayed. After additions, the hotel became the Pennsylvania House, which Samuel Waters operated. Harvey notes in his account book on May 12, 1851, "Seen Abe Lincoln run a foot race with Samuel Waters from Market to Walnut St. on Mane St. in front of the Court House. Abe beat."[17]

Lincoln had a number of important friends and allies in Champaign County. Though a staunch Democrat, Thomson R. Webber was always close to him. Born in 1807 in Shelby County, Kentucky, Webber came to Urbana in 1833 to land that his father, William Webber, had already bought. Webber the son operated Urbana's first store and was appointed postmaster by Andrew Jackson. He was county clerk, a position he held for twenty years from the day the county organized, and was circuit clerk for twenty-seven years. Webber, a delegate to the 1847 Constitutional Convention, was also a close personal friend of David Davis. President Lincoln wrote several notes endorsing Webber for paymaster of volunteers during the Civil War, including one to Secretary of War Edwin M. Stanton: "I personally know Thomson R. Webber of Illinois to be an honest and capable man having for a long time been Clerk of the courts in which I practiced."[18]

John Gere, a native of Vermont, came to Urbana in 1847 and was a prominent businessman there for nearly forty years. His brothers Asa and Lyman ran the hotel known as the Gere House and then the American House, where Lincoln and the traveling entourage frequently lodged. Whitney described the Gere hotel, "This primitive hostelry had three front entrances from the street, but not a single hall down-stairs; one of these entrances led directly into the ladies' parlor and from it an entrance was obtained to the dining-room and also from another corner a flight of stairs conducted us to our room. Close by the front and dining-room doors was kept a gong which our vulgar boniface was wont to beat vigorously, as a prelude to meals, he standing in the doorway immediately into our windows; and thereby causing us great annoyance." One day, the innkeeper became very upset because the gong had disappeared. When Whitney returned to the room he was sharing with Lincoln and Davis, he learned that Lincoln had hidden the offending implement. At Davis's urging, Lincoln replaced the gong while Whitney held the door, and the offended innkeeper remained ignorant of the culprit's identity.[19] On one visit, Lincoln and Davis stayed in a room with three beds. The portly Davis slept in one; four lawyers, including Lincoln, shared the other two. Lyman's son Asa remembered sitting on Lincoln's lap and being advised by him on choosing his life's work. As a child, he was walking out into the country with Lincoln when they encountered a team of oxen stubbornly refusing to perform. Lincoln recalled a method of motivating oxen to move by tying knots in their tails. It worked, but the riled animals suddenly turned, knocking Lincoln into a ditch.[20]

Russell, whose mother was a Gere, came to Urbana in 1847 and went to work in the hotel attending the fires in the rooms, bringing water and other items as needed, and waiting tables. He remembered all the renowned lawyers of the circuit who stayed at the hotel and particularly Lincoln's unique friendliness. Russell eventually became a stagecoach driver for the Geres. Russell married the daughter of Samuel Waters and became a prominent Urbana businessman, the first board president of the Urbana Free Library.[21]

Somers recalled the regular entertaining evenings in the judge's room, where Davis and the invited lawyers gathered to while away the evenings with stories and horseplay. He remembered an incident where Judge Davis, with his wide girth, presided before the fireplace in his room over the evening's entertainment. John Moses, a slight, balding lawyer, bent over and ran at Davis full speed, head-butting him in the midriff as the rest of those gathered convulsed in laughter. Davis finally collapsed on his bed as a defense against the repeated assaults.[22]

Lincoln enjoyed Urbana and his acquaintances there. In the 1850s, Lincoln attended every session of the Champaign County Circuit Court except in fall 1858 at the height of the senatorial campaign against Douglas.

His caseload was the same mix as in other counties.[23] A number of the community's leaders were among his clientele, including large landowner Simeon Busey and Mark Carly, politician, early entrepreneur, and builder of the first residence in the new town of West Urbana. In the temperance case of *McClatchey v. Sits and Roney,* his clients included Archibald Campbell, an early mayor of Urbana; John Gere and brother James; and Calvin Higgins, a pioneer justice of the peace and postmaster during the

Buchanan administration whose wife was an early schoolteacher in Urbana. Other defendants were William Park, builder of the town's first flour mill and sawmill; Benjamin Roney, copublisher of the *Union*, the town's first newspaper; Conrad Tobias, a leading contractor, who remodeled the third courthouse and built Urbana's first planing mill; and William H. Webber, son of William and brother of Thomson.[24]

Lincoln filled in as circuit judge in Davis's absence more in Champaign County than any other. Somers remembered that Lincoln and Davis were constant companions and characterized Lincoln as "a general favorite" of all, always taking time to be friendly and assist young lawyers and inexperienced court personnel.[25]

Some of Lincoln's most interesting Champaign County cases were criminal, including the 1842 case *People v. Weaver*, the first murder case tried in the county. Lincoln and Asahel Gridley were court appointed to represent William Weaver, who, in a drunken state, shot the victim with a rifle. The evidence against him was so overwhelming that he was convicted and sentenced to death by hanging. Fortunately for the "reckless wretch," the log jail was so poorly constructed that he escaped to Wisconsin, where he made a decent life of his second chance.[26] In 1852, Lincoln's client, "the notorious horse thief" George High, was convicted in two cases. Lincoln carried a petition for pardon to Governor William Bissell with numerous signatures, including those of the prosecutor Ward Hill Lamon and Judge Davis, citing the defendant's youth and hope of reform. Bissell granted the pardon.[27]

Joseph O. Cunningham and Whitney, who came to Champaign County in 1853 and 1854, respectively, were two of Lincoln's closest associates at the Champaign County bar. Cunningham modestly characterized himself as "mostly an observer, not a participator to any extent" in the Lincoln story, whereas Whitney was a significant "participator," though he tended to exaggerate his role.[28] Whitney, more active in the trial bar than Cunningham, handled numerous cases with Lincoln and several against him. Cunningham was born in Lancaster, New York, in 1830, Whitney in Maine in 1831, though he grew up in New York. Both attended college in Ohio, Whitney being a college roommate of Lew Wallace, author of *Ben Hur*. Both were Republicans and Lincoln supporters. Both lived long after Lincoln's death, and each became renowned for his graphic and colorful descriptions of life on the circuit and observations of Lincoln.

Attorney Joseph O.
Cunningham, one of Lincoln's
longest-surviving circuit
contemporaries, ran the
Urbana Union, a newspaper
that was staunchly supportive
of Lincoln. His writings and
lectures helped preserve the
story of Lincoln's time on
the circuit. Champaign County
Historical Archives, Urbana Free
Library, Urbana, Illinois.

On June 14, 1853, Cunningham purchased the *Urbana Union* from William M. Coler, who had started it in 1852. Cunningham converted it from a Democrat paper to an "independent" one that supported the Republicans. Cunningham sold his interest in the *Union* in August 1858 after commencing the practice of law in 1856. He continued to be involved with the newspaper well into the 1860s.[29] Cunningham's impact on Urbana is much greater than that of Whitney, who moved to Chicago in 1857, employed by the Illinois Central.[30]

Whitney was the first attorney in the newly formed town of West Urbana, now Champaign, his makeshift office located in the dining room of the home of his father, a justice of the peace. Whitney described a visit that Lincoln and other lawyers made to his office in fall 1854. Notwithstanding Whitney's youth, Lincoln and his close friends Davis and Swett accepted him as part of their inner circle. Lincoln was notably private about his inner thoughts and strategies, but his letters to Whitney display an unusual trust and closeness.[31] Lincoln and Whitney shared law business. In December 1855, Lincoln wrote Joshua Speed in Kentucky, referring business to Whitney because Lincoln had a conflict of interest. Lincoln gave Whitney a legal opinion in December 1857: "You must not think of offering me pay for this."[32] The law firm that appeared most frequently in association with Lincoln in Urbana as well as on occasion against him was Coler, Sheldon, and Sim. The firm that most frequently opposed Lincoln was that of Somers, whose nephew James later joined him in the practice.[33]

In 1850, the population of the Champaign County was 2,649, the smallest in the circuit except Piatt. In comparison, DeWitt County that year had 5,000 residents, and McLean and Edgar each had over 10,000. Cunningham gives a graphic picture of the Urbana hamlet to which he came in 1853. He estimated the town's population to be 500, mostly southerners. The frontier village was surrounded by unbroken prairie, mostly government land. Wolves preyed on farm animals out in the country, and one even roamed in town in 1854. Wild turkeys, prairie chickens, and grouse abounded. The town had an estimated seventy-five buildings, all within a quarter of a mile of the square. Cows, pigs, chickens, and geese roamed the dirt streets.[34]

Lincoln spent his idle time in Urbana in various ways, including reading and quiet meditation, as he did everywhere. He often socialized with local merchants at a nearby drugstore and would meet acquaintances outside the courthouse. In 1852, he and Davis took the "Tavern Keepers wife's Sisters" to hear the Newhall Family Singers—"an act of charity." Lincoln attended the troupe's concerts in Bloomington and Danville as well. The singers were the Hillis family of Bloomington, a couple with three daughters and a son. They seemed to have traveled the circuit to coincide with the crowds of court week and frequently traveled with the itinerant lawyers. They first met Lincoln in 1849 and performed for him, Davis, Stuart, and many of the other lawyers around the circuit over the years. Lincoln attended their concerts repeatedly in Danville during court week in May 1852 to a "good audience."[35] Lincoln played billiards; he watched young men wrestle at the courthouse square, a pursuit in which he himself had engaged as a younger man. He played euchre. He was observed to play a mouth harp and attended weddings. He was invited to teas in the homes of notables of Urbana. Whitney recalls him taking long walks in the country out to the great oaks of Big Grove.[36]

As in other towns, Urbana's newspapers played an important role in enhancing Lincoln's political stature. In addition to Cunningham's *Urbana Union*, several other newspapers were established. A strident Democratic paper, *Our Constitution*, commenced publication in July 1856. In March 1858, the colorful John W. Scroggs acquired the failed *Spirit of Agricultural Press* and started the *Central Illinois Gazette*. Scroggs, born in Ohio in 1817, left home at age ten following his mother's death. He labored for several years, ultimately becoming a doctor after matriculating at Ohio Medical College and Eclectic Medical College, both in Cincinnati. He practiced medicine from 1840 until failed health caused him to quit. Having earlier invested in the land in Champaign County, he came to the county in 1857.[37] The masthead of Scroggs's newspaper modestly proclaimed, "An Independent Paper: Devoted to Agriculture, Education, Hygiene, Temperance, Literature, Social Reform, News, and the Interests of Central Illinois."[38] For its first two years, the front page carried only agricultural news, but its avid reporting of the political scene covered page 2. Scroggs lacked newspaper experience, but he was rescued by the appearance of William O. Stoddard on the scene. A native of Rochester, New York, where he attended the University of Rochester, Stoddard migrated to Chicago in 1857 to work for a paper there. When it folded, he bought a farm south of Urbana near Tolono, attempting farming. That drove him to West Urbana, where he brazenly presented himself to Scroggs and announced that he would run the paper. Stoddard describes Scroggs as always wearing a black frock suit and a brilliant vest of many colors. He greatly admired Scroggs, terming him a fanatical temperance and antislavery man who was courageous and pugnacious.[39] Stoddard successfully ran the paper, and it became unequivocally supportive of Lincoln in his pursuit of the nomination and White House.

Lincoln made his last circuit appearance in Champaign County in October 1859.

After the usual four or five days in Urbana, the next stop for the traveling lawyers was thirty miles to the east in Danville, county seat of Vermilion County and virtually on the Indiana line. The road was the most strenuous but also the most scenic on the circuit tour. On the way to the next county, the group passed and sometimes stopped at Kelley's Tavern, a few miles east of Urbana on the north side of the road and east bank of Salt Fork. Built in the early 1830s, the split-log tavern held four rooms when first built. Travelers crossed the river here on a ford when the water was low and a ferry when it was high; a bridge, built in 1837 for $426, was swept away by high water within a year. The tavern proprietor from 1849 to 1864 was Joseph Kelley,

Kelley's Tavern, on the Salt Fork between Urbana and Danville, was a frequent stop for the traveling lawyers. This previously unpublished photo of the long-abandoned site was taken by a member of Urbana's Busey family on a 1910 outing. Champaign County Historical Archives, Urbana Free Library, Urbana, Illinois.

born in Virginia in 1802. He arrived in March 1831 from the vicinity of the namesake Urbana, Champaign County, Ohio. The tavern, named for Kelley, also served as the post office due to a passing tavern patron with influence over the postal service in Washington, D.C. Whitney recalled first meeting Lincoln, Davis, Swett, and Campbell at the tavern on June 3, 1854, as the four were traveling in a two-seated open-spring wagon.[40]

Vermilion

After passing Kelley's Tavern, the road leaves Champaign County and winds its way curving and rolling toward Danville. It passes the Smith Farm, where Davis, Lincoln, and Campbell stayed in May 1852, having been held up in Urbana by heavy afternoon rains.[41] Then the road passes north of Conkeytown, where Lincoln is said to have occasionally stayed with the Dalbey family. The road curves and descends to the picturesque crossing of Stony

Creek, out of the small valley, past the site of the Hubbard House, where Lincoln also stayed. Then it heads down a steep incline to cross the Middle Fork of the Vermilion River at the site of the Salines, commercial salt operations started in 1819 and the first settlement in Vermilion County. They were made commercially viable by John W. Vance, who arrived in 1824 from Urbana, Champaign County, Ohio, pushing production to one hundred bushels per week with nine employees. Vance was a client and political ally of Lincoln for whom Lincoln won in the U.S. District Court in Springfield in 1844; in his letter reporting on the verdict, Lincoln addressed Vance as "My dear Old Friend." On June 9, 1860, three years after Vance's death and while winding up his law practice, Lincoln wrote Vance's widow, informing her with some irritation that he was not holding any of Vance's money.[42]

After crossing the Middle Fork, the road, a portion of which still exists, climbs steeply up Kistler Hill. After several miles on the bluff, it descends to cross the North Fork of the Vermilion River. From there, the lawyers followed the river downstream almost to the junction of its two branches and ascended the fairly steep spine of a bluff to reach the edge of Danville itself. Whitney recalls an incident when he and Lincoln, with Swett and his wife in the other seat, were riding to Danville after dark in a two-seat carriage on a dismal fall day. The narrow road wound through heavily timbered bottoms with deep ditches on each side. For safety's sake, Lincoln and Whitney rolled up their pants, jumped out into the muddy road, and walked ahead to guide the wagon, at first by shouting back and then by Lincoln singing "an old Methodist Air."[43]

Danville, the easternmost reach, was in the circuit from its inclusion in 1845 throughout the balance of Lincoln's career. The court session here lasted a full week. Whitney described Danville as the most congenial, relaxed, and enjoyable stop on the circuit. Formed in 1826, Vermilion, one of the largest and most influential counties of the circuit and a Whig and then Republican stronghold, was a major source of support for Lincoln. Its residents provided him with a significant volume of legal business and steadfast and reliable political support. While in the legislature, Davis was influential in placing Danville in the Eighth Judicial Circuit in 1845 to offset the strong Democratic tilt of Shelby County.[44]

The early settlement at the Salines was not suitable for a town, so the mouth of the North Fork of the Vermilion was chosen for the county seat.

Dan Beckwith, a county surveyor, who surveyed and laid out one hundred lots and for whom the town was named, donated the land. Beckwith, a native of Pennsylvania, had arrived in 1819. He built the town's first cabin as an outpost for his fur trade with the area's Indians. The trade also drew Gurdon Saltonstall Hubbard to the area that year. In 1824, he established a trading post in Danville for the American Fur Company and platted a road from the Salines to Chicago that became known as Hubbard Trace, which is approximately present-day Route 1. In 1832, he built the courthouse in which Lincoln was to practice, a fifty-foot-by-fifty-foot building at the location of the present courthouse. A year later, he left for Chicago, where he became a pioneer developer. He traveled to Vandalia to lobby the legislature in 1834 and reconnected with Lincoln, renewing the acquaintanceship they had in the Black Hawk War. He later became an active Whig, then a Republican, in Chicago and remained in contact with Lincoln as another valuable supporter in Lincoln's rise through the years.

Like the circuit's other counties, Vermilion grew rapidly during the Lincoln years. Its population in 1840 was 4,200; in 1850, 11,500; and by 1860, 19,800. Danville's rate of growth was not as fast as those counties to the west where the railroad had arrived.[45] The town was a major point of departure for the less-settled counties to the west, and the placement of the government land office there in 1831 was a major factor in its early growth. That office was the center for the sale of government lands over the next several decades, which drew speculators flocking to town to buy central Illinois land. The town's first newspaper was started in 1833, and the State Bank of Illinois located a branch in Danville three years later. While in Vandalia, Hubbard had introduced Lincoln to William Fithian, a legislator. Lincoln's first visit to Danville (and to Champaign) was in 1841 at the invitation of Fithian, who had hired him as a lawyer.[46]

The case *Hezekiah Cunningham v. William Fithian* arose out of real-estate speculation in Milwaukee in Wisconsin Territory. In 1836, several men, including Cunningham, engaged Fithian as an agent to buy land from Solomon Juneau, pioneer developer and first mayor of Milwaukee. The three gave Fithian promissory notes to fund land purchases he made for them. They refused to pay the notes, charging Fithian with fraud. Fithian sued them in Danville in 1840 and 1841 with Lincoln as his attorney in association with Edward D. Baker. John Brown and Isaac Walker, who would one day be a U.S. Senator from Wisconsin, represented Cunningham. The jury awarded Fithian $2,500.[47]

Fithian, perhaps the most important citizen of Danville, was born in 1799 in Ohio, where he trained as a doctor, practicing in Urbana, Ohio, before arriving in Danville in 1830, where he built a cabin above the river. Hubbard and he were close friends. Hubbard boarded with Fithian, and they married sisters. Hubbard sold Fithian his trading post, which became a highly successful mercantile establishment. He also advised Fithian on real-estate investments in Chicago and Milwaukee. Fithian speculated heavily in land, acquiring vast acreage west of Danville that made him wealthy. Others he brought to Danville to work for him also became leading citizens. A hard-working doctor, he rode miles and miles across the prairie to serve his patients. Fithian, who fought in the Black Hawk War, was elected to the legislature as a Whig in 1834.

The friendship of Fithian and Lincoln benefitted both men. They served together in the legislature from 1834 to 1842. Lincoln's relationship with Fithian was a significant boost for Lincoln's legal and political career in this important corner of the circuit.[48] Lincoln handled six cases for Fithian, more than any other client in Danville.[49] Letters from Lincoln to Fithian advising on real estate in Sangamon and Menard Counties in 1850 and offering sage, concise advice on a collection matter in 1855 suggest the depth of Fithian's reliance on his Springfield lawyer. The most notable case that Lincoln handled for Fithian was the high-profile slander case of *William Fithian v. George W. Casseday*. Casseday, also a prominent Danville citizen, built the first steam mill on the river in 1836 and had a long history of bad blood with Fithian. It started with Casseday's vicious attack on Fithian in a Danville paper during Fithian's Illinois senate campaign in 1842. Another dispute started between factions of the Presbyterian and Methodist churches. As the bitterness deepened, the Methodist Church, led by Casseday, built a seminary. The Presbyterians responded by building their own seminary. Judge Davis described the incident as a "Squaw War" that had divided the people of the town: "Casseday is at the bottom of it all. The result. They built two seminaries to cost $4,000 or $5,000."[50] This led to a battle of libelous handbills between the two men. In the final one, Casseday accused Fithian of abandoning his deceased wife's body prior to burial in Paris, Illinois, referring to Fithian variously as an "inhuman monster," "vile heartless wretch," and "unfeeling reptile." These accusations were too much for Fithian, who engaged Lincoln, Oliver Davis of Danville, and Usher Linder of Charleston, Illinois, to sue Casseday for libel. Edward A. Hannegan of Covington, Indiana, defended Casseday.[51]

A charming and gifted lawyer, Hannegan had served as a Democrat in both houses of Congress and as ambassador to Prussia under President James K. Polk.[52] David Davis said of him, "Mr. Hannegan is a beautiful speaker. . . . He is as companionable pleasant gentleman as I ever associated with." Linder recalled one of these sessions when Hannegan dazzled them with stories of his time as an ambassador in Europe and when he, David Davis, Campbell, and Lincoln were all staying at the McCormack House during the Casseday trial. John Murphy and Ward Hill Lamon assisted Hannegan at the October 1851 trial, which Davis characterized as an "exciting trial. . . . The ladies of town in great number as ever present all the time." The courtroom was packed, and outside a huge crowd jammed the public square. Forty-one witnesses testified, including many of the leading citizens of the city. The suit sought $25,000. The jury rejected Casseday's defense of the truth of the statements and awarded a verdict of $547.90. Casseday paid the judgment and for many years listed on his personal-property tax schedule the following, "The character of Dr. Fithian $547.90 which I bought and paid for." Davis closed his comment on the trial, "Our passions do a great deal to make us miserable."[53] Substance abuse drew Hannegan to a tragic end. A heavy drinker, he stabbed his brother-in-law to death in a drunken brawl. He avoided prosecution because the victim forgave him before expiring. Moving to St. Louis after his wife died in 1857, he died there from a morphine overdose in 1859.

The outstanding lawyer in Danville during Lincoln's time was Oliver Davis, a brilliant attorney, who associated more with Lincoln in Vermilion County than any lawyer other than Lamon but opposed him in over one hundred cases there.[54] Lincoln referred to him as "little Davis" to distinguish him from the judge, who was no relation. Oliver Davis was born in New York City in 1819, the son of a shipping merchant. Educated at Hamilton College, he clerked for the American Fur Company for six years before coming to Danville in 1842, when he began the practice of law. He built a fine home on North Vermilion Street, which Lincoln often visited. He was a gifted and highly respected lawyer often consulted by Judge Davis. In 1854, he and three other prominent men were indicted for gambling, a case that was eventually dismissed because it was not pursued. One story about him suggests a streak of arrogance to go with his considerable talent. Whitney, about a case against Davis and Lincoln, recalled that Davis told Whitney that he and Lincoln were going to "beat me awfully" in the case. Alarmed, he went to Lincoln, who assured him it was just another case, which they might win or they might lose but not to worry.[55]

Oliver Davis's partner, Oscar F. Harmon, was another leading lawyer of Danville and a close friend of Lincoln. Born in 1827 in Monroe County, New York, Harmon attended law school and practiced briefly in Rochester, New York, before coming to Danville in 1853. He set up practice with Oliver Davis and soon married a doctor's widow, Elizabeth Hill, a cousin of Davis's wife and niece of the wealthy Paris, Illinois, Lincoln client Milton Alexander. Harmon was a temperance advocate and a man of substantial character. As a lawyer, he was highly respected for his knowledge and counsel, though he was not particularly able in court. He both associated with and opposed Lincoln on a number of cases, and they became good friends as did Lincoln and Elizabeth.[56] She, like many of the local lawyers' wives, frequently attended court, and she was a great admirer of Lincoln, attending all of his speeches in Danville.

The Harmons built a large brick home on thirty acres on East Main Street not far from the railroad tracks. One year, a contagious fever hit the hotel, the McCormack House, and the resident lawyers invited the visiting lawyers to stay in their homes. Lincoln stayed with the Harmons, and Elizabeth and Lincoln talked long into the evening about the tragic loss of his son Eddie several years earlier. The fall court session here often fell on Thanksgiving, so court was adjourned, and the Davises and the Harmons would entertain the out-of-town lawyers. Lincoln came to the Harmon home, where in addition to turkey, Elizabeth served prairie chicken. She recalled Lincoln's kindness and attention to her children on these visits.[57]

The lawyers, including Lincoln and Judge Davis, generally stayed at the McCormack House, one of the circuit's oldest and best hotels. Founded in 1833 by Jesse Gilbert, it had a relatively high-caliber clientele drawn by the land office.[58] Davis would commandeer the ladies parlor and convert it into a two-bed room. Whitney remembered an incident involving Lincoln there that is one of several accounts of such behavior on his part. Davis had one bed, and Whitney and Lincoln were sleeping in another. Whitney awakened before daylight to see Lincoln sitting up in bed talking "the wildest and most incoherent nonsense all to himself." After about five minutes, Lincoln got up and hurriedly dressed.[59]

The McCormack House was one of the circuit's oldest and best hotels. A congenial site, it was the scene of many incidents during Lincoln's stays in Danville. It was from this hotel, during his last visit there, in 1859, that Lincoln sent his acceptance of the invitation to speak at Cooper Union. Abraham Lincoln Presidential Library and Museum.

The storytelling sessions went late into the night at the McCormack House. Lew Wallace, later a Civil War general and author of *Ben Hur*, graphically recalled one such evening. Attorney Dan Voorhees, who would become a Democrat U.S. Senator, stopped by Wallace's law office in Covington, Indiana, and suggested that they rent a horse and buggy to go over to Danville because court was in session. They reached town about dusk and entered the bar room, which "was all a-squeeze with residents, spiced with parties to suits, pending witnesses and jurors." There were "bursts of laughter and now and then a yell of delight." Wallace and Voorhees worked their way into the room: "In front of us a spacious pioneer fireplace all aglow with a fire scientifically built. On the right of the fireplace sat three of the best storytellers of Indiana (including Edward A. Hannegan). Opposite them a broad brick hearth intervening with two strangers to me who inquiry presently identified as famous lawyers and yarn spinners of Illinois." He described it as a "tournament" of the five men, "only instead of splintering lances they were swapping anecdotes. As to the kind and color of the jokes submitted to the audience, while not always chaste, they never failed to hit home." This went on until midnight. Finally, one of the contestants seemed to prevail: "His hair was thick, coarse, and defiant; it stood out in every direction. His features were massive, nose long, eyebrows protrusive, mouth large, cheeks hollow, eyes gray, and always responsive to the humor. He smiled all the time, but never once did he laugh outright. About midnight his competitors were disposed to give in, either their stories were exhausted or they were tacitly conceding him the crown. From answering them story for story he gave two or three to their one. At last he took the floor and held it." That was Lincoln.[60] While such gatherings were packing the McCormack House, east on Main Street in the Lincoln-Lamon office, the hard-core drinkers were meeting around Lamon's renowned pitcher full of whiskey.

The lawyers attended shows and entertainment on occasion. Whitney tells of one occasion when Lincoln walked west down Main Street to the Academy, the Methodist seminary, where he was so enthralled by a magic light show that he went back to watch it the next night.[61] Sometimes they entertained themselves. Swett recalled a surprising scene at the McCormack House. He arrived after dark and was told that Lincoln was upstairs in Davis's room. Climbing the bannisterless stairway, he entered upon invitation after knocking to find Lincoln and Davis in their nightshirts engaged in a pillow fight. He described Lincoln's yellow, flannel nightshirt extending all the way to his ankles: "He was certainly the ungodliest figure I had ever seen."[62]

On occasion, Judge Davis and Lincoln attended the First Presbyterian Church of Enoch Kingsbury. Kingsbury was an ardent abolitionist and friend of Lincoln whom Lincoln would appoint as postmaster of Danville in 1862. Born in New Hampshire and educated at Amherst College, he was a pastor from 1831 to 1852 at the Danville church, which he even built. He traveled all over east central Illinois and on into Indiana as the Clerk of Presbytery. Notwithstanding their friendship, the conservator of one William Wilson hired Lincoln in 1851 to sue Kingsbury as the former guardian for an incompetent individual. Lincoln successfully obtained a judgment.[63] None of Kingsbury's credentials apparently impressed Davis, who told his wife, Sarah, that he observed Kingsbury's wife to be more of a woman than

Kingsbury was of a man. Once after Lincoln and Davis attended his church, Davis reported in a letter to Sarah that they had heard "a dull sermon." That afternoon after church, Lincoln and Davis "wandered about the river for at least three or four miles."[64]

The eastern end of the circuit provided a welcome home-away-from-home for Lincoln. Davis once said, "Danville looks beautiful now the foliage is very green and the river is charming."[65] It was a congenial venue, as Whitney noted. The relatively advanced town and the comfort of the superior McCormack House made the stay more comfortable. Lincoln developed particularly close friendships there: Fithian, Oliver Davis, and Oscar Harmon and his wife, Elizabeth. The relationship with Lamon generated a profitable volume of business. The political landscape made Danville a major source of political support for Lincoln. All of this contributed to present an oasis from the rigors of crossing the circuit. From Danville, it was on to the southern tier of counties, which, though accepting of Lincoln, presented a more challenging political atmosphere with which to contend.

7. EDGAR, SHELBY, MOULTRIE, MACON, CHRISTIAN, MENARD, MASON

———⊷———

Edgar

The lawyers left Danville and headed south about thirty-five miles to Edgar County. They traveled along the renowned Vincennes Trace, straight south out of Danville through Abraham Smith's Ridge Farm, where they crossed the county line. It passes through Bloomfield, where Lincoln sometimes stayed at the hotel of Alexander Sommerville. Lincoln is said to have given a temperance lecture here with George W. Riley during the 1830s. The Vincennes Trace crosses several branches of Brouilletts Creek and yet another Sugar Creek just north of Paris.[1] David Davis described the scene in 1847 from Danville: "The country the whole distance is beautiful to the eye—much better improved than in McLean and Tazewell." He notes the courthouse in the center of the Paris public square and "trees of thirteen years' growth in full bloom" around it. The town was more attractive than Danville, "with houses generally painted or whitewashed and surrounded with trees."[2]

Edgar, Shelby, and Sangamon were the only counties in the circuit whose eventual boundaries included settlers at the time of statehood in 1818. The early settlers were mostly Kentuckians, and their influence accounts for the counties' tolerance of slavery throughout the antebellum era. Edgar County was created in 1823, and the county seat was placed on twenty-six acres Samuel Vance donated. He stipulated that the town be named Paris, though the reason for the name is unknown. Its first courthouse, a frame building, was completed in 1824 at the south end of the town square.

A year earlier, Milton K. Alexander, a native of Georgia, settled in Paris and opened the county's first store. In 1826, while continuing to run the store, he also took the office of postmaster, which he held for thirty-two years. Alexander was a veteran of the War of 1812 (and the 1832 Black Hawk War in which he had also fought as a brigadier general of volunteers). He acquired considerable wealth investing in Illinois land, and in 1828, he built a grand home in Paris, the first brick building in the county, evidence of the advance of Paris compared to future circuit sites to the north and west. Lincoln stayed in this home, and Stephen A. Douglas visited there, courting Alexander's daughter, Jane.[3] Alexander, a Democrat, hired Lincoln as an attorney in cases in DeWitt County after Lincoln opposed him in two collection cases Alexander brought in 1851 in Edgar County, his attorney being Kirby Benedict.[4] Alexander's engagement of Lincoln enhanced Lincoln's professional stature in the area.

Another early settler with eventual connections to Lincoln was Elvis P. Shaw. His father, Smith Shaw, came to Paris from North Carolina in 1821 with a land grant from James Monroe and built the town's first permanent residence in 1823. Elvis, born in 1816, was in the livery and grocery business in Paris. Lincoln got to know him as a youth carrying mail from Paris to Springfield. Lincoln successfully represented Elvis in a dispute in 1842 over ownership of two mares. Elvis built a graceful vernacular I-house in 1853 with Greek Revival elements that Lincoln visited.[5]

Another leading citizen was Leander Munsell, a native of Cincinnati born in 1793 who fought in the War of 1812. He came to Paris in 1832 and built the more elaborate second courthouse, a brick, coffee-mill-style, two-story building that served throughout Lincoln's practice. With a contract price of $4,250, it was the first of four Lincoln-era courthouses, all in the coffee-mill style, that Munsell built, the others in Coles (not part of the circuit), McLean, and Macon Counties. He became a successful merchant, owning stores in four counties, and built the first steam mill in Paris in 1834. A dispute with his partner, William McReynolds, ended up in court with Lincoln and Usher Linder representing McReynolds and Benedict representing Munsell.[6]

The coffee-mill-style Edgar County Courthouse, built by Leander Munsell of Paris, Illinois, in 1832, served until 1891. It was a common design, one of five coffee mills in the circuit, including McLean, Macon, Shelby, and Vermilion. Munsell was a strong supporter of Lincoln throughout his career. Abraham Lincoln Presidential Library and Museum.

Edgar County's first attorney was Garland Shelledy, born in 1802 in Kentucky. After attending Jefferson College in Pennsylvania, Shelledy began his law practice in Paris in 1828. He asked Lincoln and Stephen T. Logan to "attend to" his bankruptcy cases in the federal court in Springfield, the state's only federal court at the time, and outlined the terms and details of the work, which Lincoln accepted in February 1842. Lincoln later worked with Shelledy on a Paris case prior to his death in 1851.[7]

Edgar County was part of the Eighth Judicial Circuit from 1845 until 1853, when Lincoln's bill removed it. Lincoln handled approximately forty-five cases in the county, the first in May 1842 and the last in 1853. Edgar's population was one of the largest in the circuit. Its leadership was longstanding and stable and its economy solid.[8]

Paris, the county seat, was a cultured city, its Presbyterian Church founded in 1824 and a school, the Paris Academy, founded in the 1830s. Its first newspaper, the *Illinois Standard*, was started in 1836 or 1837 but soon failed. In 1848, Jacob Harding began publishing the solidly Whig, then Republican, *Prairie*

Beacon. Harding, a native of Virginia, came to Paris in 1836 via Knoxville, Tennessee, and Corydon, Indiana. Twelve years later, he had enough money to buy a press in Cincinnati, Ohio. In its May 18, 1849, announcement of David Davis's election to the circuit bench, the *Prairie Beacon* described Davis as "about 30 years of age—a sound lawyer, and is blessed with a strong mind and vigorous constitution. He is quite industrious in disposing of business and while he presides with all the dignity appropriate to the bench. . . . [H]e is frank, social, and kind."[9] Accommodations in early Paris left something to be desired, according to Davis. In 1847 he reported to his wife, Sarah, "I have got quartered in about the meanest tavern you ever saw. . . . [T]he floors dont look to have been scoured for a quarter of a century. . . . Eating wretched & rooms dirty. This Kentucky cooking, just as the middling classes know how to prepare is, hardly fit for the stomach of a horse."[10] Things improved so by the early 1850s that Paris boasted a fine inn, the Green Tree Hotel with seventeen rooms, a large public room, a large dining room, a stable for sixty-two horses, and two wells.

Lincoln's Edgar County cases were the typical assortment. The cases themselves were not as interesting as the lawyers with whom Lincoln worked, both for and against him. In addition to Linder, Lincoln appeared with and against the talented and mercurial Benedict. A skilled trial lawyer, Benedict had cases with Lincoln in six counties, including Edgar, and numerous cases against Lincoln in five counties. After settling briefly in Sangamon from Mississippi, to which he had moved from his Connecticut birthplace, Benedict came to Decatur in 1836. He was a popular member of the retinue of circuit riders and close to Davis. Decatur's flagging fortunes in the late 1840s caused Benedict to follow Decatur attorney Charles Emerson's lead and move to Paris, where he remained very active with the trial bar. In both places, he was a popular figure with his fellows. Danville's *Illinois Citizen* praised him in 1850, "We have never yet met Benedict's equal. . . . As far as oratory is concerned, he transcends, by far, any member of the Bar on the Circuit." Benedict had an explosive temper and a serious problem with alcohol. Nevertheless, in 1853, President Franklin Pierce appointed Benedict chief justice of the supreme court of the Territory of New Mexico.[11]

Lincoln had a number of cases with and against attorney Charles Constable from Marshall in Clark County, who frequently attended court in

Paris. Their relationship was strained at best. Born on the Eastern Shore of Maryland in 1816, Constable was something of a dandy. Davis thought little of him, commenting to Sarah, "I don't think that he will ever do good for himself." He said that Constable's constant complaining made everyone unhappy, his commitment to the Whig party had little depth, and his interest in it was self-serving, which would have disturbed Lincoln, the loyal Whig. On the other hand, Linder described him as "one of the handsomest men I've ever seen . . . a man of fine culture and elegant manners."[12]

The proximity of Paris to Terre Haute attracted Indiana lawyers to cross the Wabash River and come over to Edgar County, and this Indiana connection to the eastern edge of the circuit would figure in Lincoln's successful pursuit of the nomination in 1860 because it gave him vital entrée to the critical Indiana Republican delegation. In May 1849, the *Prairie Beacon* reported that the circuit session included attorneys from Springfield, Decatur, Bloomington, and Danville, Illinois, and Terre Haute, Indiana; some ladies, also from Terre Haute, had come for the court session, which Davis also confirmed. The Terre Haute lawyers included future leading Republicans Thomas Henry Nelson and Richard W. Thompson. Thompson and Lincoln had become friends during their shared term in Congress in 1847.[13] Samuel Judah, a prominent Whig politician from Vincennes, Indiana, also attended the circuit court in Paris opposing Lincoln on the Dubois cases, involving Lincoln ally Jesse DuBois.[14] John P. Usher, one day to be Lincoln's secretary of the interior, was active in Paris. A native of upstate New York, Usher was admitted to the bar in New York and in 1837 came to Terre Haute. He was a prominent Whig and active in the formation of the Republican Party in his county. The practice of his law firm extended throughout west central Indiana, including Indianapolis. He was not universally liked; Linder found him to be a good lawyer but disliked him, describing him as "a grasping avaricious man."[15]

Edgar County continued to be an important political base for Lincoln, although he had little legal business there after its removal from the circuit, as he told Linder in March 1853, "The change of Circuits prevents my attending the Edgar Court this spring and perhaps generally thereafter." Lincoln said that he had been paid a "little fee" that he hated "to disgorge" in an ejectment case and asked Linder to do him a favor and finish it.[16]

Shelby

Following a week-long court session in Paris, the lawyers traveled the Stage-coach Road to Shelbyville in Shelby County, the longest leg on the circuit between county seats. They rode through Grandview, where Lincoln occasionally stayed at the Barnett Tavern, and then headed west, crossing the Embarras River and entering Charleston, where they usually stayed overnight. Lincoln frequently took business in Charleston, the seat of Coles County, which was never part of the Eighth Judicial Circuit. The thirty miles to Charleston and another thirty-five to Shelbyville took two days. In 1852, Davis described the road between Charleston and Shelbyville as "horrid. . . . We have met no such road anywhere round the Circuit. My horses were very tired & Mr. Lincoln old horse nearly gave out."[17]

About twelve miles east of Shelbyville in Ash Grove (later Cochran's Grove) stood the Tressler family's Black Horse Tavern, a noted inn for the circuit riders. About Mrs. Tressler, "a Dutch woman," Davis commented,

The Black Horse Tavern, between Charleston and Shelbyville, was a regular stop for the circuit lawyers and was known for the good quality of its accommodations. President Martin Van Buren visited here while traveling Illinois. Shelby County Historical and Genealogical Society.

"The old lady keeps an excellent house."[18] From there the road continued west to the Kaskaskia River, which is called the Okaw along this stretch. Shelbyville was reached by a ford downstream from Brewster Bluff, the elevated site of the courthouse. Later a ferry, started in 1827, served to cross the river until the first bridge was built in 1832. Unlike Paris, Shelbyville was perhaps less than refined. Davis, admittedly wont to complain as he traveled the circuit, once called it "as ragged and dilapidated a place as you ever saw." Three years later, he said, "Shelbyville looks horrid . . . a miserable town as yet." Linder called it "hog town," to which the *Shelbyville Banner* responded, "This was more truth than poetry. . . . [I]f a hog's census had been . . . taken[,] . . . the hogs would form the most numerous part of the population in Shelbyville."[19]

Perhaps, Shelby County's main contribution to Lincoln was to provide another venue where it was wise to practice moderation in expressing his views on slavery. Like other southern-tier counties, Shelby was heavily pro-Democratic and proslavery. Shelbyville's Joseph Douthit remembered, "There was a very intense partisan spirit in those days in southern Illinois and the sympathy was nearly all with the south so that an outspoken anti-slavery man was considered hardly human."[20]

On the southern edge of the Eighth Judicial Circuit, which the county was part of from 1841 to 1845 and from 1847 to 1853, Shelby was one of the older counties in the circuit. Its first settlers came in March 1818, and the state legislature established it in January 1827. Most of its residents were from Kentucky, and the county being named for Isaac Shelby, a hero of the Revolutionary War of 1812 and two-time governor of Kentucky, confirmed that bond. The three commissioners assigned to organize the county included William L. D. Ewing, Lincoln's future nemesis. The three chose the top of the bluff as the site of Shelbyville, seat of the county.[21]

Court was first held in the county in 1828 in a log courthouse, replaced in 1832 by a brick-and-stone structure, a square of forty-foot sides and twenty-three feet high, costing $1,094, to which a cupola was added in 1837. The building served the county for thirty years. The principal accommodation in Shelbyville, the two-and-a-half-story Tallman House, also known as the Tackett House, which the Tackett family from Kentucky ran, sat just east of the courthouse. Douthit remembered Lincoln sitting on the long porch that ran across the front, reading and chatting with other lawyers and citizens of Shelbyville while passing the time of day.[22] Davis reported the food to be first rate, although by 1852, when the inn had a different proprietor, he was complaining about it. The lawyers found the company to be amiable in Shelbyville. While Davis complained about the amenities in Shelbyville, he also enjoyed himself with good company, "very clever, gentlemanly people," attending occasional lavish social events and taking time to relax. He also took a group fishing at the river.[23]

The county's initial relative influence diminished from 1830 to 1860 as the state expanded northward and the other towns of the circuit grew at a faster rate. A chunk of the county was taken off the west side in 1839 to add to the new county of Christian and again in 1842, when the northeast corner was added to the newly formed Moultrie County.[24]

The two leading attorneys in Shelbyville were Anthony Thornton and Samuel Moulton. Thornton, born in Kentucky in 1814 of slave-holding parents, was educated at Centre College in Kentucky and Miami University in Ohio. After being admitted to practice in Kentucky, he visited his uncle William Thornton in 1836 on the way to Missouri, where he had planned to settle. Shelbyville had only one attorney, so sensing the opportunity, Anthony decided to stay. He traveled immediately to Vandalia to gain admittance to the practice, where he first met Lincoln. He joined the circuit riders, and he and Lincoln associated with each other and opposed each other frequently in Shelby County as well as in at least four other counties of the circuit. Tall like Lincoln, he was an imposing and handsome man, according to Linder, who gave Thornton high marks as an attorney, able and always well prepared.[25] Lincoln and Thornton first opposed each other in a slander case in Coles County in 1840. Thornton noted Lincoln's consistent fairness and honesty: "He was always earnest and forceful and could manage a case with as much power and clearness as any man I ever saw." Thornton, an ardent Henry Clay supporter and influential Whig, won the election in that Democratic stronghold to the Illinois legislature in 1850. Like Lincoln, he was a strong supporter of the railroads. He was a delegate to the Constitutional Convention in 1847 and was a strong supporter of Davis's successful pursuit of the circuit judgeship, writing to Davis, "You can rely on my feeble influence in this and Moultrie Counties."[26]

Samuel Moulton, a native of Massachusetts and son of a sea captain, was born in 1823, taught in Kentucky and Mississippi, where he married a local woman before coming to Illinois in 1845, and opened his practice in Sullivan. He moved to Shelbyville in 1849 and served four terms in the Illinois Legislature, first elected as a Democrat in 1853.[27]

Lawyer Orlando Ficklin, of Charleston, was a political adversary with whom Lincoln associated on a number of cases in Shelby County, as well as others. Born in Kentucky in 1808, Ficklin began work in 1830 as a lawyer in Mount Carmel, Illinois. He served in the Black Hawk War, was elected to the legislature, and became a prosecuting attorney for the Wabash circuit in 1834. He moved to Charleston in 1837 and practiced the rest of his life there. Although Ficklin had an extensive practice in that end of the Eighth Circuit, he rode the more southerly Wabash circuit for twenty-five years, often with close friend Linder. Linder, describing Ficklin's sense of humor and singing, said, "Ficklin was a boon companion, a little vain to be sure as perhaps I was myself."[28] Elected to the legislature from Charleston in 1840 and 1842, Ficklin opposed Lincoln's successful efforts to move the capital to Springfield. He introduced legislation to have another ballot taken on the Springfield move, which failed. At age forty, he married a daughter of prominent Georgia planter and slave owner. He served four terms in the Congress, including service at the same time as Lincoln.[29] Notwithstanding their career-long relationship as political adversaries, they practiced law cordially together and associated on many cases, including five in Shelby County alone.[30]

Lincoln's range of cases is different in Shelby County than those in other counties. The most common type of case was slander, which numbered six, but he had only four collection cases. Almost all of Lincoln's cases here occurred during the period of his most focused legal practice, between 1849 and 1854, except for the series of cases against the Terre Haute and Alton Railroad. His twenty cases in Shelby County showed him associating with Thornton on four cases and opposing him on nine, associating with Moulton on four and opposing him on eight, opposing Linder on six, and associating with Ficklin on five.[31]

Moultrie

After a week-long session in Shelbyville, the traveling band headed for Sullivan, county seat of Moultrie County, twenty miles away. The lawyers rode north from Shelbyville and then turned east, descending and ascending the oak savannah–covered bluffs of the Okaw River before they emerged onto open prairie near Sullivan. Sometimes they paused along the way, as when in June 1852, Davis, Lincoln, Thornton, Moulton, and David Campbell stopped for a leisurely lunch at John Ward's rural home, five miles north of Shelbyville. From here the trip continued for three more hours to Sullivan.[32]

The last county of the circuit to be formed, Moultrie, its population a mere two thousand, was created in 1843 out of eastern Macon and northern Shelby Counties. Some residents of what was then northeast Shelby County petitioned the legislature successfully in 1842 for a referendum about forming a new county, but a majority of residents voted against it the next year. However, the year after that, the legislature created the new county without the referendum. In 1847, the miller, Beverly Taylor, built the county's first tavern, the two-story Taylor House, on the northwest corner of the square. Five years later, Davis refused to lodge there because it was "so tough that I would have been in a bad humor to have staid there." Instead, he and Lincoln roomed at a neighboring boarding house owned by James Elder, a native of Tennessee who moved to Sullivan in 1845 and also opened a store across the street to the north.[33]

Court was held at various sites until completion of a two-story, thirty-eight-foot-square brick structure in 1848 for $2,800. The next year, a fence went up around the building to keep livestock away. Due to a paucity of business, the court sessions lasted just a few days. An 1864 courthouse fire destroyed most of the court records, so little is known of Lincoln's practice in Sullivan. In one known case, Lincoln and Thornton defended John Crockett in November 1852 for murder. He was convicted of manslaughter and sentenced to two years in the Alton Penitentiary. His father, Elliott, a nephew of Davy Crockett, worked to have his son pardoned because John, as Lincoln called him in a petition for pardon, was "not quite an idiot, being at least of the very worst grade of intellect above absolute ideocy." More than one hundred people signed the petition, including the state's attorney, jurors, and the judge. Lincoln received a promissory note in payment for his services, which Elliott never paid.[34] Lincoln's legislation in 1853 removed the county from the circuit, and Lincoln had no business there after that.

Macon

After a short session in Sullivan, the lawyers headed north and west out to Lovington, where Lincoln stayed on occasion at another Black Horse Tavern.

There the road joined the Paris-to-Springfield Road, the east-west route, which was part of the route the Lincoln family had followed during their 1830 move to Illinois. A branch off the Paris-to-Springfield Road crossed the Sangamon River to Decatur, Macon County's seat.[35]

The county had been cut out of Shelby County a year before the Lincoln family's arrival. The legislation designating the new county's seat directed Decatur be laid out like Shelbyville.[36] The Decatur to which Lincoln returned six years after his initial arrival had grown some but remained a sleepy village with a population that had tripled to about three hundred. Growth remained slow, the population increasing from 1,122 in 1830, to 3,233 in 1840, to 3,988 in 1850.[37] Lincoln appeared for the last circuit court session held in the log courthouse that had been under construction when he and his family had arrived. Located in the town's original square, it was across the street from the new brick courthouse that was nearing completion when Lincoln returned as a lawyer. The contract with builder Munsell specified that the new courthouse was to "be equal to or superior to the McLean County Courthouse," which he had built a year earlier. The $10,000 Macon County Courthouse, also in coffee-mill style, was thirty-two-foot square; the first floor held offices, and the second floor the courtroom.[38]

Edward O. Smith, a Maryland native who arrived in 1837, played a significant role in Decatur's early growth. In 1839, Smith and J. J. Peddecord, both of whom later abandoned the city for the California gold mines, started the first ox mill for grinding grain. Smith became known as the builder of Decatur, figuratively and literally, putting up many 1840s brick buildings, including the Macon House and the first Opera House. He also built Urbana's first brick courthouse. An active Whig, he was elected to the Constitutional Convention of 1848 and the Illinois State Senate and supported Abraham Lincoln as early as the 1840s. The Macon House, the city's first good hotel, started with twelve rooms on two floors in 1839 at the intersection of Franklin and Prairie Streets.[39]

The 1840s saw this minimal growth continue. Stores and a handful of other businesses were started so that by 1840, Decatur "was beginning to take on the appearance of a town."[40] In 1842, the Krones took over the Macon House for eight years, and it was an island of comfort for the traveling lawyers because of the superior quality of the food and accommodations, which Davis rated "first rate" in 1849.[41] While waiting for their home to be completed, Jane M. Johns and H. C. Johns, who had moved from their large Piatt County farm, stayed at the Macon House. During court week, a wagon pulled up to the front door of the hotel. The wagon's cargo was Mrs. Johns's piano, a Gilbert from Boston that had traveled via the Ohio and Wabash Rivers to Crawfordsville, Indiana, and by wagon to Decatur. At the suggestion of the landlord, she waited for the attorneys' return to the hotel after court for manpower to unload the instrument. Lincoln agreed to help and went to the basement to find two timbers to roll the piano from wagon to steps and into the hotel, with the help of Swett and Linder. That night, Mrs. Johns played for the lawyers of the Eighth Circuit and accompanied their singing.[42] Her colorful description of Decatur and environs gives a picture before the railroads arrived in 1854. Decatur looked like an abandoned effort to build a city, she said, and the prairie surrounding the town had wolves "lurking in thickets of tall grass." Wild turkeys, sand hill cranes, and prairie chickens roamed, all in great abundance, with "wild pigeons so dense as to cast a shadow like a passing cloud."[43]

The somnolent town did finally get its first newspaper when James Shoaf, married to Nancy, the daughter of Lincoln's cousin Dennis Hanks, started *Shoaf's Family Gazette*, which lasted from 1851 to 1856. An 1864 letter to Lincoln displays Shoaf's view of their relationship because he refers to Lincoln as "Uncle Abe," reminding Lincoln they had called him such an affectionate name when Lincoln "used to sit around our table in our humble cottage." Shoaf was seeking the position of postmaster, a request Lincoln did not honor, perhaps because few people who knew Lincoln well addressed him as "Abe." Perhaps the denial was in part because the two did not have a close relationship.[44]

Decatur had two resident lawyers at the time of Lincoln's arrival as a lawyer, both of whom left for the more promising city of Paris. Charles Emerson, who arrived in Decatur in 1834, was the county's first lawyer. A native of New Hampshire, he was educated at Illinois College in Jacksonville and practiced in Decatur until he moved to Paris in 1847, only to return to Decatur in 1850, when he was elected to the legislature. He became circuit judge when Macon County was removed from the Eighth Judicial Circuit in 1854.[45] The other resident lawyer at this time was Kirby Benedict, who practiced there for fourteen years before also moving to Paris. During that time, he served one term in the legislature, elected as a Democrat. Both attorneys were frequently involved in cases with Lincoln, both with him and in opposition to him. Emerson opposed him more than any other lawyer in Macon County.

Joel S. Post, Decatur's third lawyer, both sided with and opposed Lincoln.[46] Post was Decatur's first schoolteacher, arriving in 1839. He studied in Emerson's office before becoming an attorney in 1841, served in the Mexican War in 1846, and was elected to the state senate where he served from 1856 to 1860, a staunch Democrat.[47]

Lincoln's Macon County practice was not as extensive as that in other counties of the circuit, but it did follow the same fairly mundane pattern. His attendance at the Macon County Circuit Court was its heaviest from 1849 to 1854.[48] In 1849, William Warnick, the man for whom Lincoln had worked as a field hand in 1830, hired him and Post to recover some land taken from him to pay a judgment. In one of four cases Lincoln handled around the circuit involving Gold Rush participants, Lincoln sued Joshua Hanks, nephew to Lincoln's cousin, John Hanks. John and Joshua went to the goldfields in 1850, and John sent nephew Joshua back to Illinois with $205 in gold dust for John's wife, Susan. The errant nephew failed to deliver the gold dust, and a suit ensued. Joshua gave a note for the debt so the case was dismissed. When payment on the note was not forthcoming, a second suit filed a year later resulted in a judgment of $241.[49]

Lincoln's bill cutting the size of the circuit removed Macon County, and his work volume in the county dropped dramatically after that.[50]

Christian

After the four- or five-day court session in Decatur, the judge and his entourage moved on to Christian County. After crossing the Sangamon River for the fourth time, they rejoined the Paris-to-Springfield Road, heading west along the west-flowing river. They passed the William Warnick Halfway House, and traversed territory familiar to Lincoln from his first year in Illinois, including the family's first Illinois home on the opposite bank of the river. There is no evidence that Lincoln was ever moved enough by nostalgia to visit the deteriorating home site. They soon saw Mt. Auburn, a glacial kame that can be seen ten miles away rising seventy-five feet above the generally featureless prairie, which made up 75 percent of the county. The town of Mt. Auburn, the first in what was to become Christian County, preceded the 1839 formation of the county.[51] Lincoln's legislative bill on January 15, 1840, called for a survey and plat of Mt. Auburn.[52] From Mt. Auburn, the lawyers headed south to Taylorville.

Two other towns, Edinburgh and Allenton, older than the county seat, have ties to Lincoln. In 1836, speculators, including Ninian Edwards, Benjamin Edwards, and Stephen T. Logan, laid out the town of Edinburgh, now part of the larger city of Taylorville, and in 1844, Lincoln and Logan brought a partition suit to force a sale and division among the various owners. Prior to 1842, Lincoln had served as trustee for a mortgage his friend Joshua Speed held on the land in the Edinburgh area, which Speed later received to pay off the underlying debt.[53] Allenton was on the early stage line from Vandalia to Springfield, and Lincoln sometimes stayed at the local inn, whose proprietor, William Frink, was active in promoting the creation of Christian County.

The controversial legislation of 1839 formed Christian County, first named Dane, as well as Logan and Menard Counties. Christian was pieced together from Sangamon County on the north, Shelby on the east, and Montgomery on the south. Promoters of Allenton and Edinburgh fully expected one of these two existing towns to become the county seat, but the three commissioners whom the legislature chose picked an undeveloped site in the geographic center of the new county and called it Taylorville. The land of the new town had not seen a settler until four years earlier.[54]

Taylorville was named for John Taylor of Springfield, one of the three commissioners, an active real-estate speculator in central Illinois. He was involved in the development of Springfield as early as 1821 and platted the first addition to its original town site in 1827. An early sheriff, his real-estate activity covered a broad area, including Petersburg, for which he engaged Lincoln to resurvey the town; they worked together on several projects, including the legislative incorporation of Sangamon Fire Insurance Company in 1835 and the Bank of the State of Illinois a few years later.[55]

Horatio M. Vandeveer, soon to become Taylorville's leading citizen, built the first house, on the north side of the courthouse square in the new town. He was born in North Carolina in 1816 and with his family worked his way into Illinois via Kentucky and Indiana, arriving in Sangamon County in 1829. He studied law under John T. Stuart and became a lawyer in 1839; he would be the most prominent lawyer in Christian County. He raised a company to fight in the Mexican War and served at the Battle of Buena Vista. He associated with Lincoln on eight cases, more than any other lawyer in Lincoln's practice in the county—one case was as late as 1859—and he also opposed him more than any other lawyer, nineteen times. He also hired Lincoln to represent him several times. In an April 28, 1844, letter that starts out, "Friend Vandeveer," Lincoln asks Vandeveer, now the circuit clerk, to fill in blanks in a divorce pleading Lincoln was filing. Vandeveer, a staunch Democrat, held nine different offices in Christian County, including both houses of the legislature and finally serving as the circuit judge in the 1870s.[56]

The county was attached to the circuit from its beginning until Lincoln's 1853 circuit-reducing bill. Christian County, one of the smallest counties in the circuit, saw a population of 878 in 1840, 3,200 in 1850, and 10,500 in 1860. Campbell and James Conkling were the only attorneys at the first session of the court, held in Vandeveer's home, in the fall of 1839; other officials were Vandeveer as circuit clerk and Samuel Treat as judge. In 1840 for $2,350, Marvelous Eastham, a town founder, built the first courthouse, a frame structure set on eighteen brick pillars that raised it two feet above the ground, creating a perfect haven for the hogs that roamed the streets in those early days. During one of Lincoln's cases in the first-floor courtroom, his argument to a jury was drowned out by the rooting of the hogs immediately beneath the courtroom floor. Lincoln stopped his presentation to the jury and asked Judge Davis for a "writ of quietus" to chase the pigs from beneath the courtroom.[57]

Taylorville in the 1840s was a "new place but prettily laid out and tastefully arranged with trees and shrubs," described Davis. The lawyers stayed at the Long Inn on the square; Davis reported in August of 1850 that he roomed there with Lincoln and Thornton.[58]

In 1850, Vandeveer hired Lincoln to sue four brothers for wrongfully cutting down over three hundred trees on Vandeveer's property. After listening to twenty witnesses, the jury returned a verdict of $476 for Vandeveer, but the Illinois Supreme Court reversed it on a pleadings technicality. No doubt because of the twenty witnesses, the trial extended well into the evening. Because the courtroom was not lit, there being no chandeliers or kerosene lamps, the sheriff brought in two candles, attaching one to the wall sconce behind the judge's bench and handing the other lit candle to Lincoln. Lincoln held a law book in one hand and a candle in the other as he attempted to complete his closing argument. The light began to pale, and the candle slowly disappeared as the hot wax melted between his fingers while he hurried to finish his argument.[59]

The other lawyers from the circuit with whom Lincoln most frequently dealt in Christian County include Charles Welles, Silas Robbins, and William Ferguson of Springfield and Thornton and Moulton from Shelbyville. Lincoln and Vandeveer were trying a case against Robbins when Lincoln made a strong point to which Robbins responded, "If that is true, I will agree to eat this desk." Lincoln quickly replied, "If you do eat that desk, I hope it will come out a brand new manufactured wagon." Hiram Roundtree, second to Vandeveer in the number of cases with (seven) and against (eleven) Lincoln in the county, was probably the leading citizen as well as leading lawyer in Hillsboro, county seat of Montgomery County, immediately to the south of Christian County.[60]

In 1852, Lincoln defended Samuel Brown on a charge of assault with a deadly weapon that was ultimately dismissed. Brown chased and shot at several people who had come into his watermelon patch. Three years, later Lincoln had to sue Brown in the justice of the peace court for his $6.22 fee, which he recovered. Forty years later, Brown remembered Lincoln sitting on the wood pile on the north side of the courthouse and swapping stories in the evening after court.[61]

Lincoln's practice there was steady from 1841 through 1853 with only a smattering of cases after that. His law partner, William H. Herndon, also had a substantial number of cases here throughout the partnership. As in most counties, only a small percentage of Lincoln's Christian County cases were criminal.[62]

The excursion of almost three months was over after the brief court session in Taylorville, known as the "Last Stop," the end of the long trip around the circuit. The judge and the lawyers rode northwest to Springfield, where the journey had started.

Menard and Mason

Two counties briefly in the circuit before Lincoln's renewed vigor in his law practice were Menard and Mason, both north of Springfield. Menard was in the circuit from the time of its controversial creation in 1839 until 1847. Mason was in only from its formation, in 1841, to 1845. As the road to both went out of Springfield, it paralleled the Sangamon River and passed the abandoned site of New Salem, traveled twenty miles to Petersburg, seat of Menard County, then on twenty-five miles to Havana, Mason County's seat, on the Illinois River. A ferry crossed the Sangamon, the county line between the two counties. Because of the counties' locations, their brief court sessions were held consecutively. The Lincoln and Herndon firm had a fairly substantial practice in Menard County, though 80 percent of Lincoln's cases there occurred during the brief time that it was in the circuit. Herndon handled most of the firm's business in both counties.

Lincoln's law business in Menard County included the usual variety, though he had a higher percentage of criminal cases here than in most other counties. The lawyer who opposed Lincoln more than any other in Menard County was Thomas L. Harris, with whom Lincoln associated on a smaller number of cases.[63] Harris, who also visited other counties on the circuit, had come from his native Connecticut to Petersburg in 1842 after being admitted to the Virginia bar. He fought in the Mexican War and returned to defeat Stephen T. Logan as U.S. Representative from the Seventh District in the wake of Lincoln's unsuccessful congressional term. After serving four terms, he died at the age of forty-two.[64]

Lincoln's past acquaintances in New Salem were a source of business in the county. In 1834, the insolvent Lincoln had his personal possessions, including his surveying tools and saddle, seized by the sheriff for sale to satisfy a judgment arising out of his failed store with William Berry. "Uncle Jimmy" Short bought the items at the judgment sale and returned them to Lincoln. In 1843, the storekeeper-turned-lawyer represented Short in a suit brought against him as executor of the estate of Joshua Short, whose will Lincoln drafted in New Salem in August 1836. Lincoln won the case, as he did in a suit on Short's behalf seeking an injunction to protect his real estate in 1845.[65] That same year, Lincoln represented Nancy Green, widow of Bowling Green. The Greens had nurtured and cared for Lincoln in his New Salem years. The suit was to collect a note from Mentor Graham, New Salem's schoolmaster, to whom Lincoln was also indebted for his hours of tutoring Lincoln in grammar and mathematics. Judgment was entered for Green, which Graham paid.[66]

In 1837, the town of Athens, then located in Sangamon County, had a banquet for the successful Long Nine to celebrate the county landing the state capital; four years later, Lincoln handled a mortgage foreclosure involving the owner of the building in Athens where that 1837 celebration was held. By the time of the foreclosure, Athens was in the new county of Menard.[67] In 1842, Lincoln represented John Allen, one of the two New Salem doctors, in a suit against former New Salem resident Samuel Hill, the successful merchant who had the only two-story house in the village. The basis of the suit was Hill's assault on Allen, for which the jury awarded Allen $20. In 1842, Lincoln defended former New Salem resident Isaac Cogdal in a suit to recover for labor performed. Five years later, Lincoln sued former client John Allen for Cogdal, but the jury found for Allen. Ironically, two years after his own avoidance of the antidueling laws, Lincoln represented Jacob Williams, charged with challenging a man to a duel. The case was dismissed. In 1847, Lincoln successfully sued former resident Alexander Trent on behalf of Speed, Abner Ellis, and others to set aside Trent's sale of a lot to his son to avoid these creditors.[68]

Perhaps the most contentious case Lincoln had here involving a New Salem resident was *Eliza Cabot Torrey v. Francis Regnier*, a slander suit against the other New Salem doctor. Regnier accused Torrey, "an almost friendless school mistress," of fornication for which she sued him. His defense was the truth of the allegations, which two juries rejected. Torrey's attorneys were Lincoln, Baker, and Harris. Seventy witnesses testified in the two trials. The original $12 Menard County verdict was set aside for the retrial, which resulted in a $1,600 verdict that the Illinois Supreme Court affirmed in March, 1844. Three months later, Eliza sued Regnier and his brother Felix to set aside an alleged fraudulent conveyance of 190 acres by Francis to Felix for no consideration, allegedly to avoid payment of the judgment. The brothers denied the fraudulent motive, and the case was finally settled. Afterwards Lincoln bitterly denounced Regnier for his behavior in these transactions.[69]

Mason County was settled late compared to other parts of central Illinois, possibly because, as one county history comments, "The soil is very sandy. Its main production in the early days was sand burrs and fleas." Ossian Ross had platted the town of Havana in 1827 but did not record it until 1835. The county, carved out of Menard and Tazewell counties, is named for Mason County, Kentucky, again reflecting the Kentucky influence. The first circuit court sessions were held in the bar of Ross's hotel. In 1843, the legislature moved the county seat to Bath, which had a courthouse and where Lincoln practiced. The court terms were short because business was minimal. In 1850, James Pemberton rode down in his carriage from Havana to attend court in Bath, and "[s]ome rowdy boys took out his buggy and anointed it all over with an unsavory lot of human excrement." Pemberton, obviously not a man to be trifled with, got himself elected to the legislature and got a bill pushed through the legislature to move the county seat back to Havana, which occurred in February 1851. The courthouse square there has been the location of the courthouse since the county seat returned to Havana.[70]

The counties of the Eighth Judicial Circuit, with their talented lawyers, challenging cases large and small, aggressive entrepreneurs and adventurers, devotion to partisan politics, mix of social and racial attitudes, and joys and sorrows of the people, provided Lincoln with a context and a stage. As the counties progressed, he progressed with them. Many of these people recognized Lincoln's special quality, whether they agreed or disagreed with him politically. Those who agreed with him politically were able to advance him in a highly partisan political environment. They provided the nucleus of the supporters that captured his nomination, which ultimately elevated him to the presidency.

PART THREE

CLIMBING THE LADDER

8. THE 1840S AND THE EARLY 1850S

A s the 1840s began, with his law practice and political career firmly rooted in the circuit, Lincoln began to look to bigger things, the first being the presidential race between Whig William Henry Harrison and incumbent Democrat Martin Van Buren. Lincoln gave over twenty-five speeches for Harrison, most of them in southern Illinois over a period from mid-August to mid-October, with only two in the circuit.[1] He pursued this wide-ranging schedule even though he was himself again a legislative candidate and a Harrison presidential elector.

On May 2, 1840, in Tremont, court adjourned at noon, and Whigs and Democrats began debate. Lincoln spoke first and gave a humorous attack on Van Buren that caused "frequent and spontaneous bursts of applause." His many anecdotes convulsed the house with laughter, and he concluded with praise for the civil and military reputation of the Hero of Tippecanoe. Holding a copy of a Van Buren biography that William Fithian of Danville had loaned him, Lincoln attacked the president for his stand in favor of black suffrage. Fithian reported that Lincoln's use of the book so angered Stephen A. Douglas that he seized the book from Lincoln and threw it into the crowd.[2] Three weeks later, Lincoln and Douglas joined forces to successfully defend *People v. Spencer Turner* in DeWitt County.

The largest crowd Lincoln was to address for many years was at an early June Whig convention and rally in Springfield that drew fifteen thousand to twenty thousand people (equal to 5 percent of the Illinois population) from all over Illinois and neighboring states. In solidly Democrat Shelby County,

Lincoln made only two purely political appearances, the first on June 27, 1840, following the ubiquitous, Lincoln political adversary William L. D. Ewing's well-received speech to a "thin audience."[3] Lincoln's efforts brought little success for him and Harrison, who lost Illinois, though he won nine of the then-thirteen circuit counties. Lincoln, running as a presidential elector, ran last in a field of five, all of whom lost. His pursuit of reelection to the statehouse was successful, although he was last among the successful candidates, Harrison's race apparently detrimental to Lincoln's campaign.[4]

When the legislature convened on November 23, 1840, the Whigs again put Lincoln up as their candidate for speaker of the house against Ewing, and Ewing again prevailed. On December 5 in session, when the Democrats locked the chamber door to keep a quorum and to compel a favorable vote, Lincoln, Asahel Gridley, and Joseph Gillespie of Edwardsville jumped out the window of the First Methodist Church, the temporary quarters of the house. The chair ruled that there was still a quorum; the incident caused Lincoln embarrassment the rest of his career.[5]

Gillespie, later to join the Republicans, was one of Lincoln's most steadfast friends. The two first met during the Black Hawk War. Gillespie, son of Irish-born parents, was born in 1809 in New York City and moved at age ten with his family to Edwardsville. After working in the Galena lead mines from 1827 to 1829, he began the study of law under the noted Cyrus Edwards and attended Transylvania College in Kentucky. Admitted to the bar in 1836, he soon reconnected with Lincoln as active Whigs, and they practiced law together in the circuit. Gillespie, elected in 1846 to the Illinois senate, served ten years, during which he was a strong advocate for the railroads. He supported Lincoln in his bid for the appointment as superintendent of the General Land Office in 1849 and his pursuit of the U.S. Senate seat in 1855 and 1858.[6]

This term, Lincoln's last, was not as successful as the earlier ones. His leadership waned substantially during this session due in large part to his melancholy and depression over the breakup of his relationship with Mary Todd late in 1840 and on the "fatal first" January 1, 1841. He was totally absent from the house during vital sessions in January, abdicating his leadership role, and he never did return to his full effectiveness during the session.[7]

The eight years of legislative service, though, benefited Lincoln greatly. He mastered the art of politics and learned how to deal with issues of government, leadership, and public service. He found that he was the equal of any of the leaders of the state, particularly important considering his humble station, minimal formal education, and modest background when first elected in 1834. He was popular with his fellow legislators. His reputation for honesty and integrity was exceptional, though his creativity and imagination had not yet shown themselves. He was well-known not only within the area that would become the Eighth Judicial Circuit but also throughout the state. Many important players in Illinois politics for the balance of Lincoln's twenty years in the state were legislators during his four terms.

After he left office, Lincoln's hard-earned stature was severely threatened by intemperate letters that he wrote anonymously to the *Sangamo Journal* in August of 1842, ridiculing the state auditor, a hot-headed, egotistical, Democrat Irishman, James Shields. "Aunt Rebecca" from "Lost Township" wrote the letters. Mary Todd probably had a hand in the composition of these letters that questioned Shields's honesty and ridiculed his self-image as a desirable ladies' man. Shields eventually found out who wrote the letters. Lincoln took the blame; Shields issued a challenge to a duel to Lincoln, which Lincoln received while in court in Tremont. An ill-advised exchange of correspondence that followed failed to defuse the confrontation, and Lincoln was cornered into accepting the challenge. Custom gave the six-foot-four Lincoln the choice of weapon. He chose broad swords as the weapon with which to fight his five-foot-seven challenger.

Dueling was illegal in Illinois, so the parties chose "Bloody Island," in the Mississippi River, across from Alton and outside the borders of Illinois, as the site. The date set was September 22. Lincoln's entourage included his close friend William Butler and fellow Whig legislator Albert T. Bledsoe. Hearing of the duel, prominent Whig John J. Hardin raced to Alton from a nearby county seat, hoping to talk the combatants out of their imprudent and foolish contest. They and their respective contingents rowed to the island; cooler heads prevailed, however, and the duel was averted. The unfortunate incident was more than a great embarrassment to Lincoln. It did damage to his image as a responsible Whig leader.[8]

Lincoln recovered his stature before the legislature when long-time Illinois Supreme Court Justice Thomas C. Browne chose him as his defense attorney in impeachment proceedings. Browne is remembered for causing a stir at Lincoln's wedding on November 4, 1842, when he wisecracked during the vows, reassuring Lincoln that the matters in the vows were already covered by statute. He is the only justice of that court to ever be tried for removal from office. Browne, a colorful character, came to Shawneetown from Kentucky in 1812. An early proslavery advocate, he served on the Illinois Supreme Court from 1818 to 1848, the longest-serving justice in the history of that court.[9] Considered good and decent, Browne was a man of high integrity performing to the best of his limited ability. His alleged favorable treatment towards his son-in-law Joseph P. Hoge, a Galena attorney, angered four other Galena attorneys, who filed a petition to remove Browne from the bench. The constitution permitted removal by a two-thirds vote for mere reasonable cause as opposed to more serious charges required for impeachment. The petition was formalized and specified in a resolution that Lincoln drafted. Browne hired Lincoln to defend him in the three-day trial, which began on January 3, 1843, before the full house (acting as a committee of the whole) and a packed gallery. Legislative factions through procedural arguments and posturing consumed most of the trial. The only witness called was Sidney Breese, then on the Supreme Court of Illinois but soon to be a U.S. Senator. The charges were dismissed, and Browne won.[10]

Pursuit of a Congressional Seat

In 1843 when John T. Stuart decided not to run for reelection as the district's U.S. representative, Lincoln went after the seat in the Seventh Congressional District, the only Whig district in Illinois, whose eleven counties included the Eighth Circuit's Logan, Mason, Menard, Sangamon, Woodford, and Tazewell, with the last particularly important. Two other highly qualified candidates also immediately surfaced: Hardin of Jacksonville and Edward D. Baker of Springfield.

In February 1843, Lincoln let his friends in Tazewell know of his interest in Congress and exerted his considerable influence within the Whig Party to select the congressional candidates throughout the state through a convention system. The Whigs had been reluctant to use conventions, opponents arguing that a convention mandate was undemocratic. On the other hand, the Democrats, more successful politically in the state, had been using conventions. On March 1, Whigs meeting in Springfield resolved to use the convention system and directed Lincoln to write a report, which he did working with Stephen T. Logan and Bledsoe. The document, citing party unity, stated, "A house divided against itself cannot stand," and advocated the convention system. Lincoln then set out to get the nomination for himself.[11] But his own Sangamon County Whigs chose Baker and selected Lincoln as one of the eight delegates with instructions to vote for Baker at the state convention to be held in Tazewell County. In a letter to Joshua Speed, Lincoln described this turn of events, "I shall be fixed a good deal like a fellow who was made groomsman to the man what has cut him out, and is marrying his own dear 'gal.'" Baker's success was in part due to a whisper campaign that accused Lincoln of being the candidate of wealth and influence and in part due to raising the issue of his lack of religion. Lincoln found both charges ironic but magnanimously declined to blame Baker for the raising of these insidious issues, a scenario that was plausible, given Baker's character.[12]

On May 1, at the Whig convention in Pekin, a deadlock loomed between Baker and Hardin. It was averted when Lincoln, as requested in the interest of party unity, withdrew Baker's name from consideration, and a unanimous ballot was cast for Hardin. In turn, Lincoln introduced a resolution recommending Baker to run in 1844 when the seat was open again. By a vote of nineteen to fourteen, the delegates accepted this compromise called the "Pekin Agreement" that implied that Lincoln would have his turn after the other two had served.[13] The agreement established the rotation principle upon which Lincoln heavily relied in his later pursuit of the office. Hardin was nominated and elected, as was Baker in 1844. Lincoln strongly supported Baker for the nomination.

Lincoln was deeply devoted to the Whig presidential candidate in 1844, his hero Henry Clay running against the Democrat James K. Polk. Lincoln campaigned extensively for Clay, even going to Indiana in late October and early November, a trip during which he nostalgically revisited his boyhood haunts. His campaigning in Illinois included appearances with fellow lawyers from the circuit, although only a few events were held in the circuit. In July, he appeared with fellow circuit lawyers Linder, Thornton, Bledsoe, and Constable in Vandalia and later with Bledsoe in Hillsboro. However, Lincoln only once campaigned outside of Sangamon County for Clay on the circuit, and that was in Menard County at a Whig meeting during the June court session. Polk won, carrying Illinois and ten of the circuit's seventeen counties.[14]

In 1845, Lincoln discovered that Hardin had decided that he might like to return to Congress, thus denying Lincoln the opportunity.[15] Lincoln's friends and contacts on the circuit, especially Benjamin F. James of Tremont, were particularly important in his maneuvering to get the nomination. James was not only an attorney who had a fair number of cases with and against Lincoln—he was also editor of the *Tazewell Whig*. Lincoln's letters to James from fall 1845 to spring 1846 reveal Lincoln's political savvy and the closeness of his friendship with James. Lincoln needed Tazewell and Woodford Counties to go with Sangamon and Menard to offset Morgan and Scott, the latter two presumably for Hardin. At Lincoln's request, James's newspaper advocated the convention system and avoided mentioning Hardin as a congressional candidate. Lincoln, relying on the rotation agreement that turnabout is fair play said nothing negative about Hardin.[16] In two long letters to Hardin in early 1846, Lincoln disputed Hardin's right to ignore the Pekin Agreement and defended his own right to rely upon it.[17]

Lincoln's numerous Tazewell County supporters included his old friend Dr. Anson Henry, now of Pekin, and Thomas J. Pickett of Pekin. Pickett founded the *Tazewell Reporter* at age nineteen in 1840. His relationship with Lincoln started then and lasted throughout Lincoln's Illinois years.

An able ally in Menard County was John Bennett, circuit clerk and an influential Whig. Likewise, in Woodford County, Lincoln had strong Whig support, including his client William Davenport, the influential community leader and minister of the Christian Church in Metamora.

Because of opposition in Menard County to the convention system, Lincoln, at Bennett's suggestion, proposed placing the convention there, and it was held there.[18] During this critical period of soliciting delegate support, Lincoln was in the district on the circuit—Tazewell and Woodford in September 1845, Menard in November, and again in Tremont and Metamora in April 1846. Because of Lincoln's astute maneuvering, Hardin withdrew, and Lincoln, the only candidate, was nominated in Petersburg on March 1, 1846. In turn, he was elected to Congress over the Democrat Peter Cartwright, the circuit-riding, evangelist Methodist preacher, on August 3.[19]

Lincoln's term did not begin until December 6, 1847. While he worked diligently to establish himself as a freshman congressman, he continued to serve his clients when he could, and Herndon, in Springfield, faithfully attended to the firm's clients there. Lincoln took time to assist a long-time circuit client, Benjamin Kellogg. On April 20, 1848, Lincoln visited the Patent Office in Washington, D.C., for Kellogg, who was trying to get a patent for the manufacture of iron pumps. The following day, he reported to Kellogg, their friendship indicated by his salutation, "Dear Ben."[20]

Lincoln's constituents viewed his service in the Congress as a failure due to his opposition to the Mexican War. The war's popularity in Illinois was fanned by the gallant service of so many from the state, including Hardin, who was killed in action. Baker, who had been critical of Whig opposition to the Mexican War during his term in Congress, served in that war. Returning from the war, he relocated to Galena, a move, David Davis opined, that was motivated by political, not legal, opportunism. There, Baker was elected to Congress and served from 1849 to 1851. Lincoln had initially committed to not seeking reelection, which was academic because he had no chance to even get the nomination. When the Whigs convened to select a candidate to run to replace Lincoln, only two delegates, one of whom was Logan County's Samuel Parks, favored Lincoln. Logan, elected to the Illinois legislature in 1842, 1844, and 1846, ran to succeed Lincoln in Congress in 1848. The Whigs had held that congressional seat since Stuart's successful candidacy in 1838. However, Lincoln's unpopular criticism of the Mexican War made the election of his successor problematic; Logan's ineptitude as a candidate aggravated the already weakened candidacy. He lost many former Whig strongholds, and his opponent, Thomas Harris, won. Davis describes this outcome "as a terrible blow to Whigs all over the state." Lincoln said Logan was "worse beaten than any other man was since elections were invented."[21] With Logan's loss of the central Illinois seat, Baker was the only Whig from Illinois serving in that Congress.

In fall 1848, Lincoln campaigned vigorously for the Whig presidential candidate, Zachary Taylor. From September 9 to 22, Lincoln spoke ten times in Massachusetts on Taylor's behalf before returning to Illinois via the Great Lakes, reaching home on October 10. He gave eleven more speeches for Taylor, including in the circuit's Petersburg, Metamora, Washington, Tremont, and Pekin. For all but two of these, Henry accompanied him.[22] Taylor won the presidency on November 4 but did not carry Illinois. Ten of the circuit's seventeen counties went for Taylor and seven for his opponent. Taylor garnered 61 percent of the Tazewell County votes, his highest majority in the state.[23] In late November, Lincoln returned to Washington to complete his term, staying for the final adjournment at 7 A.M., March 4, 1849. The next day, he attended the inauguration and the inaugural ball.

Patronage Failures

On March 11, Lincoln called on Secretary of the Interior Thomas Ewing to discuss patronage and the opportunity to strengthen the Illinois Whig Party with it.[24] With a Whig president and assuming himself and Edward Baker to be the leaders of the Whig Party in Illinois, Lincoln returned to the state ready to begin building the party. What followed was six months of frustration and disillusionment caused by his inability to effectively use patronage either for the party or for himself. The events also show the weakness and division within the Whig Party.

Lincoln's support of his Tazewell County constituents and their support of him caused some of the difficulty. The highest post available to an Illinois Whig in the new government was the patronage- and prestige-loaded commissioner of the General Land Office. Initially, Lincoln was reluctant to seek the post for himself, but then he decided to do so. As early as April 6, Henry urged him to pursue this post.[25] Henry and James led Tazewell's efforts to support Lincoln's appointment. Lincoln also had strong support from Bloomington and Paris. At the same time, Lincoln supported his Tazewell constituents in their quest for office. In April, James made it clear he expected Lincoln to also get him an appointment.[26] Lincoln's friends urged him to support Turner R. King of Pekin for the job of registrar of the land office in Springfield. This gave rise to the type of patronage-driven conflict Lincoln feared when the hot-headed William Butler also sought the post, although Lincoln had recommended him for pension agent at the land office, apparently the wrong position. In an effort to appease Butler, Lincoln again wrote Ewing requesting that he alter the appointments first urged.[27] By that time Butler had begun a campaign against King, accusing him of being a drunkard, a gambler, and, even worse in that time and place, an abolitionist. Pekin merchant Philo Thompson assured Lincoln that King was none of these things. This prompted Lincoln to write Thompson in April asking that Thompson's faith in Turner be confirmed by letters of support: "I propose that you sustain me in the following manner—copy the enclosed scrap in your own handwriting (not three or four but three or four hundred) to sign it and then send it to me." It appears that the May 1 petition Lincoln received with 139 signatures was from that "enclosed scrap":

We the undersigned citisens [*sic*] of Pekin and other parts of Tazewell
County, understanding that . . . Hon. A. Lincoln has recommended the
appointment of our Townsman, Turner R. King, to fill one of the Land
Offices at Springfield, and that certain persons sixty miles from here,
are charging said King, with being an Abolitionist, a Drunkard and a
Gambler with a view of defeating his appointment, do pronounce said
charges one and all to be false—that Mr. King may sometimes drink
spirits or throw a Card for amusement is probably true, but that he is
either a Drunkard or a Gambler in any true sense we utterly deny. We
add that in our opinion his appointment would be a proper one and we
sincerely hope that it may be made.[28]

On May 10, Lincoln forwarded the petition to Ewing with a letter again
reversing the solicited appointments and asking once more that King be appointed registrar, because it had come to Lincoln's attention that Butler was
responsible for the "assault on King's character." Seeking retribution, Butler
circulated petitions against Lincoln and in favor of Chicago's less-deserving
Justin Butterfield for the post of commissioner. More than fifty Springfield
residents joined in these petitions against Lincoln, including Dr. William
Wallace and James Matheny. Lincoln had characterized Butler's efforts as "a
tirade . . . kept up against me." He told Ewing, "I am not the less anxious because of knowing the principal object of the fault-finders, to be to stab me."[29]

These actions by Springfield residents are surprising. Perhaps Lincoln's
unpopular position against the war with Mexico had contributed to this kind
of enmity in his hometown.[30] At the same time, circuit comrade Davis characterized the possible appointment of Butterfield as "outrageous." This con-
trasting attitude perhaps led Lincoln to look beyond Springfield to the rest of
the circuit for support when he again became more active politically in 1854.

The falling-out with Butler is difficult to understand considering the deep
indebtedness Lincoln had to Butler and his family for their support during
Lincoln's early years in Springfield. And Butler had been one of Lincoln's
seconds in the aborted Shields's duel in 1842.[31]

Despite the Tazewell supporters' continued efforts and Lincoln's aggressive pursuit of the post, seeking the help of Joseph Gillespie, and fruitlessly
writing Zachary Taylor himself, Butterfield received the appointment. The
fracas had done substantial harm to Lincoln's efforts, although King did get

his appointment. Lincoln repeatedly attempted unsuccessfully to get appointments for Henry, Simeon Francis, and Logan. Lincoln declined to assist
George Rives of Edgar County, though, telling him, "You overrate my capacity to serve you. Not one man recommended by me has yet been appointed
to anything little or big." Rives later indulged in "open abuse" of Lincoln for
his refusal to help him. On the Henry appointment, Lincoln sought the help
of Caleb Smith and Richard Thompson, Indiana Whig congressmen, both
of whom were lawyers on the circuit.[32] The Taylor administration eventually
offered Lincoln the post of secretary of the Oregon Territory and then the
governorship of the territory, both of which he declined, perhaps assessing
these far-flung opportunities as detours from any meaningful advance of
his political career.

Lincoln's bitterness over his lack of reward surfaced in the fall 1851 court
session while on the circuit in Paris. Davis reported that Lincoln was shaving
in their shared room when the self-serving and wavering Charles Constable
complained about his own lack of reward from the Whig party. Lincoln
turned on him with uncharacteristic anger and accused him of slowly going
over to the Democratic Party. The two had to be separated to avoid a fight.
Soon thereafter, Constable did, in fact, go over to the Democrats.[33]

This patronage-seeking period reveals an unfamiliar Lincoln. The confidence with which he had moved politically up to this point is missing.
An uncharacteristic, almost desperate tone shades his entreaties and his
flailing about and lack of direction. His methods caused offense to some
of his Springfield friends and others, such as influential Cyrus Edwards of
Alton.[34] His lack of success showed a lack of skill and adroitness, unlike the
Lincoln of the next decade. He suffered hard-earned lessons from this experience. Friendship was more fragile than the pressure generated by patronage
opportunities. Further, the circuit offered a more reliable and committed
source of political strength than Springfield. On the national stage, loyalty
and party service were only of limited value in creating spendable political
currency. He accepted these lessons without complaint and emerged better
prepared for the politics of the next decade.

Back to the Law

The combination of his failed term in Congress, the lack of support for
his pursuit of patronage, even in his hometown, and the lack of reward for

his personal efforts on behalf of Taylor caused Lincoln to intensely turn to the law, leaving little time for politics: "From 1849 to 1854, both inclusive, practiced law more assiduously than ever before."[35] Cases took him to the newly formed federal district court in Chicago, and he continued the semi-annual trips around the circuit, which allowed him to maintain the vital relationships ultimately essential to his political career. During this period of reduced direct political activity, he was able to continue to increase his personal and professional stature throughout the circuit with the very people who would one day elevate him to the leadership of the antislavery forces in the critical state of Illinois.

Lincoln did not withdraw from politics completely during this period, although his activity was limited compared to prior years. He was called upon to deliver the eulogy for Zachary Taylor at City Hall in Chicago in July 1850, which he concluded with a reading of his favorite poem, "O! Why Should the Spirit of Mortal Be Proud."[36] He was a signatory on the call for the Whig convention in December 1851.[37] On July 6, 1852, in the chamber of the Illinois House of Representatives, he delivered a eulogy to Henry Clay, his longtime political hero.[38] That year, he participated in the presidential race, which pitted Winfield Scott against Franklin Pierce, a losing effort for the Whigs. The circuit travel covered his political appearances: in August, he responded on behalf of the Scott Club to a speech by Douglas in Springfield; on September 17, he gave a major address in Peoria while across the Illinois River for the court session that week in Pekin; he also spoke briefly in Pekin on the twentieth.[39] All of this demanded far less time than the previous presidential campaigns, consistent with Lincoln's reduced political drive, although he did not abandon politics completely.

The year 1853, another year of concentrated law practice with little distraction from politics, saw Lincoln again ending the fall circuit session at "the Last Stop" on November 10. As he headed northwest to Springfield after nine weeks out on the circuit, he might have reflected on events, including the securing of the important Illinois Central Railroad taxation case that fall.[40] However, he couldn't have anticipated that 1854 would see his old adversary Douglas upset the uneasy truce between free and slave America, unleashing the forces that would lead to the abyss of Civil War and propel Lincoln from successful lawyer to leader for the ages.

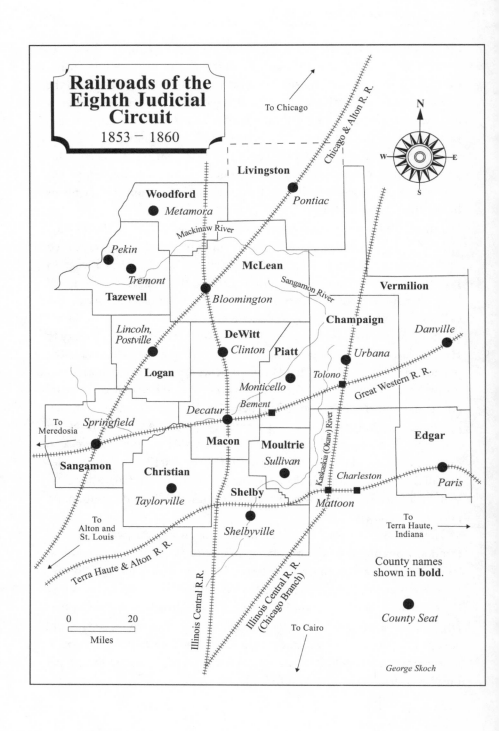

Railroads of the Eighth Judicial Circuit

1853 – 1860

To Chicago

N
W E
S

Livingston

Pontiac

Woodford

Metamora

Mackinaw River

Pekin

Tremont

Tazewell

McLean

Bloomington

Sangamon River

Vermilion

Champaign

Danville

Lincoln, Postville

DeWitt

Clinton

Piatt

Urbana

Logan

Monticello

Tolono

Great Western R. R.

Bement

Decatur

To Meredosia

Springfield

Macon

Moultrie

Sullivan

Edgar

Sangamon

Christian

Shelby

Charleston

Mattoon

Paris

Taylorville

Shelbyville

To Alton and St. Louis

Terra Haute & Alton R. R.

Illinois Central R. R.

Illinois Central R. R. (Chicago Branch)

Kaskaskia (Okaw) River

Chicago & Alton R. R.

To Terra Haute, Indiana

County names shown in **bold**.

County Seat

0   20
Miles

To Cairo

George Skoch

9. THE AWAKENMENT

⸺⬦⸺

The arrival of the railroads in the 1850s drove a decade of momentous change in the Eighth Judicial Circuit and almost overnight ended the circuit's colorful era of horseback and country inns. Urbana's Joseph Cunningham called the impact of the railroads "the Awakenment." James Matheny of Springfield characterized the coming of the railroads as "the most important event in the history of Springfield, changing that city forever." A history of early McLean County describes it as "the end of the pioneer life."[1] The railroads carried Lincoln to the vortex of all the forces swirling in the country at the time: immigration, industrialization, capitalization, rampant development, and education. The tremendous growth in population during the decade also fueled this great change. The state's population grew from 851,000 in 1850 to 1,712,000 in 1860. The growth of the fourteen counties of the circuit more than matched that rate, soaring from 107,000 to 223,000.[2] The growth came predominately from the northern section of the nation, including an influx of immigrants, particularly Germans and Irish, that diluted the southern flavor of the circuit's population, culture, and politics. The Germans, particularly, were strongly antislavery. On the one hand, the rush of immigration generated a strong backlash manifested in the American or Know-Nothing Party, which was antislavery but was also anti-immigrant. Lincoln learned how to communicate with these diverse elements and fluid attitudes within the circuit and state.

The relatively flat prairies were perfect terrain for quick and easy construction of the railroads. In 1850, 110 miles of railroad track ran through the state; by 1860, 2,860 miles served it.[3] Towns were no longer so isolated. Land for which there had been relatively little demand now skyrocketed in value. Because the railroad provided access to market for row crops, the areas of prairie under cultivation expanded, accelerating their destruction.

Virtually all aspects of life felt the effect of the railroads. Manufacturing became an integral part of many towns in the circuit because of access to raw materials from distant places and shipment of finished goods to distant markets. The county seats connected to the railroads flourished, including Springfield, Bloomington, Clinton, and Decatur. Others such as Monticello, Urbana, and Pekin went flat because the railroads passed them by. Mercantile activity increased as stores had access to a steady year-round supply of goods. Construction became more urban, and homes less primitive. More newspapers were published, and the telegraph arrived at most towns in the circuit early in the decade. Colleges and universities were established. The towns started libraries and more public school systems. Hotels improved dramatically from the rough inns of the past.

Four railroad systems built in the early 1850s crisscrossed the circuit: the two major systems, which ran more or less north and south, were the Alton and Sangamon (later called the Chicago and Alton) in combination with the Chicago and Mississippi running from Alton in the southwest of Illinois to Chicago in the northeast; and the Illinois Central with its two branches, one down the state's center and the circuit, through eastern Woodford County and the new towns of El Paso and Kappa (which had collected the remnants of Bowling Green) to Bloomington, south to Clinton in DeWitt County, on to Decatur in Macon County, and then on south out of the circuit. The other branch was located to the east basically paralleling the first, heading south from Chicago through the isolated northwestern segment of Vermilion County into Champaign County, passing two miles west of Urbana, then onto the new town of Tolono, and into Coles County out of the circuit.

The construction of the railroads was made possible by Illinois' U.S. Senators Sidney Breese and Stephen A. Douglas, who secured a grant of 2.5 million acres of federal land to the state in 1850 to subsidize construction of the Illinois Central Railroad to run the full length of the state. The Illinois Central was formed to build this railroad in exchange for the land, the sale of which financed the construction of the railroad. The railroad was to pay a certain percentage of the proceeds to the state, first 5 and then 7 percent, in lieu of local taxes. The railroad's real-estate holdings throughout the state were vast. For example, the Illinois Central owned one-fifth of the land in DeWitt County. Obviously, the route of the railroad was a major political issue, which the legislature ultimately determined in 1851.[4] Asahel Gridley, as state senator, helped steer the Illinois Central tracks not only to his hometown of Bloomington but also into Clinton.

The two lesser lines, which ran east-west, were the Great Western, running from Meredosia on the Illinois River to Springfield to Decatur, through Piatt County at Bement (ten miles south of Monticello), to Tolono, and to Danville, at the Indiana line; and the Terre Haute and Alton between Terre Haute, Indiana, and Alton, Illinois, passing through Paris across Coles County to another junction with the Illinois Central near Shelbyville, then through Pana in the corner of Christian County and on southwest. The more important of the lesser lines was the Great Western, whose predecessor was Illinois' first railroad, the Northern Cross, which had been planned to run from the Illinois River at Meredosia to Springfield, demonstrating its role as the preeminent city in the state. An overzealous legislature in the mid-1830s pushed through laws to expand "internal improvements." Serving in the legislature, William Fithian, though a somewhat reluctant supporter of most of these measures, was quick to back this one headed for Danville. Large amounts of money were spent improving the rough terrain west of Danville, beginning with large trestles and bridges across the deep-cut streams. However, the panic of 1837 caused a collapse of the entire improvement program, including the Northern Cross. The effort failed in 1844. It was almost another ten years before Springfield saw a railroad, now called the Great Western, as part of the railroad-construction boom of the 1850s, which did not reach Danville until 1856.[5]

The first railroad to reach the territory of the circuit was the Alton and Sangamon on September 9, 1852, when the first train pulled into Springfield. The tracks proceeded northeast into Logan County, encouraging new towns along the right of way, including Elkhart, Broadwell, Lincoln, and Atlanta. John Shockey, whom Lincoln represented in a number of cases, platted Elkhart in 1855. He acquired a substantial amount of land in and near Elkhart prior to his death in late 1859. He built a large frame hotel in Elkhart.[6] Broadwell was laid out in 1856 near the Tan-Tivy Lodge, a colorful log inn Lincoln visited. The tracks continued northeasterly to the newly platted town of Lincoln near Postville, the county seat before Mt. Pulaski. John D. Gillett, then of Cornland, Virgil Hickox of Springfield, and Robert Latham, then of Mt. Pulaski, founded Lincoln in 1853, with Abraham Lincoln as their lawyer. The circumstances of Lincoln's founding provide insight into two aspects of the lawyer Lincoln's career: his skills as a transactional lawyer and that he and his contemporaries here were not operating in a vacuum but were part of the larger economic forces shaping America.

Gillett, who would become the county's wealthiest citizen, was born in Connecticut in 1819, the son of a ship's captain, and educated in New Haven, Connecticut. He came to central Illinois to invest the family's money in land in the new country. His first house, a large residence that still stands, is in Cornland, which Lincoln visited frequently. He eventually acquired twenty thousand acres, including land in western Illinois that he sold to the Mormons, who constructed their city of Nauvoo there. Before farm drainage, much of the prairie was difficult to farm, so Gillett took up cattle raising. He refined the short-horned breed and would eventually ship out fifteen hundred head a year, becoming known as the "Cattle King of the World." In 1868, he purchased Elkhart Hill from John Shockey's estate, including a fine home that was destroyed by fire in 1872 and that was replaced by the stately mansion on the south side of the hill. He was a client, friend, and supporter of Lincoln. Family sources say Lincoln represented him on many of his land dealings.[7]

Hickox was the uncle of Gillett's wife. Smith Tuttle, Gillett's stepfather, a crafty, well-connected entrepreneur from New Haven, Connecticut, told Gillett that Hickox would track the railroad legislation for them.[8]

Latham was only eight years old when his father died, after which the child was sent to Peoria and then Kentucky for schooling. When Latham needed help with homework, he would go to Lincoln's office, where the two became acquainted. At age sixteen, Latham completed his education in Springfield. In 1850, he sold his inherited farm, moved to Mt. Pulaski as a real-estate speculator, and was elected sheriff of Logan County in 1850.[9]

The town's founders carefully planned strategy under Tuttle's direction.[10] Pursuant to his instruction, they chose Lincoln, with his broad range of skills, to execute their three-step plan for the town Lincoln. The first step was to determine the location of the corridor that the Alton and Sangamon would follow from Springfield to Bloomington through Logan County and to buy land along that corridor where the locomotives would need water or fuel. In 1852, Tuttle advised Gillett that Henry Dwight of New York, the financier of the railroad, had said he would ask the legislature in July for permission to build the railroad, and he foresaw "a great thoroughfare between Chicago and St. Louis," and land along this railroad would be more valuable than that along the Illinois Central down the center of the state. He advised Tuttle that it was more important to get land "near the depot" than merely along the right of way, and Tuttle warned Gillett that it was important to keep this information to himself. Lincoln's correspondence in the summer of 1852 shows his early assistance in this scheme.[11] The second step was to organize the new town at the chosen location; the third was to get the county seat moved from Mt. Pulaski to the newly formed town.

The railroad engaged Latham, who was married to one of Gillett's daughters, to acquire right-of-way through Logan County, so he knew the location of the railroad and that it would go slightly west of the languishing Postville. In July 1852, Tuttle had advised Gillett that the county seat of Logan County would be moved "to Postville," where he wouldn't mind paying more for the land if it was located near the depot.[12] Hickox and Gillett gave Latham the power of attorney to purchase the town site that they selected, 160 acres of prairie north of Postville. He traveled to Pennsylvania to purchase the quarter section directly from its owner; Lincoln drew the papers.[13] Colby Knapp, Logan County's legislator from Middletown, introduced the bill to hold a county-wide referendum in November to consider moving the county seat from Mt. Pulaski to an as yet unnamed town, a curiosity proposing a move to a nonexistent town with no name. In the referendum, the site is designated by its technical legal description. Lincoln drafted and probably lobbied on this bill as well.[14]

The next step was the formation of the town. Lincoln did all this work as well. He drafted a power of attorney of Gillett and Hickox to Latham, empowering a variety of acts that might be required to complete the founding of the new town and sale of its lots. When the three speculators met in Lincoln's office on August 24, 1853, to complete paperwork, the town still had no name. The clients proposed to their attorney that the town bear his name, Lincoln. When he filled in the blank for the town name, he wrote "Lincoln" in quotes and stated, "Nothing named Lincoln has ever amounted to much."

The owners deeded the current courthouse square to Logan County. The skillfully drawn deed included a complex condition that the conveyance would be void if the county seat was not removed to the new town and public buildings erected there.[15] The town was platted on August 26, 1853, and the next day, sale of lots began at the depot site in the middle of the prairie. A special train brought people, including Lincoln, from Springfield. Ninety lots were sold for a total of $6,000; the three speculators had paid $1,280 for the entire 160 acres of which the platted town was but a part. Lincoln prepared the contracts and deeds, expressly contingent upon voter approval in the referendum that fall of the relocation of the county seat to the new town. Following the sale, the founders invited Lincoln to toast the new town. He split two watermelons from a nearby stack, caught the juice in a cup, and poured the juice onto the ground to christen the newborn town.[16] Tuttle warned in October 1853 that the transfer of the county seat was imperative and depended on the vote of Atlanta, then called Xenia. The final piece of the puzzle fell into place as the referendum passed in the November election.

Just as the move of the county seat from Postville to Mt. Pulaski provoked a law suit, so did the move from Mt. Pulaski to the new town of Lincoln. Again the county hired Abraham Lincoln as its attorney. Lincoln's associates in the case were Samuel Parks and Stephen T. Logan. Long-time friends of Lincoln, Mt. Pulaski's founders Jabez Capps, Barton Robinson, and George Turley, represented by Benjamin Edwards and Stuart, brought the suit. Judge David Davis ruled for the county, and the supreme court affirmed his decision. The move of the county seat left a certain amount of bitterness, although Lincoln's popularity in the county remained undiminished by his part in these moves.[17]

The town of Lincoln grew rapidly. Its first schoolhouse was erected in 1854. The circuit court started operating in Lincoln in spring 1854, after lawyer Lincoln's successful conclusion of the relocation litigation. In 1855, the town's first public meeting hall, Musick's Hall, was built, and the town's first newspaper, the *Herald*, began publication. Hickox, Latham, and Gillett built the first hotel, the Lincoln House, at the southeast corner of Broadway and Chicago, where Lincoln and the other traveling lawyers generally stayed. The first courthouse went up on the current site, though fire destroyed it on April 15, 1857. Arson was never ruled out. The new building served as the county courthouse until its replacement by the current building in 1907. Lincoln owned two lots on the square in his namesake town, which he acquired from his old Postville friend James Primm in payment of a $400 debt.[18]

In early fall of 1853, the tracks reached the new town of Atlanta, which was platted on March 22, 1853, before the town of Lincoln. Atlanta's founder was Richard Gill, Kentucky native and former sheriff of Tazewell County. He discovered the area and its potential when he drove a stagecoach through the now defunct town of New Castle. He and his brother Thomas learned of the coming of the railroad and purchased several thousand acres from which they sold the railroad its right-of-way in 1852. The tracks had to veer slightly to the west to find a gentler grade up the steep side of the moraine that had provided the horseback-riding lawyers a spectacular view of miles of tall-grass prairie.

Atlanta was off to a running start with lot sales in May 1853 and with the tiny town of New Castle packing up and moving to Atlanta. By 1855, Atlanta had three hotels and the county's first newspaper, the *Logan County Forum*. By 1856, it had seven doctors, four lawyers, and churches of eight different denominations. Hezekiah Armington built the first public meeting place. With the sizable amount of money he had made in his land dealings, Thomas M. Gill started Atlanta's first bank, Thomas M. Gill Company, which Lincoln represented. Other early settlers included George N. Angell from Rhode Island, who attracted a number of people from that state to the booming new town. Lemuel Foster, Yale Theological Seminary graduate, influential Congregational minister, and outspoken abolitionist, was also an early resident, having moved from Bloomington. He and Angell immediately pushed for free education in Atlanta and started the Atlanta Seminary in 1855.[19] Lincoln, a frequent visitor to Atlanta, was closely acquainted with its residents and served as attorney for other residents of Atlanta in addition to Gill, including the Hoblit family.[20]

The railroads transformed Bloomington. The Chicago and Alton reached Bloomington in mid-October 1853, about five months after the Illinois Central had arrived from the north. Over the years, with the influx of northerners and Europeans, McLean County shifted from an Andrew Jackson majority in 1832, to a slight Whig majority in 1840, and to a stronger Republican majority in 1856. Bloomington became a center of antislavery sentiment. By 1860, Bloomington's population had attained 7,100. Lincoln played a role in this transformation. When the city's public school system was chartered in

1857, Charles P. Merriman, editor of the *Pantagraph*, was elected its president. The law mandated that the city levy taxes to support the district, but the city refused to follow through. The district hired Lincoln to bring a suit compelling the levy; the city relented. In 1857, Shelbyville attorney Samuel Moulton introduced legislation to found Illinois State Normal University, the state's first public university. Jesse Fell was the prime mover in bringing the university to North Bloomington, which required McLean County to pledge $70,000. Lincoln drafted the bond needed to support that pledge.[21]

Getting the Illinois Central Railroad, whose legislative incorporation Gridley had introduced in the state senate, was a great benefit for the city but also for Gridley. Elected to the Illinois senate in 1852, Gridley was able to bring the two railroads into Bloomington. The railroad appointed Gridley as one of its agents to sell the land granted from the state, his sales inventory being all the railroad land between LaSalle on the Illinois River to the north and the southern edge of McLean County to the south. Assisted by trusted aides, he was the most successful sales agent the railroad had.

Gridley was also instrumental in other areas. In addition to bringing the telegraph to Bloomington in 1854, he founded the city's first bank in 1852, the McLean County Bank, the building where Lincoln spent a considerable amount of time.[22] Lincoln represented that bank in a case in which it unsuccessfully sought to stop the city from taxing the bank's property. In 1857, Gridley acquired ownership of Bloomington Gas, Light, and Coke Company, which made Bloomington one of the state's first gas-lit cities, in a case in which Lincoln, assisted by Logan, represented him. The owners from whom Gridley took the company in a judicial sale charged him with collusion. Judge Davis and the Supreme Court both upheld the judicial sale.

Bloomington's growth and resultant prosperity brought back the newspaper. Fell's paper, the *Bloomington Observer*, had discontinued publication in 1839, but in 1846, Charles Merriman resumed publication of the *Western Whig*. Fell joined him, and in 1851, they changed the name to the *Bloomington Intelligencer*. In 1854, Merriman, a classical scholar, changed the name to the *Pantagraph*, which by the mid-1850s was one of the state's leading newspapers. It was unabashedly partisan, strongly supportive of the Republican cause and the party's leaders, especially Lincoln.[23]

The main hotel in the 1850s was the Pike House, a large, four-story, frame structure. People remembered Lincoln relaxing on the porch and in the lobby as he told stories and discussed politics. In 1856, Lincoln and Gridley unsuccessfully sought recovery for Meshach Pike, who allegedly had been defrauded in the sale of Pike House that year.

The newfound affluence in Bloomington led to fine, even luxurious homes, the grandest being Gridley's, built in 1859 for the then astounding sum of $40,000. When Lincoln saw the house, he supposedly asked, "Do you want everyone to hate you, Gridley?"[24]

Bloomington became a manufacturing center. William Flagg and John Ewing, the one-time innkeeper, employed as many as 150 men in the manufacture of reapers. John Lewis Bunn and Abraham Brokaw made plows. Cyrenius Wakefield, a close friend and political ally of Lincoln, developed and made the nationally renowned Wakefield's Blackberry Balsam. The Chicago and Alton Railroad located its shops in Bloomington in 1857. It was one of the city's major industries for almost one hundred years after Fell accompanied the railroad's superintendent, Richard Price Morgan, on horseback to Joliet to select a site. Morgan and Lincoln became friends in 1853 in Bloomington when Lincoln arrived late at the rooming house where Morgan was staying. No vacant rooms were to be had, so Morgan shared his large room with the stranger.[25] Morgan, who settled in Livingston County and founded the town of Dwight along the path of the Chicago and Alton, would become an effective supporter of Lincoln though the balance of the decade.

From Bloomington, the railroad continued northeast to Pontiac, which had remained a rough frontier town until the railroad arrived on July 4, 1854, which, an 1878 county history states "was a grand holiday and fuller of importance than any had dreamed."

To the south, the Illinois Central traveled into DeWitt County, whose population doubled from 5,000 in 1850 to 10,800 in 1860, and on to Clinton. Commerce and the law business picking up considerably. The city's first newspaper, the highly partisan pro-Democrat *DeWitt Courier*, was launched in 1854. In 1856, Isaac Coltrin founded a Republican paper, provoking the *Courier* to observe "an heir was born to the Black Republican Party that bore the name Central Transcript."[26]

The coming of the railroad was not all beneficial, however. In 1853, railroad-construction gangs created a growing crime problem, and the citizens gathered at a town meeting in Clinton to try to solve it. The railroad rode roughshod through the county in its goal to run the entire length of the state and caused a substantial amount of damage to neighboring landowners' property.[27]

The Illinois Central reached Decatur from Clinton on October 18, 1854. Edward O. Smith convinced railroad officials to bring it to Decatur rather than six miles west of the city as originally planned. Six months earlier, the Great Western had arrived from the west, its progress slowed by the filling of the Stephens Creek valley, difficult work that crews of Irish and Germans, who often skirmished, did. Once-sleepy Decatur became an important junction that Lincoln frequently used while making his way around the state. A story has it that in 1857, Lincoln missed his train, so an Illinois Central section hand helped him propel a handcar the twenty-two miles from Clinton to Decatur.[28]

Soon the town had various manufacturing concerns, lumberyards, a brewery, and wood mills. In 1855, publisher William J. Usrey founded the town's second newspaper, the *Illinois State Chronicle*, and at the intersection with the Great Western, the Illinois Central built a large depot, which both railroads shared, and a hotel, the Junction House. The Macon House added a third floor and wings on the east and south ends, increasing it to sixty rooms. In 1854, another major hotel, the Cassel House, went up at the courthouse square's southeast corner. All of this activity the railroads sparked made Decatur a convenient site for the coming political activity of the volatile 1850s and caused its population to quadruple.[29]

Throughout Lincoln's career, it seems almost providential that a Lincoln supporter was in a vital position to advance Lincoln's course. Such a man was Richard J. Oglesby, Decatur's leading political figure who was to become a giant in Illinois politics of the second half of the nineteenth century. Although not one of the inner circle of Lincoln's supporters, Oglesby was to play a key role in Lincoln's rise to power. His life in some respects parallels Lincoln's: He was born in 1824 in Kentucky, had minimal schooling, and was orphaned, coming to Decatur in 1836. He was admitted to the practice of law in 1845 and went on to enjoy great political success in Illinois, becoming governor in 1864. He served with valor in the Mexican War. After a short period as an attorney, he joined others from Decatur going to the California goldfields, and with the small fortune made selling equipment to miners, delivering mail, and hauling for them in California, Oglesby returned to the law in Piatt and Macon Counties. He formed a partnership in 1853 with

Sheridan Wait, and they frequently opposed and associated with Lincoln.[30]

When the Illinois Central's eastern branch reached the vicinity of Urbana in 1854, it transformed Champaign County but not Urbana itself. The county's population exploded but at the new town that sprang up where the rails went, not in Urbana. The route chosen for the tracks ran two miles west of Urbana, a decision based on cost because the relatively flat land there had no significant streams to cross. Unlike Bloomington, Clinton, and Decatur, it was not a concern of the Illinois Central to go to Urbana—it was too small to matter. The railroad had no plans to create a new town and continued to call the stop "Urbana" until 1860. However, the new town that started up at once was called the Depot until it became known as West Urbana two years later. In less than three years, the new town's population exceeded Urbana's. With extensive remodeling of the courthouse in 1859 to make it economically impractical to remove the courts, Urbana's leaders successfully resisted an effort to relocate the county seat. The new town's name was officially changed to Champaign in 1861, although West Urbana's new newspaper, the *Central Illinois Gazette*, first referred to the town as "Champaign City" on May 16, 1860.[31]

The railroads also created the town of Tolono, ten miles south of West Urbana. In 1856, the Great Western came through Champaign County south of the Urbanas, creating a junction that fueled optimism for growth there. History has not justified this optimism, but the junction made Lincoln an occasional visitor to Tolono. In order to go north or south, he could take the train from Springfield to Tolono and switch trains. The town had a fairly large depot and hotel, the Marion House, at the southeast corner of the intersection of the Great Western and the Illinois Central. Early residents recalled Lincoln whiling away his time at the junction waiting for a connecting train, sometimes playing chess or throwing horseshoes. Adelaide Chaffee, the town doctor's sixteen-year-old daughter at the time, remembered going to meet Lincoln in the hotel's parlor as he waited for a train.[32]

Lincoln took full advantage of the seismic change thrust upon the circuit by the railroads. The railroads' arrivals coincided with his reentry into politics and the maturing of his law practice. He understood how to exploit the increased mobility the well-placed junctions of Springfield, Decatur, and Tolono created, making the entire state more accessible, including the booming city of Chicago. His new mobility substantially expanded the horizons of his practice, bringing him in contact with significant entrepreneurs and financial interests. The Illinois Central Railroad's hiring of Lincoln affirmed his preeminent stature among Illinois lawyers. The lack of agenda noted in Lincoln's practice is also seen in his railroad practice: Over the years, he handled seventy-one cases for railroads and sixty-two against them, and he represented seven different railroads in litigation, but he also sued six of them.[33]

Lincoln handled three cases for the railroads, two in the circuit and one in Chicago, that had significant impact on the vitality and viability of the railroads not only in Illinois but also nationally. The first of these arose in 1853 and threatened the foundation of the financing of the Illinois Central Railroad. The state transferred thousands of acres to the railroad, not only for right-of-way but also land for the railroad to sell to subsidize construction. The massive transfer involved alternating one-square-mile sections within six miles on each side of the right-of-way throughout the track's entire length in Illinois. The 1851 legislation authorizing the transfer provided that the state would receive a percentage of the sales proceeds or a percentage of the land's value, whichever was greater. It also provided that the land was exempted from county taxation. Each county stood to lose the tax revenue from thousands of acres along its portion of the right-of-way. The counties, not willing to lose tax revenues, contended that the exemption was unconstitutional; the issue was critical to the railroads' financial viability and to the potential explosive growth dependent on the railroads' arrival.

Lincoln's involvement in this important case speaks to his objective approach to his law practice. Thomson R. Webber, Champaign County circuit clerk, asked Lincoln to represent that county to contest the exemption and to tax the railroads. On September 12, 1853, Lincoln told Webber that McLean County was also attempting the taxation and that the Illinois Central offered to engage him there; he stated his "feeling that you have the prior right to my services; if you choose to secure me a fee something near such as I can get from the other side. The question, in its magnitude, to the Co. on the one hand, and the counties in which the Co. has land, on the other, is the largest law question that can now be got up in the state; and therefore, in justice to myself, I cannot afford, if I can help it, to miss a fee altogether."[34] The Illinois Central formally hired him in October 1853. When the McLean County assessor tried to levy the tax, Lincoln filed suit seeking to prevent the taxation by means of an injunction to keep the county from levying the tax. Gridley assisted in the trial court; John M. Scott represented the county. Judge Davis held for the county; Lincoln appealed to the Illinois Supreme Court and won. The court held that the railroad's charter was constitutional, and the legislature could exempt the lands from local taxation. Lincoln charged $5,000 for his services, an incredibly large fee at the time ($116,000 in today's money), the railroad refused to pay, and Lincoln successfully sued in McLean County Circuit Court in 1857. He relied on an affidavit as to the fee's fairness that well-known attorneys, including Norman Judd of Chicago, Norman Purple of Peoria, and Orville Browning of Quincy, signed.[35] The fee became an issue in the Douglas senatorial campaign of 1858 when, ironically, Douglas, who had the full support of the Illinois Central Railroad and its chief engineer George B. McClellan, depicted Lincoln as the railroad's agent against the people's interest. In response, Lincoln said, "The decision, I thought, and still think, was worth half a million to them [$11,558,000 in today's money]. I wanted them to pay me $5,000, and they wanted to pay me about $500. I sued them and got the $5,000. This is the whole truth about the fee; and what tendency it has to prove that I received any of the people's money, or that I am on very cozy terms with the Railroad Company, I do not comprehend."[36]

In the second case, the Illinois Central again hired Lincoln in another major tax case, this time by the state. When the case arose, in 1857, Lincoln was not only a prominent member of the Republican Party but also enjoyed a long-standing, close political and personal friendship with Jesse DuBois, the state auditor. Lincoln was also a special adviser to Governor William H. Bissell. Maybe the specter of a significant tax case and a desire to have Lincoln's representation were factors in the railroad ultimately paying Lincoln's $5,000 fee in the McLean County case without further appeal. Lincoln's efforts in the McLean County tax case sustained the legislation that provided for an annual tax in the amount of 7 percent of the value of railroad assets. Based upon the information provided by the railroad in its 1857 return, DuBois filed suit in the Illinois Supreme Court to recover the claimed shortfall in a peculiar procedure created under the railroad's charter. When the state and the railroad could not agree on a valuation, DuBois proposed a trip around the entire system, which Lincoln, Logan, Ozias M. Hatch, state treasurer William Butler, and DuBois took for nine days from July 14 to July 22, 1859.

Still unable to agree on a valuation, Lincoln prepared to try the case. His strategy was to shift the issue from construing the legislation to the validity of the valuation. The trial consisted primarily of ten witnesses offering opinions on the valuation of railroad land. Lincoln was successful again in saving the railroad substantial taxes, for which he received a $500 fee.[37]

The third case was the momentous *Hurd v. Rock Island Bridge Company*, which Lincoln tried in 1857, about the construction of a railroad bridge across the Mississippi River at Rock Island, Illinois.[38] Completed in April 1856, the bridge carried its first train on the twenty-first of that month. On May 6, the *Effie Afton*, a steamboat owned by Jacob S. Hurd, crashed into the bridge, the boat became engulfed in flames, and a bridge span ignited and collapsed into the wreckage of the boat. The boat owners sued the bridge company in the federal court in Chicago for obstructing the river. Attorney Norman Judd, secretary of the bridge company, was lead counsel; Lincoln joined him. In a similar case, Lincoln, representing the boat's insurance company trying to recover its loss, had taken the opposite side in *Columbus Insurance Company v. Peoria Bridge Company*, in 1851 when a barge on the Illinois River struck a bridge at Peoria, and the barge owners claimed wrongful obstruction of the river; after a hung jury, the case was settled.[39]

The newspapers of the day avidly followed the *Hurd* trial, which lasted from September 8 to September 23, 1857. National attention focused on the pitting of river against rail and river-transportation capital St. Louis against rail-transportation capital Chicago. As part of his trial preparation, Lincoln went to the bridge site, hired a boat to pass under the bridge, and floated debris past the span as he studied the currents. In his day-and-a-half closing argument, Lincoln pointed out that between September 8, 1856, and August 8, 1857, 12,386 freight cars and 74,179 passengers had passed over the bridge, and he emphasized the importance of rail traffic to the nation's future. The jury could not reach the necessary unanimous verdict but favored Lincoln's side 9-3; a mistrial was declared. Lincoln's mastery of the complex scientific and legal issues raised in this case placed him clearly at the top of his profession in the state. The lack of a verdict finding the bridge to be an obstruction solidified the railroad bridge's role in the new era of transportation. It also cemented Lincoln's place in the forces shaping the face of America. For his efforts, Lincoln received $400, which, as always, he split with Billy Herndon.

Much of Lincoln's railroad litigation involved landowners, who won far more often than the railroad in lawsuits brought. Lincoln's circuit cases arose first from railroad construction, such as diversion of streams and damage to the landowners' fences, crops, and land caused by the crews as well as the livestock kept to feed the crews as they worked their way south, and then from the operation of the railroads, for example, typically for lost goods or an engine destroying a cow. The Illinois Central particularly was the target of lawsuits, including in McLean, Champaign, and DeWitt Counties.[40] In March 1854, Lincoln wrote the railroad's general counsel, Mason Brayman, of the discontent caused by its failure to keep its fencing agreements. He advised, "A stitch in time may save nine in the matter."[41] In late summer, the Illinois Central Railroad requested that Lincoln not take cases against it. Lincoln began turning down cases against the railroad so as not to jeopardize the railroad's steady stream of business.[42]

Lincoln, who always associated with a local attorney for the railroad, worked in DeWitt County with Clifton H. Moore. Most of the landowner cases there pitted Lawrence Weldon and Leonard Swett against Lincoln and Moore. DeWitt cases demonstrate the mundane nature of much of this litigation, which began in 1854. A litigious man named Wilson Allen brought seven separate suits against the railroad between 1854 and 1859 over such disputes as removal of fifty thousand cubic feet of earth for construction, damaging his fields, and blocking a stream creating a pond that, Allen claimed, caused disease in his family. A neighbor of Allen remembered that Lincoln came to her family's house, put his horse in their barn, had dinner, and walked through the timber to the Allen place only to find the Allen family using the water from the pond because their well had failed. Lincoln used this information in his cross-examination of Allen that afternoon. The tactic was only moderately successful because Allen won his lawsuit in which he had asked for $2,000 and was awarded $286. Davis, who was friends with Allen, had visited in Allen's home. In July 1853, Davis reported to Sarah that "my old friend Wilson Allen is quarreling bitterly with railroad officers and contractors." This relationship did not prevent Davis from presiding in all seven of Allen's suits against the railroad.[43]

If the local newspaper reflected community attitude toward the railroad, these cases were difficult ones in which to represent the Illinois Central. The *Clinton Democratic Courier* reported on one of Allen's cases,

"Nothing short of victory however gross, wrong, and absurd can satisfy the morbid cravings of that huge and unprincipled monopoly known by the title of I.C.R.R. Company."[44] However, this community ill will toward the railroad seems to not have spilled onto Lincoln, who remained highly regarded in the community even though he was the railroad lawyer, judging from the political support he continuously received from DeWitt County throughout the decade.

Railroad litigation introduced Lincoln to McClellan, later vice president of the Illinois Central. Within five years, President Abraham Lincoln would appoint General McClellan to head the Army of the Potomac, a job that McClellan fumbled; he ran against Lincoln in the bitter election of 1864. A West Point graduate, McClellan had been one of the U.S. Army's highly favored young officers until his surprising resignation in 1856 to join the railroad. As chief engineer, he came to DeWitt County to testify on the railroad's behalf.[45] Later, he wrote, "Long before the war when Vice President of the Illinois Central Railroad, I knew Mr. Lincoln. More than once I have been with him in out of the way county seats where some important cases were being tried and had to sit up all night listening to the incessant flow of anecdotes from his lips." The arrogant McClellan's contempt for Lincoln was thinly veiled: "He was not a man of strong character and he was destitute of refinement—certainly in no sense a gentleman—he was easily wrought upon by the coarse associates whose style of conversation agreed so well with his own." His opinion never changed. McClellan was a close friend and ardent supporter of Douglas.[46]

Lincoln's representation of the railroads included seven cases of issues surrounding railroad-stock subscriptions. Individuals would subscribe to railroad stock based on the railroad's initially proposed location, only to refuse to pay when the railroad moved the route of its tracks. In 1851, the Alton and Sangamon Railroad engaged Lincoln to sue in Sangamon County Circuit Court against several shareholders, including James A. Barrett, who had refused to pay their subscriptions for this reason. Lincoln asserted the railroad's right to make the change and still enforce the subscriptions. Logan defended Barrett. Judge Davis ruled for the railroad, and the Illinois Supreme Court affirmed it, significant results for railroad interests. Nevertheless, in 1856, on an apparent referral from attorney and friend Anthony Thornton, Lincoln defended seventeen of Shelbyville's leading citizens, including Thornton, who refused to pay for stock to which they had subscribed because the Terre Haute and Alton Railroad, which Joseph Gillespie represented, was not coming through downtown Shelbyville. Lincoln took the cases although the opposite side of the *Barrett* case. He won the cases in the trial court but lost in the supreme court when the court cited his *Barrett* case as authority against him.[47]

Lincoln's cases against railroads included suits in other counties. In McLean County, he sued the Illinois Central and the St. Louis, Alton, and Chicago Railroads for damage to land during construction.[48] In Sangamon County, he represented a brakeman whose leg was amputated when the engineer allegedly prematurely started the train. The suit against Great Western Railroad for negligence was settled.[49] In Vermilion County, he opposed the Great Western, which Oliver Davis represented. Lincoln and Lamon, for landowners in about fifteen cases from 1853 to 1855, handled the acquisition cases that the railroad filed to obtain right of way; the principal issue was assessment of damages.[50] In Macon County, Lincoln filed a suit in 1855 for three plaintiffs against the Great Western Railroad over property they had given to the railroad for the depot, but his clients dropped the case in 1857. Two of the plaintiffs, William Martin and Henry Prather, were among Decatur's most prominent citizens, and the third was Richard J. Gatling, inventor of the legendary Gatling gun, patented in 1862. When the weapon was turned down for testing by the War Department, Gatling appealed directly to President Lincoln, apparently to no avail.[51]

The railroads' arrival in Illinois raised a wave of change that swept the circuit. To those who saw the wave coming and rode it, it was a time of unparalleled opportunity—careers were created, fortunes were made, and the national spotlight was drawn to Illinois. With his circuit network in place, Lincoln was one of those, more than most, who saw the wave coming. It inflated and grew his law practice and his stature as a politician.

10. THE REPEAL . . . AROUSED ME AGAIN

Despite privately holding a deep-seated antipathy toward slavery, Abraham Lincoln expressed himself publicly on the question only once before 1854. In the Illinois legislature in 1837, he took his first public stand against slavery. At the request of the legislatures of four southern states, the governor of Illinois asked the legislature to pass a resolution against abolitionism. On January 20, Lincoln's vote was the first nay as the roll call unfolded, and in the end, the vote in favor of condemning abolitionism was seventy-seven ayes and only six nays. Two weeks later, Lincoln and his colleague Dan Stone, who also voted nay, explained their reasons for their votes: "They believe that the institution of slavery is founded on both injustice and bad policy," although they went on to note that they did not think abolitionism was the answer to the problem of slavery.[1] The potential political fallout from this open stand against slavery was considerable. To side with the abolitionists would have been political suicide. In 1844, for example, the McLean County Commissioners denied access to the courthouse for a meeting of abolitionists, declaring that abolitionists were the "enemies of the country."[2]

Lincoln's reluctance to speak out against slavery was twofold. Foremost were the racist attitudes of a sizable number of the people of central Illinois. They held little sympathy for the plight of African Americans, whether in bondage or free. Although the issue was looming nationally, no real racial issues were before the voters of the circuit throughout the 1840s and into the 1850s, so there was little reason for Lincoln to be publicly vocal. He knew the people from his trips among them and found no practical reason to raise the issue. This silence does not reflect his revulsion of the institution of slavery.

At the same time, Lincoln's values were firmly rooted in the sanctity of the laws and the Constitution. In his Lyceum address in 1838, he urged that every American should never violate the laws of the country and further encouraged his audience "to support the Constitution and the Laws, let every American pledge his life, his property, and his sacred honor."[3] Until the Missouri Compromise was repealed in 1854, Lincoln, like many other opponents of slavery, believed that as long as slavery did not expand its territory, it would gradually expire within the framework of existing law. They saw the ultimate demise of slavery as dependent on stopping its expansion. Thus, Lincoln could maintain his fervent hatred of slavery alongside his strong commitment to the law and Constitution. This tension of these two entrenched values allowed him, like many opponents of slavery, to be content with the slow but orderly extinction of slavery. In 1845, Lincoln outlined this strategy to Hennepin attorney Williamson Durley, "I hold it to be equally clear, that we should never knowingly lend ourselves directly or indirectly, to prevent slavery from dying a natural death—to find new places for it to live in, when it can no longer exist in the old."[4] The Kansas-Nebraska Act, which Stephen A. Douglas introduced in January 1854 and which passed in May, shattered this complacency. The law opened the door to the dreaded expansion of slavery and threatened its anticipated demise. "I was losing interest in politics, when the repeal of the Missouri Compromise aroused me again," Lincoln revealed.[5]

Ottawa's T. Lyle Dickey was rooming with Lincoln at Bloomington's Pike House at the time Lincoln learned of the U.S. Senate's passage of Douglas's act. Dickey recalled that he and Lincoln discussed the situation the act created late into the night until Dickey finally fell asleep. He awakened in the morning to find Lincoln still sitting up, and when he saw that Dickey was awake, he immediately resumed the discussion as if there had been no interruption.[6] Lincoln spent the summer researching the history of slavery and its course in America. In late summer, he emerged and reentered politics with a vengeance. Gone was the frequent, somewhat frivolous reliance on humor in his speeches as his speeches became more serious and focused on that single issue of slavery. He demonstrated a morally driven commitment and a single-minded direction from which he did not stray. To further that effort, he marshaled the resources he had accumulated over the years, the venues and the talented men of the Eighth Judicial Circuit.

The circuit provided Lincoln the perfect platform from which to launch this effort. His longtime presence in the communities of the circuit gave him standing and contacts to create opportunities to speak. His law practice allowed him to visit the locations as part of his routine travel and to continue to make a living as he also began his campaign against the extension of slavery. Because he had become part of the communities, he could reasonably anticipate a friendly reception to his appearances in them. He knew his moderate approach to the elimination of slavery, control of its expansion, would not offend the conservative sensibilities of his circuit audiences.[7] The strategic moderation of Lincoln's approach to this issue should not obscure the passion of his hatred of slavery or his ultimate goal for its extinction.[8] Although he held no office or position of authority from which to speak, his appearances were justified by his local stature earned by the years of semi-annual visits to each community.

Lincoln was like Paul Revere riding across central Illinois arousing complacent Illinoisans to the imminent threat the Kansas-Nebraska Act would cause. He began developing and honing a basic anti-Nebraska speech that would reach maturity in Peoria on October 16. As Shelby Foote said, "And now the Lincoln music began to sound." After speaking in Winchester, Scott County, on August 26, he debated longtime friend and opponent John Calhoun regarding the Nebraska question on September 9 in Springfield. He traveled to Bloomington for the beginning of the fall term in McLean County Circuit Court, where he handled a variety of cases, including several for the Illinois Central Railroad. He also successfully sued Asahel Gridley and his McLean County Bank on behalf of the Chicago and Mississippi Railroad.[9] While there, on September 12, Lincoln addressed a German antislavery meeting at the courthouse in the evening. Two weeks later, accompanied by Jesse Fell and Lawrence Weldon, he met Douglas at the National House, a Bloomington hotel, to discuss Fell's proposal that Lincoln and Douglas debate each other about the issues Douglas's legislation had raised. With some irritation, Douglas declined, and he spoke at the courthouse in the afternoon. In a pattern that was repeated throughout their future Illinois confrontations, Lincoln responded that evening at the courthouse. Lincoln's speeches had the same themes and points as the more fully developed speech he would give in Peoria in October.[10]

Next stop was Metamora, where he appeared on the explosive *Pearl* cases after a change of venue from Tazewell County. The political storm caused Lincoln to interrupt his circuit rounds as he returned to Springfield and attended Douglas's speech on October 3 at the Illinois State Fair. He announced that he would answer on the next day. The response lasted three hours, though it was only briefly reported in Springfield's *Illinois State Journal*. One witness stated that as Lincoln proceeded in the speech, "he took on an air of unconscious majesty."[11] Because the audience included leaders from all over the state, word of the speech spread throughout Illinois. His stature was enhanced by this speech, which has been favorably compared to the better-known Peoria speech. Following Lincoln's speech, a group of more than twenty of the state's more radical antislavery leaders met in Springfield for two days to attempt to form the Republican Party in opposition to the Douglas bill. In order to gracefully avoid this meeting because of its anticipated extreme stance, Lincoln left on October 5 for the court session in Pekin, two days away, where he handled a substantial volume of other cases, including eight appearances on October 12. Unbeknownst to Lincoln, he was named to the twelve-member central committee of the new party back in the Springfield meeting. However, he was not yet ready to participate in the new party to this extent.[12]

From Pekin, he crossed the Illinois River to Peoria, where four days later he gave the complete version of his anti-Nebraska speech. The Peoria speech, which was printed and widely disseminated, was the longest speech Lincoln would ever deliver. He reached a newfound eloquence in defining his moral repugnance to the institution of slavery as he spoke at length on the ramifications of the repeal of the Missouri Compromise. He condemned its repeal as wrong. He expressed his hatred of the "covert zeal" for the spread of slavery "because of the monstrous injustice of slavery itself" and its reflection on the democratic principles of America. He indicated that the repeal threatened the uneasy truce in the sectional dispute over slavery and, therefore, threatened the very Union. While not urging political or social equality of African Americans, he eloquently offered "that no man is good enough to govern another man, *without that other's consent*. I say this is the leading principle—the sheet anchor of American Republicanism." This speech, refining the themes developed in the earlier speeches that fall, marks his first significant step toward the presidential nomination and the White House.[13]

He resumed the circuit and moved on to Urbana for the regular court session. There he repeated a variation on the speech in Urbana on October 24, 1854, at the courthouse. Henry Clay Whitney recalled going to their room at the Pennsylvania House with David Davis and Lincoln, early in the evening before the speech and the banter between the two as they awaited the meeting. When the time came, they crossed the street to the courtroom, now lit by eleven tallow candles. Without introduction, Lincoln gave his speech "with no ostentation, no preparation, and no labored effort." After the speech, which Whitney called one of Lincoln's best efforts, the three men returned to the room to continue their joking and camaraderie until midnight. Joseph O. Cunningham later recalled being disappointed by the moderate tone of Lincoln's speech that night. However, it reflected the antislavery views of the majority of opponents of slavery in Illinois and, as it turned out six years later, the majority of Republicans nationally. The next day, Lincoln filled in for Judge Davis on eleven Urbana cases.[14]

First U.S. Senate Race

Until the adoption of the Seventeenth Amendment in 1913 providing for the direct election of U.S. Senators, they were selected by the legislatures of each state. Senate campaigns used to be directed at the legislators, not the electorate, and started in earnest after a new legislature was elected. Democrat James Shields's U.S. Senate term was about to end in 1855. By November 1854, Lincoln had decided to aggressively pursue that seat. Earlier that fall, Springfield Whigs had nominated him for the General Assembly, to which he was elected before circuit associate and Peoria lawyer E. N. Powell advised him that the office rendered him ineligible for election to the U.S. Senate. Lincoln resigned as representative-elect, necessitating a special election in which Norman Broadwell, prominent Springfield attorney, was upset by a Democrat, and, thus, the anti-Nebraska forces lost a vote in the selection of the new U.S. Senator. Later that month, Lincoln declined the position on the new party's central committee to which he had been named because, as he explained in his November 27 response to Powell's advice regarding the Senate race that he was reluctant to join the movement at this early date, "I fear some will insist on a platform which I cannot stand upon."[15]

These developments, which did not endear Lincoln to the more-aggressive antislavery forces, harmed his bid for the Senate, and Lincoln turned to his comrades from the Eighth Circuit for support in the race. Leonard Swett went to northern Illinois to canvass legislators for Lincoln, and David Davis also strongly lobbied legislators. Samuel Parks, running primarily to vote for Lincoln for the Senate, was elected to the legislature from Logan County. He wrote to Lincoln, assuring him of his support and volunteering to assist in any way, as did William Fithian about Vermilion County. Joseph Gillespie joined in the efforts to assist Lincoln, although Lincoln's circuit companion Samuel Moulton of Shelbyville voted against him. Jesse DuBois wrote from Lawrenceville of the uphill battle there, "I am for you against the world."[16]

The race was hotly contested in the legislature. The anti-Nebraska forces, a combination of Whigs and anti-Nebraska Democrats, held a majority in the house and senate 57-43. On the first ballot, Lincoln had forty-five votes, and Lyman Trumbull, the candidate of the anti-Nebraska Democrats, had but five. Fifty votes were needed to win. As the voting went on through nine ballots, Lincoln's support waned, and Democratic Governor Joel Matteson's support for the Senate seat continued to grow, which raised a severe threat to the anti-Nebraska proponents. When Lincoln's number of votes slipped to fifteen, he finally urged his supporters, including Gillespie, Parks, and Stephen T. Logan, to vote for Trumbull, which they did with great reluctance. Lincoln generously put the anti-Nebraska cause above his own personal ambition.[17]

The Trumbull forces were led by Norman Judd, a Democratic state senator from Chicago, and the outcome caused many of Lincoln's circuit supporters to harbor a life-long grudge against Judd. Lincoln magnanimously bore no ill will for Judd or Trumbull. On the other hand, Trumbull's wife, Julia, who was the maid of honor for Mary Lincoln, fell out of her good graces. Mary would not speak to her for years and never forgave her for her husband's success over Lincoln in 1854. Lincoln's refusal to carry a grudge enabled him to work with all factions of the antislavery forces and emerge as the party's leader later in the decade.[18]

Once the senatorial race was resolved early in the year, Lincoln had little political activity for most of 1855. In March, he did join twenty-four Springfield lawyers to publish an open letter to Judge Davis, requesting his announcement for reelection to which Davis affirmatively responded immediately.[19] Lincoln worked hard in the courts, making the circuit rounds in both the spring and the fall, and he traveled to the courts in Chicago, his mobility, like the other lawyers', greatly enhanced by the still-spreading railroads.

Toward the end of the year, the circuit presented Lincoln with one more opportunity to speak out against the Kansas-Nebraska Act. During his busy fall session in Vermilion County, he appeared at the Danville courthouse on the evening of October 31 to speak. The courtroom was crowded with spectators, including Oliver Davis, Swett, Whitney, and Elizabeth Harmon.[20]

The Illinois Republican Party Is Born

As 1855 grew to a close, pressure was mounting to bring together the diverse factions in Illinois opposing the Kansas-Nebraska Act. They were former opponents, primarily Whigs and Democrats, now sharing common opposition to the extension of slavery. This pressure resulted in two meetings that led to the formation of the Republican Party in Illinois. Lincoln and his circuit allies controlled both meetings, both of which were held in the circuit. The first of these was in Decatur in February, which set up the second in Bloomington in May.

Paul Selby, in his Jacksonville newspaper, the *Morgan Journal*, called for all the Illinois anti-Nebraska editors to meet to consider uniting opponents of the Douglas legislation. On December 6, William Usrey of the *Illinois State Chronicle* in Decatur called for such a meeting in Decatur because of its convenient railroad access and central location and proposed that all the sympathetic newspapers issue a call for such a meeting. Twenty-five other newspapers endorsed the idea, including Springfield's *Illinois State Journal* and the increasingly influential *Chicago Press and Tribune*. The organizers made sure Lincoln was able to attend; he was the only non-newspaper man invited. Thus, he was moving forward, reversing his refusal to attend a similar meeting in 1854. Usrey formed a committee of Decatur leaders, including Lincoln's friends Hiram C. Johns, Edward O. Smith, and Isaac Pugh, to put on a dinner after the meeting. A major snowstorm reduced the number of editors attending the February 22 meeting at the Cassell House on the courthouse square to twelve.[21]

The committee on resolutions, in whose deliberations Lincoln was permitted to participate, laid down the relatively moderate principles that would chart the course for the new fusion party throughout the next four years. Its moderate terms were consistent with those of Lincoln. First, there was to be no interference with the institution of slavery where it already existed. Second, there was to be strong opposition of the extension of slavery into any other territories, and the line of the Missouri Compromise should be restored. In other action, a state delegate convention was set in Bloomington in May 1856 in anticipation of the national convention of the anti-Nebraska forces. The productive meeting was followed by a banquet over which the eloquent Richard J. Oglesby presided. Lincoln spoke after Oglesby, taking advantage of the unique opportunity to promote his leadership to the influential editors present. The Bloomington *Pantagraph* opined regarding the success of the meeting on February 27: "We rejoiced that the movement has manifested a firm and moderate spirit, such as will confute their enemies and secure the sympathies and confidence of the people."[22] Soon afterward, Oglesby took himself out of any key role on the central committee when he resigned in order to take a trip to Europe and the Holy Land that lasted almost two years. Significantly, the national anti-Nebraska leaders met in Pittsburgh at the same time and issued a call for a national convention to be held in Philadelphia in June 1856.[23]

Between the important February meeting and the Bloomington convention, Lincoln continued busily with his law practice in the federal court in Springfield and the courts of the circuit in six counties.[24] On May 20 in Urbana, he defended a slander case, *Spink v. Chiniquy*, representing one of his most bizarre clients, Charles Chiniquy, a charismatic French Canadian priest. He had come from Quebec to Illinois to minister to several French Canadian communities located in southern Kankakee County and Saint Anne and L'Erable in northern Iroquois County. Chiniquy repeatedly stated from the pulpit that Peter Spink had perjured himself in statements about Chiniquy. After Spink was cleared of those charges, he sued Chiniquy for slander in Kankakee County and obtained a change of venue to Champaign County. The trial in May 1856 drew large contingents supporting each side, overrunning the town with colorful crowds including "musicians, parrots, pet dogs, and all." The hotels were full, and some of the visitors camped out. The entire bar of Iroquois County attended the trial. Lincoln's co-counsel included Whitney. Spink's attorneys included Danville's Oliver Davis. Portions of the trial were conducted in French, so an interpreter was necessary. The three-day trial consumed the balance of the court session but resulted in a hung jury, so a mistrial was declared, and the case was set over to June.[25]

Momentum for the convention was building as the May 29 date approached. On May 10, Danville lawyer Joseph Peters, who would attend the convention, presided over an anti-Nebraska meeting in Danville to protest the extension of slavery and to plan participation in the convention. That same day, the citizens of Sangamon County were asked to hold a county convention in Springfield on May 24 to choose delegates. William H. Herndon included himself and Lincoln as signatories, which Lincoln sanctioned even though his role as an organizer stirred controversy. The *Urbana Union* asked all those who opposed the repeal of the Missouri Compromise to meet at the courthouse on May 18 in order to select delegates to the Bloomington convention. The signers of this important invitation included attorneys William D. Somers, Jarius C. Sheldon, James Jaquith, and Cunningham.[26]

Following the Chiniquy trial, Lincoln moved on to Danville on May 24. He was busy in court for three days before he departed for the Bloomington convention. First he traveled to Tolono, where he caught the train to Decatur in order to take a northbound train the next day to Bloomington. A number of attorneys from the eastern part of the state including Cunningham and Whitney were with him. Lincoln was pleased to see his old friend DuBois on the train, assuaging some of Lincoln's concerns that Whigs from farther south would not join in the new political movement. Upon arrival in Decatur, Cunningham and Whitney recalled casually strolling from Union Depot to the courthouse square where they were staying at the Cassell House. Lincoln pointed out the spot on the square where he spent that first night in Illinois twenty-six years earlier. He told them where he had crossed the Sangamon to enter the tiny hamlet of Decatur in 1830, and then he reminisced about his early days in the pioneer community. The entourage strolled to the timber along the Sangamon River, where they relaxed, and Lincoln continued to share recollections of his younger days.[27]

Lincoln and his companions took the train to Bloomington the next day, where he stayed at Clover Lawn. That evening he walked downtown with Whitney. He bought his first pair of spectacles on the way and informally addressed a crowd from the balcony of the Pike House.[28] Bloomington attorney Ezra Prince saw Lincoln for the first time that day from Swett's office on the west side of the courthouse square. Lincoln was crossing the courthouse lawn, and Prince described him as "a tall, gaunt man with a sallow complexion, coarse dark hair, an old battered stovepipe hat on the back of his head, coarse rough boots, innocent of blacking, baggy pants, much too short for his long legs, and a rusty bombazine coat that hung loosely about his frame."[29]

Major's Hall, the first public meeting hall in Bloomington, was the site in May 1856 for the organizing convention of the Kansas-Nebraska antislavery forces in Illinois, which evolved into the Illinois Republican Party. Lincoln made his legendary "Lost Speech" here. McLean County Historical Society.

The next day, 270 delegates assembled on the third floor of Major's Hall, built by William Major, brother of Woodford County's Ben Major. A number of Bloomington Lincoln supporters at the convention included Major, James Ewing, Fell, Isaac Funk, Gridley, William McCullough, Charles P. Merriman, William Orme, James Routt, John M. Scott, and Swett. Lincoln supporters from all over the circuit at the convention included attorney J. H. Dart from Livingston County, Leander Munsell from Edgar, Parks from Logan, Usrey, and J. C. Pugh from Decatur, and Herndon and James C. Conkling from Sangamon County. James Miller of McLean County was named treasurer, and DuBois as auditor. Lincoln circuit supporters also captured some important duties: Parks as a member of the resolutions committee, a committee for the permanent organization, and as an assistant elector; electors chosen included Fithian and Herndon; Logan as a member of the nominating committee; and Gridley as a member of the central committee.

The platform was essentially the same as the one drafted by Lincoln at the Decatur meeting.[30] Business completed, Lincoln was called upon to make the closing remarks. Lincoln gave what all agreed was the most effective speech he had ever given. There is no record of it, so it is known as the Lost Speech. One explanation of its lack of recording is that it was so inspiring that even the reporters forgot to write it down. A more likely explanation is that the tone was so explosive that Lincoln did not want it disseminated beyond the four walls of the meeting hall, where the sentiments expressed would not offend as they might if spread beyond those in attendance. Lincoln urged that all who opposed the extension of slavery and stood for the preservation of the Union should unite. Scott described what transpired: "The scene in that old hall was one of impressive grandeur. Every man, the venerable as well as the young and the strong, stood upon his feet. In a brief moment, everyone in that incongruous assembly came to feel as one man, to think as one man, and to purpose and resolve as one man." The *Pantagraph* stated, "Mr. Lincoln surpassed all others—even himself."[31] Dickey recalled that Lincoln expounded the controversial opinion that the government could not last half slave and half free, as he was to state two years later in his famous "House Divided" speech. Dickey, who roomed that night with Lincoln at the Pike House, criticized him for the tone of the speech. While defending the validity of his opinion, Lincoln acknowledged that spreading that doctrine at that point in time could do harm.[32]

The Republican Party in Illinois was born, and Lincoln emerged as its leader. Herndon stated that Lincoln's speech was the "grand effort of his life."[33] This speech stands as Lincoln's second significant step toward the nomination and election because it elevated him to the leadership of the Illinois Republican Party, which meant a high profile in the newly formed national party.

Frémont for President

Six days after the convention, Lincoln was back on the circuit in Decatur with former Whig ally Anthony Thornton on the case of *Overholt & Squier v. County of Christian* and writing the petition for dismissal of *People v. Longnecker*. Lincoln addressed to a crowd at the courthouse, the *Illinois State Chronicle* reporting "his exposition . . . produced an excellent effect." Back in his hometown on June 10, Lincoln gave an address, about which the local *Democratic Register* reported, "Except from the squad of claquers we have mentioned, Mr. Lincoln's remarks were received with coldness. He convinced nobody of his own sincerity."[34]

On June 17, Lincoln went to Urbana for a special circuit court session necessitated by the lengthy *Chiniquy* mistrial in May. During his stay, the National Republican Convention in Philadelphia nominated John C. Frémont for president. Whitney, after reading the news in Cunningham's *Urbana Union*, informed Lincoln that he had received 110 votes for vice president. Lincoln's response to the surprising news was to act amused, but both James Matheny and Whitney later expressed the opinion that this nomination first planted the seed of presidential ambition and possibility.[35] The Illinois delegation at the national convention was well represented with circuit contacts: J. B. Tenney of Atlanta, Johns of Decatur, Henry Grove of Peoria, Pekin's Thomas J. Pickett, now of Rock Island, and the always supportive Parks of Lincoln.[36]

On June 23, Lincoln addressed a political gathering at the Congregational Church in Champaign known as the Goose Pond Church. The church's membership rules barred anyone who supported slavery in word or deed. He endorsed Frémont, about which the *Urbana Union* stated three days later, "As a persuasive and convincing speaker the equal of Mr. Lincoln cannot be found."[37] While in Urbana for court business and this political appearance, Lincoln learned that the partially handicapped son of John Johnston, his stepbrother and boyhood friend, was under arrest. The young man, aiding a drover taking horses from Coles County to northern Illinois, passed through Champaign and stole a valuable gold watch from an elderly watchmaker's shop. Whitney arranged for Lincoln to quietly visit the young miscreant in jail. Lincoln was saddened but assured the lad that he would attempt to help.[38]

Lincoln's wide-ranging campaign for the Republican Party and John Frémont included two campaign appearances in Edgar County on August 6 and 7 with Henry P. H. Bromwell of Charleston, candidate for Congress and a partner of Usher Linder. About Lincoln's August 6 appearance, the Paris *Prairie Beacon* said, "When Abe got up, that is to say he undoubled his great, long gangly legs and stood almost erect before the audience." He urged that the blame for the discord over slavery fall on those who wish to extend it, contrary to the wishes of the founding fathers.[39] The next day, he and Bromwell traveled to Grandview, a few miles west of Paris, where they addressed a large crowd, but their speeches were overshadowed by two spontaneous addresses that followed when a Republican lawyer from nearby Marshall and a doctor from nearby Kansas, Illinois, both of whom prided themselves on their oratorical skills, announced their intentions to speak. Their florid rhetoric was fueled by emotion and anger that steadily rose as they exchanged heated insults to the amusement of all. The speakers' shared display of exaggerated eloquence lasted from 4:00 P.M. until dinner when they quit from sheer exhaustion. The laughter of many witnesses, including Lincoln and his companions, continued far into the night.[40]

On August 9, Lincoln ventured into politically hostile territory in the strongly Democratic Shelby County. No one from Shelby had attended the Bloomington convention. The handful of Shelby County Republicans Lincoln described as "[b]ut sixteen Republicans in Shelby County."[41] Two of them,

This scene, taken from Robert Root's painting in the Shelby County Circuit courtroom, depicts the August 9, 1856, debate between Lincoln and Shelbyville Democrats Samuel Moulton (to Lincoln's right) and Anthony Thornton (to his left). Moulton, as a state senator, had introduced the bill creating Illinois State Normal University. Thornton was the first president of the Illinois State Bar Association, serving in 1877, 1878, and 1879. From the author's collection; scanned by Susan Hartzold.

George Durkee and Charles Woodward, invited Lincoln and Thornton to debate in Shelbyville, which both men agreed to do. When the Whig Party broke up over slavery, Thornton was one of those who became a Democrat and political adversary of his friend and former ally Lincoln. Lincoln described Thornton and other former Whigs as having "conservative feelings and slight pro-slavery proclivities." Typical of the two, however, they remained cordial. At the debate, held in the Shelby County courthouse, Moulton, longtime Democratic legislator, proposed that he should speak first, which he did at great length. Lincoln then spoke for three hours. The *Illinois State Register* carried the only news account of the event, reporting that Lincoln's speech was "prosy and dull in the extreme—all about 'freedom,' 'liberty,' and 'niggers.'" Thornton recalled that he declined to deliver a lengthy response, in light of the length of Lincoln's speech, and spoke only briefly after repeating one of Lincoln's anecdotes.[42]

The ability of Lincoln and his close circuit comrades to separate law and politics is illustrated by the case of *Lincoln v. Alexander*. Anthony Thornton, on Lincoln's behalf, filed the case in Shelby County court four months after the Lincoln-Thornton debate between them. Elliot Crockett, who had signed a note for Lincoln's fee in the 1852 Moultrie County case of *People v. Crockett*, had died, so Lincoln sued the administrator of his estate. Judgment was $64.12.[43]

As a moderate within the politically diverse antislavery forces, Lincoln took heat from all sides. In addition to losing the long-standing support of one-time Whigs like John T. Stuart and Thornton, Lincoln felt the wrath in late 1854 and 1855 of the abolitionists for his caution and risked losing the support of other moderates by attempting to placate all sides. His hard-core Bloomington support was divided as well, with Fell more radical in his views than Davis, Swett, and Gridley. Swett sought the Republican nomination in the race for the Third District's congressional seat against Owen Lovejoy of Princeton, brother of newspaper publisher Elijah Lovejoy killed for his abolitionist writings and a radical in his own right. The Bloomington contingent strongly disliked Lovejoy and viewed his radical views as a threat to the party's success. Lincoln was surprised how strong Lovejoy's support was in his own part of the district. When Lovejoy won the nomination, Lincoln expressed his reaction to both David Davis and Whitney in similar language. With uncharacteristic candor, he demonstrated his trust in

Whitney by writing on July 9, 1856, "It turned me blind when I heard Swett was beaten, and Lovejoy nominated; but after much anxious reflection I really believe it best to let it stand. This, of course, I wish to be confidential."[44] These letters illustrate Lincoln's ability to set aside personal feelings in analyzing professional and political issues, a trait that allowed him to be objective in dealing with both friend and foe.

Lincoln's busy speaking schedule that fall illustrates how he used his circuit schedule to support his political speaking engagements. On August 30, he was in Petersburg, in Lincoln on September 2, Atlanta on September 4, Springfield on the sixth and eighth. The Bloomington court session began September 9, where he worked on the "chicken bone case" and *Pike v. Shaffer*. The day of September 12 he defended his temperance vigilantes in the "Whiskey-Zootic" case; that night, he was back in Major's Hall giving an address for Frémont. On September 16, Lincoln and Swett attended Douglas's speech in Hinshaw's Grove, where the Democrat stated bold fabrications about abolitionist John Brown; Lincoln's friends put out handbills there advertising his spirited response that night at Major's Hall, which, the *Pantagraph* reported, was "[a] most masterly speech in which he tore the day-time speeches of the Bucks at their great meeting into ribbons."[45]

Early the next day, Lincoln went to Monticello, where his reception reflected his lesser reputation and the limited appeal of the Republican cause in Piatt County. Responding to an insistent invitation from an old Whig friend, Lincoln was greeted only by the friend and one other person. They formed a three-man procession, even carrying a flag as they walked to the meeting place, where a small crowd awaited. Lincoln endured racial epithets provoked by his opposition to slavery, using his quick humor to deter some egg-bearing youths. This crowd of thirty doubled by the end of the speech. The reception was mirrored by the Piatt County election results, in which Frémont received only 85 votes to his opponent's 660.[46]

From there, it was on to Champaign County for its major rally of the campaign on the afternoon and evening of September 17. The *Urbana Union* reported an audience of five thousand. The crowd started gathering from all over the county in early morning. Its size forced the proceedings to move to Webber's Grove, east of Urbana. A brass band and thirty young women representing the thirty states led the procession. Two stands accommodated all the speakers, eight in number besides Lincoln, the main attraction. His speech aroused the crowds in favor of the Frémont candidacy: "Before him the sophistic 'little giant' Douglas quaked (got sick) and others of his party fly like a flock of birds," the September 25, 1856, *Urbana Union* said. After a sumptuous dinner, the glee club closed what then was the county's largest gathering ever. Fithian's appearance on the platform with Lincoln in Urbana (and in Paris) demonstrated Fithian's popularity throughout the region. Frémont outpolled James Buchanan in Champaign County 722 to 556, although the total for Buchanan and Millard Fillmore together was greater than that of Frémont.[47]

Lincoln's next appearance in the circuit was his major rally of the campaign in Decatur before a relatively small crowd of fifteen hundred. After arriving on the Illinois Central Railroad, he dined at the home of Hiram and Jayne Martin Johns and then attended the rally with Weldon and spoke briefly. Democrats threw eggs through the windows of the hall during the meeting. The consistently supportive *State Chronicle* reported on the event, asking rhetorically, "And who in Macon County does not know and respect Abe Lincoln?"[48] Next was Springfield on September 25 for a major rally before thousands in a grove west of town. On October 3, Lincoln took the train to Bloomington, where Prince took him by carriage west to Tremont. They passed numerous covered wagons heading west for Kansas along the way and engaged the intrepid travelers in conversation as they passed. That night, Lincoln and Prince slept at Micken's Tavern near Danvers and visited with other, numerous, Kansas-bound immigrants who were camping in the vicinity and were all Frémont supporters.[49] Lincoln spoke the next day in Tremont and appeared in Pekin court for Clinton's Thomas Snell. During the court session, he was in Clinton on October 13 for the major DeWitt County campaign event, reported by the *Pantagraph* as "an anti-Nebraska mass meeting on a cold, gloomy, windy day on the courthouse square." The Wapella Brass Band entertained prior to the speakers, who included circuit attorneys Scott, Swett, Weldon, and Lincoln.[50]

Lincoln returned to Urbana on October 20 for the regular court session and the retrial of *Spink v. Chiniquy*. The crowd of onlookers and supporters invaded Urbana again. Lincoln convinced his client to recant in a statement written in Lincoln's hand, in which Chiniquy stated that he had never believed Spink to be guilty of perjury; each party paid his own cost. That evening, Lincoln addressed an enthusiastic crowd at the courthouse, and the next night, he spoke at the Goose Pond Church, accompanied by Swett and Bloomington's Harvey Hogg, both of whom also gave speeches to the enthusiastic audience. While awaiting his turn, Lincoln visited the nearby residence of the shopkeeper whose watch John Johnston's son had stolen. Lincoln persuaded the shopkeeper to request dismissal of the case, and the charges were dropped.[51]

Lincoln spoke at only two colleges during his political career: Knox College in Galesburg, scene of the fifth Lincoln-Douglas debate in 1858, and Aurora College in Woodford County during the 1856 campaign. In October, Lincoln gave a speech on a moonlit evening in the chapel that had been the Eureka College's original academy building. Student Benjamin J. Radford vividly recalls the large crowd that overflowed the relatively small hall onto the lawn and the powerful speech that quickly silenced a fairly hostile audience. Lincoln was back in Logan County speaking in Armington Hall in Atlanta on October 23, accompanied by the Mt. Pulaski Brass Band.[52]

Throughout the campaign, Lincoln was trying to woo Fillmore voters, whose support of the Know-Nothing Party was hopeless and taking votes away from Frémont. In September 1856, Lincoln wrote a form letter to numerous supporters of Fillmore, the Know-Nothing nominee. His letter urged voters not to waste their vote on Fillmore because it would in essence be a vote for Buchanan, the Democratic candidate (who did ultimately win). The *Dewitt Courier* published the letter, but it is not known if a recipient of this letter gave it to the paper or if Lincoln did.[53]

Lincoln spoke over fifty times all over Illinois during the campaign, but in the election on November 4, Buchanan carried the state. Frémont won only Livingston, McLean, Champaign, and Vermilion Counties of the seventeen of the circuit. The fears of Lincoln and his fellow Republicans regarding the Fillmore threat were justified. Fillmore had more votes than Frémont in eight of the circuit's counties. However, the Republicans had made huge strides carrying a number of state offices, including governor, secretary of state, public auditor, and state treasurer.[54] The Republican Party was firmly established.

With the long, demanding campaign behind him, Lincoln resumed the law practice with the defense of *People v. Anderson and Anderson* in Springfield. Lincoln, Logan, and Stuart collaborated in the defense of Theodore Anderson and Jane Anderson. George Anderson's nephew Theodore moved

in with George and his wife, Jane. In June, George was killed, beaten outside his home with a club; evidence also revealed a slow case of strychnine
poisoning. The circumstances suggested an illicit relationship between Jane
and Theodore. The sensational case was tried in November, resulting in jury
verdicts of not guilty.[55]

Lincoln continued with a substantial amount of business in the December
circuit court session in Sangamon County and sat in for Judge Davis on December 1 on forty-five cases. He attended a large Republican banquet at the
Tremont House in Chicago that month while attending court in Chicago's
federal court.[56] As the year drew to a close, Lincoln found himself not only
one of the outstanding lawyers in the state but also the leader of the new
and rising anti-Nebraska party.

1857

The year 1857 was a year without any significant election activity so Lincoln aggressively pursued his law practice, which included busy times on
the circuit in both sessions. In the spring, he appeared in all of the counties
of the downsized Eighth Judicial Circuit.

His March visit to Bloomington included the sensational five-day trial of
People v. Wyant, Lincoln's most important criminal case in McLean County.
The case is renowned because it is among the earliest that raised the insanity
defense. In summer 1855, the defendant, Isaac Wyant, had a heated land-
boundary dispute with Anson Rusk in DeWitt County. Rusk shot Wyant in
an arm, necessitating its amputation. Several months later, Wyant calmly
followed Rusk into the DeWitt county clerk's office in Clinton and shot him
four times in front of several witnesses. State's Attorney Ward Hill Lamon
filed charges. Wyant retained Swett and his partner, Orme, to defend him.
Lamon hired Lincoln, Hogg, and Clifton H. Moore to assist in the prosecution. Venue was transferred to Bloomington.

The April 15, 1857, *Weekly Pantagraph* provides a gripping account of the
trial, reporting that the court room was constantly "thronged" and detail-
ing the testimony of every witness. Lincoln opened with a straightforward
prove-up of the murder case, ignoring the insanity issue. Swett, not disputing the shooting, countered with substantial testimony as to the insanity
defense, using lay witnesses describing the conduct and demeanor of the
defendant before and after losing his arm. He also called medical witnesses

to support the defense. Lincoln responded with witnesses who testified to the rational behavior of the defendant around the time of the shooting. After midnight on April 4, the jury returned a verdict of not guilty by reason of insanity and recommended Wyant's commitment to the Hospital for the Insane at Jacksonville.[57]

The demands of Lincoln's practice are demonstrated by the fact that for the three days following *Wyant*, he tried the complicated medical malpractice case known as the "chicken bone case."[58] His practice brought him back to Bloomington in June for the suit against Illinois Central Railroad to recover his $5,000 fee, which collection efforts took him to New York in July. Most of summer was otherwise consumed by preparation for the case of *Hurd v. Rock Island Bridge Co.*, which was tried from September 8 to 24 in Chicago.[59]

In October, Lincoln was in Metamora for the defense of Melissa Goings. The seventy-year-old Goings was married to the abusive Roswell Goings, a heavy drinker. During what was their last of many quarrels, Roswell grabbed his wife by the neck. Freeing herself, Melissa grabbed a piece of firewood and struck him twice and fractured his skull. It appeared that the judge, James Harriott, was eager to see her tried and convicted. The injustice of the case can be inferred from the fact that the sureties on her bond included two relatives of the deceased, Josephus Goings and Armstrong Goings. Lincoln took on the defense of Mrs. Goings in association with local attorney Welcome Brown and attorney Henry Grove of Peoria. During a recess in the trial, Lincoln consulted with his client in a first-floor room of the courthouse, returning to the courtroom without her. What happened to cause her disappearance cannot be known with certainty, but local court officials told the story that Lincoln said she had asked for a drink of water, and he opened the window and responded that there was good water in Tennessee. After Lincoln left the room, she supposedly climbed out the window, never to be seen in Illinois again. Local court officials thought enough of the veracity of the story to later spread it on the court records of the county. Three years earlier, William Ricketts had hired Lincoln to sue Josephus Goings and his sureties, including Roswell Goings, for money Josephus owed. Lincoln got a judgment for $220.[60]

After a substantial amount of work in DeWitt and Sangamon Counties, Lincoln was in Urbana in late October and on to Danville for the Vermilion

County session, which lasted into November. His busy year of trial work concluded with an extra session in Bloomington in December in which he and Gridley lost the case of *Pike v. Shaffer* on December 23.[61] He stayed in Bloomington until the session ended on December 28.

The year 1857 had been relatively uneventful in politics, but Lincoln's allies had attained places of influence within the new party throughout the state. This included Whitney, who had moved to Chicago, thus giving Lincoln a trusted operative and observer in the morass that was the Republican Party in Cook County.

11. THE TALL SUCKER AND THE LITTLE GIANT

The year 1858 began with Lincoln focusing on politics, assessing his chances to upset Stephen A. Douglas's reelection bid for the U.S. Senate in the fall. At the same time, Lincoln was focused on his busy law practice with his elevated stature as a leading lawyer in Illinois.

Lincoln's leadership of the Illinois Republicans and prominence as a lawyer merged in his representation of the Illinois Republican Party in January before the Illinois Supreme Court in *People ex rel. Lanphier and Walker v. Hatch*. The legislature, still heavily Democratic, had voted along party lines to pass the Democrat bill for district reapportionment that Shelbyville's Democratic Senator Samuel Moulton had introduced. Newly elected Republican Governor William H. Bissell, who intended to veto the Democratic bill, mistakenly signed it. He immediately stated his error, but the Democrats ignored his claim and brought suit in the Illinois Supreme Court to force recognition of their reapportionment act, litigation crucial to both parties. Lincoln, aided by Joseph Gillespie, successfully defended the Republican position, and the intended veto stood, leaving the districts in place.[1]

Early in the year, Lincoln began to gather the separate parts that were necessary to meet his goal to oppose Douglas. Norman Judd was now also the state Republican chairman and an ally of Lincoln, thanks to Lincoln's notable magnanimity after Judd and a handful of former Democrats had pulled the other Illinois senatorial seat out from under him four years earlier. Lincoln's circuit friends neither understood nor accepted Lincoln's embrace of Judd.[2] On February 18, Lincoln met with Judd in Chicago to plan

Lincoln's run. Judd agreed with Lincoln that central Illinois, which included the Eighth Judicial Circuit, was the significant battleground.[3] It was also necessary that Judd join with Lincoln to eliminate the threat to Lincoln's selection as the antislavery party's nominee that, oddly enough, was posed by Douglas himself as a possible nominee. Douglas and the Buchanan administration had fallen out over the questionable proslavery Lecompton constitution in Kansas, which had been adopted by proslavery advocates contrary to the apparent popular will in Kansas. While Douglas was clearly not antislavery, he did favor fair elections to determine this issue in the new territories. This placed him against Buchanan, who favored the Lecompton constitution.[4] While this schism between Douglas and Buchanan measurably enhanced the Republicans' chance of success, the split also posed a threat to Lincoln's candidacy because eastern Republicans were flirting with supporting Douglas. It was important that the party unite behind Lincoln to end the specter of collaboration with Douglas, an alliance unthinkable to Lincoln and most Illinois Republicans, including Judd. The meeting solidified Judd's support of Lincoln for the nomination.

Notwithstanding the impending senatorial race, Lincoln actively pursued the law on the circuit for the spring session, appearing in seven counties. In Woodford County, he filed documents to discharge the bond of the missing Melissa Goings. He appeared in Bloomington for the circuit court session, where on April 6, he delivered his lecture "Discoveries and Inventions."[5] Lincoln gave this lecture on only a few occasions, and it was never particularly well received.

On April 21, the Democrats' division became fixed by holding two conventions in Springfield: one by the Douglas wing that was inspired by Usher Linder's fiery speech and another convened by the Buchanan wing. That evening, Lincoln caucused with over twenty other Republican leaders in the State Library. He was ecstatic about the Democratic split and the Republican leaders' clear indication that they would not support Douglas. The next day, the group encouraged county conventions to endorse Lincoln to ensure party unity behind him before the June 16 state convention in Springfield.[6]

As these political winds swirled around him, Lincoln traveled on May 7 to Beardstown, Cass County, where he defended Duff Armstrong, son of the widow Hannah Armstrong, Lincoln's long-time New Salem friend, in

The only picture of Lincoln in a white suit was taken as an ambrotype by amateur photographer Abraham Byers on May 7, 1858, in Beardstown following the verdict of acquittal in the Duff Armstrong "Almanac Trial." Abraham Lincoln Presidential Library and Museum.

the celebrated case known as the "Almanac Trial." The killing took place in neighboring Mason County, but Lincoln had the venue changed to Cass County for trial. His skillful cross-examination discredited the witness who had relied on the light of a full moon to identify Duff. Lincoln used the almanac to show that the moon was near setting at the time of the murder. His closing argument was heavy with nostalgia and sentimentality describing his relationship with the widow and her son. Duff was acquitted. The case demonstrates not only Lincoln's trial skills but also his strong commitment to his profession and his loyalty to friends from his early days in Illinois. Eighteen-year old, amateur photographer Abraham Byers preserved Lincoln's appearance there when he stopped Lincoln on the street and requested that he pose on the evening of the verdict.[7]

Lincoln's old friend George Rives had been his correspondent on developments in the spring in Edgar County, reporting on the competition for the legislative seat so critical in the coming senatorial race. On May 20, Champaign County's *Urbana Union* reported an earlier *Chicago Press and Tribune* endorsement of Lincoln as "talents so commanding and for the influence of a character so exalted . . . the highest ideal of mankind." Later that month, the Edgar County Republicans chose Leander Munsell and Robert Mosley, who was to be the candidate for the house, as delegates to the critical upcoming state convention in Springfield.[8]

Jesse Fell introduced an endorsement resolution in the McLean County Republican Convention on June 5: "Lincoln is our first, our last, and only choice for the vacancy soon to occur in the United States Senate. . . . The Republicans of Illinois as with the voice of one man are unalterably so resolved." By the time of the state convention, Republican county conventions in all but five counties had passed such resolutions.[9] In early June, an effort to unseat the radical Owen Lovejoy threatened this unity; a number of more moderate circuit friends of Lincoln, including David Davis and Leonard Swett in McLean County, Ward Hill Lamon, and T. Lyle Dickey of Ottawa, led the attempt. They felt that Lovejoy's abolitionist views threatened the new party's efforts. With the help of William Fithian and Oliver Davis, Lincoln diverted his friends' effort, thus preserving Lovejoy's incumbency. The Lovejoy candidacy pushed longtime ally Dickey into the ranks of other Whigs defecting to Douglas.

On June 16, the state Republican convention brought 578 delegates along with numerous spectators to Springfield, jamming the hallways and the house chamber in the capitol. The executive committee of five including two circuit associates, James C. Conkling of Springfield and Asahel Gridley of Bloomington, Danville's Fithian, James Kilpatrick, and Hiram Beckwith were there, as well as other Lincoln circuit associates. Fourteen counties, including Piatt and Moultrie, did not report to the convention because of lack of support for the Republican cause. A resolution unanimously adopted echoed the tone of Fell's McLean County resolution: "Resolved that Abraham Lincoln is the first and only choice of the Republicans of Illinois for the United States Senate."[10] After the gathering reconvened at 8 P.M., Lincoln delivered his famed "House Divided" speech, the third major step toward the White House. He had read it to a handful of close advisers the night before, including Samuel Parks of Lincoln and Swett of Bloomington. Swett later said Lincoln lost the campaign in the first ten lines of this speech.[11] Lincoln gained national recognition, both favorable and unfavorable, as a result of this speech and its perceived extreme tone.

This nominating convention and the candidates' aggressive, direct approach to the people were unprecedented in the history of Senate races because the people did not vote directly for senator. Usually, as in 1854, the campaign started after, not before, the legislative election, and the campaigns had been directed at the voting legislators, not the people. Lincoln aggressively led his candidacy throughout the campaign. Sensitive to outside interference in his own race due to budding support for Douglas in the eastern part of the country, he lashed out at the *Chicago Press and Tribune* for a similar offense, that is, interfering in an intraparty contest in Indiana. On June 27, he wrote Charles Ray of the *Chicago Press and Tribune* a surprisingly harsh criticism of a position the paper had taken: "How in God's name do you let such paragraphs into the Tribune, as the enclosed cut from the paper yesterday. . . . I confess it astonishes me."[12]

The momentous campaign directly to the people began on July 9 with Douglas speaking from a balcony of the Tremont House in Chicago. As would be typical during the four-month campaign, Lincoln attended Douglas's speech and spoke the next night from the same location.[13] The campaign was marked by its ugly racial tone. For Lincoln, there was only one issue—ultimately ending slavery by limiting its expansion into the territories. In trial tactics noted by his fellow lawyers, Lincoln was always willing to concede the lesser points in order to emphasize the important ones. Here, the lesser points were those of civil rights and racial equality, while the vital issue was the eventual end of slavery. Lincoln's tactic was to prevent Douglas from obscuring the issue of slavery by arguing these lesser issues. Racial equality would not be relevant until slavery was exterminated.[14]

Throughout the campaign, Douglas appealed directly to the racial prejudices of the voters, attempting to overwhelm the basic issue of the spread of slavery. He described the government as being solely for white people, its protections no more applicable to "negroes" than to farm animals. Douglas proclaimed that the "negro" was not a man within the meaning of the Declaration of Independence's fiat that declares, "All men are created equal," and he emphasized that slavery was permissible when the enslaver was white and the enslaved of an "inferior race." Further, he constantly raised the specter of white wives and daughters consorting with black men and the threat of intermarriage with the resulting amalgamation of the races.[15]

The two men made use of the new web of railroads crisscrossing the state. Lincoln traveled 4,350 miles and gave sixty-three speeches; Douglas 5,227 miles and gave seventy-six.[16] Because of the division of the state—south for Douglas—north for Lincoln—central Illinois, including the circuit, in particular, was the real battleground. Following the Chicago exchange, Douglas was in Bloomington on July 16, again with Lincoln in attendance. Before the speech, Lincoln had gone to the Pike House to pay his respects to Douglas and his wife. As usual, Lincoln declined an invitation from his partisans in the crowd to speak on the spot but promised to return for his own appearance later in the campaign.[17]

The Challenge to Debate

Lincoln's strategy of following Douglas dated back to the initial skirmishes between the two in 1854. Now it was not playing well and caused the campaign a slow start. With some justification, Democrats ridiculed Lincoln for attempting to take advantage of Douglas's larger crowds and stature. It made Lincoln appear a shadow of the Little Giant. On July 19, Decatur's William J. Usrey quoted an old farmer to Lincoln: "'Douglas is taking advantage of Lincoln . . . with a sort of Napoleon air of that of a conqueror. . . . Douglas takes the crowd and Lincoln the leavings.' If Douglas desires to Canvass the state, let him act the honorable part by agreeing to meet you in regular debate giving a fair opportunity to all to hear both sides. . . . It struck me that Mr. Douglas was rather getting the start of you and that if you would make a proposition for a Canvass immediately you could stop the prestige of these triumphal entries which he is making."[18]

On July 21, Lincoln met in Chicago with the central committee and Judd to plan a major change in direction for the lackluster campaign. Pursuant to Usrey's advice and that of the committee, Lincoln drafted a five-line letter to Douglas that Judd personally delivered on July 24.[19] The letter proposed that they debate but contained no details. On July 27, Douglas and Lincoln were both in Clinton, where Douglas's forces were strong, well organized, and outnumbered Lincoln's for Douglas's major speech that day in a west-side grove. Lawrence Weldon, who had invited Lincoln to Clinton for the event, Clifton H. Moore, and Swett listened as Douglas aggressively attacked Lincoln for three hours in a powerful, dynamic speech. At the end of the speech, calls for a reply from some of Lincoln's supporters went up, but Lincoln declined, citing courtesy to Douglas, but invited the crowd to the courthouse square that night to hear his reply. A smaller crowd heard Lincoln respond strongly to Douglas's assertions and question his opponent's honesty on the issues.[20]

On the evening of July 28, the two candidates dined in either Clinton or Decatur, but it is not known if they discussed the debates. Lincoln returned home to find Douglas's response to his July 24 letter; Douglas expressed surprise that Lincoln had waited so long to propose such "an arrangement." Douglas agreed to "a discussion between us" in each of the seven specified sites where the debates were ultimately held. He proposed sites in seven of the nine congressional districts, omitting the districts that contained Chicago and Springfield because the two men both had already spoken there. Thus, none of the debates occurred in the Eighth Circuit, although both candidates made frequent, separate appearances in the circuit throughout the campaign. In closing, Douglas noted the necessity of conferring on the details of these combined appearances.[21]

Douglas made his planned Piatt County campaign appearance on the afternoon of the July 29 speaking to between one thousand and two thousand people and accompanied by three brass bands. Handbills distributed announced Lincoln's appearance at the courthouse at 5:00 that afternoon.

Following his speech, Douglas departed for Bement to spend the night at the home of his good friend former Democratic legislator Francis Bryant before taking the train to his next campaign appearance the following day. On the way, about a mile south of Monticello, he met Lincoln, who was coming north from the train at Bement for his own speech.[22]

There on the road, Lincoln handed Douglas a letter, also dated July 29, agreeing to Douglas's proposal and indicating he would no longer appear at Douglas's "exclusive meetings." Douglas did not take the time to read it then or respond. He continued to Bryant's cottage, and Lincoln continued to Monticello, where he read the Douglas correspondence to the audience and briefly reiterated his views on the principal issues. The next day, Douglas wrote to Lincoln from Bement repeating the seven sites but with dates and proposing a format in which he would open and close four times and Lincoln three. Lincoln agreed by letter the following day.[23]

The meeting on the road has been called "accidental," but circumstances suggest it was intentional.[24] Lincoln's brief appearance that day was a hastily arranged event with little planning, and the speech he gave was notable for its brevity and lack of content.[25] Because he had already scheduled his major campaign appearance in Piatt County for September, it seems unlikely that he would have planned another appearance in the circuit's smallest county. The correspondence before that day had been vague and without detail. Time was running out for making specific arrangements, given the scheduling demands imposed on both candidates by the intense campaign. It appears that Lincoln boldly made this appearance in Monticello to chase Douglas down and corner him with the debate challenge. The public appearance provided cover for the real purpose of the visit that day. In any event, these July 29 contemporaneous visits to Monticello by the two candidates provided for a confrontation that was to have a lasting impact not only on the campaign but on American politics. An item in the Lincoln loyalist *Urbana Union* on August 5 demonstrates the further efforts of the Lincoln forces to induce Douglas to debate and perhaps gives an insight into why Douglas decided to do so: "Since the celebrated flight of Douglas in 1854 from before the ever-conquering Lincoln, Republicans have charged that the Little Giant, with all his boasted prowess, was afraid to meet Lincoln face to face on the stump." The newspaper then printed verbatim the Lincoln challenge of July 24 and the Douglas reply, both of which the Lincoln men supplied.[26]

The Campaign Heats Up

The next time the two met in the circuit was in Mason County, when Lincoln followed Douglas to Havana on August 13. After a long speech at Beardstown the day before, Lincoln took a riverboat to Havana. A large contingent of supporters met him at the wharf and escorted him to the home of Francis Law. His two-hour speech the next day was reported most fully in the *Chicago Daily Press and Tribune*. He resorted to humor to make light of Douglas's aggressive, pugnacious speech the previous day. He was followed by freshman Republican Congressman William P. Kellogg of Canton. During Lincoln's appearance, a delegation from Bath invited him to speak there the following Monday.[27]

The *Chicago Daily Press and Tribune* characterized the Bath speech as a warm and nostalgic occasion: "Mr. Lincoln said he had seen many things since coming into Mason County to remind him that he had ceased to be a young man. Among the old men, he had met more than half a dozen who were in the same company with him 27 years ago in the Black Hawk War. ... On this very spot, 22 years ago, he had with his own hands staked out the first plat of this town of Bath, then a wooded wilderness. But what more reminded him of his advancing age was the number of young men around him, now, and for years past, voters, who were the sons of his friends of early years, and who are now of the age he was when he first knew their fathers." He stated that Douglas had never suggested there was any wrong in slavery, and citing Henry Clay, Lincoln said he favored "the ultimate emancipation of slavery, and pronouncing the institution the greatest of evils."[28]

The first debate took place in Ottawa on August 21. Lincoln pointedly and specifically refuted statements that he had heard Douglas make in Clinton in July. On the day following the debate, Lincoln wrote to Joseph O. Cunningham to invite him to come to Monticello on September 6 to plan his Urbana campaign appearance later in the fall. It reflects their friendship when he confided, "Douglas and I, for the first time this canvass, crossed swords here yesterday; the fire flew some, and I am glad to know I am yet alive."[29]

Following the second debate in Freeport on August 27, Lincoln took the Illinois Central Railroad south to El Paso in Woodford County, then caught a westbound train to Peoria. Lincoln's formerly solid Whig base in Tazewell County had become shaky because of its strong Kentucky-based conservative elements. On August 3, 1858, Pekin newspaper man Thomas J. Pickett advised restraint and urged that any rallies be called "friends of Lincoln" rather than "Republican" because Lincoln was stronger than "Republicanism." Davis consistently cautioned how tenuous Tazewell was. He reminded Lincoln that Congressman Kellogg had lost in that county in 1856. In August, Davis urged that all pro-Lincoln orators who went to the county disavow Negro suffrage and other measures of equality and later advised that any man who had "the taint of abolition" must not go to Tazewell.

Lincoln's former principal supporter in Tazewell, Benjamin F. James, agreed, writing from Chicago that either Davis or Gridley should campaign there. Samuel Parks stumped for Lincoln in Tazewell as well as Logan County throughout the campaign. On August 7, Lincoln's old friend John A. Jones warned Lincoln of being labeled an abolitionist there and advised him to speak in the county soon.[30] The county was important enough that Lincoln went there twice, first on August 30, three days after the second debate at Freeport, at the county Republican convention in Tremont, which had been called to nominate the candidate for the house. Introduced by Jones, Lincoln spoke for two hours in front of the courthouse. The *Chicago Press and Tribune* described Lincoln as "occupied in talking, familiarly and often eloquently to old Whig friends." He stated that there was no difference between the Republicans and the old-line Whigs of Henry Clay.[31] Lincoln's second appearance in the county was with Kellogg at the big Lincoln rally held in Pekin on October 5, two days before the fifth debate in Galesburg. Pursuant to James's earlier advice, it was billed as a meeting of "Lincoln men," not Republicans. The *Chicago Press and Tribune* described Lincoln's speech as "the most forcible argument against Mr. Douglas' Democracy and the best vindication of an eloquent plea for Republicanism, that we ever listened to from any man." The rally was Lincoln's last appearance in Tazewell County.[32] The campaign effort was for naught as the Democratic candidate for representative, R. M. B. Wilson, won, vindicating Davis's fears of the volatile slavery issue. Wilson and Lincoln's fellow lawyer Democrat Samuel Fuller, a holdover in the state senate, voted for Douglas in the legislative selection of a U.S. Senator. The two Tazewell votes against Lincoln proved to be significant in the outcome. As Davis lamented to Lincoln by November 7 letter, "Poor Tazewell, falling from her high Estate grieves me greatly."[33]

Isaac Coltrin, John Warner, and Alex Argo planned Lincoln's September 2 appearance in Clinton. Delegations from outside the county included five railcars of supporters from Bloomington with Pullen's Brass Band. Lincoln arrived in Wapella on the train from Decatur in order to be part of the long procession that wound its way to Snell's Hill, where as many as ten thousand spectators gathered. The Bloomington delegation led the colorful parade that took an hour to pass. When it reached the hill, Weldon's introduction of Lincoln was "eloquent, pointed, and appropriate," and "Lincoln made one of his usual happy and humorous responses." At 2 P.M., the procession headed to the grove west of Clinton, where Moore introduced Lincoln. Lincoln aggressively attacked Douglas and again raised questions of the truthfulness of Douglas's campaign. Afterward, the crowd retired to the dinner tables and "made an irresistible attack upon the eatables." When the festivities concluded, the procession formed and returned to town, brass bands playing.[34] Lincoln spent the night at Moore's home.[35]

Tradition has it that Lincoln said one of his most famous lines at Clinton at one of his two campaign appearances there: "You can fool all the people some of the time and some of the people all the time, but you cannot fool all the people all the time." The line is not included in any contemporary account of either speech, nor did any of his active supporters who were present ever report it. The first known account of the quote is a 1904 secondhand recollection. In 1909, Richard Price Morgan recalled that Lincoln had said it at the Pike House in Bloomington in the summer of 1856. Nevertheless, the legend continues, and it expresses the spirit of what Lincoln said in Clinton as he attacked the integrity of Douglas in an increasingly bitter campaign. In the 1880s, Moore remembered Lincoln being in his office on the day of one of these speeches and stating that he recalled with regret that Lincoln said, "Douglas will tell a lie to ten thousand people one day, even though he knows he may have to deny it to five thousand the next."[36]

As promised, Lincoln returned to Bloomington on September 4. A huge procession formed and went to the Davis home, where Lincoln was staying, to accompany him to the speech site. William McCullough, Lamon, and Charles P. Merriman led several bands in the procession as it proceeded down Washington Street to the courthouse, where seven thousand people gathered to hear Lincoln speak. Davis introduced Swett, who introduced Lincoln, who gave such a speech that the *Pantagraph*'s headline read, "The tall Sucker exposes the sophistries of the Little Giant." The *Pantagraph* summarized Lincoln's closing remarks, "And when you have stricken down the principles of the Declaration of Independence, and thereby consigned the negro to hopeless and eternal bondage are you *quite* sure that the demon will not turn and rend you? Will not the people then be ready to go down beneath the tread of any tyrant who may wish to rule them?"[37]

Later that day, Lincoln returned by train to Springfield, stopping on the way in Lincoln. overflowing with Douglas supporters going to a large Douglas rally. The huge procession started at the Lincoln House, across which a banner proclaimed: "Stephen A. Douglas: Champion of Popular Sovereignty," and passed under an arch spanning Main Street, bearing the legend "Douglas Forever." Then it proceeded several blocks on to the rally site, a large tent where the circus was also appearing. The *Pantagraph* ridiculed Douglas because his rally was scheduled between two performances of Spaulding and Rogers, a New Orleans circus. On September 8, 1858, the newspaper reported that the daylight performance of the circus would be concluded before Judge Douglas's speech: "Where Judge Douglas is classed we are not informed, whether he's among the 'riders,' 'acrobats,' 'gymnasts,' 'voltiguers,' 'equilibrists,' 'calisthenics,' or one of the three clowns, the bill leaves us in blissful ignorance." The *Pantagraph* reported that the 11:30 performance would conclude prior to Douglas's speech.[38] Lincoln unceremoniously stepped off the back of the train and hung back, mostly unnoticed on the fringes of the crowd. S. Linn Beidler of Mt. Pulaski recalled seeing Lincoln by himself, with no friends or supporters nearby. Lincoln followed the crowd to the tent where attorney Lionel Lacey introduced Douglas, who spoke to an enthusiastic audience. After the meeting, Beidler boarded a train for Springfield and walked through several cars before coming across an empty seat, which happened to be next to Lincoln. Lincoln chatted about his friendships in Mt. Pulaski and the folks with whom he had stayed there, including Thomas Lushbaugh and Jabez Capps.[39]

Lincoln returned to Monticello on September 6, a banner day in Piatt County. Seven hundred came from Champaign alone, including Cunningham, at Lincoln's August 22 invitation to plan a campaign event in Champaign County later in September. Henry Clay Whitney rode in a carriage with Lincoln on his way to the rally. The Champaign delegation included two bands; large contingents from DeWitt and Macon Counties attended as well. A long procession formed with the usual array of pretty girls, colorful banners, band music, alcohol, and fights. After a generous meal, Weldon started the proceedings with a speech. Attorney Thomas Milligan introduced Lincoln, who spoke for three hours. The reporter for *Chicago Press and Tribune* commented, "I never heard him make a finer speech except at Ottawa when he skinned Dug." The large crowd and warm reception contrasted significantly with the reception Lincoln had received in Monticello two years earlier, when two people greeted him and his audience swelled to only sixty people.[40]

Next, Lincoln traveled by train to Edgar County. He had been invited by the county's Republican Central Committee—Rives, A. J. Baber (a Lincoln client in an 1850 ejectment case) and merchant and politician William P. Dole—to campaign in Paris on September 7. Dole, who had been a successful merchant in Vigo County, Indiana, location of Terre Haute, had served in both the house and senate in Indiana. Upon his wife's death in 1850, he moved to Paris, where he set up a successful mercantile establishment. He was an early active Republican with substantial influence on both sides of the Wabash River.[41] On that day, Lincoln was running on a tight schedule, speaking at Mattoon at noon and arriving by train at 2:30 in Paris. A procession with a brass band took Lincoln to Alexander Grove on East Washington Street, where Douglas had spoken on July 31. Several little girls, Douglas supporters sitting on the top row of a fence along the platform's north side, were yelling and making noise when the rail broke, and all of them fell in the grass. Said Lincoln, "I'm glad to see that some of my little friends who at the beginning of this meeting were against me are now falling for me."[42]

In his two-hour speech, Lincoln made it clear that he did not favor Negro equality, much as he was to do at the Charleston debate on September 22. The *Prairie Beacon* reported this with approval.[43] The racist tenor of the electorate is suggested by the quote that the pro-Republican and antislavery *Beacon* carried on the masthead every week during the campaign from the Democratic Congressional candidate James Robinson, "Robinson on Negro Equality 'I would rather sleep with a Nigger than a Republican.'" The ugly racism of the time was reflected in the *Beacon*'s pro-Lincoln coverage of his speech in Paris: "If the Douglasites don't believe Abraham Lincoln is for non-interference where it exists and opposed to Negro equality, either social or political and to amalgamation, then we know not what would satisfy them unless indeed, he would arm himself with a huge cleaver, and at the next meeting between himself and his competitor, with appropriate formality and due solemnity kill at least one Nigger." Although the *Beacon* was quick to point out Lincoln's statements suggesting the inequality of blacks, no mention of these statements was made by the Democratic *Weekly Valley Blade* in Paris.[44]

Notwithstanding that Lincoln was the railroad's attorney, George B. McClellan, a close friend of Douglas, saw that the railroad's resources were strongly aligned with Douglas's candidacy. The candidates repeatedly traversed the state during that campaign, Douglas on special trains with McClellan's private car at his disposal and Lincoln generally on regularly scheduled trains as an ordinary passenger. Lamon, with Lincoln on the trip to Jonesboro in deep Southern Illinois for the September 15 Lincoln-Douglas debate, recalled that in order to get there, he and Lincoln had to take a ride in the caboose of a freight train. Their train pulled over to a siding to allow the Douglas train to pass, including his luxurious special car and the platform car for the cannon that was part of his campaign appearances. This Lamon reminiscence sounds apocryphal, but it illustrates the favoritism of the Illinois Central during the campaign, courtesy of McClellan.[45]

The Campaign Wears Thin

The fourth debate, at Charleston on September 18, was the closest debate site to the circuit. Eight or nine carloads of passengers traveled there from Terre Haute and Paris. When they disembarked, the passengers formed two lines, one of Douglas supporters carrying banners that read, "Edgar County, 500 majority for Douglas." The Lincoln men sported banners reading, "Old Edgar for the Tall Sucker." Again, Lincoln's racist remarks were favorably reported in the Republican *Prairie Beacon* account but not in the Democratic *Weekly Valley Blade*. While the *Beacon* reported the gist of Lincoln's speech in detail, the *Valley Blade* called it a mere rehash of charges Republican Senator Lyman Trumbull had made earlier against Douglas.[46]

One of the more bizarre events of the debates occurred in Charleston. In addition to baiting Lincoln over slavery, Douglas continually attacked him for his congressional stand against the Mexican War, misrepresenting Lincoln's position. Orlando Ficklin, who had introduced Douglas at the Charleston debate, was seated on the platform. As Lincoln defended his position on the Mexican War, asserting his opposition to the war but his support of appropriations for the troops, he went back to where Ficklin was seated, brought him forward, and demanded that he confirm Lincoln's version. Ficklin responded, "Mr. Lincoln and myself are just as good personal friends as Judge Douglas and myself," equivocating artfully as to the conclusion Lincoln sought. The descriptions vary on the degree of force Lincoln used to get Ficklin forward. One version said Lincoln "led him forward." Another asserted, "He turned to Ficklin, . . . and seizing him by the collar, dragged him by main force before the audience."[47]

Lincoln responded to Douglas's racial baiting at Paris and at the Charleston debate with surprisingly racist statements of his own. He denied that he had ever favored the social and political equality of the races, including the right to vote, hold office, and intermarry. Lincoln acknowledged the physical difference between the races and stated, "I am in favor of having the superior position assigned to the white race."[48] Not only did he unequivocally assert the superior status of whites but also his condemnation of slavery was tepid at best, although his condemnation of slavery was blunt and more outspoken at the northern debate venues, Freeport and Galesburg, and there he had toned down the racial statements.[49]

Why did Lincoln say these things at Charleston and other sites? One possible reason is that he was simply pandering to the prejudices of the electorate. Douglas's blatant disparaging of black persons would have been well received by many of the voters in Illinois, and, possibly, Lincoln felt he had to counteract that with his own pejorative opinions as to the rights of black people. The other possible reason is that given the time and place where Lincoln had spent his life, his views coincided with those of the vast majority of central Illinois white residents. He simply believed these things to be true. Either or both of these reasons might have been what motivated him to make these statements.[50] Whatever the explanation is, they did not hurt his chances of election. Regardless, Lincoln remained steadfast and unwavering in his belief that slavery was wrong. He stated that while the races might not allow perfect social and political equality, "that in their right to 'life, liberty, and the pursuit of happiness' as proclaimed in that old Declaration, the inferior races are our equals."[51]

The acrimony and passion of the campaign heated to the boiling point in Moultrie County, two days after the contentious debate at Charleston. As early as September 10, Douglas had planned a campaign appearance in Sullivan. Once again, Lincoln scheduled an appearance to follow him in the same town. The night before, Douglas stayed with John Ginn, an Irish immigrant farmer who lived about five miles east of Sullivan. That morning, a crowd as large as two thousand people greeted Douglas. It is uncertain whether Lincoln stayed with relatives in Coles County the night before or with James Elder, his old circuit host, at his new home a mile east of Sullivan. Reportedly, Lincoln was at the Elder home observing the Douglas procession as it passed on its way into Sullivan.[52]

What happened from that point on depends on which one of the highly partisan newspaper accounts is believed. Confusion arose because originally Douglas was to speak at 10:00 but was delayed, so he rescheduled his appearance for 1:00 on a bunting-draped platform constructed on the east side of the courthouse square. Lincoln planned to speak at Freeland's Grove on the north edge of town. While Douglas rested at the Eagle House, Lincoln sent him a hastily drafted note, advising that he would delay his 2:00 P.M. speech until 3:00 P.M. if Douglas would announce that at his own speech.[53] John Eden, a Sullivan Democrat, introduced Douglas, who then made the announcement he had assured Lincoln that he would make. Lincoln's procession was forming two miles east of Sullivan at Addison McPheeters's home. Though smaller, it included the usual brass band, this time from Bowling Green, Indiana, and a giant wagon with wheels sliced off a hickory tree 3½ feet in diameter. Thirty-six yoke of oxen pulled a thirty-four-by-sixty-four-foot platform on which one hundred people rode.

The noise of the band in Lincoln's procession interrupted the Douglas meeting, at last underway; the Douglas crowd, already on edge because of the delay, turned angry. The Republican version of the occurrence is that many in the Douglas crowd attempted to leave for the Lincoln site and were stopped by Douglas enforcers. The Democrat version is that Lincoln's more aggressive supporters and their procession invaded the Douglas crowd. Whichever version is accurate, alcohol played a role. The Lincoln contingent proceeded along the west and south ends of the courthouse square. Then, either accidentally or intentionally, it plowed into the Douglas crowd filling the east side of the square, wagon and all. A free-for-all ensued, including the exchange of brick bats, fence rails, and other missiles. The Lincoln wagon displayed a tableau that included wooden moving figures of two slaves being mistreated by an overseer. The figures were powered by a ten-foot windmill. When that power failed, the proud creator of the display turned the shaft by hand, only to be struck with a brick during the fracas.[54] The melee lasted a short time before cooler heads prevailed, and the Lincoln procession turned and headed back to the grove, where Lincoln gave his address. Douglas finished his speech, and Lincoln's old friend Anthony Thornton of Shelbyville concluded the Douglas meeting, speaking in support of Douglas, Thornton described by the partisan press as "an old line Whig who refuses to be abolitionized."[55]

One undetermined question is whether Lincoln was in the procession as it encroached on the Douglas meeting. Some eyewitnesses reported that Lincoln's carriage was in the procession, but this was never verified. Regardless of which candidate's supporters were to blame for this ugly confrontation, it is fortunate for the elevated image of the campaign and the participatory democracy it represents that order was restored. This occurrence was as close to mayhem as occurred during the storied campaign.

The next campaign stop was Danville in Vermilion County. Douglas was speaking on the afternoon of September 21, followed by Lincoln the next day. Because he was speaking in the afternoon, Douglas had to take the night train to Danville. To save his beautiful wife, Adele, the strain of this forced trip, he asked Lincoln to accompany her on the train the next day, which Lincoln graciously agreed to do. Lincoln and Adele arrived in Danville at 7:00 P.M. A large crowd of Lincoln supporters, including a band and thirty-seven young girls dressed in white, met the train to be part of a procession to accompany Lincoln to Fithian's home, where he was to spend the night. A committee including Beckwith greeted him as he disembarked. Lincoln advised them, "He had a lady in his care whom he must first put in the hands of her waiting friends." Lincoln accompanied Mrs. Douglas to her cab, which would take her to Douglas's suite at the McCormack House.[56] Then Lincoln joined his crowd and the procession to Fithian's.

Later that evening, a large throng had gathered there to hear Lincoln. He stepped out of the long window of his second-floor guest room at the Fithian house onto a balcony, from which he made a brief address in his stocking feet.[57] The next day, he made his major Danville campaign speech in the same sugar-maple grove in which Douglas had spoken, about a mile southeast of the square. Both drew large and festive crowds. The procession accompanying Lincoln was almost a mile long. Elizabeth Harmon recalled that while waiting for his speech, a Lincoln emissary asked her over to

Lincoln's carriage to visit, an invitation she accepted. Lincoln spent that night at Fithian's again before traveling to Champaign County the next day. Before leaving, he wrote to Norman Judd, suggesting a German speaker would be effective in Danville, evidence of the large influx of Germans to the area.[58]

The campaign brought Lincoln back into contact with Abraham Smith, the Ridge Farm abolitionist and temperance advocate. Smith wrote Lincoln on May 31, chastising him for working against abolitionist Owen Lovejoy: "I don't like Linclon (sic) personally" and acknowledged working against Lincoln in the Trumbull race for the senate in 1854, although he did concede that he considered Lincoln trustworthy. However, Lincoln's "House Divided" speech turned him. In July, Smith wrote him, "I am rejoiced that by thy speeches at Springfield and Chicago thou art fairly mounted on the eternal and vulnerable bulwark of truth."[59] Smith's change from his original negative attitude toward Lincoln may relate to Lincoln's assistance of Lovejoy's candidacy for reelection to Congress.

From Danville, the candidates moved on to Champaign County, where the *Central Illinois Gazette* had endorsed Lincoln in June. The opponents squared off on separate days, Douglas speaking at the fairgrounds on September 23, the last day of the county fair, and Lincoln the next day. Douglas drew a huge crowd and received a generous reception from the audience, including a large contingent of Republicans who treated him courteously. Lincoln arrived that afternoon, making an appearance at the Doane House, a hotel in West Urbana next to the depot. Many friends and supporters greeted him, accompanied by bands from Danville and Urbana. On this campaign visit, he spent one night in West Urbana and one night in Urbana. Perhaps he sensed the already brewing rivalry between the two towns. While in West Urbana the first night, he stayed at merchant John W. Baddeley's home, a center of the young town's social life. The lawyers dined there at least once at each term of court. Ironically, this strong supporter of Lincoln had a history with him. It was Baddeley who had discharged Lincoln on his first trip to Bloomington in 1838, appalled by Lincoln's callow appearance and demeanor.[60]

In Urbana the next night, Lincoln stayed at Mayor Ezekiel Boyden's house. Boyden was one of the early successful manufacturers in Urbana, owning a large plant that Lincoln had visited during his years on the circuit.

Lincoln's friends knew of this connection; in fact, Whitney addressed an urgent letter dated September 23, 1858, from Chicago to Lincoln at Boyden's home. The next day, an elaborate procession with three bands and a delegation of young women met Lincoln in West Urbana and proceeded to the fairground. The two-mile-long parade reached the fairground for a meal before the speech.[61] Lincoln recognized an elderly woman known as "Granny" standing nearby who had been a waitress and dishwasher at one of the hotels in Urbana where Lincoln had stayed over the years. At his insistence and over her protestations, Lincoln gave Granny his seat at the head table and ate lunch sitting on a stump under a tree.[62] Following the meal, Lincoln spoke for an hour and a half, his speech rehashing the points given in the debates. Lincoln operated under a distinct disadvantage that day, as his appearance followed the close of the three-day fair. The crowd was not quite what it might have been and was not quite as large as the Douglas crowd. However, the ever-loyal *Union* noted, "The enthusiasm was ten times as great." Following the speech, the procession then accompanied Lincoln to Boyden's home. That night, he walked over to the courthouse and delivered a speech condemning the Kansas-Nebraska Act once again.[63]

After the Champaign County appearances, the next stop was also in the circuit, this time in Woodford County. Each candidate appeared at Metamora in a field on the south edge of town, Douglas on September 30 and Lincoln on October 4. Several thousand people gathered to hear each of the candidates, the crowds much larger than the town. While in Metamora, Lincoln met with the prosecuting attorney and convinced him to discharge the bond of Melissa Goings and to dismiss the case, which had been pending since her escape a year earlier.[64]

The fifth debate took place at Knox College in Galesburg on October 7. Lincoln ran into his old Tazewell friend Pickett and asked him to compare the carrying power of Lincoln's voice to that of Douglas. From the fringe of the crowd, Pickett reported, "Mr. Lincoln's thin, wiry voice was much better adapted for outdoor speaking."[65] The last two debates were at Quincy on October 13 and Alton two days later, to which Lincoln traveled by boat down the Mississippi River from Quincy. After the Alton debate, Lincoln took the train to his namesake town for a Logan County appearance, where five thousand people showed up from all the towns of the county. The procession included fifty wagons from Mt. Pulaski alone. Lincoln spoke from the west side of the new courthouse after having been introduced by the faithful Samuel Parks.[66]

Lincoln spoke in Petersburg on October 29 and again briefly at a huge Republican rally, numbering perhaps ten thousand in Springfield the next day, which drew thirty-two train cars from McLean and Logan Counties. The noise of the crowd made a speech impossible. Lincoln merely said, "My friends, today closes the discussions of this canvass. The planting and the culture are over; and there remains but the preparation, and the harvest." His final appearance of the campaign on November 1 was his only appearance in Decatur. He had made campaign appearances in every county of the Eighth Circuit except the Democratic strongholds Shelby and Christian, where showing up would have been time ill spent.[67]

On Election Day, November 2, Douglas won a majority in the legislature, 54-46, though Lincoln candidates narrowly carried the popular vote. Lincoln carried eight of the counties that were ever part of the Eight Judicial Circuit, and Douglas, nine. Lincoln won seven of the districts that included circuit counties to Douglas's six; however, Douglas won Sangamon County, which elected two representatives, so the circuit counties elected seven representatives for each candidate. All but three of the counties had no senatorial race because of holdover incumbents.[68] Of those three, Vermilion and Edgar supported the successful Republican candidate, and Woodford County voted for the Democrat who lost to the Republican district-wide. A few votes in a few districts would have resulted in a different outcome. One of these districts was Tazewell County, which Lincoln lost by fewer than two hundred votes. This is an instance where his circuit practice may have hurt him. The county was a stronghold for Lincoln and his political career ten years earlier, but the basis of his political strength had weakened. His practice had placed him on the wrong side of the bitter county-seat dispute, in which Tremont lost to Pekin, his influence waning because of the shift of the county seat. Tremont was the real core of his support in that county. One of his principal supporters, Benjamin James, had moved to Chicago. Also, Lincoln quit making his regular circuit trips there in 1857, giving him less contact with the people of that county.

The Paris *Prairie Beacon* reported that popular vote favored the Republican statewide ticket carried by three thousand to five thousand votes, yet Lincoln still lost. The newspaper's astute analysis of the election returns points out the impact of the shape of the districts: "For a Legislature favorable to his aspirations, Mr. Douglas is indebted more than all else to the most atrocious gerrymander that ever violated popular supremacy." If it is assumed those who voted for Lincoln-leaning legislators intended to vote for Lincoln, he would have won the house races with 52 percent of the vote and the senate races with 54 percent. The Paris *Weekly Valley Blade* prophetically stated on November 10, 1858, "Never before, perhaps in the history of the country, has a state election assumed such an importance in the eyes of the people of the whole union as did this race in Illinois."[69] Lincoln's campaign elevated his stature to the national level; as the *Chicago Press and Tribune* noted, "He has created for himself a national reputation that is both envied and deserved. His speeches have become landmarks in political history."[70]

However, Lincoln was discouraged by the outcome, though not particularly surprised: "Though I now sink out of view, and shall be forgotten."[71] However, his commitment to the antislavery cause never wavered. On November 20, he advised, "The fight must go on. We are right, and can not finally fail. There will be another blow-up in the so called democratic party before long. In the mean time, let all Republicans stand fast by their guns."[72] Lincoln's letters of encouragement to many diverse supporters following the election show a strong desire to continue the fight and not to quit. He used "The fight must go on" in six letters that month.[73] However, the tone is that of a party leader rallying his troops, rather than a candidate. The flame was flickering but was not extinguished. Lincoln's consideration of his future had begun with his request to Charles H. Ray at the *Chicago Press and Tribune* to send him two sets of the *Tribune* version of the debates as reported for a "scrapbook." When Ray failed to respond, Lincoln turned to Whitney with the same request on November 30, which Whitney dutifully did. On Christmas Day, Lincoln wrote Whitney to thank him and offered him a copy of the book when published: "There is some probability that my Scrap-book will be reprinted."[74]

Perhaps pessimistically, Lincoln felt his political resources were depleted, but the campaign had left his financial resources depleted. Shortly after the election, he wrote Norman Judd, "I have been on expenses so long without earning anything and I am absolutely without money now for even household purposes . . . all which be added to my loss of time and business bears pretty heavily upon one no better off in the worlds goods than I."[75] Lincoln's liquidity was not helped by his loan of almost half of his large fee from his Illinois Central case to Judd in September the year before. Judd paid neither principal nor interest but renewed the note for $3,000 on September 1, 1859. He paid nothing on the note until after Lincoln's death, when he paid it in full, $5,400.[76]

As he had done in times of past political setbacks, Lincoln returned to the law, appearing in the Sangamon County Circuit Court as early as November 6 and for the rest of that week. In December, he was off to Bloomington for a special session of the McLean County Circuit Court.[77] While there, an encounter with longtime friend and supporter Jesse Fell breathed fresh oxygen on that flame of political ambition.

12. A LITTLE SKETCH

━━━◦━━━

L ate in an afternoon during the special session of the McLean County
Circuit Court that began in late December 1858, Jesse Fell watched Abraham Lincoln leave the Bloomington courthouse and cross the street. Fell
intercepted Lincoln and invited him up the stairs to his brother Kersey's
office for a much-needed pep talk. During the Douglas campaign, Fell had
traveled throughout New England and the mid-Atlantic states and observed
substantial interest in Lincoln as a presidential candidate because of his
strong showing against Douglas. Fell told Lincoln of this in detail, extolling
the potential for his candidacy that Fell observed and characterizing Lincoln
as a formidable candidate. Fell told Lincoln the people wanted to know
more about him and his personal life than just his notable speeches, which
had already been published around the country. Fell asked for a personal
history to answer those inquiries for the eastern press. Lincoln admitted
his ambition for the office but saw little chance of success, so he declined.[1]

The Illinois legislature convened to formalize the selection of Stephen
A. Douglas as U.S. Senator on January 5. The exhilaration of the victorious
Douglas forces swept over Lincoln's hometown. Douglas's loyal, career-long
confidante and friend Charles H. Lanphier telegraphed him in Washington,
D.C.: "Glory to God and the Sucker Democracy . . . town wild with excitement . . . guns, music, and whiskey rampant."[2] This contrasted sharply with
the pall that hung over Lincoln forces. Henry Clay Whitney was in Springfield to keep Lincoln company on this difficult day, spending ten hours
alone with Lincoln from two in the afternoon till bedtime. He describes

Lincoln as being "gloomy, dejected, dispirited . . . radically and thoroughly depressed, so completely steeped in the bitter waters of hopeless despair."[3]

However, the next day, Lincoln displayed his resilience at a meeting in the state capitol's library. The meeting included his circuit cadre—Leonard Swett, Fell, and David Davis—as well as other supporters. The subject of the meeting was the coming presidential race and which candidate to support. The attendees skirted the issue until Lincoln brusquely and directly asked his team to consider him as that candidate, which turned the focus of the meeting back to Lincoln and strategies to advance his candidacy. Thus began Lincoln's quiet testing of his candidacy and his patient wait for the right time to openly make his move.[4]

While he spent the better part of 1859 keeping himself a prominent figure without appearing to be a candidate, Lincoln also carefully and adroitly continued to mold the Illinois Republican Party and to keep it together. The contentious threads had to be held together but not so close as to rub and fray each other: the Free Soilers versus the abolitionists, antislavery Germans versus the nativists, former Know-Nothings and the old Whigs versus the former Democrats, each suspicious of the other. Lincoln understood the need to keep all of these elements supportive. The Republican Party in Chicago continued to grow in significance as the population of the city expanded. The bitter struggle within the Chicago party between former Democrat Norman Judd and former Whigs, the slippery John Wentworth and rival Charles Wilson, created a difficult situation. Judd's friendship was a constant burden to Lincoln due to the continuing rumors of his disloyalty to Lincoln and his mismanagement in directing the campaign against Douglas.[5] It took a deft touch on Lincoln's part to maintain the unity of this alliance. Throughout, he gained strength from his team of Eighth Circuit friends whose principal motivation was personal loyalty to their longtime leader. In early 1859, Lincoln had to also deal with Douglas's appeal during the senatorial campaign to certain elements of the Republican Party because of his split with the almost treasonous Buchanan administration. On March 1, Lincoln and Swett appeared jointly in Chicago speaking against the Douglas flirtation, one of his few political appearances early in the year.[6]

Throughout the year, Lincoln carefully juggled his somewhat competing professional and political lives. He became more selective in choosing his speaking engagements. He attended the spring sessions of the Eighth

Judicial Circuit, appearing in court in Sangamon, DeWitt, Logan, McLean, and Champaign Counties. His strategy was to stay visible, which traveling the circuit allowed him to do. Another way was the publication of a book of the debate transcripts. In March, he wrote William Ross of Washington in Tazewell County a detailed letter outlining his ideas for the publication.[7] Perhaps because Lincoln preferred that the book be printed in Springfield, the project never went any further with Ross.

In early April, Lincoln was in Bloomington for the court session, a meeting of the state central committee, and another presentation of "Discoveries and Inventions." J. H. Burnham was in attendance at the event in Phoenix Hall and reported, "[F]or some reason not explained, only about 40 persons were present, and Old Abe would not speak to such a small crowd." Accordingly, the twenty-five-cent admission fee was refunded.[8] The state central committee, with essentially the same players as the January meeting, confirmed the strategy designed then. Four days before the meeting, Lincoln wrote Bloomington's Asahel Gridley of the central committee, for whom he also had legal business, to confirm his coming. Lincoln wanted to continue his portrayal as a prominent noncandidate but was always looking for appropriate opportunities to remain in view.

On April 11, he reported to Gustave P. Koerner, a prominent German-immigrant advocate of his candidacy: "The meeting of the Central Committee was at Bloomington, and not here. I was there attending court, and, in common with several other outsiders, one of whom was Judge Trumbull, was in conference with the committee, to some extent. . . . I am right glad the Committee put in operation, our plan of organization which we started here last winter. They appointed Mr. Fell of Bloomington, as Secretary."[9] Fell's appointment gave Lincoln's candidacy a significant advantage within the Illinois party. Fell spent much of the balance of 1859 traveling across the state and carrying out plans for a more thorough organization of the Republican Party. He personally visited a large number of the counties and strongly pushed Lincoln's candidacy. Lincoln's old Tazewell County supporter Thomas J. Pickett, now editor of the Rock Island, Illinois, *Weekly Register*, helped keep Lincoln's profile raised during 1859. In April, Pickett proposed that all of the pro-Lincoln newspapers do a simultaneous announcement of Lincoln's candidacy for president. Lincoln expressed his gratitude but vetoed the idea.[10]

On April 21 in Urbana in Champaign County, Lincoln, Swett, and Whitney combined to defend a manslaughter case, *People v. Thomas Patterson*, which had been delayed for six months due to the Douglas campaign. The defendant, a storekeeper in Sadorus and member of a prominent family, threw a two-pound scale weight at the intoxicated victim, killing him. Controversy surrounded the incident and the character of the defendant, who was found guilty in the high-profile trial and sentenced to the Alton Penitentiary for three years.[11]

Lincoln improved his already solid relationship with the *Central Illinois Gazette*, meeting with owner John Scroggs and editor William O. Stoddard that week. The paper had endorsed Lincoln for the U.S. Senate and covered Lincoln's campaign appearance in detail. Stoddard, who met Lincoln for the first time the previous fall at the *Gazette* offices, said Lincoln dazzled him with his feel for the county's politics: "He seems to know my prairie neighbors almost man for man." Stoddard described Lincoln in glowing terms in the May 4 issue, which he widely disseminated to promote Lincoln.[12]

Lincoln further used the newspapers to address two other initiatives. First, in his continuing efforts to solidify the support of the German community, he purchased a printing press for Springfield's *Staats-Anzeiger*, a German-language newspaper, on the condition that its publisher, Theodore Canisius, would publish the paper and that it would be pro-Republican.[13] Second, Lincoln's efforts to promote party unity are reflected in a July 3 letter to the editor of the *Clinton Central Transcript*, a paper always loyal to Lincoln. He chastised the editor for his negative remarks about the northern Illinois Republican Party and urged unity.[14]

Lincoln remained busy maintaining his circuit relationships that summer. Sylvester Strong of Atlanta, in Logan County, a friend of Lincoln since 1839, when he served as a juror in Clinton on a Lincoln case, invited Lincoln to speak at the town's Fourth of July celebration. Lincoln recommended James Matheny instead, but he did agree to attend. The procession, about a mile long, included seven War of 1812 veterans as it proceeded from town to Turner's Hill. Following Matheny's rousing speech, Strong presented Lincoln a specially made cane of orangewood with silver buttons and each of the fourteen letters of Lincoln's name on fourteen knots down the length of the cane. "Mr. Lincoln responded to the personal compliment in a short speech abounding with beauty, wit, and feeling," the *Pantagraph* reported.

"Just such a speech as this distinguished gentleman can give utterance to as such a one as goes home to the hearts of his audience."[15] Following the celebration, Lincoln repaired to the Strong home, to Richard Gill's for dinner, and then to the Lemuel Foster's Congregational Church for an ice-cream social held to raise money for pews in the church. Samuel Parks gave one of several toasts offered for the occasion. A local baker presented Lincoln with a cake, which Lincoln gave to the ladies of the church so that they could auction it off for the church's benefit.[16]

Law and Politics

From July 13 to 22, Lincoln traveled the entire Illinois Central system, representing the railroad on a taxation case before the Illinois Supreme Court. Although he declined speaking invitations in Morris, Illinois, and Minnesota due to legal business, his travel beginning in August raised his national profile. From August 9 to 18, he was in Saint Joseph, Missouri, and Council Bluffs, Iowa, combining business with a substantial amount of politics and hoping to further his still thinly disguised presidential bid. In Council Bluffs, he stayed with former Springfield residents W. H. M. Perry and Thomas Office.[17]

This travel was sandwiched around his defense of Peachy Quinn Harrison in a renowned Sangamon County murder case. On July 16, 1859, Harrison and Greek Crafton got into a fight in a drug store in Pleasant Plains, and Harrison stabbed Crafton, who died two days later. The son of Peyton Harrison, who was a political ally of Lincoln, Peachy was also the grandson of Lincoln's longtime antagonist Peter Cartwright. Peachy was indicted, and Lincoln, Logan, and Shelby Cullom, who represented him, asserted self-defense; the prosecution team was John M. Palmer and Norman Broadwell. The trial, which began on August 31, lasted four days, during which twenty-seven witnesses were called. The drama of the proceedings peaked when Lincoln called his old foe to the witness stand to testify on behalf of his grandson. One can imagine the scene as Lincoln questioned the old circuit rider, now seventy-four, who told of being called from his home to pray with the dying victim, who declared to Cartwright, "I have brought it upon myself and I forgive Quinn." Not surprising, there was no cross examination. The next day, after deliberating just over an hour, the jury returned a verdict of not guilty.[18] Once again, Lincoln's commitment to his calling as an attorney is demonstrated by his taking a difficult case in the middle of intense political activity.

Lincoln continued to combine law and politics. His significant speaking tour to Ohio in Columbus, Dayton, Hamilton, and Cincinnati and to Indianapolis, Indiana, took from September 16 to 20. He returned for court in Logan County before leaving again for the important and successful speeches in Wisconsin at Milwaukee, Beloit, and Janesville from September 29 through October 4. On October 5, he resumed the circuit in DeWitt County. The October 6 *Clinton Transcript* states, "The old familiar face of Abraham Lincoln is again amongst us and we cannot help noticing the peculiarly friendly expression with which he greets everybody and everybody greets him. He comes back to us after electrifying Ohio, 'with all his blushing honor thick upon him,' yet the poorest and plainest amongst our people fears not to approach and never fails to receive a hearty welcome from him."[19] In court there for most of the week, he substituted for Judge Davis on October 12 and 14 in twenty-five cases.

That week, the Republicans captured major statewide victories in Ohio, Pennsylvania, Iowa, and Minnesota, foretelling the tide that would sweep Lincoln into power a year later. The evening of the fourteenth, Lincoln spoke in the courtroom, which was "rammed, jammed and crammed from stem to stern," and urged patience and persistence in pursuing the principles of the party. Lawrence Weldon, who also addressed the meeting, referred to Lincoln as the next candidate for president. The *Clinton Transcript* commented, "Last Friday night will long be remembered by the Republicans of this place." That night, Lincoln's last in Clinton, he stated, "But I do hope that as there is a just and righteous God in heaven, our principles will and shall prevail sooner or later."[20]

The next day, he returned to Springfield. He was accompanied by a brass band and several hundred Republicans as he walked from his residence to the capitol, where he delivered a speech. By the end of October, he was again on the circuit in Urbana. After returning home to vote in the congressional election, he resumed the circuit in Danville for its regular session in mid-November. While there, he received an invitation from a supporter of presidential hopeful Salmon P. Chase to speak in New York, which he accepted on McCormack House stationery, "I am here at court, but my address is still at Springfield, Ills."[21]

The Pieces Begin to Fall into Place

On November 30, he was again off to speaking engagements in Saint Joseph, Missouri, and in volatile Kansas territory, from which he returned on December 9. As December drew to a close, he tied up some long-standing loose ends, finalizing the arrangements for publication of his book of the debate transcripts in Columbus, Ohio, instead of a hometown publisher, and finishing the sketch of his life.[22] It was almost one year since Lincoln had declined Fell's request for a personal history. Lincoln now sent the two-page document to Fell with a note dated December 20, 1859, "Herewith is a little sketch, as you requested. There is not much of it, for the reason, I suppose, that there is not much of me." In doing so, he was perhaps acknowledging what he had previously denied, the viability of his presidential candidacy. As Fell said of the delivery of the autobiographical sketch, Lincoln himself now felt that "perhaps it would pay."[23]

At the same time, Lincoln's operative on the Republican National Central Committee, Judd, traveled to New York for the committee meeting to decide the location and timing of the 1860 national convention. Locating the event in Chicago was critical for Lincoln's chances of success, and he so advised Judd by letter, "I find some of our friends here [Springfield] attach more consequence to getting the National Convention into our State than I did, or do. Some of them made me promise to say so to you. As to the time, it must certainly be after the Charleston Fandango; and I think, within bounds of reason, the later the better." The possible sites in contention were narrowed down to Chicago and St. Louis, the latter being home base of nomination rival Edward Bates. Lincoln's official noncandidacy made it easier for Judd to promote Chicago, which received eleven votes to St. Louis's ten. The convention site was in hand.[24]

Following the May 1859 praise of the *Gazette*, various newspapers of the circuit throughout the fall openly discussed Lincoln's suitability for the presidency, some even endorsing the noncandidate. The Bloomington *Pantagraph* reported in October that the *Lincoln Herald* endorsed Lincoln for president; the *Pantagraph* itself would not formally endorse him until the following spring.[25] The *Vermilion County Press* discussed him as a viable presidential candidate as early as November of 1859, although its endorsement was not until the following February. The *Clinton Transcript* endorsed

Lincoln for president on November 3, followed by Champaign's *Gazette*'s "Abraham Lincoln for President" on December 21.[26]

That year, Lincoln's stature in the circuit was both demonstrated and enhanced by the construction of Lincoln Hall in Danville, an opera house and the town's tallest structure. Prominent merchant W. R. Woodbury built it and named it for Lincoln, who was somewhat embarrassed by that. He told Woodbury he hoped the enterprise would do better than a dog whose name was changed to Lincoln, after which he failed to win another dogfight.[27]

Lincoln and his supporters had been remarkably successful during 1859. From the despair felt at the time of the Douglas victory in the legislature in January, Lincoln had molded the central Illinois support into a viable candidacy that expanded beyond the confines of the circuit to include the increasingly important Chicago and then beyond the confines of Illinois due to his selective regional travel and future appearance at Cooper Union in New York City in February. He had done so without exposing the threat of his candidacy to the more prominent candidates. Selection of Chicago as the convention site enhanced his chance for the nomination. Lincoln had placed himself in the perfect position as the race came off the last turn into the home stretch.

PART FOUR

NOMINATION, ELECTION, AND THE PRESIDENCY

13. NO STONE UNTURNED

s 1860 began, the field of candidates for the Republican presidential nomination included William H. Seward of New York; Salmon P. Chase of Ohio; Edward Bates of Missouri; U.S. Senator Simon Cameron, a powerful Pennsylvanian; and elderly conservative Justice John McLean of Ohio. Frontrunner Seward was the most prominent with the best credentials, but he was perceived, perhaps unfairly, as more radical on antislavery. Chase was the most radical on that crucial issue. Bates offered the most competition for Lincoln and his moderate image because of Bates's own moderation, but his reluctance to actively pursue the nomination ultimately proved to be his undoing.[1]

Although the field did not yet really include Lincoln, in January his candidacy began to gain momentum. On the fourteenth, the *Illinois State Journal* finally endorsed Lincoln. The next day, Lincoln released his autobiography, in effect, when he advised a Chicago supporter to contact Jesse Fell for any information he wanted. On January 20, Fell sent the autobiography to prominent Pennsylvania newspaper editor Joseph J. Lewis for publication, which occurred in the *Chester County Times* on February 11, 1860. Lewis was the brother of the editor of Fell's *Pantagraph*, Edward J. Lewis. This piece provided the basis for other biographical sketches in 1860.[2]

Lincoln was busy in Springfield in the federal court and the Illinois Supreme Court, court sessions that brought many of the Lincoln cadre to Springfield. During the last week of January, a secret meeting in Secretary of State Ozias M. Hatch's office included Leonard Swett, Jesse DuBois,

Lawrence Weldon, William Butler, John W. Bunn, Ward Hill Lamon, Norman Judd, and Fell. Quincy's Jackson Grimshaw started the meeting out as an effort to promote Cameron for president and Lincoln for vice president. Lincoln made it clear he was not interested in the second spot so with some prodding from the others, particularly Swett, he openly agreed to be considered a contender for the presidency, still quietly, so as not to excite any opposition from the other contenders.[3]

On January 27, 1860, Lincoln gave his lecture, not a political speech, to the Young Men's Literary Association of Pontiac at the Presbyterian Church.[4] By telegram, Lincoln abruptly accepted a long-standing invitation and took a train to get there in time for the lecture the same day. In spite of the short notice, a crowded hall awaited him. One attendee observed, "I think the people generally were disappointed in his lecture as it was on no particular subject and was not well-connected," expressing his wish that Lincoln had spoken about politics.[5] Attorney Jason Strevell, a locally prominent Republican, introduced him; later that night, the two sat up until midnight discussing politics as Lincoln awaited the train for his return to Bloomington. As the evening wore on, they began comparing their relative heights; Strevell proposed they measure, and Lincoln agreed. His height in stocking feet—six-foot-four—was measured on a door jamb.[6] Strevell was a Livingston County delegate to the Republican State Convention in Decatur in May, as was Lincoln's old friend Richard Price Morgan, now living in Dwight.[7]

Another important piece fell into place on February 8 when the central committee chose Decatur as the site for the state convention in late May. Just as the location of the national convention in Chicago was considered vital to Lincoln's success, so was the location of the state convention. Northern Illinois was Seward country, southern Illinois was Bates territory, and central Illinois was strongly for Lincoln. Lincoln later described this to Cincinnati's Richard N. Corwine but stated, "I feel disqualified to speak of myself in this manner."[8] The date was later advanced to May 9 because of the advancement of the date of the national convention. The *Chicago Press and Tribune* questioned the choice of convention site to no avail, although on February 16, the newspaper endorsed Lincoln. Lincoln's success at the Republican National Convention in May would depend on unit control of the Illinois delegation, which first had to happen at the state convention.[9]

Chicago Mayor John Wentworth and Judd became embroiled in a festering dispute for control of the Republican Party in Cook County. The bitter feud exploded in late 1859 when Judd sued Wentworth for libel. The dispute threatened the party's ability to carry the state in November, a key for Lincoln's presidential aspirations. Lincoln set aside his reluctance to become involved and quietly attempted to bring the parties together to mediate their differences. When that failed, he openly defended Judd, which convinced Judd to drop his lawsuit and curtail his attacks on Wentworth.[10]

With his hold on Illinois firmly established, Lincoln left on February 23 for New York, where he delivered his masterful Cooper Union speech on the twenty-seventh. This speech was the last of the four that cumulatively put Lincoln in the White House.[11] A triumphant tour of New England followed, during which he gave twelve speeches in thirteen days. Exhausted by his efforts but satisfied by the results, he returned home on March 15 with the *New York Tribune* declaring, "Mr. Lincoln has done a good work and made warm friends. . . . [I]n this quarter he will long be gratefully remembered."[12] He continued to work in Springfield, attending to political details and correspondence. Follett, Foster, and Company, Columbus, Ohio, finally published the debates in late March. Lincoln gave presentation copies of the book to a variety of friends and supporters, including Oscar Harmon, Hatch, Stephen T. Logan, Thomas Milligan, Samuel Treat, and Horatio M. Vandeveer. The book sold fifty thousand copies nationwide.[13]

Lincoln's friends in McLean County rallied around him. In mid-March, Bloomington Republicans had organized one of the earliest Lincoln clubs. On April 2, Republicans there held a mass meeting to appoint twelve delegates to the coming state convention. Eight days later, Lincoln traveled to Bloomington for his final circuit session and his last political speech before his successful nomination. From twelve hundred to fifteen hundred people braved rain and mud to jam into Phoenix Hall to hear his speech, of which the *Pantagraph* reported, "Several of his home thrusts went through the sophisms and duplicities of the Shamocracy with damaging effect."[14]

The State Republican Convention

His Illinois strategy was working. On May 2, he wrote to Corwine, "Illinois will be unanimous for me at the start."[15] Decatur's Richard J. Oglesby was not a delegate, but he was placed in charge of arrangements for the Decatur

gathering, raising $257 from local businessmen, of which he spent $170 for
convention expenses. Oglesby hired a local builder to solve the problem of
finding a place large enough to accommodate the crowd. Oglesby borrowed
the lumber needed to construct a frame between two existing downtown
buildings, and he borrowed a large circus tent to drape over the frame. The
speaker's platform was at the back wall of the makeshift structure, which
was one hundred feet across and seventy feet deep. The canvas ceiling was
so low that a tall man on the platform almost touched it. It was called the
Wigwam, as was the more permanent structure under construction for the
Chicago convention, the name borrowed from New York State to designate
a building constructed for political meetings.[16]

The Wigwam, the temporary structure built under Richard J. Oglesby's super-
vision, held the Republican State Convention in Decatur in May 1860. Here
Oglesby introduced the display of the Rail-Splitter. From a painting by Marge Wilson
in the collection of the Macon County Historical Museum; photo by Patrick McDaniel.

Visitors jammed trains and roads as they flocked into the city of four
thousand, the convention drawing perhaps five thousand to the largest meeting of its type in the state's history. Decatur citizens opened their homes to
accommodate some of those who were unable to find hotel rooms. Delegates

started arriving on May 7. Lincoln arrived on the next day and ended up sharing a room with two delegates at the Junction House.

The convention started on May 9 with seven hundred delegates from all counties of the state except one in southern Illinois. As with the other important state conventions of 1856 and 1858, the delegations from the circuit counties were filled with lawyers and other friends of Lincoln from his days on the circuit. Reports claimed twenty-five-hundred to three thousand people packed the Wigwam hall.[17] The convention was loaded for Lincoln from the beginning; its permanent president was Joseph Gillespie. The only threat to the party unity was Judd's pursuit of the gubernatorial nomination, which conflicted with Lincoln's circuit support and Swett's candidacy for the same slot. Both Judd and Swett were eliminated from the race before the divisiveness damaged Lincoln's bid.

Lincoln was just inside the back door as the afternoon session started. From the floor, Oglesby introduced Lincoln, and the crowd erupted. Lincoln was thrust forward; some reports say he was actually even lifted over the crowd and passed to the platform. What followed is one of the signature moments of the entire campaign. Oglesby again arose, and this time he introduced "an old Democrat," Lincoln's cousin John Hanks. Hanks entered the hall with a friend carrying two split rails, a banner stretched between them that proclaimed:

Abraham Lincoln, The Rail Candidate in 1860
Two rails from a lot of 3,000 made in 1830 by Thos.
Hanks and Abe Lincoln whose father was the
first pioneer of Macon County

The inaccuracies in the banner were irrelevant. All accounts describe the "prolonged" and "deafening" response of the crowd, which lasted for more than fifteen minutes. The cheers didn't raise the canvas roof—they caused part of it to collapse. Lincoln acknowledged that if these were not the actual rails, they certainly were like many that he had split, which detonated another explosion of cheering.[18]

After the convention had adjourned that first day, Lincoln met with several friends in a grove near the Wigwam. Relaxing in the grass, Lincoln handpicked the at-large delegates for the national convention, including David

Just before the unanimous endorsement of Lincoln by the Illinois Republicans in Decatur in May 1860, Lincoln found time on May 9 to pose for Decatur photographer Edward A. Barnwell. Decatur Public Library, Decatur, Illinois.

Davis and Judd. Lincoln and his advisers planned the strategy for the next day, including submitting to the full convention a resolution that the entire delegation vote as a unit. Somehow, Lincoln found time during all this to pose for a photograph at the request of Decatur photographer Edward A. Barnwell.[19]

The convention was a lock: Not only did it nominate Lincoln the next day, as had been anticipated but it also did so unanimously with instruction to the delegation to vote as a unit without mention of any alternate candidate. An effort by Seward supporters to object was drowned out in the tidal wave of Lincoln sentiment stoked by the intense Lincoln demonstrations. Decatur banker Lowber Burroughs recounted that after the nomination resolution was passed, he went to retrieve Lincoln and found him asleep on a couch in the back of the Peake Jewelry Store next door. Lincoln was rushed to the convention for a brief statement of thanks.[20]

The Decatur convention gave Lincoln a substantial advantage over rival Chase, who had some minority division within his own Ohio delegation. The unit vote for Lincoln made him a stronger and more viable candidate for the coming national convention. He was no longer just a politician seeking the nomination, he was the Rail-Splitter. Oglesby's simple ploy instantly created the image of the common man, one of the people and the advocate of free labor, a powerful force in that time. Historian William C. Harris said, "Much depended on Republican unity in the Illinois State Convention. . . . [It] played a surprisingly important role in American political history."[21]

The National Republican Convention and the Circuit Lawyers

After a brief sojourn at home in Bloomington on Friday, May 11, Davis traveled to Chicago the next day to execute the plan devised in Decatur. The strategy was to keep Lincoln's candidacy inconspicuous, urging that he be considered the second choice of the supporters of all the other candidates pursuing Seward, who was the clear favorite. The goals on the first ballot were to stop a Seward victory and get a hundred votes for Lincoln and on the second ballot to gain votes on the way to victory on the third. Davis was the quarterback of the team of Lincoln operatives in Chicago, mostly lawyers from the Eighth Circuit. The three decades of building relationships in central Illinois, twenty-three years as a lawyer, the countless days on the prairie roads and in the county seats, the evenings in the taverns, the thousands of cases all culminated in those crucial five days in Chicago.

The May 12, 1860, centerfold of *Harper's Weekly* shows the wide range of candidates and demonstrates the uphill battle that Lincoln and his circuit team faced in capturing the nomination. From the author's collection.

The Republican National Convention of 1860 took place in the Wigwam, two stories high, 100 feet by 180 feet, constructed specifically and barely completed in time for the meeting. Mayor Wentworth had appointed Gurdon Hubbard, the Danville pioneer and old friend of Lincoln and now a Republican alderman in Chicago, to supervise its construction. The stage, which ran the width of the building, held all 460 delegates and 60 reporters. The rest of the ground floor was for spectators and offered no seating. Women and their companions watched from the gallery, which seated about 1,200. The building, which cost between $5,000 and $6,000, had a total capacity of approximately 10,000. Chicago's Republican women had decorated the hall's interior for the building's dedication with a reception on Saturday evening, May 12. Judd, in charge of seating of the delegates, cleverly placed the influential New York delegation so the committed Illinois and Indiana contingents separated it from the doubtful delegations.[22]

For each session, the crowd of ten thousand inside was a half or even less than the numbers outside.[23]

When Davis arrived in Chicago, he was surprised that Lincoln had no headquarters, unlike the other candidates. The Chicago contingent, led by Judd had failed to make such arrangements, but Davis was somehow able to rent two rooms at the Tremont House at this late date. Davis was well equipped to direct pursuit of the nomination, both within and without the tight circle of Eighth Circuit lawyers, who were accustomed to their respected judge directing and controlling them. His commanding interpersonal skills were well suited to the give and take of the difficult and sometimes heated cajoling of those outsiders who had to be persuaded to cast their ballots for Lincoln. His lieutenants were Swett, Logan, and DuBois; the actual delegates from the circuit counties were himself, Oliver Davis, William P. Dole, Henry Grove, and Logan. In addition to DuBois, Logan, and Swett, circuit associates on the Lincoln team were William Butler (by then state treasurer), Oliver Davis, Dole, Fell, William Fithian, Grove, Harmon, William H. Herndon, Lamon, Clifton H. Moore, Oglesby, William Orme, Samuel Parks, Henry Russell, Weldon, and Henry Clay Whitney. It is unclear whether Asahel Gridley attended.[24] As was the custom, Lincoln as a candidate did not attend the convention.

The first order of business was to nail down Indiana's anticipated support. Lincoln had said earlier that month, "The whole of Indiana might not be difficult to get." His circuit relationships through Vermilion and particularly Edgar Counties were important tools in capturing the support of the Indiana delegation; Vice President Adlai Stevenson later said Lincoln's circuit relations with several Indiana delegates "proved the opening wedge." A day earlier, Lincoln wrote to Cyrus Allen, the speaker of the Indiana house, who was from Vincennes, across the Wabash from DuBois' Lawrenceville, asking Allen to meet Davis or DuBois in Chicago on the twelfth and urging him to contact John Usher.[25] Usher had been mildly supportive of Bates, like some other Indiana Republicans, until spring 1860, when he visited his old friend Lincoln in Springfield. Though practicing in Terre Haute, Usher had a long-distance partnership with Caleb Smith, longtime friend of Lincoln from their shared time in the Congress. Smith, from Indianapolis, was one of the most influential members of the Indiana delegation. One-time Hoosier Dole, now of Paris, was a circuit delegate and the "perfect liaison agent to the Indiana forces." By May 15, the day before the opening session, Indiana was ready to cast all its twenty-six ballots for Lincoln. Davis later told Lincoln, "Without Smith's active art and cooperation, the Indiana Delegation would not have been as a unit to go for you."[26] By a large margin, this vital Indiana unit vote was the largest cast for any candidate by a state other than his own.

Now that Indiana was in the fold, the next step was to shake loose additional votes for Lincoln. Davis's plan was to send his team to the delegations where they had connections, some being their birthplace states. Some advance work had been done. Lincoln had written former Springfield resident Hawkins Taylor on April 21 thanking him for planning on coming from Iowa to attend the convention. In April, Moore had written to his brotherin-law in Iowa for a letter of introduction to the Iowa caucus.[27]

The demanding Davis worked tirelessly and drove his men. At the convention, Moore worked the influential William Green of Dayton, sergeant at arms of the Ohio senate (and at the end of the year, Moore sent letters thanking the central Ohio delegates for their support). Because Weldon was a native of Zanesville, Ohio, he also focused on the Ohio delegation, including a delegate from his hometown. Swett was assigned to his home state of Maine and Parks to his native state of Vermont, which had a delegate from Parks's hometown of Middlebury. David Davis was well connected in Massachusetts through his wife's family. Fell's close friend Lewis from West Chester, Pennsylvania, was a key member of that state's delegation. Lamon, besides serving as the amiable entertainer and gracious host at the Tremont, worked Virginia, his home state. Kentucky natives Oglesby, born near Louisville, which sent eight delegates, and Logan talked to the Kentucky delegation. Butler's job throughout was to regularly update Lincoln.[28] The politicking was furious between the twelfth and the opening of the convention. Swett later reported that he had averaged two hours of sleep a night for the whole week.[29]

The convention convened on May 16 in a session dedicated to its organization, including the designation of a vice president and secretary from each state. David Davis was named Illinois vice president and Oliver Davis as Illinois secretary; Logan was on the committee on credentials. On May 17, the delegates adopted the platform; the driven and dedicated Lincoln team continued the campaigning, convincing, and cajoling. Judd's other significant contribution to the week was to influence the railroads to charge only half fares for passengers from central Illinois and Indiana to pack the crowd. The crowds thus drawn for Lincoln were matched by the huge number of Seward partisans brought to the Midwest by the certainty of victory. The din from the two sides was deafening.[30]

The party leaders, regardless of whom they favored, generally agreed that the keys to victory in the November election were Illinois, Indiana, New Jersey, and Pennsylvania, states lost in 1856. On the afternoon of May 17, delegates from those four states got together and at Judd's suggestion created a committee of twelve, three from each state. The committee included Caleb Smith and David Davis, who persuaded the Pennsylvania and New Jersey delegates to caucus separately that evening to decide whether all four delegations should support Lincoln. That day, Davis wired Lincoln, "Am very hopeful dont be Excited nearly dead with fatigue telegraph or write here very little."[31]

The New Jersey delegation by 1 A.M. had agreed to support Lincoln after the first ballot vote for their favorite son, William Dayton. But, under the influence of the conniving Cameron, the Pennsylvania delegation was not so easily persuaded. Swett and Davis hammered away at the delegates, but the promise of a cabinet post for Cameron was the price. Earlier in the day, Lincoln had admonished, "Make no contracts that will bind me." Davis is said to have commented, "Lincoln ain't here and don't know what we have to meet, so we will go ahead, as if we hadn't heard from him, and he must ratify it."[32] Early Friday morning, Cameron was promised his cabinet post, and Lincoln had the Pennsylvania vote. While there is some dispute about this deal, all the contemporary evidence supports the striking of a bargain. There is speculation that the Lincoln forces had to promise a cabinet seat to Smith and the commissioner of Indian affairs to Dole for the Indiana vote, although there is no documented evidence of a deal.[33] Lincoln's longtime circuit friendships in western Indiana and his preconvention work offer a more plausible explanation.

While David Davis and Swett negotiated the night away, other Lincoln supporters were putting together one more device to maximize their home-field advantage. The Seward forces had placed substantial numbers of rooters in the hall who were doing all they could to influence the voting. To counter this, the Lincoln men schemed to pack the hall with their supporters, who had poured into the city during the week. It is claimed that at the suggestion, Fell, with the sanction of the Illinois Central Committee, issued hundreds more tickets illicitly the night prior to the balloting for distribution to the Lincoln forces. Another story is that Lamon got ahold of Indianapolis attorney Alexander Hamilton Connor, who knew the man who printed the tickets. Lamon and Russell obtained a supply of the tickets and spent the night forging official signatures on them.[34] In any event, on the fateful day of the balloting, May 18, the complacent Seward men, recovering from a night of celebrating the victory that most observers thought imminent, casually sauntered over to the Wigwam for the session. They arrived only to find many of their places had been taken by the Lincoln crowd. Accompanied by raucous roars from the crowds of spectators, first Seward and then Lincoln were each placed in nomination. Ebullient eyewitness accounts searched for words to describe the noise during the proceedings. The roar reached its crescendo in response to Lincoln's nomination by Judd, with significant seconds from Smith and Columbus Delano of Ohio.[35]

As the balloting began, Seward was expected to be strong in New England, whose votes were particularly significant because those states were first in the roll call. However, the cracks in the Seward façade became evident as soon as the voting began with the loss of New England votes. Lincoln received a surprising 6 votes from Swett's Maine, the first state to be called, compared to Seward's 10. New Hampshire gave 7 of its 10 votes to Lincoln. The 10 Vermont votes went to their Senator Jacob Collamer. Lincoln received 4 votes from Massachusetts and 2 from Connecticut. As expected, Seward got all of New York's 70 votes and Dayton, all of New Jersey's 14. Pennsylvania cast 4 votes for Lincoln and 47½ for Cameron with only one-half ballot vote going to Seward. Seward's presumed lock on the southern states dissolved with Lincoln's 14 of 23 votes from Lamon's Virginia compared to Seward's 8. Lincoln outpolled Seward in Kentucky 6 to 5 out of the total of 23 votes. Chase was not as fortunate with his own Ohio delegation as Lincoln and Seward had been with their respective delegations. Ohio gave Lincoln 8 votes compared to Chase's 29 and none for Seward. Lincoln and Seward each received 2 of Iowa's 8 ballots. Thanks to Seward's loss of expected votes and the relative success of Bates, Cameron, and Chase, Seward, though leading with 173½ votes, had been headed off—Davis and Lincoln's first goal was met. Lincoln came in second with his solid 102 votes—thus meeting his second goal. He was well ahead of the remaining three, whose totals were approximately 50 ballots each.[36]

The Davis-Lincoln forces met their goal for the second ballot as Lincoln picked up 79 votes to total 181 votes while Seward picked up only 11 to reach 184½. The additional Lincoln votes included 2 from New Hampshire, 3 from Rhode Island, 2 from Connecticut, all 10 from Parks's Vermont, and a whopping 44 from Pennsylvania, a result of the Davis-Swett negotiation. Delaware added 6, Kentucky 3, Ohio 6, and Iowa 3. The chairman had to quiet the roar from the Lincoln partisans as the vote total was announced on the second ballot.[37]

On the dramatic third ballot, Massachusetts gave Lincoln another 4 votes, New Jersey 8, Pennsylvania 4, David Davis's Maryland 9, Kentucky 5, and Oregon 4. Significantly, Ohio gave Lincoln another 15 votes, and Iowa contributed a curious ½ vote. When the count finished, Lincoln was at 231½ and only ½ vote short. It is generally agreed that David Cartter, the chairman from Ohio, announced the change of four of his delegations' ballots, which put Lincoln over the top.[38] Pandemonium broke loose as wild cheering and foot stomping filled the hall. An official shouted through the skylight, "Fire the salute, Abe Lincoln is nominated!" The cannon, placed on the roof and ready to announce the final vote, boomed, and David Davis wept.[39]

Beside the circuit lawyers, others contributed to the victory. Senator Orville Browning was one, although throughout the spring of 1860, he was still urging Lincoln and the party to support Bates. The *Chicago Press and Tribune* had endorsed Lincoln, although its editor Joseph Medill quietly urged support for Justice McLean.[40] The most significant contributor from outside the circuit was Judd, although his support always came at a cost. Among those were his bitter feud with Wentworth, his hunger for the Republican gubernatorial nomination in 1860, and his borrowing in 1857 out of Lincoln's share of the large Illinois Central fee, which aggravated Lincoln's strained finances. Judd's support of Lincoln never interfered with his own personal ambition. Thomas J. Pickett recalled a visit from Judd a few months before the convention as Judd sought support for his gubernatorial candidacy. When Pickett named Lincoln as his presidential choice, Judd sneered and named others he preferred. Lincoln's closest circuit confidantes neither liked nor trusted Judd.[41]

Without the effort and skill of the lawyers of the Eighth Judicial Circuit and their steadfast unilateral loyalty to their colleague, Lincoln would not have captured the 1860 Republican nomination for president. Had it not been for the effort of the indefatigable Davis, Lincoln would not have won it, something Lincoln himself acknowledged as he weighed Davis's U.S. Supreme Court nomination, Swett recalled. Pickett said, "David Davis performed the work of a score of ordinary men." Fifteen years later, Cameron recalled that Davis and Swett had done more for Lincoln than anyone.[42] The lawyers of the Eighth had much of which to be proud. Swett wrote on May 27, 1860, "The lawyers of our circuit went there determined to leave no stone unturned, and really they, aided by some of our State officers and a half dozen men from various portions of the state, were the only tireless, sleepless, unwavering, and ever vigilant friends he had."[43]

The Election

Although the convention adjourned, Davis and Swett were not done. They immediately met with Thurlow Weed to begin unifying the November effort, inviting him to Springfield to meet Lincoln personally before returning to Albany. The May 24 meeting went a long way towards solidifying the campaign. On June 6, Lincoln resumed his law practice, appearing in the federal court; his last court appearance was two weeks later.[44]

Because custom confined Lincoln to Springfield, the efforts of Swett and Davis were important for success. The custom of the day was that the candidates themselves did not campaign, so Lincoln made no speeches or campaign appearances during the campaign. Republicans had to carry Pennsylvania, but it was badly fractured between the pro-and anti-Cameron forces. Lewis, a leader of the anti-Cameron side, was in regular communication with Fell to help narrow this breach. At the request of the Republican Central Committee, Davis went in August, stopping in Indiana to evaluate that campaign, to meet with the leaders of the Republican Party in Pennsylvania, including Cameron himself. Davis visited Pittsburgh, Harrisburg, Philadelphia, and Scranton and then on to New York City and Albany for similar meetings, returning through tenuous Indiana. Swett, likewise, served at Lincoln's direction to assist in keeping the new party's disparate parts pulling in the same direction.[45]

Following the nomination, biographies of Lincoln were published, including W. D. Howell's volume on July 5. Samuel Parks loaned Lincoln his copy, which he read and carefully corrected in handwritten notes, a volume that remains an important biographical source. In August, Lincoln joined in a petition for pardon of his client Thomas Patterson of Champaign County, convicted of manslaughter a year earlier. A petition to the governor, which cited in part "absence of previous bad character . . . the necessities of his family," brought the pardon on August 30, 1860.[46]

Working from the governor's office on the capitol's second floor, Lincoln corresponded with Republicans all over the country, quietly doing what he could to keep the party together. Fithian decided to run against Harmon for the Republican nomination for the legislature from Vermilion County. The race had significance because the legislature still selected U.S. Senators, and Republican Lyman Trumbull was up for reelection. Lamon wrote Lincoln on August 17 asking that he intervene. Lincoln had already written Fithian several days earlier requesting that he find a way to restore party harmony. The problem was solved when Fithian and Harmon both withdrew in favor of a compromise candidate. Lamon, quoting Oliver Davis, agreed that Harmon's magnanimity defused a delicate problem that the obstreperous Fithian had caused.[47]

A highlight of the campaign was a huge, August 8 rally in Springfield that Lincoln attended. He was overcome with the outpouring of support but declined to speak. "The prairies are on fire for Lincoln," the *Illinois State Journal* said.[48]

Little is known as to the source of funding for the Lincoln campaign. What information there is points again to the support of the circuit. The expenses of the Chicago effort included $300 for the Tremont House, which Davis paid, and $34.50 for whiskey, $60 for wine, $77 for brandy, $125 for quarters, and $25 for cigars, all paid by Hatch and Lamon. A less-credible source, Asahel Gridley biographer Robert H. Browne, claims that Gridley was the heart and soul of the "Ways and Means" and that Swett told him that Gridley had advanced over $100,000 for Lincoln. This claim is uncorroborated, but it is consistent with Gridley's means and the close relationship he and Lincoln had.[49]

Early elections in Pennsylvania, Ohio, and Indiana went for Lincoln. On October 10, Lamon reported to Lincoln from Clinton on the circuit,

It has become my melancholy duty to inform you that Judge Davis is in a d—l of a fix: he was seized with a griping about noon to day which has greatly endangered the roots of the hair of all the members of this Bar: His unfortunate condition was produced by Telegraphic Despatches received from Penn, & Ind. When he first received the Election news, he was trying an important criminal case, which terminated in his Kicking over the Clerk's desk, turned a double somersault and adjourned court until after the presidential Election—and in his delirium he actually talks of Lincoln's Election as being a fixed fact—and says he knows that Douglas is sorry he did n't die when he was little.[50]

On Election Day, November 6, Lamon and Elmer Ellsworth, Lincoln and Herndon's law clerk, accompanied Lincoln to the polls. That night, Lincoln, Davis, and a few others went to the telegraph office, where he received after midnight the momentous news of victory with remarkable calm.[51] The opportunistic Edward D. Baker showed up to share in the triumph—his first visit to Springfield in a decade since moving to San Francisco, where he was defeated for Congress and then on to Oregon where he was elected to the U.S. Senate.[52]

Lincoln's Ladder to the Presidency

The Eighth Judicial Circuit's most direct contribution to Lincoln's ascension to the White House was obtaining the Republican nomination for him in Chicago. The nomination presented a greater hurdle than the election that followed. Lincoln's circuit colleagues went to Chicago on behalf of the heavy underdog and defeated the favorites. These circuit lawyers, all recently converted to the Anti-Nebraska Party like Lincoln, were brilliantly organized and directed by their judge David Davis. These men executed the strategy that Lincoln and Davis and their colleagues had planned through the spring of 1860, finalizing that plan in Decatur on May 9 and 10. These men controlled the Illinois state convention in Decatur and led the effort at the national convention in Chicago.

The nomination victory had been a more difficult challenge than the general election was because of the schism of the Democrats that started in their April convention in Baltimore with the party's inability to select a nominee. As a result of the stalemate, the northern faction agreed to reconvene in Baltimore in June, and the dissident southerners would reconvene in Richmond that same month. Each nominated its own candidate to run against the other nominees, the northerners nominating Stephen A. Douglas, and the southerners John Breckinridge. This dramatically increased the odds of Republican success and, accordingly, the significance of the Republican nomination.[53]

The *New York Times'* Republican editor, Henry Raymond, said, "The action of the Democracy at Baltimore seems, with reasonable diligence on the part of the Republicans, to have insured the success of the Republican ticket."[54] Lincoln himself offered the same opinion later in the summer in a letter to old friend and former editor of the *Springfield Journal*, Simeon Francis, who had moved to Oregon, "When you wrote, you had not learned of the doings of the democratic convention at Baltimore; but you will be in possession of it all long before this reaches you. I hesitate to say it, but it really appears now, as if the success of the Republican ticket is inevitable."[55]

The long days of travel across the prairies and in the courtrooms and the nights of camaraderie in the taverns in the years on the circuit rooted the zeal, dedication, and commitment of the Lincoln coterie. The concurrent politics of the day further forged these bonds. These men had shared hard-earned, narrow political success, first as Whigs and then as Republicans, working together within the party and against the statewide strength of the Democrats. The most important meetings and conventions of the 1850s—Decatur and Bloomington in 1856, Springfield in 1858, and Decatur in 1860—were all held in the circuit, heavily attended by circuit residents in support of Lincoln. The circuit relations were not only important within the Illinois delegation but were also considerable assets with the Indiana delegation as well, giving Lincoln a head start with that vital swing state. His long-standing circuit-based friendships with key members of the delegation created this opportunity. The convention delegates viewed Indiana as one of four key states that had to be won in November in the general election. The Indiana delegation's decision to cast a first-ballot, unit vote for Lincoln gave a significant boost to the Lincoln forces, sending a message that his candidacy was viable. The unit vote, more than twice that of any other delegation's votes cast for a nonnative son, added considerably to Lincoln's vote total.

The nomination victory came from intraparty relationships and Lincoln's stature and strength within the party. There is no comparable strength in Lincoln support across the circuit in the general elections, either in 1858,

1860, or 1864. The circuit's election results are not as important in the outcome because the circuit vote was a relatively small percentage of the total. The 1858 senatorial race has to be viewed separately because the electorate voted for legislative candidates, rather than Lincoln and Douglas themselves. The evenness of the 1858 results demonstrates the circuit's racism and the division of opinion on slavery with which Lincoln always had to contend. [56]

The Eighth Judicial Circuit's popular vote had less potential to have real impact on Lincoln's ascension, regardless of voting trends. The circuit's election results in the presidential elections of 1860 and 1864 were only 16 percent of the total votes cast in the state. In 1860, he carried Illinois by over 10,000 votes, but only eight of the seventeen circuit counties voted for him. His largest plurality was 1,000 votes in McLean County; he was defeated by more than 2-1 in Shelby County. It is difficult, perhaps impossible, to measure the impact on the outcome, if any, of Lincoln's stature and popularity within the communities of the circuit.

Comparison with John C. Frémont's results in the 1856 presidential election somewhat answers this question in the 1860 race. At first it appears that Lincoln's stature in the circuit did favorably affect his vote totals. Frémont gained 40 percent of the statewide vote in Illinois as opposed to 32 percent in the circuit, an 8 percent gap. In 1860, Lincoln carried the state as a whole with 50.7 percent to 49.3 percent, a 1.4 percent margin, and the circuit with 50.2 percent to 49.8 percent or 0.4 percent gap. Thus, Lincoln reduced the state-versus-circuit difference from Frémont's 8 percent to his own 1.4 percent in 1860, or a 7 percent reduction in the gap. However, 1856 was the new Republican Party's first national election. More important, many former Illinois Whigs were Know-Nothings who voted for Millard Fillmore instead of Frémont. Fillmore carried 16 percent of the popular statewide vote and 22 percent in the circuit. This 6 percent discrepancy almost erases the 7 percent difference between Frémont and Lincoln, suggesting that Lincoln's circuit-wide popularity and personal connection to the circuit were of little consequence when the voters of the circuit cast their ballots in 1860.[57]

Just as his politics had little impact on his personal popularity and professional standing around the circuit, it appears that these two attributes had little impact on the entrenched politics. The popular votes in the seven Republican, antislavery counties of Champaign, DeWitt, Livingston, Logan, McLean, Piatt, and Vermilion were cast for Lincoln in 1858, 1860, and 1864.

Likewise the seven Democratic proslavery counties, Christian, Mason, Menard, Moultrie, Sangamon, Shelby, and Woodford, voted against Lincoln in all three elections. Only three counties switched. Macon voted for Lincoln in 1858, Douglas in 1860, and Lincoln again in 1864. Tazewell voted for Douglas in 1858 and 1860, when anti-abolitionist feeling beat Lincoln, who finally prevailed there in 1864. Edgar County voted for Lincoln in 1858 due to a popular legislative candidate and an exceptional campaign but against him in 1860 and 1864.

Lincoln's reliable support from key circuit counties contrasted sharply with his lack of support from his hometown in Sangamon County, on which he could never rely. This lack of support first showed in the Whig congressional primary in 1842 and resurfaced in his patronage contests in 1849. It was repeated in the elections of 1858, 1860, and 1864, in which he never carried Sangamon County. His team at the 1860 Chicago convention, made up almost entirely of circuit lawyers, included only Logan and non-lawyer Butler from Sangamon. The county results confirm that unlike the nomination process, the popular voting in the circuit contributed minimally, at best, to Lincoln's rise. Even in 1864, with the favorable turns in the war effort in the late summer and fall, Lincoln would narrowly carry the seventeen counties in total votes and only eight of the seventeen counties individually.[58] It was the circuit-led nomination process that vaulted Lincoln to the presidency.

While the divergence of views on race and slavery within the general population eliminated any meaningful contribution to Lincoln's electoral success, it did provide an important contribution to Lincoln's ascension. These divergent views trained Lincoln in moderation, notwithstanding his fervent and passionate abhorrence of slavery. He gained political skill in this very competitive political arena.[59] He also observed that decent, God-fearing people were tolerant of slavery. He had to live and work with respected, bright lawyers who opposed his political views—John T. Stuart, Orlando Ficklin, Anthony Thornton, Usher Linder, and Vandeveer, to name a few. Lincoln's renowned magnanimity toward the South and those in the North who differed with him on slavery was enhanced and kindled by the broad range of views with which he dealt throughout his political career on the circuit.

Lincoln's initial choice of the Whig Party in a Democratic-dominated state placed him behind a huge political barrier statewide. On the other hand, he attained the leadership of the Whig Party and its offspring, the Anti-Nebraska or Republican Party, in a section of the state where its leadership was strong. This association aligned him with some of the most astute and talented politicians in the state, who were often the most influential in their communities. It was to these communities that he turned for the leadership of his team of supporters in the 1850s, particularly Bloomington and Danville.

This circle of close, dedicated friends gave Lincoln an asset within his party that was unique to his nomination effort. Chase's Ohio support was never particularly solid, as shown by the warm reception Lincoln received in Ohio in 1859. That lack of support proved fatal to Chase when Lincoln received Ohio votes on the first ballot in Chicago. Although Seward had the unanimous vote of the New York delegation on all ballots, his enemies in his home state created significant difficulty for his nomination. Anti-Seward forces had invited Lincoln to Cooper Union, opening the door wider for his candidacy.[60]

At the Chicago convention, the relentless opposition of Horace Greeley, the powerful editor the *New York Tribune*, was quite damaging to Seward's efforts. Douglas had to contend with a sharp division in the Democratic Party in 1858 caused by the Buchanan administration's enmity to him.[61] Lincoln's support within the Illinois antislavery forces was solid and unflagging because it was driven by the zeal generated by personal friendship and admiration arising from the years of close association in the Eighth Judicial Circuit.

14. WE SAW HIM NO MORE

B efore leaving for Chicago, the president-elect almost lost his new whiskers to the razor of Springfield barber William Florville, but Lincoln stopped his friend in time. On the trip north to Chicago to meet his newly elected vice president, Hannibal Hamlin, the train stopped in Lincoln, Atlanta, Bloomington, and Lexington, where Lincoln offered brief remarks from the back of the train. He was never to return to these towns. On November 21, 1860, he arrived in Chicago, and at the request of Henry Clay Whitney, he had his picture taken again by Samuel Alschuler, the first showing the beard. Following the trip, he wrote to Whitney on November 26, "I regret not having an opportunity to see more of you. Please present my respects to Mrs. W and to your good Father and Mother."[1]

Leonard Swett and David Davis continued to assist Lincoln. Working with their new ally Thurlow Weed, they helped Lincoln in his cabinet formation. In January, Lincoln sent Swett to Harrisburg, Pennsylvania, and Washington, D.C., to assist in this and included former rival William H. Seward in these discussions. During this time, Lincoln worked on his first inaugural address in the state capitol office, submitting the draft to Davis for review.[2] Lincoln's old friend Joseph Gillespie, in Springfield on business, visited Lincoln at his law office. At Lincoln's invitation, he stayed several days, having lengthy personal conversations with the president-elect, discussing the crisis facing the nation and reminiscing about their shared past. Gillespie recalled Lincoln saying to him, "I wish I could take all you lawyers down there with me, Democrats and Republican alike, and make a cabinet

On November 25, 1860, in Chicago, when Lincoln met his vice president, Hannibal Hamlin, for the first time, photographer Samuel Alschuler, formerly of Urbana, took the first of Lincoln's still-emerging beard. Abraham Lincoln Presidential Library and Museum.

out of you. I believe I could construct one that would save the country, for then I would know every man and where he would fit. I tell you there are some Illinois Democrats whom I know well I would rather trust than a Republican I would have to learn, for I'll have no time to study the lesson."

Those Democratic lawyers he identified for Gillespie included Usher Linder and Orlando Ficklin.[3]

On January 30, Lincoln traveled by rail across the circuit to Tolono and then south to visit his stepmother, Sarah Bush Lincoln. He spent the next day with Coles County friends and visited his father's grave. On February 1, he made a last visit to Sarah and returned to Springfield in late afternoon.[4] At last the agonizing wait was over. On February 10, Lincoln went by the office to bid farewell to Billy Herndon. As Lincoln started out the door, he noticed the sign board with the firm name hanging at the foot of the stairway: "Let it hang there undisturbed. Give our clients to understand that the election of a President makes no change in the firm of Lincoln and Herndon. If I live I'm coming back sometime and then we'll go right on practicing law as if nothing had ever happened."[5]

The Trip East

On February 11, 1861, a cold and gloomy day, Lincoln left Sangamon County for the last time. In his sentimental and touching farewell address from the back of his train at the Great Western depot, Lincoln said, "To this place and the kindness of these people I owe everything. . . . I bid you an affectionate farewell." The *Clinton Central Transcript* on February 14, 1861, noted, "The man they had known so long and loved so well was about to go from them, perhaps forever."[6] Next the train stopped in Decatur. James Shoaf, now editor of the *Democratic Magnet*, urged all to come to see the man who would "save the Union." Several thousand gathered at the Union Station, where the train stopped for a few minutes. Lincoln spoke briefly from the back and then stepped down to shake hands around, including that of a small boy who had cut across a field and through a ditch full of water to get close to him. Lincoln said to him, "My boy, you must have wanted to see me pretty bad." The people lined the tracks in the country as well as in the towns to bid the president-elect farewell.[7] The eastbound train rolled through Bement, where people stood in the drizzle in order to pay tribute to him, and entered Champaign County for his last appearance there where it stopped in Tolono. He spoke briefly, powerful in his brevity: "I am leaving you on an errand of national importance, attended, as you are aware, with considerable difficulties. Let us believe, as some poet has expressed it: 'Behind the cloud the sun is still shining.' I bid you an affectionate farewell."[8]

The train continued east for Lincoln's final trip to Danville. Ward Hill Lamon was on board in his colorful uniform as Lincoln's bodyguard. Approximately a thousand people, including William Fithian, Oliver Davis, Joseph Peters, James Kilpatrick, and Elizabeth Harmon, gathered in the drizzle to bid farewell. Lincoln greeted those friends whom he could see and asked for Davis, who had been pushed too far back by the press of the crowd, and for Oscar Harmon, who was watching with his daughter Lucy from a window at their nearby home. The *New York Herald* reported, "Mr. Lincoln again stepped out and addressing himself to the enthusiastic gathering, remarked, that if he had any blessings to dispense, he would certainly dispense the largest and roundest to his good old friends of Vermillion county." As the train approached the state line, John Hay observed that Lincoln had become abstracted, sad, and thoughtful.[9] For him, the familiar landscape disappeared over the horizon for the last time.

As Lincoln's train wound its way from major city to major city for eleven days on its way to Washington, rumors and reports of an assassination attempt as he passed through Baltimore increased in frequency and gravity. After some intense discussion, it was decided that the danger was sufficient reason for Lincoln to sneak through the city on a separate train. Lamon, armed to the teeth, guarded him, and they departed Philadelphia at 11 P.M., arriving safely but unceremoniously in Washington at 6 A.M. on February 23.[10] Between his arrival and inauguration, Lincoln was busy meeting with numerous callers, including members of Congress and foreign representatives, finalizing cabinet appointments, and getting acquainted again with the capital. During this time, he finalized the final version of his inaugural address with Seward's input. W. H. Bailhache of the *Illinois State Journal* traveled to Washington to aid with the printing of copies of the address.

March 4, Inauguration Day, dawned cloudy and chilly, but the weather improved as the day progressed. Ubiquitous Edward D. Baker was there riding with Lincoln and James Buchanan from the Willard Hotel to the Capitol for the ceremony. Baker introduced Lincoln to the crowd of thirty thousand. Also on the stand with Lincoln was Stephen A. Douglas, who was said to have taken Lincoln's hat and held it during his speech, sparing Lincoln the awkward moment of having nowhere to place his hat as he commenced his speech.[11] He successfully finished the speech, but fast-moving events left him no time to savor the moment. Questions regarding Lincoln's

preparedness had swirled around him since his election. Now his preparedness was immediately put to the test.

Lincoln's lack of training in government is well known, consisting only
of service in the frontier Illinois legislature two decades earlier and one unsuccessful term in the U.S. House of Representatives more than one decade
earlier. His resume included no administrative, diplomatic, or meaningful
military service but only twenty-three years as a practicing lawyer riding the
circuit in Illinois. That arena had trained him in human nature, mediation,
quick absorption of facts, and assessment of alternatives. The circuit practice
required rapid response to often-ambiguous choices and demanded decisive
and irrevocable action.[12] His many years on the circuit had taught him to
listen. The adequacy of this training to ready him for the more complex challenges he would face was now to be tested. As he walked away from the day's
festivities, one of the most difficult, sensitive issues a president ever faced
was thrust upon him, the Fort Sumter crisis. He had no time to feel his way
into his new role of the nation's political leader and commander in chief.
That day, he learned that Sumter had to either be supplied or evacuated.
The commander of the fort advised abandonment; his chief military adviser,
the venerable Winfield Scott, advised abandonment; all of his newly formed
cabinet except one advised abandonment. Lincoln intuitively understood
that the stakes were far higher than the mere fort itself.

The fort was a looming symbol that created a seemingly unsolvable quan-
dary. On the one hand, surrender would elevate the stature and prestige
of the neophyte secessionist leadership and marginalize the power of the
government of the United States. On the other hand, reinforcement would
be the act of aggression he had pledged he would not commit, and the Union
would be the provocateur of the unthinkable war. He devised a narrow third
course, which was to reprovision the fort with nonmilitary supplies delivered
by an unarmed flotilla. This would demonstrate the Union's resolve without
military aggression. He notified the secessionists of his chosen course of
action. They took the bait and fired upon the fort. It was the secessionists
who fired the first shot because the federal government would not back
down. The war was on. The new president of questionable preparation had
successfully met his first challenge.[13]

Lincoln's legal training and experience are reflected in his manner of dealing with the complicated issues thrust upon him throughout his presidency,

approaching these matters with a lawyerly analysis.[14] The fundamental issue of secession was viewed by him in contractual terms. A party to a contract cannot unilaterally decide to back away from his binding commitment, and Lincoln spoke in such terms in the first inaugural address and later in his first address to Congress.[15] Lincoln's loathing of slavery conflicted with the contractual commitment in the Constitution made initially to the slaveholding states. Their breach of that contract permitted the federal government to renounce the unholy pact. The Emancipation Proclamation has been criticized for its dry language.[16] It was drafted by Lincoln as a legal document with a view toward withstanding constitutional attacks in court.[17]

Throughout his years in the White House, the problem of the pardon of court-martial convictions confronted Lincoln. The repeated, painstaking oversight of these convictions required legal analysis. He even had occasion to use his specific circuit experience with the defense of temporary insanity with the case of David Wright, whom he refused to pardon.[18] Likewise, his understanding of the writ of habeas corpus was constantly applied to the need for its suspension under the doctrine of military necessity. The delicate balance between individual rights and the action necessary to save the union placed a constant issue in front of Lincoln and his analytical ability developed on the circuit.[19]

Lincoln's familiarity with the press and his ability to use the press to serve his presidency were other skills honed on the circuit, a product of his friendship with the variety of editors around the circuit and the many hours spent with them in the newspaper offices. His long-standing habit of reading and absorbing newspapers served him well in the White House. He had developed an underlying appreciation of the utility of the newspapers as a means to promulgate his message to a wider audience.[20]

The President and the Circuit Lawyers, Friends, and Associates

Lincoln rewarded many of the circuit lawyers for their work in helping to nominate and elect him. Lamon had wanted to be appointed ambassador to France, but instead Lincoln wisely appointed him U.S. Marshal for Washington, D.C. Thus, Lincoln could keep his court jester and loyal companion close by him. This appointment put Lamon in charge of law enforcement in the District and the operation of its jails. As marshal, Lamon strictly enforced the Fugitive Slave Law, making him an easy target of the radicals in Congress. In furtherance of their goal to control Lincoln, they constantly attacked Lamon, either to depose him or to severely cut his income so as to force him out of office. During his presidency at considerable cost, Lincoln stood by Lamon. On the other hand, Lamon was his ears on the streets of the dangerous city and served with "blind fidelity" as he tried desperately to protect his friend and president.[21]

Other circuit figures played a prominent role in the administration. Whether as a pay-off or not, Caleb Smith became secretary of the interior, and William P. Dole was named commissioner of Indian affairs, a position he held with distinction throughout Lincoln's presidency. When Smith began to consider resignation, Lincoln appointed John Usher as assistant secretary for the interior in December 1862. Lincoln then appointed Smith to the U.S. District Court in Indiana, and Usher became the secretary of the interior in January 1863. With the assistance of Leonard Swett, Seward was persuaded to accept Lincoln's invitation to serve as secretary of state, and he served the nation and Lincoln well during the entire administration. Keeping Davis's Chicago deal, Lincoln appointed Simon Cameron as secretary of war, a near disaster due to Cameron's corruption and incompetence.

Lincoln's capacity for magnanimity allowed him to appoint Edwin M. Stanton to replace Cameron. Forgotten—or more likely ignored—was the grievous insult Lincoln had suffered at the hands of Stanton the lawyer in Cincinnati in 1855 who shunned and insulted Lincoln in a patent case where they were supposed to serve as co-counsel.[22] Similarly, notwithstanding George B. McClellan's insulting behavior in the circuit days, Lincoln placed him—and kept him—in command of the Army of Potomac—even though the demeaning behavior intensified.

Lincoln's treatment of his one-time dueling opponent and long-time bitter political adversary, James Shields, provided a further demonstration of this magnanimity. The peripatetic Shields had landed in California as the Civil War erupted from where he sought appointment in the Union army. Accordingly, on August 19, 1861, Lincoln directed Cameron to appoint Shields a brigadier general of volunteers. Shields led a division against Stonewall Jackson in the Shenandoah Valley campaign. Lincoln then recommended him for a promotion to major general, but the Senate failed to confirm. This failure led Shields to go back to Lincoln and request transfer to California in order to gracefully withdraw from the service. Again, Lincoln obliged him, ending Shield's military career.[23]

Edward Bates was appointed attorney general. James Speed of Louisville, brother of Joshua, was appointed attorney general in December 1864,
replacing Bates, who had resigned. Swett served as an invaluable adviser
and emissary for the president, screening and negotiating appointments.
General John C. Frémont, in command in Missouri, had become a difficult
problem there for Lincoln in fall 1861, disobeying orders and issuing his
own emancipation order, a grievous mistake that threatened the loyalty
of Missouri and the other Border States. He had to be removed, but he resisted, evading Lincoln's orders of termination. Lincoln sent Swett on the
all-important mission to deliver these orders, an assignment he skillfully
executed. Swett's report to Lincoln details the difficulty he had getting the
order to Frémont through the barriers the general had raised. Swett used an
old circuit acquaintance on duty there, Urbana's Captain Ezekiel Boyden,
former mayor and past host of Lincoln, to accomplish this and successfully
delivered the order discharging the recalcitrant general.[24]

In July 1862, Lincoln summoned Swett to Washington for the sole purpose of listening to the president debate with himself over the critical issue
of emancipation, less than two months prior to its public announcement.
When Lincoln completed his monologue, he thanked Swett and excused
him without seeking his reaction. Later that year, Swett ran for Congress,
but John T. Stuart defeated him, part of the wave of anti-Lincoln backlash
in Illinois, following the September announcement of the Emancipation
Proclamation. Swett and his young son, Herbert, were present at Gettysburg,
Pennsylvania, for the address on November 19, 1863. Herbert's diary affirms
the resemblance of Lincoln in Swett as he noted that several people mistook
Swett for Lincoln. In 1864, Swett played a significant part in diffusing the
dissident Union party members in their effort to dump Lincoln.[25]

Before Lincoln left Illinois, William O. Stoddard boldly asked him for an
appointment as a secretary. With the competent and skilled John Hay and
John Nicolay already in place, Lincoln had no room for Stoddard then, so
he placed him in a position in the Department of the Interior and eventually
appointed him as the third secretary in the White House.[26] In the summer
of 1863, the anti-Lincoln sentiment continued to grow, aggravated by the
use of black troops in the war effort. James C. Conkling invited Lincoln to
speak at a mass rally in Springfield on September 3, 1863. He was unable to
do so and instead wrote an eloquent defense of the proclamation and the

use of the black troops. He read it first to Stoddard and then sent it to Conkling with instructions to "Read it slowly" at the rally, which Conkling did. The eloquent letter was praised nationwide and served to soften the outcry against the emancipation and Lincoln's use of black troops.[27]

William Orme became a brigadier general, commanding a brigade at Vicksburg. Jesse Fell, who helped Lincoln with screening and reviewing appointments, was appointed an army paymaster, as was Whitney. Army paymaster was a noncombatant post and the most lucrative military appointment the president could make without congressional confirmation. Benjamin F. James was appointed an examiner in the U.S. Patent Office in Washington. Lincoln appointed Samuel Parks to the territorial supreme court of Idaho in 1862. "Uncle Jimmy" Short became agent for the Round Valley Indian Reservation in California.[28] Asahel Gridley's family later claimed he had been offered the post of ambassador to the Court of Saint James and then later ambassador to Russia, both of which he declined.[29] Kirby Benedict came up for reappointment in 1862 to the supreme court of the Territory of New Mexico. Benedict had stayed in touch with David Davis through all of the controversy and sent him copies of the Santa Fe newspaper that praised Benedict, some of which he himself had written. His own appointment hanging, Davis took the time to write Lincoln from Clinton, on the circuit, urging him to reappoint Benedict, which Lincoln did over objections from New Mexico complaining of Benedict's excessive drinking. In December 1863, Lincoln received a report from New Mexico's secretary of state about Benedict's public drunkenness, but Lincoln refused the demands to remove Benedict: "He may imbibe to excess, but Benedict drunk knows more law than all others on the bench in New Mexico sober." President Andrew Johnson failed to reappoint him in 1866, and Benedict died, a hopeless alcoholic, broken and penniless in 1874.[30]

Lawrence Weldon, appointed U.S. District Attorney for the southern district of Illinois, prosecuted Charles Constable, by then circuit judge of Clark County. Constable had presided over the kidnapping prosecution of Union soldiers who were rounding up deserters in that county in 1863. Federal troops from Indianapolis surrounded the courthouse and arrested Constable from the bench, taking him to Springfield for the prosecution in 1863. Federal Judge Samuel Treat ultimately dismissed the charges. Constable died in 1865, probably a suicide.[31]

At Lincoln's request, in March 1861, Cameron appointed Thomas J. Pickett as agent for the government to manage Rock Island in the Mississippi River, and a year later, he was removed on charges he was selling timber and stone for his own profit. In April 1862, his protests of innocence reached Lincoln, who urged Usher to investigate. In April 1863, Lincoln, describing Pickett as "an old acquaintance and friend of mine," contacted the postmaster of the city of Rock Island, Illinois, and directed him to set up a hearing to take evidence from Pickett and his accusers. On May 4, he communicated to the quartermaster general, "It appears to me that Mr. Picketts [sic] fault is more apparent than real. It is my wish that he be restored to his place."[32]

Not all Lincoln's friends were rewarded. In 1860, Linder moved his practice to Chicago, a move that did not work well for him. Seeking a job in March 1864, he sent Lincoln an almost pitiful letter, obsequious in tone to his one-time equal and comrade at the bar. Since coming to Chicago, he said, "No prosperous wind has yet filled my sail. . . . You may consider me as a humble applicant. . . . Offer me a place. . . . I will accept it, however humble or insignificant it may be."[33] There is no evidence that Lincoln ever did so. In fairness to Lincoln, Linder had, in fact, opposed him politically consistently through the 1850s. A year earlier, Lincoln had assisted Linder with his son Daniel. In 1856, when Daniel was eighteen, he shot a companion in Paris, Illinois, which led to charges of assault that were later dismissed, a prosecution in which Lincoln had refused to participate out of deference to his old friend Usher. Daniel enlisted in the Confederate army and was taken prisoner. Linder entreated Lincoln to obtain his release. On December 22, 1863, Lincoln asked the officer in charge of Daniel's impoundment to have him brought to Lincoln, a request he renewed the next day. After Lincoln met with Daniel, he ordered his discharge, advising Linder, "Your son Dan, has just left me, with my order to the Sec. of War, to administer to him the oath of allegiance, discharge him & send him to you."[34] In Linder's *Reminiscences*, he discusses Lincoln but not Lincoln's treatment of him.

Lincoln's treatment of some of his closest supporters exposed an unattractive side of him that seems inconsistent with his warm public persona of the circuit. Lincoln seemed to take the support of those closest to him for granted; it wasn't necessary to reward them, because their loyalty was assured without reward. Lamon complained, "Lincoln's weak point is to cajole and pat his enemy's [sic] and to allow his friends to be sacrificed."[35] Jesse DuBois had been one of Lincoln's most steadfast supporters as early as Lincoln's first session in the legislature, yet he never received any appointment. In correspondence with Lincoln through the White House years, he quarreled about the president's appointments.[36] Shortly before Lincoln's death, he complained bitterly to Whitney, "Lincoln is a singular man and I must Confess I never knew him: He has for 30 years past just used me as a plaything to accomplish his own ends:—Knows no one and the road to favor is always open to his Enemies whilst the door is hymetically sealed to his old friends."[37]

Lincoln's disregard of Davis and Swett, his closest supporters, to whom he owed the most, is even more difficult to understand. The appointment of Davis to the U.S. Supreme Court was arguably Lincoln's most significant. However, he was very slow to reward his manager. When Lincoln was inaugurated, already one vacancy was on the Court; within sixty days were two more caused when Justice McLean of Ohio died and Alabama's Justice Campbell resigned. Admittedly, there were complications to the Davis candidacy. One was his own questioning of his ability given his background as only a trial judge in central Illinois, a concern that Lincoln might have shared: "I often doubt whether I could sustain myself on the Supreme Bench—it may be that I am not self-confident enough."[38] Abolitionists objected to Davis as too conservative. Additionally, there were the issues of reorganizing the Court and the geographic distribution of the judges. These latter arguments did not seem to hinder Norman Judd and Orville Browning of Illinois, both of whom intensely pursued the seat.[39] None of these were insurmountable obstacles if Lincoln was eager to reward his friend. Instead, he filled two of the three open seats with others, leaving his old friend hanging. Davis became agitated about this neglect. Surprisingly, there is no evidence Lincoln ever communicated with his old friend about any of this.

The Davis issue caused the "band of brothers" to once again form up for one of their own. Numerous lawyers of the Eighth Judicial Circuit wrote Lincoln and were particularly vocal in early 1862, including Clifton H. Moore, Weldon, Logan, Stuart, Treat, John M. Scott, William Butler, DuBois, Fell, Oliver Davis, and E. N. Powell. The Champaign County Bar and the Macon County Bar each sent petitions filled with names familiar to Lincoln.[40] The Bloomington lawyers were busy generating support for their judge. Lamon was there close to Lincoln, but even Lamon was unable to communicate with Lincoln about the appointment.[41] In an August 15, 1861, letter to Lincoln,

Swett was unrelenting in his advocacy of the Davis appointment: "Davis is my friend and if you can honor him I will consider it a favor to me and you can plead what is done for him as an estoppel to me." On January 28, 1862, he asserted, "No one has done more for you." In summer 1862, Swett even went to Washington to plead Davis's cause. Finally, on August 27, 1862, Lincoln advised Davis that he would make that appointment.[42]

Curiously, Swett never received any appointment. No one labored harder for longer on behalf of Lincoln than Swett. No one on the circuit was closer to Lincoln than Swett. Yet, Lincoln had displayed his calculating nature when he brushed aside Swett's defeat by Owen Lovejoy in 1856. In May 1861, his law partner Orme visited Lincoln to promote Swett and then reported to Swett, "The result was anything but satisfactory to me and lessened my ideas of Lincoln's character so far as his friendship for you is concerned. . . . [A]s I talked with him and mentioned your name, his face indicated somewhat a displeasure at the topic . . . but the whole interview seemed to be distasteful to him as far as the subject was concerned."[43]

Perhaps Lincoln took Swett's statement literally that the appointment of Davis to the Supreme Court would likewise satisfy any debt Lincoln owed Swett. Perhaps the pragmatic Swett's explanation is more credible:

> He never wasted anything, and would always give more to his enemies than he would to his friends, and the reason was, because he never had anything to spare, and in the close calculation of attaching the factions to him; he counted upon the abstract affection of his friends as an element to be offset against some gift with which he might appease his enemies. Hence, there was always some truth to the charge of his friends that he failed to reciprocate their devotion with his favors. The reason was that he had only so much to give away—"He always had more horses than oats."[44]

Lincoln had a great deal of patronage to dispense given the fact that the new Republican Party had swept into power. However, he had already awarded a disproportionate amount of patronage to Illinois. He told Orme, "Illinois already had over 50% of her share of appointments."[45] Whatever the reason, the gracious and generous Swett never complained about the failure of Lincoln to reward him.

When the Civil War broke out, Richard J. Oglesby raised ten companies and became a brigade commander fighting at Forts Henry and Donelson before being seriously wounded at Corinth, Mississippi. He continued to serve after recuperating until he ran for governor of Illinois in 1864. He was swept into office, the first of three times he was elected. His forceful leadership caused racist Illinois to become the first state to ratify the Thirteenth Amendment, constitutionally affirming the Emancipation Proclamation, a significant endorsement of Lincoln's momentous edict coming from his home state.[46] The successes of the war and the support of Union troops created a huge reversal of the electorates' attitude toward Lincoln, who easily won reelection over McClellan that fall. He carried Illinois but again only eight of the seventeen counties of the circuit. McLean County again had the largest plurality, and the biggest vote against Lincoln was in Shelby County.[47]

Other of Lincoln's friends, current and former, went varied ways. As the circuits became reshaped, several of Lincoln's contemporaries became circuit judges, Oliver Davis and Gillespie in 1861 and John M. Scott in 1862. Anthony Thornton, elected to the Illinois Supreme Court in 1870, eventually became the first president of the Illinois State Bar Association.[48] Albert T. Bledsoe, Lincoln's political mentor from the 1840s, who had left Springfield to teach at the University of Mississippi, taught at the University of Virginia, from which he resigned to accept a commission in the Confederate army. He eventually became assistant secretary of war in the Jefferson Davis administration. During the war in 1865, Lincoln issued a pass to Bledsoe's wife to allow her to reenter the Confederate lines, returning from a trip to the north to buy clothes for her children. Bledsoe was a bitter critic of his old friend Lincoln. His extensive writings made him one of the most prominent defenders of the Southern position on slavery and secession. He remained steadfast until his death in 1877.[49]

Throughout his presidency, Lincoln had visitors from the circuit, recalling simpler days back in Illinois. Benjamin Harris from Champaign recalled that in May 1861, he visited to encourage Lincoln during those early bleak days of the war. He went to the White House first and saw Mary Lincoln and the couple's two sons. He attended a cabinet meeting the next day at Lincoln's invitation that led to a dinner that night at the home of Montgomery Blair, a center of influence on the national scene. In March 1865, Henry P. H. Bromwell and Paris lawyer James Steele called on Lincoln at the White House, where Secretary of State Seward joined them. To the great amusement of all, Lincoln proceeded to recount the story of the debate between the

Marshall lawyer and the Kansas doctor in Grandview during the Frémont campaign in 1856. As part of his telling of the story, Lincoln mimicked the speakers to the great amusement of all. Whitney, another visitor of Lincoln in Washington, related, "At the White House his approachability, manners, habits, and behavior were the same as at Danville, Urbana, or Springfield."[50]

Like hundreds of thousands who mourned the loss of associates, friends, and loved ones, Lincoln endured personal loss throughout the war. On May 24, 1861, Elmer Ellsworth, his law clerk and political aid, entered a hotel in Alexandria, Virginia, to remove a Confederate flag that could be seen from the Capitol and was causing particular offense to Union supporters. The proprietor of the hotel stepped forward and shot the unguarded Ellsworth, who was given a hero's funeral in the East Room of the White House. Lincoln was reduced to tears by the death of his young friend, to whose parents he wrote, "In the untimely loss of your noble son, our affliction here is scarcely less than your own."[51]

On June 3, Lincoln lost a fierce rival. Douglas died, his health broken by exhaustion and probably excessive drinking as he barnstormed across the country, imploring support for the Union. In his last speech on May 1, Douglas declared, "Every man must be for the United States or against it. There can be no neutrals in this war, only patriots—or traitors." Lincoln learned by telegram that same day from Chicago of Douglas's death: "Hon Stephen A. Douglas is dead." The rivalry of more than twenty years' duration was over. In November 1861 at the request of Douglas's widow, Adele, Lincoln intervened on behalf of Douglas's minor children to save property of theirs in the South from confiscation. Two years later, he saved Adele's brother, Captain James M. Cutts, from discharge for conduct unbecoming an officer. The charges included fighting with a superior officer and peeking "at a comely lady in his hotel." Lincoln had the penalty reduced to a reprimand, advising Cutler to avoid dogfights: "Even killing the dog would not cure the bite." He privately referred to the young officer as "Count Peepers."[52]

Several circuit men close to Lincoln fell in battle. Baker raised a regiment in California. Lincoln attempted to appoint him as a brigadier general of volunteers in July 1861, which Baker declined because it would have required resignation from the U.S. Senate. Instead, he took the rank of colonel, which allowed him to retain his seat. On October 21, 1861, Baker was killed at the Battle of Ball's Bluff, forty miles from Washington. Stoddard noted that Lincoln "loved him like a brother and mourned his untimely death bitterly." At the time of Baker's death, there were questions about $10,000 that was unaccounted for in the raising of his regiment.[53] In summer 1862, Lincoln's young professional and political associate Harvey Hogg returned to his native state of Tennessee as a Union officer and was killed leading a cavalry charge in Bolivar, Tennessee. On December 5, 1862, Lincoln's old friend with one arm and one good eye, William McCullough, was killed covering a cavalry retreat in Coffeeville, Mississippi. His young daughter Fannie, whom Lincoln remembered from his time in McLean County, was overcome with grief. At the suggestion of David Davis, Lincoln wrote a touching letter of condolence that spoke to many besides Fannie: "You are sure to be happy again. To know this, which certainly is true, will make you some less miserable now. I've had experience enough to know what I say; and you need only to believe it, to feel better at once."[54] In 1862, Oscar Harmon raised a regiment of Illinois volunteers and as colonel led them at Prairieville, Stone's River, Chickamauga, Missionary Ridge, and Knoxville before he was killed during an assault on Kennesaw Mountain in January 1864. His death visibly affected Lincoln; when he received the news from the fallen soldier's brother, the saddened President expressed concern for Harmon's widow, Elizabeth.[55]

April 1865

Robert Latham wrote Lincoln in March 1865 about the remarkable progress of the town bearing his name, reporting a population of twenty-eight hundred residents and the founding of the university there also bearing the Lincoln name.[56] This letter was never answered. Robert E. Lee had surrendered his Army of Northern Virginia on Palm Sunday, April 9. Two days later, Lincoln delivered a speech from a window in the White House, in which he discussed the problems of reconstruction and suggested the possibilities of granting "the elective franchise . . . to the colored man." Lincoln's attitude toward citizenship rights for African Americans had transformed since 1858. In 1864, he had proposed that certain black men be allowed to vote, a theme he advanced in the speech of April 11. The audience that evening included John Wilkes Booth, who stated, "That is the last speech he will ever make."[57] That same day, Lincoln issued a pass for Lamon to go to Richmond, Virginia, to work on arrangements for a reconstruction convention.

Lamon had served as Lincoln's self-appointed bodyguard in Washington, although there was no formal appointment. Because of his role as marshal, he understood more than most the grave danger that hung over Lincoln. Lamon was always heavily armed, frequently patrolling the White House grounds at night, even sleeping on the floor outside of Lincoln's room. He constantly warned Lincoln and urged him to mend his careless ways as to his own safety. He even tendered his resignation to get Lincoln's attention when Lincoln had gone unattended to the theater.

On the eve of his departure for Richmond on April 13, Lamon visited Lincoln in the company of John Usher. Lamon attempted to elicit Lincoln's promise that "he would not go out after night when I was gone, particularly to the theatre." Lamon never recovered from the guilt caused by his absence at Ford's Theatre the next night.[58]

On April 14, Lincoln had a long day, including a cabinet meeting, during which he wrote eleven brief notes to various people including Dole, commissioner of Indian affairs, and James Speed relative to the resignation of his appointee, circuit lawyer Parks.[59] Later, he was once again visited by friends and associates from the circuit. Governor Oglesby arrived that day to seek reduction of the Illinois troop quotas. After checking into the Willard Hotel, he, I. N. Haynie, and Decatur attorney Sheridan Wait walked to the White House, arriving a little after 5:00. The president, his wife, and son Tad had just returned from a carriage ride. Lincoln spotted his old friends and called them to join him. They followed him into his quarters, where they discussed the war and the coming peace. Lincoln protested as Oglesby proposed leaving and invited him to sit down while he read from the popular humorist Petroleum V. Nasby. Lincoln laughed and joked as he read it. Finally, after refusing to be interrupted by three increasingly insistent calls to dinner, Lincoln allowed Oglesby to take his leave, and they shook hands, Lincoln relaxed and contented. "We saw him no more," said Oglesby later.

That evening, Oglesby heard the terrible news at the Willard within a half an hour after Booth's shot. Oglesby and Haynie rushed to the Petersen House, where Oglesby was admitted at 11 P.M. to that now-hallowed room. He, along with a number of others, stayed by the fallen leader's side until he drew his last breath at 7:22 A.M., April 15, when Stanton uttered the awful truth, "Now he belongs to the Ages."[60] It was altogether appropriate that Oglesby, the governor of Illinois and a denizen of the old Eighth Judicial Circuit, was

Local ministers in Bloomington called an "Indignation Meeting" for Easter Sunday afternoon, April 16, 1865, behind the McLean County Courthouse in shocked response to Lincoln's death. McLean County Historical Society.

there. He was surrogate for all the people and institutions of central Illinois to whom Lincoln had given so much and, perhaps more important, who had given so much to Lincoln. That afternoon, the president's son Robert Lincoln telegraphed Davis, "Please come at once to Washington and take charge of my father's affairs." Davis did so, becoming the estate's administrator.[61]

The circuit, like the rest of the nation, was stunned by the horrific news, except that this was the murder of a respected and admired friend. In Bloomington, an "Indignation Meeting," organized by local ministers, drew about five thousand people to mourn at the courthouse on Sunday, April 16. Fell presided that day; the speakers included Gridley and Swett. The *Pantagraph* edged its columns in black. On April 18, the paper said, "Mr. Lincoln has been so well known personally by so large a number of our people, and has so long been regarded as one of our own people, and has so long been regarded as one of our own citizens, that his death seemed to fall with the most crushing severity upon our inhabitants."[62]

Urbana recorded similar shock and dismay. Joseph O. Cunningham in the *Gazette* on April 21 described the community response to the calamity: "Saturday April 15th was the most mournful day ever witnessed in Urbana." The following Wednesday, businesses closed, funeral bunting draped homes and businesses, and virtually the entire community attended the memorial services. Cunningham described the county's loss: "He was not only our President and Chief Magistrate, but our fellow citizen. Since the early settlement of this county, he has, from his frequent visits upon professional business, been intimately and well known to very many—his great kindness and urbanity of manner here, as everywhere else, had won for him a warm corner in every heart."[63]

The Final Train Ride

The Lincoln funeral train left Washington on April 21. On May 3, it came to Bloomington from Chicago on its long, deliberate passage from Washington to Springfield. An arch placed over the track bore the inscription, "Go to thy Rest." A *Pantagraph* reporter rode the train from Chicago, which departed at 10 P.M. It was scheduled to arrive at 3 A.M. but was two hours late. Eight thousand people met the train in Bloomington to pay their last respects to their revered, now martyred, friend.[64]

The train on the tracks that Lincoln had ridden so frequently continued in a southwesterly direction through the Eighth Judicial Circuit. It reached Atlanta at 6:00 A.M. as the sun rose over the prairies he had traversed for so many years. A grandstand had been erected on the side of the track he had helped bring to the town. The train reached Lincoln at 7:00, and a large crowd sang a requiem as the train passed the black-draped depot and went under an arch bearing the legend, "With malice toward none, with charity for all." It proceeded on to Elkhart, passing under a span that simply stated, "Ours the cross, thine the crown."[65] The train continued, returning Lincoln to the circuit for the last time. Springfield mourners flocked by the casket for twenty-four hours, and the next day, Lincoln was buried in Oak Ridge Cemetery.

The prairie that had delivered him up to save the nation now received his remains.

NOTES

BIBLIOGRAPHY

INDEX

NOTES

Abbreviations

ALPLC Robert Todd Lincoln Collection of the Papers of Abraham Lincoln, Library of Congress, Washington, DC.

ALPLM Abraham Lincoln Presidential Library and Museum, Springfield, Illinois.

CW Lincoln, Abraham. *The Collected Works of Abraham Lincoln.* Edited by Roy P. Basler. 9 vols. New Brunswick, NJ: Rutgers University Press, 1953–55.

DDFP David Davis Family Papers. Manuscripts Division, Abraham Lincoln Presidential Library and Museum, Springfield, Illinois.

HI Wilson, Douglas L., and Rodney O. Davis, eds. *Herndon's Informants: Letters, Interviews, and Statements about Abraham Lincoln.* Urbana: University of Illinois Press, 1998.

HL Herndon, William H., and Jesse W. Weik. *Herndon's Lincoln: The True Story of a Great Life . . . the History and Personal Recollections of Abraham Lincoln..* Ed. Douglas L. Wilson and Rodney O. Davis. Urbana: University of Illinois Press, 2006.

LDD Miers, Earl Schenk, ed. *Lincoln Day by Day, a Chronology, 1809–1865.* 3 vols. Washington, DC: Lincoln's Sesquicentennial Commission, 1960.

LPAL Benner, Martha L., and Cullom Davis, eds. *The Law Practice of Abraham Lincoln Complete Documentary Edition.* DVD-ROM. Champaign: University of Illinois Press, 2000. Springfield: Illinois Historic Preservation Agency, 2009, http://www.lawpracticeofabrahamlincoln.org.

PAL Stowell, Daniel W. *The Papers of Abraham Lincoln, Legal Documents and Cases.* 4 vols. Charlottesville: University of Virginia Press, Illinois Historic Preservation Agency, 2008.

UIL Illinois History and Lincoln Collection. University of Illinois Library, Urbana, Illinois.

Foreword

1. Fraker, "Real Lincoln Highway," 76–97.
2. [Scott], "Lincoln on the Stump."

3. Ibid.
4. Ibid.
5. Ibid.
6. Hiram W. Beckwith, "Lincoln: Personal Recollections of Him, His Contemporaries and Law Practice in Eastern Illinois," *Chicago Tribune*, December 29, 1895.
7. Zall, *Abe Lincoln Laughing*, 118–19; Whitney, *Life on the Circuit*, 179. Treat told this to Henry Clay Whitney. Lincoln also told Whitney that John S. Hacker of Union County, whom he had known in the legislature, was the source of almost all his funny stories. Ibid.
8. Scott, "Lincoln on the Stump."
9. Leonard Swett, speech, "The Life of Lincoln," *Chicago Times*, October 23, 1887. Swett delivered this speech at the dedication of the St. Gaudens statue of Lincoln in Chicago.
10. G. W. Harris, "My Recollections of Abraham Lincoln," 15.
11. William H. Herndon to Isaac Newton Arnold, Springfield, Illinois, October 24, 1883, Herndon Collection, Chicago History Museum.
12. David Davis, interview with Herndon, September 20, 1866, in Wilson and Davis, *Herndon's Informants*, 350.
13. Sandburg, *Abraham Lincoln*, 2:297.
14. David Davis, interview with Herndon, September 20, 1866, in Wilson and Davis, *Herndon's Informants*, 349.
15. Whitney, *Lincoln the Citizen*, 189.
16. Herndon and Weik, *Herndon's Lincoln*, 257.
17. David Davis, interview with Herndon, 349.
18. William H. Herndon to Jesse W. Weik, Springfield, Illinois, February 24, 1887, Herndon-Weik Collection.
19. Leonard Swett, lecture delivered in Chicago, February 20, 1876, *Chicago Times*, February 21, 1876.

Introduction

1. Duis, *Good Old Times*, 287. This anecdote is part of a biographical sketch of David Davis in Duis. It is not attributed nor is the incident dated. The scene described would have been in the spring when the rivers were swollen; it would have been between 1848 and 1853, the period of Davis's tenure as judge while Decatur was in the circuit. The description of Davis's weight elsewhere in the book may raise a question as to the mobility demonstrated in this incident. Pictures of Davis when he first took the bench show him to lack the great girth he carried later in his life. Davis's stamina and physical ability during this period are noted in a letter to his wife where he reports helping hay for three or four hours a day for two or three days. David Davis to Sarah Davis, July 23, 1853, DDFP.
2. Reference, Court Structure, Circuit Courts, *LPAL*.
3. Fehrenbacher, *Prelude to Greatness*, 5 (original emphasis).
4. Ibid., 9, 10.

1. A New Country

1. Fehrenbacher, *Prelude to Greatness*, 17.
2. "Maps of Circuit, 1845–47," and "Maps of the Circuit, 1847–53," *LPAL*; Moses, *Illinois Historical*, 2:1137, 1156.
3. Howard, *Illinois*, 142; J. White, *Origin and Evolution of Counties*, 35 (map).
4. A. T. Rice, *Reminiscences*, 308.
5. Davis, "Lincoln and Macon County," 64, 65.
6. Ibid., 73.
7. Kyle, *Abraham Lincoln in Decatur*, 18–20.
8. Ibid., 21, 22.
9. Ibid., 22; Dean T. Austin, about William Warnick, letter to Guy C. Fraker, November 13, 2004.
10. "Petition to Macon County Commissions Court," May 26, 1839, *CW*, 1:2; "Appraisal of an Estray," December 16, 1830, *CW*, 1:3.
11. Kyle, *Abraham Lincoln in Decatur*, 23–25.
12. Ibid., 29.
13. Ibid., 32, 33.
14. Burlingame, *Abraham Lincoln*, 1:56–57.
15. B. P. Thomas, *Lincoln's New Salem*, 41–71. This small volume remains the best treatment of Lincoln's time in New Salem.
16. "Autobiography Written for John L. Scripps," June 1860, *CW*, 4:65.
17. Steiner, *Honest Calling*. See Steiner's excellent treatment of Lincoln's legal training, 26–54.
18. *HL*, 78, 79; H. E. Dummer interview, [1865–66], item 331, *HI*, 442.
19. "Communication to the People of Sangamon County," March 6, 1832, *CW*, 1:8.
20. Burlingame, *Abraham Lincoln*, 1:97.
21. Winkle, *Young Eagle*, 95.
22. Ibid., 321; Simon, *Lincoln's Preparation for Greatness*, 49.
23. The two senators were Job Fletcher and Archer Herndon, the members of the General Assembly in addition to Lincoln were John Dawson, William Elkin, Ninian Edwards, Andrew McCormick, Daniel Stone, and Robert L. Wilson.
24. Winkle, *Young Eagle*, 156.
25. Faragher, *Sugar Creek*, 33; Angle, *Here I Have Lived*, 4, 35.
26. Power, *History of the Early Settlers*, 41, 43; Harper, *Lincoln and the Press*, 3; Burlingame, *Abraham Lincoln*, 1:139–45.
27. Patton, *Glory to God and the Sucker Democracy*, 1:1–135; Krause, Boston, and Stowell, *Now They Belong to the Ages*, 39.
28. Simon, *Lincoln's Preparation for Greatness*, 290; Angle, *Here I Have Lived*, 109.
29. Winkle, *Young Eagle*, 121, 166, 169, 170, 212. Little note has been taken of Lincoln's lifelong relationship with Butler, remarkable for its instability with its alternating closeness and discord. Burlingame, *Abraham Lincoln*, 1:213, 2:81.
30. Krause, Boston, and Stowell, *Now They Belong to the Ages*, 108.
31. Garraty, Carnes, and Berwinger, "Edward Dickinson Baker," in *America National Biography*, 2:7, 8.

32. Selby, *Historical Encyclopedia*, 2:1.650; Krause, *From Log Cabins to Temples of Justice*, 68; F. S. Barringer, *Tour of Historic Springfield*, 24.
33. "Address before the Young Men's Lyceum of Springfield, Illinois," January 27, 1838, *CW*, 1:108–15.
34. Power, *History of the Early Settlers*, 52; Winkle, *Young Eagle*, 160. Winkle writes a concise description of the intricate network of Kentuckians in Springfield. 207.
35. Winkle, *Young Eagle*, 208–12.
36. *HL*, 122; Duff, *A. Lincoln, Prairie Lawyer*, 35.
37. Duff, *A. Lincoln, Prairie Lawyer*, 51–62; *People v. Truett*, L04327, *LPAL*; *Early v. Bradford et al.*, L03212, *LPAL*.
38. *Logan v. Adams*, L00410, *LPAL*; Angle, *Here I Have Lived*, 68.
39. *People v. Cordell*, L05536, *LPAL*; *Abrams v. Cordell*, L05546, *LPAL*.
40. *Kellogg v. Crain*, L01234, *LPAL*; Hill, *Lincoln the Lawyer*, 80; Duff, *A. Lincoln, Prairie Lawyer*, 199.
41. Jesse W. Fell to David Davis, December 15, 1885, *Illinois State Journal*, January 14, 1886; AL to John T. Stuart, January 20 and 23, 1841, *CW*, 1:228, 229.
42. Krause, Boston, and Stowell, *Now They Belong to the Ages*, 45; *HL*, 122.
43. AL to John T. Stuart, March 30, 1861, *CW*, 4:303; AL to Hanson A. Risley, March 6, 1865, *CW*, 8:337.
44. Duff, *A. Lincoln, Prairie Lawyer*, 78, 80; *HL*, 168.
45. *People v. Trailor and Trailor*, L04765, *LPAL*; Duff, *A. Lincoln, Prairie Lawyer*, 81–85; AL to Joshua Speed, June 19, 1841, *CW*, 1:254; "The Trailor Murder Case," April 15, 1846, *CW*, 2:371; *Trailor v. Radford*, L04679, *LPAL*; *Trailor v. Radford*, L04680, *LPAL*; *Traylor and Myer v. Saunders*, L04681, *LPAL*. The letter to Speed and the 1846 newspaper account are Lincoln's description of the bizarre case.
46. *PAL*, 1:139–90. These pages are a complete, detailed description and summary of that session.
47. *Klein et al. v. Mather*, L00864, *LPAL*.
48. *Memorials of the Life and Character of Stephen T. Logan*, 29; David Davis to Sarah Davis, March 23, 1851, DDFP.
49. Duff, *A. Lincoln, Prairie Lawyer*, 80; *HL*, 168; Lincoln quoted in Burlingame, *Abraham Lincoln*, 1:186.
50. Abraham Lincoln, March 26, 1862, quoted in Stowell, "Almost a Father to Me," 1. *Nisi prius* means a trial lawyer.
51. Duff, *A. Lincoln, Prairie Lawyer*, 104, 105; Donald, *Lincoln's Herndon*, 101, 126.
52. Donald, *Lincoln's Herndon*, 100–104, 71.
53. Duff, *A. Lincoln, Prairie Lawyer*, 108; Donald, *Lincoln's Herndon*, 37.
54. Turley Cemetery, rural Elkhart, Illinois, grave site of A. L. Dalby; *Dalby v. Hickox*, L00950, *LPAL*; *St. Louis Alton & Chicago Railroad v. Dalby*, L01027, *LPAL*.
55. *Menard County Illinois v. Jones and Manning*, L05815, *LPAL*; *Lesure & Bliss v. Menard County Illinois*, L03843, *LPAL* and L00369, *LPAL*; *Petersburg Illinois v. Maupin et al*, L00402 and L00403, *LPAL*; *Petersburg Illinois v. Metzger*, L00371, *LPAL*; *Petersburg Illinois v. Moon*, L00406, *LPAL*; *Petersburg Illinois v. Pemberton and Gregory*, L00404, *LPAL*; *Petersburg Illinois v. Pillsbury et al.*, L00405, *LPAL*; *Petersburg Illinois v. Wright*, L00360, *LPAL*; *Shields v. Taylor*, L00143, *LPAL*.

56. Duff, *A. Lincoln, Prairie Lawyer*, 100.
57. *HL*, 121.
58. Donald, *Lincoln's Herndon*, 126, quoting Henry C. Whitney to Herndon, July 18, 1887, Herndon-Weik Collection.
59. Review by author of Vermilion County Circuit Court cases in *LPAL*.
60. "Recommendation," May 28, 1862, *CW*, 5:247.
61. Hamand, *Ward Hill Lamon*, 50. This thoroughly documented thesis offers the most complete biography of Lamon.
62. Pratt, "Abraham Lincoln in Bloomington," 56; R. R. Wilson, *Intimate Memories of Lincoln*, 113; *Pantagraph* (Bloomington, Illinois), April 20, 1859; Hamand, *Ward Hill Lamon*, 50, 52, 56.
63. Lamon to AL, August 25, 1860, *ALPLC*.
64. Review by author of circuit court cases in Edgar, Vermilion, Coles, and Shelby Counties in *LPAL*.
65. J. Gillespie, introduction, 9–20; Palmer, *Bench and Bar of Illinois*, 1:181.
66. AL to Usher Linder, February 20, 1848, *CW*, 1:453; AL to Usher Linder, March 22, 1848, *CW*, 1:457–58.
67. King, *Lincoln's Manager*, 83; C. H. Coleman, *Abraham Lincoln and Coles County*, 124.
68. Eckley, "Lincoln's Intimate Friend," 31; Wheeler, "Road to Illinois."
69. Whitney, *Life on the Circuit*, 85.
70. AL to John T. Stuart, February 14, 1839, *CW*, 1:143.
71. Simon, *Lincoln's Preparation for Greatness*, 168.
72. Ibid., 162–64; *Journal of the House of Representatives of the State of Illinois*, 1839, 242.
73. L. B. Stringer, *History of Logan County*, 149.
74. Fowkes, *History of Christian County*, 2:654; Drennan, Gardner, and Broverman, *Illinois Sesquicentennial Edition*, 39, 40.
75. Edward D. Baker to William Butler, January 26, 1839, *CW*, 1:138, 139; AL to William Butler, January 26, 1839, *CW*, 1:139, 140.

2. As Happy as He Could Be

1. Thomas, *"Lincoln's Humor,"* chapter 10, "Abraham Lincoln Country Lawyer," and chapter 11, "Lincoln and the Courts, 1854–61" (139–88), which contain excellent descriptions of life and practice on the Eighth Judicial Circuit during the Lincoln era.
2. Krause, *From Log Cabins to Temples of Justice*, 5–7. This small book contains essays with photos of every Illinois courthouse in which Lincoln appeared.
3. Krause, *Judging Lincoln*, 62, 63.
4. King, *Lincoln's Manager*, 1–63. This excellent biography of David Davis contains graphic descriptions of circuit travel from 1849 to 1852, 70–88, and from 1853 to 1861, 85–98. The home was located at the site of today's Davis Mansion State Historic Site. 69.
5. Ibid., 76. Their loving relationship shows through clearly in their touching correspondence while Davis traveled the circuit.

6. Sarah Davis to David Davis, December 2, 1850, DDFP.

7. King, *Lincoln's Manager*, 69.

8. David Davis to Sarah Davis, August 8, 1857, DDFP.

9. *Urbana (IL) Union*, April 23, 1857, 3, and April 15, 1858, 3.

10. Whitney, *Life on the Circuit*, 67–69.

11. King, *Lincoln's Manager*, 87–95, 91.

12. "Resolutions on the Death of David B. Campbell," April 17, 1855, *CW*, 2:310; April 9 and 17, 1855, *LDD*, 2:142.

13. Duff, *A. Lincoln, Prairie Lawyer*, 179.

14. Schnell, *Stovepipe Hat and Quill Pen*, is another in the series of small books that the Papers of Abraham Lincoln published. Schnell's book is a detailed inventory and description of the items Lincoln used in his practice.

15. Thomas, *Abraham Lincoln*, 92–94; Thomas, *"Lincoln's Humor,"* 117–20; Duff, *A. Lincoln, Prairie Lawyer*, 168–220. Duff devotes pages 168–220 to trips around the circuit.

16. Burlingame, *Abraham Lincoln*, 322–32.

17. *News Gazette* (Urbana-Champaign, Illinois), February 12, 1945; Urbana-Lincoln Hotel menu notes, Champaign County Historical Archives; Obituary of Henry Mann, *Clinton (IL) Transcript*, March 20, 1891; Felts, "A. Lincoln in Piatt," 50; R. R. Wilson, *Intimate Memories*, 141; Stringer, *History of Logan County*, 216.

18. Davis and Wilson, *Lincoln-Douglas Debates*, 10.

19. Sandburg, *Abraham Lincoln*, 2:71, 72; *Memories of Abraham Lincoln in Edgar County*, 22.

20. Donald, *Lincoln*, 105.

21. Pratt, *Personal Finances*, 28; Friedman, *Inflation Calculator*.

22. Swett, *David Davis*, 4; People v. Morgan and Craig, L01996, *LPAL*.

23. Thomas, *"Lincoln's Humor,"* 3–22.

24. Pratt, *Illinois as Lincoln Knew It*, 30.

25. Ostendorf, *Lincoln's Photographs*, 8, 9. Richter, *Lincoln*, 128. Richter cites the date as "April 1858."

26. Cunningham, "Some Recollections of Abraham Lincoln," 13; Ostendorf, *Lincoln's Photographs*, 10, 11.

27. Stowell, *In Tender Consideration*, 37, 38.

28. Whitney, *Life on the Circuit*, 436; King, *Lincoln's Manager*, 69.

29. King, *Lincoln's Manager*, 75; David Davis to William Orme, May 2, 1862, Papers of William Orme, UIL. In the Davis letter, he advises that Sarah Davis is accompanying him to Danville.

30. AL to Mrs. Orville H. Browning, April 1, 1838, *CW*, 1:17.

31. Phillips, *Abraham Lincoln by Some Men Who Knew Him*, 157, 158.

32. Pratt, *Illinois as Lincoln Knew It*, 34.

33. Interview of David Davis, September 20, 1866, item 242, *HI*, 349, 350.

34. Moses Allen to David Davis, November 28, 1847, DDFP.

35. Browne, *Abraham Lincoln*, 2:84.

36. Entry for April 11, 1845, *LDD*, 1:249; Stringer, *History of Logan County*, 319.

37. David Davis interview, September 20, 1866, item 241, *HI*, 349, 350.

38. Ibid., 348.

39. *HL*, 348–61.

40. Phillips, *Abraham Lincoln by Some Men Who Knew Him*, 151.

41. Elizabeth Todd Edwards interview, 1865–66, item 332, *HI*, 443, 445.

42. Ninian Edwards interview, 1865–66, item 334, *HI*, 446.

43. Holzer, *Lincoln as I Knew Him*, 75.

44. Wilson and Davis, *Honor's Voice*, 188.

45. Leonard Swett to William H. Herndon, January 17, 1866, item 24, *HI*, 162, 166.

46. Guelzo, "Come Outer and Community Men," 23; Harris, *Lincoln's Rise to the Presidency*, 16.

47. Pratt, *Illinois as Lincoln Knew It*, 33.

48. Whitney, *Life on the Circuit*, 122.

49. See Robert Bray's *Reading with Lincoln*, an excellent treatment of what Lincoln read and its impact on him.

50. *HL*, 257; Frank, *Lincoln as a Lawyer*, 168; AL to William H. Herndon, July 10, 1848, *CW*, 1:487; Burlingame, *Abraham Lincoln*, 1:327.

51. John T. Stuart interview, December 20, 1866, item 409, *HI*, 519.

3. Purely and Entirely a Case Lawyer

1. William H. Herndon quoted in Donald, *Lincoln*, 157.

2. AL to Albert G. Hodges, April 4, 1864, *CW*, 7:281.

3. John Hanks interview by William H. Herndon, 1865–66, item 344, *HI*, 453, 457.

4. Caleb Carman to William H. Herndon, November 30, 1866, item 317, *HI*, 429; Joseph Gillespie to WHH, January 31, 1866, item 132, *HI*, 180, 183; Samuel C. Parks to WHH, March 25, 1866, item 180, *HI*, 238; John T. Stuart, WHH interview, December 20, 1866, item 409, HI, 519, and late June 1865, item 46, HI, 63–64; Orlando Ficklin to WHH, June 25, 1865, item 40, *HI*, 58.

5. AL to Mary Speed, September 27, 1841, *CW*, 1:259.

6. AL to Joshua Speed, August 24, 1855, *CW*, 2:320.

7. *In Re Bryant et al.*, L00714, *LPAL*. Mark E. Steiner excellent treatment fully analyzes this case in *An Honest Calling*, chapter 5, 102–36.

8. Hendrick and Hendrick, *On the Illinois Frontier*, 134.

9. Weik, "Lincoln and the Matson Negroes," 756.

10. Ibid.; *People v. Kern*, L01267, *LPAL*; *People v. Pond*, L00335, *LPAL*; *People v. Scott*, L01266, *LPAL*.

11. J. E. Davis, *Frontier Illinois*, 54, 182, 167.

12. Cole, "Era of the Civil War," 3:225.

13. Ibid., 3:335, 337.

14. *Bailey v. Cromwell and McNaughton*, L01213, *LPAL*.

15. *Dungey v. Spencer*, L00567, *LPAL*. PAL 3 devotes chapter 39, 133–48, to this case.

16. *Patterson v. Edwards*, L0884, *LPAL*; *Sanders et al. v. Dunham*, L01583, *LPAL*; *Benson v. Mayo*, L00760, *LPAL*.

17. David Davis to Sarah Davis, November 3, 1851, DDFP; *Smith v. Campbell*, L02072, *LPAL*.

18. "Speech Delivered to the Springfield Washington Temperance Society," *CW*, 1:271.

19. *People v. Sickler et al.,* L04956, *LPAL; Pearl & Pearl v. Graham et al.,* L01114, *LPAL; People v. Pearl,* L01804, *LPAL. PAL* 2 devotes chapter 34, 460–79, to these cases.

20. *Reynolds & Fuller v. Steele et al.,* L01681, *LPAL; McClatchey v. Sits and Roney et al.,* L01960, *LPAL.*

21. *People v. Shurtleff et al.,* L05599, *LPAL;* "Statement of Andrew H. Goodpasture," March 31, 1869, item 458, *HI,* 572.

22. *PAL,* 2:425; *Alexander v. Brown & Wilcox,* L01203, *LPAL.*

23. Review of cases by author, *LPAL.*

24. Burlingame, *Abraham Lincoln,* 1:332; King, *Lincoln's Manager,* 89.

25. "Fragment: Notes for a Law Lecture," *CW,* 2:81.

26. Ibid.

27. Wakefield, *How Lincoln Became President,* 102; *Browning & Bushnell v. Price and Fell,* L05560, *LPAL.*

28. *Campbell v. Allin,* L01635, *LPAL.*

29. Ibid.; *Atchison for the Use of Allen v. Pekin, Illinois,* L01181, *LPAL; Hamilton v. Pekin, Illinois,* L01259, *LPAL; Pekin, Illinois v. H. Myers & Co.,* L01102, *LPAL; Daven v. Armington,* L01090, *LPAL; Armington v. Skates,* L01060, *LPAL.*

30. *PAL,* 1:xxxv, xxxvi.

31. *Allin v. Douglas,* L05732, *LPAL.*

32. Table 15, "Standard Portrait, Common Subjects: Breach of Contract," *LPAL.*

33. Horwitz, *Transformation of American Law,* 160–210; Simpson, introduction, xiv.

34. Frank, *Lincoln as a Lawyer,* 141.

35. *Dubois v. Ryan,* L00784; *LPAL; Dubois et al. v. Wise,* L0786 *LPAL;* Biographical Directory, *PAL,* 4:345; Simon, *Lincoln's Preparation for Greatness,* 82; Boas, *Seaport Autographs,* item 26, 16.

36. Stowell, *In Tender Consideration,* 28.

37. *PAL,* 2:163; *Popejoy v. Wilson,* L02070, *LPAL.*

38. *Jacobus v. Kitchell,* L001063, *LPAL.*

39. *PAL,* 1:43; *Dobbs v. Dobbs,* L01231, *LPAL; Helmick v. Helmick,* L01914, *LPAL.*

40. *Dunn v. Carle,* L01339, *LPAL; Dunn v. Carle,* L01340, *LPAL; People et al. v. Dunn v. Carle,* L01340, *LPAL.*

41. *PAL,* 2:377, 382.

42. *St. Louis, Alton & Chicago Railroad Company v. Dalby,* L01017, *LPAL; Browning v. Springfield, Illinois,* L02794, *LPAL.*

43. *Fleming v. Crothers,* L01566, *LPAL;* Duff, *A. Lincoln, Prairie Lawyer,* 437–42.

44. *Evans v. Briggs,* L01236, *LPAL; Hall v. Briggs,* L01238, *LPAL; Labago v. Briggs,* L01239, *LPAL; Haines v. Jones and Gaither,* L01255, *LPAL; Finley v. Keyes,* L01763, *LPAL; Taylor v. Red,* L00438, *LPAL; Young v. Stevens,* L01613, *LPAL; Gaines v. West,* L00286, *LPAL.*

45. *Adams v. Woodford County, Illinois,* L01736, *LPAL; Edgar County, Illinois v. Mayo,* L00775, *LPAL.*

46. *Christian County Illinois v. Overholt and Squier,* L00579, *LPAL.*

47. Table 15, "Statistical Portrait, Common Subject: Legal Actions, Murder," *LPAL.*

48. Burlingame, *Abraham Lincoln,* 1:352.

49. David Davis to Sarah Davis, June 3, 1852, DDFP; "A Bill for an Act to Reduce the Limits of the Eighth Judicial Circuit and to Fix the Time of Court There," in Basler and Basler, *Collected Works of Abraham Lincoln, Second Supplement*, 7; *PAL*, 4:224, 225.

50. Donald, *Lincoln*, 149.

51. H. W. Beckwith, "Lincoln: Personal Recollections of Him, His Contemporaries and Law Practice in Eastern Illinois," *Chicago Tribune*, December 29, 1895; "Fragment: Notes for a Law Lecture," *CW*, 2:81.

52. Samuel Parks to William H. Herndon, March 25, 1866, item 180, *HI*, 238 (original emphasis); Ewing, "Address on Abraham Lincoln," 7; H. W. Beckwith, "Lincoln: Personal Recollections of Him, His Contemporaries and Law Practice in Eastern Illinois," *Chicago Tribune*, December 29, 1895; David Davis to Sarah Davis, March 23, 1851, DDFP.

53. Hill, *Lincoln the Lawyer*, 211; Jacob Harding, "Harding's Tribute to Lincoln," *Prairie Beacon* (Paris, Illinois), June 29, 1860, 2, repr. in *Paris (IL) Daily Beacon*, March 26, 1923, 1.

54. H. C. Whitney quoting Leonard Swett, August 29, 1887, item 522, *HI*, 635; Holzer, *Lincoln as I Knew Him*, 75.

55. H. W. Beckwith, "Lincoln: Personal Recollections of Him, His Contemporaries and Law Practice in Eastern Illinois," *Chicago Tribune*, December 29, 1895; Frank, *Lincoln as a Lawyer*, 98, 170; Joshua Speed to William H, Herndon, December 6, 1866, item 394, *HI*, 498, 499.

56. *HL*, 209.

57. Jacob Harding, "Harding's Tribute to Lincoln," *Prairie Beacon* (Paris, Illinois), June 29, 1860, 2, repr. in *Paris (IL) Daily Beacon*, March 26, 1923, 1.

58. Danville *Illinois Citizen*, quoted in Duff, *A. Lincoln, Prairie Lawyer*, 210; *HL*, 203.

59. Logan, "Stephen T. Logan Talks about Lincoln," 3; *HL*, 208.

60. Logan, "Stephen T. Logan Talks about Lincoln," 1, 3, 5.

61. Thomas, *"Lincoln's Humor,"* 142.

62. Hill, *Lincoln the Lawyer*, 238.

63. Duff, *A. Lincoln, Prairie Lawyer*, 243, 244.

64. *PAL*, 1:xxxvi; Duff, *A. Lincoln, Prairie Lawyer*, 247, 248.

65. Logan, "Stephen T. Logan Talks about Lincoln," 5.

66. Thomas, *"Lincoln's Humor,"* 165, 163; Woldman, *Lawyer Lincoln*, 46.

67. Phillips, *Abraham Lincoln by Some Men Who Knew Him*, 167; Duff, *A. Lincoln, Prairie Lawyer*, 366, 367.

68. Chicago *Journal*, November 3, 1854, quoted in Harper, *Lincoln and the Press*, 15.

69. Duff, *A. Lincoln, Prairie Lawyer*, 366.

4. Sangamon, Tazewell, Woodford

1. Review by author of Sangamon County Circuit Court cases, *LPAL*; Biographical Directory, *PAL*, 4:337.

2. Virgil Hickox, Reference Biography, *LPAL*; review by author of Sangamon County Circuit Court cases; Calabro, *Perilous Journey of the Donner Party*, 14; *Reed & Radford v. Phillips et al.*, L04434, *LPAL*; *Reed & Richard v Early et al.*, L04435, *LPAL*.

3. Angle, *Here I Have Lived*, 159, 171, 174; John W. Bunn in Phillips, *Abraham Lincoln by Some Men Who Knew Him*, 167.

4. *Thomas v. Wright*, L04728, *LPAL*; Verduin, "New Lincoln Discovery," 3–11; David Davis, Herndon interview, September 20, 1866, item 242, 398. Herndon and Weik's *Herndon's Lincoln* has a thorough description of this case (see 212, 213).

5. J. White, *Origin and Evolution of the Illinois Counties*, 48, 51, 53, 55, 57, 59; entry for July 15–16, 1839, *LDD*, 1:29.

6. *CW*, 1:24 (map following); Bills Introduced in the Illinois Legislature, relative to location of said road, December 15, 1834, *CW*, 1:29, December 11, 1835, *CW*, 1:39, and July 19, 1837, *CW*, 1:85.

7. Pratt, *Illinois as Lincoln Knew It*, 31, 32.

8. Federal Writers Projects, Delavan, 13–17; Mark Walsh, interview by author, October 30, 2005; original Lincoln registration for the night of September 12, 1843, private collection; *Frink, Walker & Co. v. Hall*, L01240, *LPAL*.

9. Lincoln to William Doughty, November 2, 1839, *CW*, 1:154.

10. Kraus, *From Log Cabins to Temples of Justice*, 72.

11. *History of Tazewell County*, 247, 564, 565, 250, 255.

12. Krause, *From Log Cabins to Temples of Justice*, 74.

13. E. J. Hunt, *My Personal Recollections*, 13–15, 17; R. R. Wilson, *Intimate Memories*, 123; Reminiscences of James T. Jones, July 8, 1908, Lincoln Centennial Association, ALPLM. The Red Brick and the Harris home where Lincoln occasionally stayed still stand. Sarah Butler and Susan Sears, interview by author, April 7, 2008.

14. *History of Tazewell County*, 249–50; Lincoln to a Gentleman in Tremont, July 31, 1843, *CW*, 1:329.

15. Benjamin F. James to AL, April 16 and April 29, 1849, ALPLC; *Harris v. Shaw et al.*, L01232, *LPAL*.

16. Review by author of Tazewell County Circuit cases, *LPAL*; *Alexander v. Brower & Wilcox*, L01203, *LPAL*; *Charles Walker and Son v. Porter and Higginson*, L04986, *LPAL*; *Crittenden v. Sweeney*, L01100, *LPAL*; *Flint & Matthews v. Kellogg*, L01211, *LPAL*.

17. Review by author of Tazewell County Circuit Court cases, *LPAL*; *History of Tazewell County Illinois* (1879), 387.

18. *Jones v. Maus*, L01065, *LPAL*.

19. David Davis to Sarah Davis, September 22, 1852, DDFP; David Davis to Sarah Davis, September 14, 1851, DDFP.

20. David Davis to Sarah Davis, April 5 and September 7 and 14, 1851, May 8, 1854, DDFP.

21. *Portrait and Biographical Record, Tazewell*, 457; review by author of Tazewell County Circuit Court cases, *LPAL*.

22. Norman Purple, Judge, item 1337, *Peoria Daily Transcript*, August 11, 1863, Peoria Historical Society.

23. J. M. Rice, *Peoria City and County*, 181.

24. *Selak v. Saltonstall*, L01157, *LPAL*; Holder, "Saltonstalls in Tazewell County"; Dan Holder, interview by author, March 5, 2005; William Holder, interviews by author, March 5, 2005 and August 7, 2006.

25. Thompson, "George W. Minier," 23, 31; Eckley, "Lincoln's Intimate Friend," 32; Duff, *A. Lincoln, Prairie Lawyer*, 124; George W. Minier, statement, April 10, 1882, item 605, *HI*, 707; Bray, *Reading with Lincoln*, 189, 190. The last case, *Case v. Snow Brothers*, does not appear in *LPAL*. The town of Minier, named for George W. Minier, was platted in 1867.

26. *People v. Delny*, L01235, *LPAL*; Stowell, *In Tender Consideration*, 184; *People v. Beal*, L0116, L0117, *LPAL*.

27. King, *Lincoln's Manager*, 74, 75.

28. Lincoln to Lyman Porter and Company, July 19, 1857, *CW*, 2:411.

29. *Past and Present of Woodford County*, 289; Nancy Steele Brokaw, "Metamora," *Bloomington (IL) Pantagraph*, November 29, 1999, A3.

30. Krause, *From Log Cabins to Temples of Justice*, 77.

31. Wolfe, *Metamora*, 16; David Davis to Sarah Davis, September 22, 1851, DDFP.

32. J. B. Martin, *Adlai Stevenson*, 11. Stevenson is a grandfather of the two-time presidential candidate in 1952 and 1956.

33. Review by author of Woodford County cases, *LPAL*.

34. Adams, *History of Eureka College*, 15–34, 35.

35. *People et al. Davenport v. Brown ex rel.*, L01807, *LPAL*.

36. Wakefield, *How Lincoln Became President*, 53.

37. R. L. Moore, *History of Woodford County*, 174.

38. Carlock, *Compilation*, 22.

5. McLean, Livingston, Logan, DeWitt

1. Kraus, *From Log Cabins to Temples of Justice*, 48.

2. Logan and DeWitt were the other two counties.

3. Florence Bloomer, interview by author, Bloomington, Illinois, November 6, 2004; Whitney, *Life on the Circuit*, 78; King, *Lincoln's Manager*, 52. Bloomer tells of an altercation between the two. Lincoln stayed at the Davis home, Clover Lawn, which was replaced by the current mansion in 1872 and which, in 1959, the family gave to the State of Illinois.

4. Duis, *Good Old Times*, 262–76. This is the most complete biography of Asahel Gridley, most of it written by his friend Jesse W. Fell for Duis.

5. Morehouse, *Life of Jesse W. Fell*, 36. Morehouse's book is the most complete biography of Jesse Fell.

6. Lincoln's endorsement of April 17, 1861, *CW*, 4:336.

7. Obituary of Asahel Gridley, *Daily Pantagraph* (Bloomington, Illinois), January 25, 1886; *Daily Pantagraph* (Bloomington, Illinois), February 15, 1881; Asahel Gridley to Lincoln, January 16, 1860, ALPLC; Pratt, "Abraham Lincoln in Bloomington," 46.

8. Morehouse, *Life of Jesse W. Fell*, 74.

9. Prince, "Gen. William Ward Orme"; Packard, "Old Bar of McLean County," 1:421; Lincoln to Henry W. Halleck, August 2, 1862, *CW*, 5:353.

10. Baldwin, "Colonel Harvey Hogg," 302.

11. Bajuyo, *John Milton Scott*, 2–4.

12. Palmer, *Bench and Bar of Illinois*, 727.

13. Duis, *Good Old Times*, 201.

14. Ewing, "Address," 5.

15. E. D. Jones, *Lincoln and the Preachers*, 5.

16. Pratt, "Abraham Lincoln in Bloomington," 63.

17. Winkle, *Young Eagle*, 268; *Florville v. Allin et al.*, L01647, *LPAL*; Lincoln to Major Packard, February 10, 1860, *CW*, 3:518; William Florville to Lincoln, December 27, 1863, ALPLC. William Florville's name is also seen spelled "Fleurville." The spelling used here is most commonly used.

18. Prince and Burnham, *Historical Encyclopedia*, 1:715.

19. Merriman, *History of McLean County*, 1:490–95; *Bloomington (IL) Pantagraph*, February 6, 1909, 15; Elizabeth Champlin, Mrs. (Noah) Sarah Franklin, Emily Shade (three of Jacob Spawr's daughters), Barbara Alsup, and John Franklin, interviews with author, October 4, 2005, and November 3, 2006; "Opinion concerning the Will of John Franklin," December 30, 1858, *CW*, 3:347, 348; Franklin, "Address to the Illinois Senate."

20. Pearre, *History of Livingston County*, 12, 31, 72, 75.

21. *Wilson v. Popejoy*, L05571, *LPAL*.

22. Pearre, *History of Livingston County*, 84.

23. Cavanagh, *Funk of Funk's Grove*, 86–92, 142, 158; *Iles v. Funk*, L05550, *LPAL*; *Funk and Funk v. Taylor et al.*, L03286, *LPAL*. A substantial portion of the grove still remains, protected by a private trust and the State of Illinois Nature Preserve Dedication.

24. "John T. Stuart (WHH Interview)," December 20, 1866, item 409, *HI*, 519.

25. Price and Adams, *Twelve Momentous Years*, 4; Susan Hoblit, interview with author, December 2, 2003. Family members still talk of "Uncle Linc," and the shed still stands on the family farm, Hoblit relates.

26. Stringer, *History of Logan County*, 52–56.

27. Ibid., 153, 560.

28. Duff, *A. Lincoln, Prairie Lawyer*, 203; Stringer, *History of Logan County*, 216.

29. Krause, *From Log Cabins to Temples of Justice*, 30. A faithful replica now stands in the footprint of the original building.

30. Duff, *A. Lincoln, Prairie Lawyer*, 203.

31. Stringer, *History of Logan County*, 216, 177, 587.

32. Ibid., 587.

33. Krause, *From Log Cabins to Temples of Justice*, 3

34. *Adams et al. v. Logan County Illinois*, L00937, LPAL; Duff, *A. Lincoln, Prairie Lawyer*, 205.

35. *Edmunds v. Mayers and Mayers*, L01001, *LPAL*; *Edmunds v. Hildreth et al.*, L01003, LPAL; *Hildreth v. Turner*, item 01006, *LPAL*; Duff, *A. Lincoln, Prairie Lawyer*, 259–61.

36. Duff, *A. Lincoln, Prairie Lawyer*, 205, 206.

37. Reference Biographies, *LPAL*; Stringer, *History of Logan County*, 324.

38. Swett, *David Davis*, 4; David Davis to Sarah Davis, April 24, 1851, DDFP. This is a reference to a sorcerer in the Old Testament, 1 Samuel 28:3–25.

39. Capps, *Early Recollections of Abraham Lincoln*, 2, 3.

40. Schwartz, "You Can Fool All of the People," 1, 3, 6. That Lincoln actually said this famous quotation is disputed.

41. *History of DeWitt County, 1839–1868*, 4; *History of DeWitt County*, 1882, 44; Morehouse, *Life of Jesse W. Fell*, 32.
42. *Biographical Record of DeWitt County*, 110; "Joshua F. Speed (WHH interview)," 1865–66, item 370, *HI*, 474.
43. Illinois, General Assembly, Senate, *Journal of the Senate of the Eleventh General Assembly*, 453.
44. Krause, *From Log Cabins to Temples of Justice*, 20, 21.
45. *History of DeWitt County*, 1882, 64; *LDD*, 1:119, Duff, *A. Lincoln, Prairie Lawyer*, 400.
46. Porter, *Portrait of a Prairie Lawyer*, 2; review by author of DeWitt County Circuit Court cases, *LPAL*.
47. Porter, *Portrait of a Prairie Lawyer*, 107; King, *Lincoln's Manager*, 101; Porter, *Portrait of a Prairie Lawyer*, 140; deed copy in possession of current owners. The home is a beautifully restored private residence.
48. King, *Lincoln's Manager*, 97; review by author of DeWitt County Circuit cases, *LPAL*. Moore's first home and office still stand. His grand second home, built after Lincoln's death, is a museum.
49. Porter, *Portrait of a Prairie Lawyer*, 130, 134, 141.
50. Hasbrouk, *History of McLean County*, 1:501; grave site of Lincoln Weldon, Evergreen Cemetery, Bloomington, Illinois.
51. *History of DeWitt County*, 1882, 83; *Biographical Record of DeWitt County*, 45; *People v. Turner*, L00583, *LPAL*.
52. Duff, *A. Lincoln, Prairie Lawyer*, 70; *Lincoln v. Turner and Turner*, L00506, *LPAL*.
53. Pratt, "Lincoln and Douglas as Counsel on the Same Side," 214. Pratt disputes the aspect of the case. On the other hand, Clifton H. Moore, a man known for his credibility, cites this information as true. *History of DeWitt County*, 1882, 80.
54. *People v. Loe*, L00630, *LPAL*; "Endorsement of Petition for Pardon of Moses Loe," August 18, 1857, *CW*, 2:414.
55. *History of DeWitt County*, 1892, 163.
56. *Campbell v. Warner*, L00527, *LPAL*; *Warner and Moore v. Slatten*, L00634, *LPAL*. The trial result of *Campbell v. Warner* is unknown.
57. *Biographical Record of DeWitt County*, 456; *Snell v. Kelly*, L00634, *LPAL*.
58. Pratt, "Beginner," 247.

6. Piatt, Champaign, Vermilion

1. Leonard Swett to sister Rose, March 13, 1851, quoted in Pratt, "Beginner," 246.
2. David Davis to Sarah Davis, May 1, 1851, DDFP.
3. David to Sarah Davis, May 7, 1852, and May 1, 1851, DDFP.
4. Piatt, *History of Piatt County Illinois*, 131–33; *Urbana (IL) Union*, July 29, 1858, 2.
5. *People v. Longnecker*, L00448, *LPAL*.
6. *Paine v. Shaw*, L00752, *LPAL*; *Hollingsworth et al. v. Moraine et al.*, L03572, *LPAL*; *Hollingsworth v. Thomas Milligan*, L03570, *LPAL*; *Hollingsworth v. Moraine and Buffet*, L03574, *LPAL*; *Hollingsworth v. Moraine et al.*, L03573, *LPAL*; *Hollingsworth v. Savage*, L03580, *LPAL*; *People v. Hollingsworth*, L01712–15 and L04240, *LPAL*.

7. Krause, *From Log Cabins to Temples of Justice*, 64; Henry Clay Whitney quoted in Felts, "A. Lincoln in Piatt," 50.

8. Felts, "A. Lincoln in Piatt," 51.

9. Piatt, *History of Piatt County*, 145; review by author of Piatt County Circuit Court cases, *LPAL*; *Ford v. Thorp*, L01704, *LPAL*.

10. Johns, *Personal Recollection*, 67–69.

11. B. F. Harris, *Harris*, 56, 57.

12. Lothrop, *Champaign County Directory*, 117.

13. Cunningham, *History of Champaign County*, 717, 724–27.

14. *LDD*, 1:159.

15. Lothrop, *Champaign County Directory*, 33.

16. Cunningham, *History of Champaign County*, 731, 728. During the construction, Smith corresponded with Lincoln from Urbana, regarding Lincoln's pursuit of patronage. E. O. Smith to Lincoln, June 16, 1844, ALPLC.

17. Stewart, *Standard History of Champaign County, Illinois*. 150; *Champaign (IL) News Gazette*, February 12, 1945; Urbana Lincoln Hotel menu notes, Champaign County Historical Archives. The news article states that the Harvey volume containing this entry was presented to the University of Illinois Library.

18. Thomson R. Webber, journal, May 30, 1833, private collection; *History of Champaign County*, 1087; Lincoln to Edwin Stanton, August 28, 1862, *CW*, 5:395.

19. Whitney, *Life on the Circuit*, 94, 95.

20. *Champaign (IL) News Gazette*, September 26, 1932, 5, col. 2.

21. "Reminiscences of Henry M. Russell," August 14, 1908, Lincoln Centennial Association; *History of Champaign County*, 1020.

22. "Reminiscences of William Somers," December 7, 1908, Lincoln Centennial Association.

23. Review by author of Champaign County Circuit Court cases, *LPAL*.

24. Mathews and McLean, *Early History and Pioneers of Champaign County*, 129; *McClatchey and Sits v. Roney et al.*, L01960, *LPAL*.

25. "Reminiscences of William Somers," December 7, 1908, Lincoln Centennial Association. Review by author of the Champaign County Circuit Court cases in LPAL shows Lincoln sitting for Davis on approximately seventy cases.

26. *People v. Weaver*, L01426, *LPAL*; *History of Champaign County*, 32; Cunningham, *History of Champaign County*, 734.

27. *People v. High*, L01418, L01419, *LPAL*.

28. Cunningham, "Some Recollections," 1; Angle, introduction, 22.

29. O'Donnell, *Life of Judge Joseph O. Cunningham*.

30. Henry Clay Whitney's impact on the Lincoln story is probably greater because of his book published in Boston in 1892. It is the most complete and credible contemporary account of this part of Lincoln's life. Unfortunately, Whitney's book includes a great deal of questionable material extraneous to the circuit, thus diminishing the total impact of this important book.

31. Whitney, *Life on the Circuit*, 148; AL to Whitney, July 9, 1856, *CW*, 2:347.

32. AL to Joshua Speed, December 12, 1855, *CW*, 2:328.

33. Mathews and McLean, *Early History and Pioneers of Champaign County*, 69, 4.

34. Cunningham, *History of Champaign County*, 744–59.

35. David Davis to Sarah Davis, May 7, 1852, DDFP.

36. Whitney, *Life on the Circuit*, 54, 59; "Reminiscences of Henry M. Russell," January 14, 1909, Lincoln Centennial Association; Cunningham, "Some Recollections," 4, 5.

37. Cunningham, *History of Champaign County*, 838; *History of Champaign County*, 69.

38. *Champaign (IL) Gazette*, March 10, 1858, 1. The newspaper is still published as the *News-Gazette*.

39. Burlingame, introduction, viii.

40. *LDD*, 1:264; Smalling, *St. Joseph Illinois*, 7; "Henry C. Whitney (statement for WHH)," item 535, *HI*, 647. Kelley's Tavern is also known as Bailey's Tavern.

41. Whitney, *Life on the Circuit*, 72; David Davis to Sarah Davis, May 11, 1852, DDFP. Whitney comments that they frequently stayed at farmhouses between Urbana and Danville and Charleston and Paris.

42. Tilton, "John W. Vance," 5; AL to John Vance, July 7, 1844, *CW*, 1:340; AL to Deziah Vance, *CW*, 4:74.

43. Whitney, *Life on the Circuit*, 436.

44. Ibid., 64; *LDD*, 1:159; "1841–45," "1845–47," maps, *LPAL*; King, *Lincoln's Manager*, 80.

45. Beckwith, *History of Vermilion County*, 350; Moses, *Illinois Historical*, 2:216.

46. Beckwith, *History of Vermilion County*, 311–36; Richter, *Lincoln*, 7.

47. Richter, *Lincoln*, xi, 19; *Fithian v. Cunningham et al.*, L01893, *LPAL*. The town of Fithian, in Vermilion County east of Danville, is named for William Fithian.

48. W. R. Elghammer, "William Fithian, M.D.," 19, 20.

49. Review by author of Lincoln's cases in the Circuit Court of Vermilion County, *LPAL*; AL to William Fithian, February 16, 1850, *CW*, 2:74; AL to William Fithian, March 8, 1855, *CW*, 2:307.

50. *Fithian v. Casseday*, L01891, *LPAL*: Richter, *Lincoln*, 98–111, King, *Lincoln's Manager*, 81.

51. Richter, *Lincoln*, 105, 106; *Fithian v. Casseday*, L01891, *LPAL*.

52. Garraty, Carnes, and Berwanger, *American National Biography*, 10:14, 15.

53. Richter, *Lincoln*, 110; David Davis to Sarah Davis, October 27, 1851, DDFP.

54. Review by author of Lincoln's cases in the Circuit Court of Vermilion County, *LPAL*.

55. Beckwith, *History of Vermilion County*, 394; "Oliver Davis," in Stapp, *Footprints in the Sands*, 35; Linder, *Reminiscences*, 274; "Henry Clay Whitney to JWW," September 17, 1887, item 529, *HI*, 642.

56. Pavey, *O. F. Harmon*, 24; review by author of Lincoln's cases in the Circuit Court of Vermilion County, *LPAL*.

57. Harmon, *Mrs. Harmon's Reminiscences of Lincoln*. The Harmon home still stands.

58. Beckwith, *History of Vermilion County*, 307.

59. Whitney, *Life on the Circuit*, 68; Burlingame, *Abraham Lincoln*, 1:332; King, *Lincoln's Manager*, 89.

60. Wallace, *Lew Wallace Autobiography*, 221–23.

61. Hamand, *Ward Hill Lamon*, 44; Whitney, *Life on the Circuit*, 69.

62. Leonard Swett (JWW interview), ca. 1887–89, item 631, *HI*, 731.

63. "Enoch Kingsbury," in Stapp, *Footprints in the Sands*, 21; *Wilson et al. v. Kingsberry et al.*, L02060, *LPAL*.

64. David Davis to Sarah Davis, October 20, 1851, DDFP.

65. Ibid. and May 17, 1852.

7. Edgar, Shelby, Moultrie, Macon, Christian, Menard, Mason

1. *Memories of Abraham Lincoln*, 13.

2. King, *Lincoln's Manager*, 82.

3. *History of Edgar County, Illinois*, 227, 233; Milton Alexander Biographical File, Edgar County Historical Society. This house still stands. Douglas's efforts were unsuccessful, as Jane married John TenBrook, a prominent physician in 1840.

4. *Alexander v. Warner*, L00493, LPAL; *Alexander v. Metcalf*, L00747, LPAL; *Alexander v. Parrish*, L00748, *LPAL*.

5. *Paine v. Shaw*, L00752, *LPAL*; *Champaign (IL) News Gazette*, July 1, 2008; Elvis Shaw, biographical file, Edgar County Historical Society. This house still stands.

6. Krause, *From Log Cabins*, 22; *Paris (IL) Daily Beacon*, December 21, 1938, 1; *Munsell v. McReynolds*, L00791, *LPAL*.

7. AL to Garland B. Shelledy, February 16, 1842, *CW*, 1:270; *People for the Use of Barber v. Stanfield et al.*, L05808, *LPAL*. Lincoln and Logan had an extensive bankruptcy practice in federal court under the Bankruptcy Act of 1841, filing over seventy cases.

8. Review by author of Edgar County Circuit Court cases, *LPAL*; Alcorn, "Leadership and Stability," 701.

9. Stanfield, "Lincoln the Lawyer," *Paris (IL) Evening Beacon*, February 12, 1974, 3; Jacob Harding file, Edgar County Historical Society; Paris, Illinois, *Prairie Beacon*, May 18, 1848.

10. David Davis to Sarah Davis, October 10, 1847, DDFP.

11. Hunt, *Kirby Benedict*, 39, 50; review by author of cases in all counties of the circuit, *LPAL*.

12. David Davis to Sarah Davis, October 20, 1851, DDFP; Linder, *Reminiscences of the Early Bench and Bar of Illinois*, 282, 283.

13. *Prairie Beacon*, May 18, 1848; David to Sarah Davis, May 20, 1850, and May 17, 1852, DDFP; Bradsby, *History of Vigo County, Indiana*, 963; Linder, *Reminiscences*, 293.

14. *DuBois et al. v. Nabb*, L00783, LPAL; *DuBois et al. v. Wise*, L00786, *LPAL*.

15. Richardson and Farley, *John Palmer Usher*, 4; Taylor, *Biographical Sketches*, 58, 64, 628, 700; Linder, *Reminiscences*, 290; R. R. Wilson, *Intimate Memories*, 373.

16. AL to Usher Linder, March 8, 1853, *CW*, 2:191.

17. David Davis to Sarah Davis, May 24, 1852, DDFP.

18. *Memories of Abraham Lincoln in Edgar County*, 19; David Davis to Sarah Davis, May 20, 1850, May 24, 1852, and November 3, 1851, DDFP; Gordon, *Here and There*, 49.

19. David Davis to Sarah Davis, May 26, 1848, and October 31, 1851, DDFP; *Urbana (IL) Union*, April 12, 1855.

20. Douthit, *Jasper Douthit's Story*, 49.

21. J. White, *Origin and Evolution*, 48, 63; Bateman, *Historical Encyclopedia of Illinois and History of Shelby County*, 2:626, 632, 633.

22. Krause, *From Log Cabins*, 70; Douthit, *Jasper Douthit's Story*, 49.

23. King, *Lincoln's Manager*, 85.

24. J. White, *Origin and Evolution*, 56, 58.

25. Bateman, *Historical Encyclopedia of Illinois and History of Shelby County*, 2:728, 730; Linder, *Reminiscences*, 115.

26. Anthony Thornton to David Davis, April 13, 1848, DDFP. Thornton was one of three lawyers prominent in this story who served as president of the Illinois State Bar Association. The others were David Davis (1884) and Lyman Trumball (1892). "Early Leaders," 52.

27. Bateman, *Historical Encyclopedia of Illinois and History of Shelby County*, 2:730.

28. Linder, *Reminiscences*, 112.

29. *Portrait and Biographical Album of Coles County, Illinois*, 187.

30. Review by author of Shelby County Circuit Court cases, *LPAL*.

31. Ibid.

32. David Davis to Sarah Davis, June 3, 1852, DDFP.

33. *Combined History of Shelby and Moultrie Counties, Illinois*, 65–67; Lloyd, "William Williamson," 7.

34. *Combined History*, 48, 71; Krause, *From Log Cabins*, 60; *People v. Crockett*, L00661, *LPAL*; AL to A. C. French, Nov. 22, 1852, *CW* 2:161.

35. Abraham Lincoln Memorial Highway Association, *Route Traveled*, 17.

36. Richmond, *Centennial History*, 26; E. T. Coleman, *History*, 10. Coleman's book is a volume of a series of consecutive columns that ran from 1924 to 1929 in the *Decatur Herald Review*. Chapter 7 deals specifically with Lincoln in Macon County.

37. L. G. Stevenson, *Blue Book of Illinois*, 1915–16, 508.

38. Richmond, *Centennial History*, 63; Krause, *From Log Cabins*, 52.

39. *Portrait and Biographical Record of Macon County*, 195; Richmond, *Centennial History*, 160.

40. Richmond, *Centennial History*, 160, 105.

41. King, *Lincoln's Manager*, 86.

42. Johns, *Personal Recollection*, 64, 65.

43. Ibid., 259.

44. Richmond, *Centennial History*, 197; James Shoaf to AL, November 18, 1864, ALPLC.

45. Obituary of Charles Emerson, *Decatur (IL) Republican*, April 21, 1870; J. W. Smith, *History*, 258.

46. Review by author of Macon County Circuit Court cases, *LPAL*.

47. Joel S. Post, Biographies, Reference, *LPAL*.

48. Review by author of Macon County Circuit Court cases, *LPAL*.

49. *Warnick v. Ekel*, L00443, *LPAL*; *Hanks v. Hanks*, L00450, *LPAL*; *Noblitt v. Dick* (Edgar County), L00750, *LPAL*; *Coon v. Lloyd et al.* (Sangamon County), L03052, *LPAL*; *Johnson v. Hardy*, (Shelby County), L00671, *LPAL*.

50. Review by author of Macon County Circuit Court cases, *LPAL*.

51. Drennan, Gardner, and Broverman, *Illinois Sesquicentennial*, 26; Rogers, *Christian County History*, 49.

52. "Bill Introduced in Illinois Legislature to Legalize Survey and Town Plat of Mount Auburn," January 15, 1840, *CW*, 1:183.

53. *Opdycke et al. v. Godfrey et al.*, Lo1561, *LPAL*; Christian County Title Co., Abstract of title to these premises, entries 7, 8, 9, private collection.

54. Fowkes, *History of Christian County*, 815; J. White, *Origin and Evolution*, 50; Rogers, *Christian County History*, 61, 62.

55. Angle, *Here I Have Lived*, 11; B. P. Thomas, *Lincoln's New Salem*, 37.

56. "Vandeveer, Horatio M.," Biographical Directory, *PAL*, 4:383; Biographies, Reference, *LPAL*; review by author of Christian County Circuit Court cases, *LPAL*; AL to Horatio M. Vandeveer, April 28, 1844, *CW*, 1:336.

57. Basler and Basler, *Collected Works of Abraham Lincoln, Second Supplement*, 7; Stevenson, *Blue Book*, 509; Spears, *Courthouses*, 9–13. John McClary's recently dedicated statue of Lincoln and a small pig now commemorates the event.

58. David Davis to Sarah Davis, June 9, 1848, and August 28, 1850, DDFP.

59. *Whitecraft et al. v. Vandeveer*, Lo2503, *LPAL*; Spears, *Courthouses*, 13; Drennan, Gardner, and Broverman, *Illinois Sesquicentennial*, 56.

60. Review by author of Christian County Circuit Court cases, *LPAL*; Fowkes, *History of Christian County*, 2:680; Strange, *Historical Encyclopedia*, 694.

61. *People v. Brown*, Lo1565, *LPAL*; *Lincoln v. Brown*, Lo1616, *LPAL*; Samuel Brown, Reminiscence, n.d., *Taylorville (IL) Daily Breeze*, February 8, 1909; Lincoln Centennial Association, ALPLM.

62. Review by author of Christian County Circuit Court cases, *LPAL*.

63. Reference, Maps, "1841–1845," "1845–1847," *LPAL*; review by author of Menard County cases, *LPAL*.

64. "Thomas L. Harris," Reference, Biographies, *LPAL*.

65. B. P. Thomas, *Lincoln's New Salem*, 72–74; *Short for use of Short v. Short*, Lo0310, *LPAL*; *Short v. Caldwell*, Lo0311, *LPAL*; Winkle, *Young Eagle*, 82.

66. B. P. Thomas, *Lincoln's New Salem*, 48, 49, 69; *Green v. Graham*, Lo0299, *LPAL*.

67. Simon, *Lincoln's Preparation*, 102, 103; *Rogers v. Francis et al.*, Lo4459, *LPAL*. John Eden owns this building, now a well-preserved museum.

68. *Allen v. Hill*, Lo0150, *LPAL*; *Barnett v. Cogdal*, Lo0162, *LPAL*; *Cogdal v. Allen*, Lo0253, *LPAL*; *People v. Williams*, Lo0257, *LPAL*; *Ellis et al. v. Trent et al.*, Lo0123, *LPAL*.

69. *Regnier v. Cabot & Torrey*, Lo0158, *LPAL*; *Torrey et. ux. v. Regnier & Regnier*, Lo0272, LPAL; Samuel Parks to WHH, March 25, 1866, item 180, *HI*, 238.

70. Ruggles, "History of Mason County," 408, 424, 427.

8. The 1840s and the Early 1850s

1. *LDD*, 1:138–46.

2. "Speech at Tremont, Illinois," May 2, 1840, *CW*, 1:209, 210; Richter, *Lincoln*, 37; Simon, *Lincoln's Preparation*, 214.

3. *LDD*, 1:138–40.

4. Pease, *Illinois Election Returns*, 117–19.

5. "Joseph Gillespie to WHH," Edwardsville [Illinois], January 31, 1866, item 132, *HI*, 180–88.

6. Obituary of Joseph Gillespie, *Edwardsville (IL) Intelligencer*, January 7, 1885. The town of Gillespie in Macoupin County, founded in 1854, is named for Joseph Gillespie.

7. Simon, *Lincoln's Preparation*, 236–41; AL to John Todd Stuart, January 23, 1841, *CW*, 1:229; Burlingame, *Abraham Lincoln*, 1:196.

8. Burlingame, *Abraham Lincoln*, 1:190–94; "The 'Rebecca' Letter," August 27, 1842, *CW*, 1:291–97; AL to James Shields, September 17, 1842. *CW*, 1:299; James Shields to AL, September 17, 1842, *CW*, 1:299–300, nn 1, 4; "Memorandum of Duel Instructions to Elias H. Merryman," September 19, 1842, *CW*, 300–301.

9. Pratt, *In Defense of Mr. Justice Browne*, 1–8. He was also the only jurist to serve the entire period of the 1818 constitution.

10. *Journal of the House of Representatives of the Thirteenth General Assembly*, 142, 145, 147–50.

11. AL to Alden Hall, February 14, 1843, *CW*, 1:306; Resolutions at a Whig Meeting, March 1, 1843, *CW*, 1:307, 308; *Extra Journal* (Springfield, Illinois), April 20, 1843, 2, col. 3; Campaign Circular from Whig Committee, March 4, 1843, *CW*, 1:309–18.

12. AL to Joshua F. Speed, March 24, 1843, *CW*, 1:319; AL to Martin S. Morris, March 26, 1843, and April 14, 1843, *CW*, 1:319–21, 322.

13. "Resolution Adopted at Whig Convention at Pekin, Illinois," May 1, 1843, *CW*, 1:322; *Extra Journal* (Springfield, Illinois), May 30, 1843, 1:4.2.

14. *LDD*, 1:229–35; Bartelt, "There I Grew Up," 51–55; Pease, *Illinois Election Returns*, 117–19.

15. Findley, *A. Lincoln*, 28.

16. AL to Benjamin F. James, November 17, 1845, *CW*, 1:349; November 24, 1845, *CW*, 1:351; December 6, 1845, *CW*, 1:351–52; January 14, 1846, *CW*, 1:353–54; January 16, 1846, *CW*, 1:355–56; January 27, 1846, *CW*, 1:359–60; February 9, 1846, *CW*, 1:365–66.

17. AL to John J. Hardin, January 19, 1846, *CW*, 1:356; February 7, 1846, *CW*, 1:360.

18. R. R. Wilson, *Intimate Memories*, 189; AL to John Bennett, January 15, 1846, January 16, 1846, *CW*, 1:355.

19. Burlingame, *Abraham Lincoln*, 1:235–41. The reference to Peter Cartwright as a "circuit rider" was a description of him as one of the wide-ranging ministers of the day who covered vast areas to spread their denomination. It is not a reference to the circuit-riding attorneys.

20. AL to Benjamin Kellogg, April 21, 1848, *CW*, 1:466.

21. Burlingame, *Abraham Lincoln*, 1:271, 272; David Davis to Julius Rockwell, May 11, 1848, DDFP; Donald, *Lincoln's Herndon*, 185.

22. *LDD*, 1:318–23.

23. Allen and Lacey, *Illinois Elections*, 121–23.

24. *LDD*, 2:3–9.

25. R. C. White, *A. Lincoln*, 295; Anson Henry to AL, April 6, 1849, ALPLC.

26. Benjamin F. James to AL, April 16, 1849, ALPLC.

27. AL to Thomas Ewing, April 7, 1849, and April 13, 1849, *CW*, 2:40, 42.

28. Philo H. Thompson to AL, April 23, 1849, ALPLC; AL to Philo H. Thompson, April 25, 1849, *CW* 2:44; "Pekin, Illinois, Citizens to Abraham Lincoln," May 1, 1849, ALPLC.

29. AL to Philo H. Thompson, April 25, 1849, *CW*, 2:44; AL to Thomas Ewing, April 26, 1849, *CW*, 2:44.

30. Petition of Mathews and Others to Thomas Ewing, June 1849, and Petition of William Butler and others to Thomas Ewing, June 1849, both in entry 14, box 31, RG48, Central Office Appointment Papers, Records of the Department of Interior, NACP, in Stowell, "Abraham Lincoln and the Contest"; David Davis to AL, June 2, 1849, DDFP; Burlingame, *Abraham Lincoln*, 1:300.

31. Burlingame, *Abraham Lincoln*, 1:192.

32. AL to Joseph Gillespie, May 19, 1849, *CW*, 2:50; AL memorandum to Zachary Taylor, June 15[?], 1849, *CW*, 2:54; AL to George W. Rives, May 7, 1849, and December 15, 1849, *CW*, 2:46, 69; AL to Caleb B. Smith, May 1, 1849, *CW*, 2:46; AL to Richard W. Thompson, May 25, 1849, *CW*, 2:51.

33. King, *Lincoln's Manager*, 83–84.

34. Donald, *Lincoln*, 140–41; AL to Joseph Gillespie, July 13, 1849, *CW*, 2:57; Donald, *Lincoln's Herndon*, 185.

35. Autobiography, December 20, 1859, *CW*, 3:511, 512.

36. Eulogy on Zachary Taylor, *CW*, 2:83.

37. Call for Whig Convention, November 29, 1851, *CW*, 2:113.

38. Eulogy on Henry Clay, July 6, 1852, *CW*, 2:121.

39. "Speech to the Springfield Scott Club," August 14, 26, 1852, *CW*, 2:135; "Speech at Peoria, Illinois," September 17, 1852, *CW*, 2:153; *LDD*, 2:83.

40. *LDD*, 2:109.

9. The Awakenment

1. Cunningham, *History of Champaign County*, 766; Prince and Burnham, *Historical Encyclopedia*, 2:650; Matheny, "History of Springfield," 11.

2. Moses, *Illinois Historical*, 2:1137.

3. Fehrenbacher, *Prelude to Greatness*, 16, 17.

4. Howard, *Illinois*, 243–45.

5. Ibid., 200–202.

6. *History of Logan County*, 361.

7. *Biological Record of Logan County*, 587; Gillette Ransom and Lisa Pasquesi, interviews by author, Elkhart, Illinois, December 2, 2003. Ransom's descendants still occupy the stately home; the Cornland residence likewise is still standing and occupied.

8. Smith Tuttle to John Dean Gillett, May 13, 1852, Gillett Family Papers.

9. *History of Logan County*, 361; Smith Tuttle to John Dean Gillett, July 23, 1852, Gillett Family Papers.

10. Smith Tuttle to John Dean Gillett, July 23, 1852, Gillett Family Papers; Stringer, *History of Logan County*, 566; Tuttle to Gillett, April 5, May 1, May 10, 13, 17, July 23, 1852, February 19 and October, 3, 1853, Gillett Family Papers.

11. Smith Tuttle to John Dean Gillett, May 10, 1852, and May 13, 1852, Gillett Family Papers.

12. *History of Logan County*, 361; Smith Tuttle to John Dean Gillett, July 23, 1852, Gillett Family Papers.

13. Stringer, *History of Logan County*, 566, 569.

14. Beaver, *Abraham Lincoln*, 55.

15. Deed of conveyance, Recorder of Deeds, 11:379, Lincoln, Logan County, Illinois.

16. Beaver, *Abraham Lincoln*, 59; John S. Stephens to Lawrence B. Stringer, April 30, 1926, in Dooley, *Namesake Town*, 15. The notice of the sale of lots dated August 16, 1853, is reproduced in Beaver.
17. *Turley et al. v. Logan County, Illinois*, L00927, *LPAL*.
18. Stringer, *History of Logan County*, 570; Krause, *From Log Cabins to Temples of Justice*, 42; Hickey, *Collected Writings*, 1–4.
19. Price and Adams, *Twelve Momentous Years*, 7, 49, 33, 19, 50.
20. *Herley v. T. N. Gill & Company*, L01040, *LPAL*; *Hildreth v. Gill*, L01050, *LPAL*; *Gill et al. v. Hoblit*, L01037, *LPAL*; Hill, *Lincoln the Lawyer*, 225–27.
21. *People ex rel. Board of Education of Bloomington, Illinois, v. Bloomington, IL*, L05545, *LPAL*; Pratt, "Abraham Lincoln in Bloomington," 53.
22. Gates, *Illinois Central Railroad Company*, 59–64; Schlenker, "Resurrection of General Asahel Gridley," 39.
23. *McLean County Bank v. Bloomington Illinois & Moore*, L01668, *LPAL*; *Bloomington Light and Gas Co. v. Charles Herrich & Co.*, L01630, *LPAL*; Reinking, *Lincoln in Bloomington-Normal*, 15. Gridley's home still stands, as does his bank building.
24. *Daily Pantagraph* (Bloomington, Illinois), May 11, 1860.
25. Phillips, *Abraham Lincoln by Some Men Who Knew Him*, 95; *Pike v. Shaffer*, L01670, *LPAL*
26. Pearre, *History of Livingston County*, 84; Reinking, *Lincoln in Bloomington-Normal*, 15; Gates, *Illinois Central Railroad Company*, 59–64; *History of DeWitt County* (1882), 63; *Clinton (IL) Democratic Courier*, September 29, 1856.
27. *History of DeWitt County*, (1910), 314.
28. Richmond, *Centennial History*, 138, 209; "Lincoln Helped Pump Handcar," *Decatur (IL) Daily Herald*, February 7, 1909, 15.
29. Richmond, *Centennial History*, 212, 158.
30. Plummer, *Lincoln's Railsplitter*; review by author of Lincoln's Macon County Circuit Court cases, *LPAL*. Plummer's book is a comprehensive biography of this significant figure in the history of the nineteenth-century Illinois.
31. Cunningham, *History of Champaign County*, 760–66. The Alexander Bowman map shows the development and status of the two towns in 1858.
32. Daugherty, "Lincoln at Tolono"; M. Moore, "Lincoln in Tolono," 58, 59.
33. "Statistical Portrait, Peers and Clients," Reference, *LPAL*; Starr, *Lincoln and the Railroads*, 67.
34. AL to Thompson R. Webber, September 12, 1853, *CW*, 2:202. This letter is still owned by Webber's descendants in Urbana.
35. "Brief of Argument in Abraham Lincoln vs. Illinois Central Railroad," *CW*, 2:397; Friedman, *Inflation Calculator*. Volume 2 of *PAL* devotes chapter 31 to *Illinois Central Railroad v. McLean County, Illinois, & Parke*, L01655, and *Lincoln v. Illinois Central Railroad*, L01660, both also in *LPAL*.
36. "Speech at Carthage, Illinois," October 22, 1858, *CW*, 3:331.
37. Steiner, *Honest Calling*, 154–58; *People v. Illinois Central Railroad*, L02468, *LPAL*.
38. *Hurd v. Rock Island Bridge Co.*, L02289, *LPAL*. Volume 3 of *PAL* devotes chapter 46 to a full description of this case and its significance.
39. *Columbus Insurance Company v. Peoria Bridge Company*, L03310, 3311, *LPAL*.

40. Review by author of the cases against these railroads in the circuit courts of those three counties, *LPAL*.
41. AL to Mason Brayman, March 31, 1854, *PAL*, 1:8.
42. AL to Mason Brayman, September 23, 1854, *CW*, 2:233; AL to James Joy, March 23, 1854, *CW*, 2:326.
43. *Allen v. Illinois Central Railroad*, L00662, 663, 664, 767, 768, 769, *LPAL*; David Davis to Sarah Davis, July 23, 1853, DDFP.
44. Review by author of the DeWitt County Circuit Court cases brought against the IC Railroad, *LPAL*; *Clinton (IL) Democratic Courier*, November 2, 1855, 2.
45. Corliss, *Main Line*, 90, 91; A. T. Rice, *Reminiscences*, 201.
46. Starr, *Lincoln and the Railroads*, 66; Sears, *George B. McClellan*, 59.
47. *Barrett v. Alton & Sangamon Railroad*, L02610, *LPAL*. Volume 2 of *PAL* devotes chapter 25 to *Terre Haute and Alton Railroad v. Armstrong* and sixteen additional defendants in seventeen separate suits, L00980 and L00680 through L00695, *LPAL*.
48. *Bishop v. ICRR*, L01628 (1854), and *Scott v. St. Louis, Alton, and Chicago RR*, L01686, *LPAL*.
49. *Harris v. Great Western R.R.*, L03753, *LPAL*.
50. See, for example, the following landowners against the Great Western Railroad: *Campbell*, L01866; *Frazier*, L01899, 1900; *McKenson*, L01946, 47, 48; *Hickman*, L01916, all in *LPAL*.
51. *Gatling et al. v. Great Western R.R.*, L00480, *LPAL*; Bruce, *Lincoln and the Tools of War*, 290, 291.

10. The Repeal . . . Aroused Me Again

1. Simon, *Lincoln's Preparation for Greatness*, 131–34; W. L. Miller, *Lincoln's Virtues*, 116–28; "Protest in Illinois Legislature on Slavery," March 3, 1831, *CW*, 1:74.
2. Prince and Burnham, *Historical Encyclopedia*, 2:834.
3. "Address before the Young Men's Lyceum of Springfield, Illinois," January 27, 1838, *CW*, 1:108–15, 112.
4. AL to Williamson Durley, October 3, 1845, *CW*, 1:347.
5. AL to Jesse W. Fell, enclosing autobiography, December 20, 1859, *CW*, 3:511–12.
6. Wakefield, *How Lincoln Became President*, 37, 38; Hill, *Lincoln the Lawyer*, 263–64.
7. Harris, *Lincoln's Rise to the Presidency*, 67, 87.
8. Oakes, *Radical and the Republican*, xx; Striner, *Father Abraham*, 2.
9. "Speech at Peoria, Illinois," October 16, 1854, *CW*, 2:247–83; "Speech at Winchester, Illinois," August 26, 1854, *CW*, 2:226–27; "Speech at Springfield, Illinois," September 9, 1854, *CW*, 2:229; Foote, *Civil War*, 1:27; "Speech at Bloomington, Illinois," September 12, 1854, *CW*, 2:230, 233; "Speech at Bloomington, Illinois," September 26, 1854, *CW*, 2:234–40; *McLean County Bank & Gridley v. Chicago and Mississippi Railroad*, L01669, *LPAL*.
10. A. T. Rice, *Reminiscences*, 198; Pratt, "Abraham Lincoln in Bloomington, Illinois," 53.
11. *LDD*, 2:128; "Speech at Springfield, Illinois," October 4, 1854, *CW*, 2:240–47; Burlingame, *Abraham Lincoln*, 1:387; *Pearl & Pearl v. Graham et al.*, L01114; *People v. Sickler et al.*, L04956, *LPAL*. For a description of the *Pearl* cases, see chapter 3, the current volume.

12. *LDD*, 2:129.

13. "Speech at Peoria, Illinois," October 16, 1854, *CW*, 2:247–83 (original emphasis).

14. Whitney, *Life on the Circuit*, 209; Cunningham, "Some Recollections of Abraham Lincoln," 5; *LDD*, 2:130.

15. AL to Elihu N. Powell, November 27, 1854, *CW*, 2:289.

16. Burlingame, *Abraham Lincoln*, 1:390–406; Jesse K. Dubois to AL, November 21, 1854, ALPLC.

17. Swett to AL, December 19, 1854, ALPLC; King, *Lincoln's Manager*, 103; Samuel Parks to AL, December 13, 1854, ALPLC.

18. Burlingame, *Abraham Lincoln*, 1:404, 405; Leonard Swett to William H. Herndon, January 17, 1866, item 24, *HI*, 166; William Fithian to AL, December 20, 1854, ALPLC.

19. Attorneys to David Davis, March 30, 1855, *CW*, 2:310.

20. Goodwin, *Team of Rivals*, 174, 175; Burlingame, *Abraham Lincoln*, 1:340, 341; *LDD*, 2:156.

21. Selby, "Editorial Convention," 30–47.

22. *Bloomington (IL) Pantagraph*, February 27, 1856, 2.

23. Gienapp, *Origins of the Republican Party*, 254, 259.

24. *LDD*, 2:163–69.

25. *Spink v. Chiniquy*, L01448, *LPAL*; Whitney, *Life on the Circuit*, 73–75.

26. Richter, *Lincoln*, 176; *Urbana (IL) Union*, May 22, 1856, 2.

27. Richter, *Lincoln*, 180; Kyle, *Abraham Lincoln in Decatur*, 77–79.

28. Whitney, *Life on the Circuit*, 92.

29. Pratt, "Abraham Lincoln in Bloomington," 54.

30. "Official Account of the Convention," May 30, 1856, 3. The appendix to Chrissey's book has biographical sketches of those persons the author asserts were present. Prince, *Meeting of May 29, 1900 Commemorative of the Convention of May 29, 1856*, contains the most complete account on this momentous meeting.

31. "Speech at Bloomington, Illinois, as Reported in the *Alton (IL) Weekly Courier*," *CW*, 2:341; Scott, *Lincoln on the Stump*, 20; Wakefield, *How Lincoln Became President*, 65; Foote, *Civil War*, 1:29; *Weekly Pantagraph* (Bloomington, Illinois), June 4, 1856.

32. T. Lyle Dickey to William H. Herndon, item 398, *HI*, 504.

33. *HL*, 236.

34. *LDD*, 2:170; Kyle, *Abraham Lincoln in Decatur*, 81; "Speech at Springfield, Illinois," June 10, 1856, *CW*, 2:344, quoting the *Illinois State Register* (Springfield), June 12, 1856.

35. Whitney, *Life on the Circuit*, 94–97; O'Donnell, *Life of Judge Joseph O. Cunningham*, 19–21; Burlingame, *Abraham Lincoln*, 423; Beveridge, *Abraham Lincoln*, 4:39.

36. *Proceedings of the First Three Republican Conventions*, 41; Burlingame, *Abraham Lincoln*, 423; Harper, *Lincoln and the Press*, 20.

37. Wilson, *Cherishing the Past*, 2; *Urbana (IL) Union*, June 26, 1856, 2.

38. Whitney, *Life on the Circuit*, 419–21.

39. *Prairie Beacon* (Paris, Illinois), August 8, 1856, 2.

40. *Memories of Abraham Lincoln in Edgar County*, 22–27.

41. D. C. Smith, "Lincoln-Thornton Debate," 97–100.

42. "Speech at Shelbyville, Illinois," August, 9, 1856, *CW*, 2:359, quoting the *Illinois State Register*, August 19, 1856; Cooper, "Lincoln-Thornton Debate," 105.
43. *Lincoln v. Alexander*, L01656, *LPAL; People v. Crockett*, L00661, *LPAL*.
44. King, *Lincoln's Manager*, 114; AL to Henry C. Whitney, July 9, 1856, *CW*, 2:347; AL to David Davis, July 7, 1856, in Basler, *Collected Works of Abraham Lincoln, Supplement*, 27.
45. *LDD*, 2:177, 78, 79; "Speech at Bloomington, Illinois," September 12, 1856, *CW*, 2:375.
46. Felts, "A. Lincoln in Piatt," 55, 56; Piatt, *History of Piatt County*, 505, 640; Allen and Lacey, *Illinois Elections 1818–1990*, 135–37, 1856 returns.
47. *Urbana (IL) Union*, September 25, 1856; Allen and Lacey, *Illinois Elections 1818–1990*, 135–37, 1856 returns.
48. Kyle, *Abraham Lincoln in Decatur*, 85–93, 90.
49. Prince, *Day with Abraham Lincoln*, 5–6.
50. *LDD*, 2:180, 181, *Bloomington (IL) Pantagraph*, October 27, 1856.
51. *Spink v. Chiniquy*, L01448, *LPAL*; McDermott, "*Spink, and Chiniquy*," 2–4; Chiniquy promissory note, in McDermott, "*Spink, and Chiniquy*," 3; *LDD*, 2:170–82; Whitney, *Life on the Circuit*, 420.
52. *Metamora (IL) Herald*, August 24, 1928, 6; *LDD*, 2:182.
53. "Form Letter to Fillmore Men," September 8, 1956, *CW*, 2:374; *Dewitt Courier*, Clinton, Illinois, October 15, 1856, 2.
54. Moses, *Illinois Historical and Statistical*, 2:1140.
55. *People v. Anderson and Anderson*, L04190, *LPAL*. See also Fenster, *Case of Abraham Lincoln*, an informative book that fully examines the case in the context of the circuit and its politics.
56. *LDD*, 2:185.
57. *People v. Wyant*, L01676, *LPAL; Bloomington (IL) Weekly Pantagraph*, April 15, 1857, 3; Duff, *A. Lincoln, Prairie Lawyer*, 304–7.
58. *Fleming v. Rogers and Crothers*, L01566, *LPAL*.
59. *Lincoln v. the Illinois Central Railroad*, L01660, and *Hurd v. Rock Island Bridge Company*, L03310, L03311, all in *LPAL*.
60. *People v. Goings*, L01800, *LPAL*; Duff, *A. Lincoln, Prairie Lawyer*, 347–49; Myers, *Justice Served*, 1–4; *People v. Goings and Beck*, L01801, *LPAL; Ricketts v. Goings*, L01158, *LPAL*.
61. *LDD*, 2:181–87; *Pike v. Schaffer*, L01678, *LPAL*.

11. The Tall Sucker and the Little Giant

1. *People ex rel. Lanphier and Walker v. Hatch*, L04112, *LPAL*. Volume 4 in *PAL* devotes chapter 50, 64–92, to this case.
2. King, *Lincoln's Manager*, 129–30.
3. *LDD*, 2:211; Beveridge, *Abraham Lincoln*, 4:196.
4. Johannsen, *Stephen A. Douglas*, 576–613.
5. "First Lecture on Discoveries and Inventions," April 6, 1858, *CW*, 2:61; Pratt, "Abraham Lincoln in Bloomington," 61. Centre Hall is still standing.
6. Burlingame, *Abraham Lincoln*, 1:454–56; Wakefield, *How Lincoln Became President*, 79.
7. Ostendorf, *Lincoln's Photographs*, 14.

8. AL to Thomas A. Marshall, April 23, 1858, *CW*, 2:443; *Urbana (IL) Union*, May 20, 1853, 3; *Prairie Beacon* (Paris, Illinois), May 29, 1858, 2.

9. Pratt, "Abraham Lincoln in Bloomington," 56; Guelzo, *Lincoln and Douglas*, 54.

10. Burlingame, *Abraham Lincoln*, 1:456; *Proceedings of the Republican State Convention*, June 16, 1858; Guelzo, *Lincoln and Douglas*, 56.

11. "'A House Divided' Speech at Springfield, Illinois," June 16, 1858, *CW*, 2:461–69; Guelzo, *Lincoln and Douglas*, 59; Leonard Swett to William H. Herndon, item 24, *HI*, 162.

12. AL to Charles H. Ray, June 27, 1858, ALPLC.

13. Burlingame, *Abraham Lincoln*, 1:468–69; "Speech at Chicago, Illinois," July 10, 1855, *CW*, 2:484.

14. Striner, *Father Abraham*, 61.

15. Douglas, quoted in Guelzo, *Lincoln and Douglas*, 47–78.

16. Guelzo, *Lincoln and Douglas*, 293, 299; Johannsen, *Stephen A. Douglas*, 680.

17. Burlingame, *Abraham Lincoln*, 545; Pratt, "Abraham Lincoln in Bloomington," 56.

18. William J. Usrey to AL, July 19, 1858, ALPLC.

19. Guelzo, *Lincoln and Douglas*, 89; AL to Stephen A. Douglas, July 24, 1858, *CW*, 2:522.

20. Guelzo, *Lincoln and Douglas*, 106; A. T. Rice, *Reminiscences*, 205–7.

21. Stephen A. Douglas to AL, July 24, 1858, *CW*, 2:528n1.

22. Felts, "A. Lincoln in Piatt," 58–61; Bryant Cottage, Bement, Illinois, brochure. These sources claim that Lincoln and Douglas met at the Bryant cottage, an existing Illinois historic site, on July 29. This meeting is disputed.

23. AL to Stephen A. Douglas, July 29, 1858, *CW*, 2:528; AL to Stephen A. Douglas, July 31, 1858, *CW*, 2:531–32 (footnote 1 includes Douglas's July 30 response to Lincoln's letter of July 29); AL to Stephen A. Douglas, July 31, 1858, *CW*, 2:531.

24. Harris, *Lincoln's Rise to the Presidency*, 107.

25. "Speech at Monticello, Illinois," July 29, 1858, *CW*, 2:527.

26. *Urbana (IL) Union*, August 5, 1858, 2.

27. *LDD*, 2:224; "Speech at Havana, Illinois," August 14, 1858, *CW*, 2:541–43.

28. "Speech at Bath, Illinois," August 16, 1858, *CW*, 2:543–44.

29. Davis and Wilson, *Lincoln-Douglas Debates*, 26, 28; AL to Joseph O. Cunningham, August 22, 1858, 37, *CW*, 3:37.

30. *LDD*, 2:226; Thomas J. Pickett to AL, August 3, 1858, ALPLC; David Davis to AL, August 31, 1858, ALPLC; David Davis to AL, August 10, 1858, ALPLC; Benjamin F. James to AL, August 25, 1858, ALPLC; John A. Jones to AL, August 7, 1858, ALPLC.

31. "Speech at Tremont, Illinois," August 30, 1858, *CW*, 3:76, quoting the *Chicago Press and Tribune*, September 2, 1858.

32. "Speech at Pekin, Illinois," October 5, 1858, *CW*, 3:206; *LDD*, 1:231, quoting the *Chicago Press and Tribune*, October 7, 1858.

33. David Davis to AL, November 7, 1858, ALPLC.

34. *Bloomington (IL) Daily Pantagraph*, September 3, 1858, 1; "Speeches at Clinton, Illinois," September 2, 1858, *CW*, 3:81–84.

35. Starr, *Lincoln and the Railroads*, 140, 141. This house stills stands on the outskirts of Clinton.

36. Schwartz, "You Can Fool All of the People," 1, 3, 6; Phillips, *Abraham Lincoln by Some Men Who Knew Him*, 102; Clifton H. Moore interview, item 630, *HI*, 731.
37. *Daily Pantagraph* (Bloomington, Illinois), September 6, 1858, 2; "Speech at Bloomington, Illinois," September 4, 1858, *CW*, 3:85–90; Wakefield; *How Lincoln Became President*, 35, 90.
38. *Daily Pantagraph* (Bloomington, Illinois), September 8, 1858, 2.
39. Stringer, *History of Logan County*, 281.
40. Felts, "A. Lincoln in Piatt," 61–63; Whitney, *Life on the Circuit with Lincoln*, 59; *Chicago Press and Tribune*, September 9, 1856; Piatt, *History of Piatt County*, 640.
41. Paris Republican Central Committee to AL, August 4, 1858, ALPLC; McCormick, "Wabash Valley Resident William P. Dole."
42. Day, *Museum Minutiae*, 46.
43. *Prairie Beacon* (Paris, Illinois), September 7, 1858, 2.
44. *Weekly Valley Blade* (Paris, Illinois), September 8, 1858–November 10, 1858.
45. Hamand, *Ward Hill Lamon*, 103; Johannsen, *Stephen A. Douglas*, 658, 659.
46. *Weekly Valley Blade* (Paris, Illinois), September 22, 1858, 2, and September 29, 1858, 2.
47. Sparks, *Lincoln-Douglas Debates*, 307; *Chicago Democrat*, September 22, 1858, quoted in ibid., 318.
48. "Fourth Debate with Stephen A. Douglas at Charleston, Illinois," September 18, 1858, *CW*, 3:145–201, 146.
49. "Second Debate with Stephen A. Douglas at Freeport, Illinois," August 7, 1858, *CW*, 38–76; "Fifth Debate with Stephen A. Douglas, Galesburg, Illinois," October 7, 1858, *CW*, 3:207–44.
50. Richard Striner examines Lincoln's manner of dealing with the electorate's racism in chapter 3, "Lincoln and Free Soil 1854–1858," *Father Abraham*, 35–88. Allen Guelzo addresses it in a direct manner in his discussion of the Charleston debate in *Lincoln and Douglas*, 191–95.
51. "Fifth Debate," *CW*, 219, 222.
52. *Sullivan (IL) Express*, October 1, 1858, quoted in Stone, *Untitled Compilation of Newspaper Accounts*, 2.
53. AL to Stephen A. Douglas, September 20, 1858, *CW*, 3:201, 202.
54. *Sullivan (IL) Express*, October 15, 1858; "Reminiscences of F. N. Green," February 8, 1823, *Illinois State Register*, September 23, 1858, all quoted in Stone, *Untitled Compilation of Newspaper Accounts*, 9–14, 19.
55. *Illinois State Register*, September 23, 1858, as quoted in Stone, *Untitled Compilation of Newspaper Accounts*, 14.
56. AL to William Fithian, September 3, 1858, *CW*, 3:84; Hiram Beckwith, "Lincoln: Personal Recollections," *Chicago Tribune*, December 29, 1895.
57. *Danville (IL) Press*, September 29, 1858, quoted in Richter, *Lincoln*, 213; Gary, *Following in Lincoln's Footsteps*, 53. The Fithian home, including Lincoln's room and the balcony, still stands.
58. Harmon, *Mrs. Harmon's Reminiscence*, 3; AL to Norman B. Judd, September 23, 1858, *CW*, 3:202.
59. Abraham Smith to AL, May 31, 1858; July 20, 1858, ALPLC.

60. Cunningham, *History of Champaign County*, 792; *Central Illinois Gazette* (Champaign, Illinois), September 29, 1858, 2; Hill, *Lincoln the Lawyer*, 80; Whitney, *Life on the Circuit*, 57.

61. Berlochler, "Illinois Lincoln Site Rediscovered," 211–22; *Central Illinois Gazette* (Champaign, Illinois), September 29, 1858, 2; Henry C. Whitney to AL, September 23, 1858, ALPLC; Whitney, *Life on the Circuit*, 59. The Boyden house still stands.

62. Cunningham, "Some Recollections of Abraham Lincoln," 10.

63. *Urbana (IL) Union*, September 29, 1858; Cunningham, *History of Champaign County*, 795.

64. R. L. Moore, *History of Woodford County*, 140; *People v. Goings and Beck*, L01801, *LPAL*.

65. R. R. Wilson, *Intimate Memories*, 193.

66. Guelzo, *Lincoln and Douglas*, 238; Stringer, *History of Logan County*, 281.

67. *LDD*, 2:234, 235; "Fragment: Last Speech of the Campaign at Springfield, Illinois," October 30, 1858, *CW*, 3:334; Barrett, *Lincoln's Last Speech*, 17, 18.

68. Illinois, General Assembly, Senate, *Journal of the Senate of the Twenty-First General Assembly*, January 6, 1859; Clayton, *Illinois Fact Book and Historical Almanac*; 1858, Illinois House and Senate Return in Guelzo, *Compilation of 1858 Election Returns*, 1–9.

69. *Prairie Beacon* (Paris, Illinois), November 12, 1858, 2; Guelzo, *Lincoln and Douglas*, 286; *Weekly Valley Blade* (Paris, Illinois), November 10, 1858, 2.

70. Harper, *Lincoln and the Press*, 27, quoting the *Chicago Press and Tribune*, November 10, 1858.

71. AL to M. M. Inman, November 20, 1858, *CW*, 3:341.

72. AL to Anson G. Henry, November 19, 1858, *CW*, 3:339.

73. AL to Norman B. Judd, November 15, 1858, *CW*, 3:336; AL to Henry Asbury, November 19, 1858, *CW*, 3:339; AL to Anson S. Miller, November 19, 1858, *CW*, 3:340; AL to Eleazar Paine, November 19, 1858, *CW*, 3:340; AL to B. Clark Lundy, November 26, 1858, *CW*, 3:342.

74. AL to Charles H. Ray, November 20, 1858, *CW*, 3:341; AL to Henry C. Whitney, November 30, 1858, *CW*, 3:343, and December 25, 1858, *CW*, 3:347.

75. AL to Norman Judd, November 16, 1858, *CW*, 3:337.

76. Pratt, *Personal Finances*, 54, 78, 79.

77. *LDD*, 2:235, 238.

12. A Little Sketch

1. R. D. Richardson, *Abraham Lincoln's Autobiography*, 37; Ecelbarger, *Great Comeback*, 2, 3; W. E. Barringer, *Lincoln's Rise to Power*, 65–68.

2. Charles H. Lanphier, quoted in Patton, *Glory to God and the Sucker Democracy*, 1:108.

3. Whitney, *Life on the Circuit*, 51.

4. Ecelbarger, *Great Comeback*, 13–16; Whitney, *Life on the Circuit*, 411, 412.

5. Burlingame, *Abraham Lincoln*, 1:553.

6. Ecelbarger, *Great Comeback*, 26–31; *LDD*, 2:244; "Speech at Chicago, Illinois," March 1, 1859, *CW*, 3:365–70.

7. AL to William A. Ross, March 26, 1859, *CW*, 3:372.

8. J. H. Burnham to his father, May 19, 1860, quoted in Pratt, *Concerning Mr. Lincoln*, 22.

9. Pratt, "Abraham Lincoln in Bloomington," 56; AL to Asahel Gridley, April 4, 1859, in Basler, *Collected Works of Abraham Lincoln, Supplement*, 39; Ecelbarger, *Great Comeback*, 38; AL to Gustav P. Koerner, April 11, 1859, *CW*, 3:376.

10. R. D. Richardson, *Abraham Lincoln's Autobiography*, 7; AL to Thomas J. Pickett, April 16, 1859, *CW*, 3:337.

11. *People v. Patterson*, L01488, *LPAL*; Whitney, *Life on the Circuit*, 466.

12. Burlingame, introduction, viii; Holzer, *Lincoln's White House Secretary*, 179–93.

13. Ecelbarger, *Great Comeback*, 40, 41; "Contract with Theodore Canisius," May 30, 1859, *CW*, 3:383.

14. "To the Editor of the *Central Transcript*," July 3, 1859, *CW*, 3:389.

15. *Bloomington (IL) Pantagraph*, July 5, 1859.

16. Price and Adams, *Twelve Momentous Years*, 74, 75; Stringer, *History of Logan County*, 227.

17. Ecelbarger, *Great Comeback*, 48, 49.

18. *People v. Harrison*, L04306, *LPAL*; Bray, *Peter Cartwright*, 248–57. This is the only Lincoln trial that is transcribed.

19. *LDD*, 2:258–62; *Clinton Central Transcript*, October 6, 1859, 2.

20. *LDD*, 2:263; *Clinton Central Transcript*, October 20, 1859, 2; "Speech at Clinton, Illinois," October 14, 1859, *CW*, 3:487.

21. "Speech at Springfield, Illinois," October 15, 1859, *CW*, 3:489; Holzer, *Lincoln at Cooper Union*, 10; AL to James A. Briggs, November 13, 1859, *CW*, 3:494.

22. Leroy, *Mr. Lincoln's Book*, 49–51; AL to Samuel Galloway, December 19, 1859, in Basler, *Collected Works of Abraham Lincoln, Supplement*, 47.

23. R. D. Richardson, *Abraham Lincoln's Autobiography*, 7; AL to Jesse Fell, enclosing autobiography, December 20, 1859, *CW*, 3:511, 512.

24. AL to Norman B. Judd, December 14, 1859, *CW*, 2:509; Ecelbarger, *Great Comeback*, 112–14.

25. *Bloomington (IL) Daily Pantagraph*, October 18, 1859, 1.

26. Richter, *Lincoln*, 241, 243; *Clinton (IL) Central Transcript*, November 3, 1859, 2; *Champaign Central Illinois Gazette*, December 21, 1859, 2.

27. Stapp, *Footprints in the Sands*, 41; Richter, *Lincoln*, 45.

13. No Stone Unturned

1. W. C. Harris, *Lincoln's Rise*, 204. Doris Kearns Goodwin's *Team of Rivals*, already a classic, is a well-documented treatment of the relationship of these four and includes lively biographies of the four candidates and their pursuit of the presidency as well as their relationships in Lincoln's cabinet.

2. W. E. Barringer, *Lincoln's Rise to Power*, 136; AL to Fernando Jones, January 15, 1860, *CW*, 3:514; R. D. Richardson, *Abraham Lincoln's Autobiography*, 8, 9, 17.

3. *LDD*, 2:269–73; W. E. Barringer, *Lincoln's Rise to Power*, 142–44; Ecelbarger, *Great Comeback*, 117, 118.

4. Two versions of Lincoln's lecture "Discoveries and Inventions" exist, according to Roy Basler, the editor of *Collected Works of Abraham Lincoln*. "First Lecture on Discoveries and Inventions" was given in Bloomington on April 6, 1858. *CW*, 2:437–42. His revised "Second Lecture on Discoveries and Inventions" was first given on February 11, 1859, in Jacksonville and repeated on several occasions. *CW*, 3:356–63. Some historians believe that it was all part of one lecture dividing the manuscript. Wayne C. Temple, "Discoveries and Inventions," special twelve-page supplement, *Jacksonville (IL) Journal Courier*, May 23, 1982. *Collected Works* omits the Pontiac rendition. It is not known which version was given in Pontiac.

5. Bateman, *Historical Encyclopedia of Illinois and History of Livingston County*, 726; *Pontiac (IL) Sentinel*, January 31, 1860, 3; "Gus to Mary P. Christian," January 28, 1860, quoted in Pratt, *Concerning Mr. Lincoln*, 21.

6. Jason Strevell to his son Charles, March 21, 1901, in Sanken, "Abraham Lincoln Slept Here"; Strevell, *Story of the Strevell Museum*, 48. A photograph of the door jamb is on page 49 of Strevell, *Story of the Strevell Museum*.

7. Temple, "Delegates," 294.

8. AL to Richard M. Corwine, April 6, 1860, *CW*, 4:36.

9. Ecelbarger, *Great Comeback*, 121, 124.

10. W. C. Harris, *Lincoln's Rise*, 154–58; Burlingame, *Abraham Lincoln*, 1:578, 579.

11. The first three were the Peoria speech of October 16, 1854, the Bloomington "Lost Speech" of May 29, 1856, and the "House Divided" speech of June 16, 1858.

12. *New York Tribune*, March 12, 1860, quoted in Holzer, *Lincoln at Cooper Union*, 201.

13. Leroy, *Mr. Lincoln's Book*, 75, 97, 153–66.

14. Wakefield, *How Lincoln Became President*, 106, 107; *Bloomington (IL) Daily Pantagraph*, April 11, 1860, 2.

15. AL to Richard M. Corwine, May 2, 1860, *CW*, 4:47.

16. Plummer, *Lincoln's Rail-Splitter*, 41.

17. Temple, "Delegates," 290–97; Kyle, *Abraham Lincoln in Decatur*, 100–118.

18. Plummer, *Lincoln's Rail-Splitter*, 42, 43; *Springfield (IL) Daily State Journal Register*, May 11, 1860; Ecelbarger, *Great Comeback*, 180, 185.

19. Ecelbarger, *Great Comeback*, 187; Ostendorf, *Lincoln's Photographs*, 40, 41.

20. Kyle, *Abraham Lincoln in Decatur*, 114.

21. W. C. Harris, *Lincoln's Rise*, 197.

22. Burlingame, *Abraham Lincoln*, 1:602; Doris Kearns Goodwin, interview, *Lincoln: Prelude to the Presidency*; Ray, *Convention That Nominated Lincoln*, 5–10; Ecelbarger, *Great Comeback*, 204.

23. Ecelbarger, *Great Comeback*, 218.

24. Burlingame, *Abraham Lincoln*, 1:602; Angle and Miers, *Fire the Salute!* 53–61; King, *Lincoln's Manager*, 135–36. Angle and Miers lists all of the officers and delegates.

25. King, *Lincoln's Manager*, 135; W. E. Barringer, *Lincoln's Rise to Power*, 193; Hill, *Lincoln the Lawyer*, 285, 286; AL to Richard M. Corwine, May 2, 1860, *CW*, 4:47; AL to Cyrus M. Allen, May 1, 1860, *CW*, 4:46.

26. Richardson and Farley, *John Palmer Usher*, 10, 11; W. E. Barringer, *Lincoln's Rise to Power*, 215; Burlingame, *Abraham Lincoln*, 1:611; R. Thomas, "Caleb Blood Smith," 139–46.

27. W. E. Barringer, *Lincoln's Rise to Power*, 230; AL to Hawkins Taylor, April 21, 1860, *CW*, 4:45; Porter, *Portrait of a Prairie Lawyer*, 139, 140.

28. King, *Lincoln's Manager*, 135–36; Ecelbarger, *Great Comeback*, 193.

29. Leonard Swett to J. H. Drummond, May 27, 1860, in R. R. Wilson, *Intimate Memories of Lincoln*, 296.

30. Angle and Miers, *Fire the Salute!* 53–61; Ecelbarger, *Great Comeback*, 204.

31. Ecelbarger, *Great Comeback*, 206; W. C. Harris, *Lincoln's Rise*, 208; David Davis to AL, telegram, May 17, 1860, ALPLC.

32. "Endorsement on the Margin of the *Missouri Democrat*," May 17, 1860, *CW*, 4:50; King, *Lincoln's Manager*, 139–42; Whitney, *Lincoln the Citizen*, 289.

33. Burlingame, *Abraham Lincoln*, 1:609.

34. Ecelbarger, *Great Comeback*, 219; Hamand, *Ward Hill Lamon*, 116, 117; R. R. Wilson, *Intimate Memories of Lincoln*, 125; Henry M. Russell, reminiscences, January 14, 1909, Centennial Association Papers, ALPLM; W. C. Harris, *Lincoln's Rise*, 208.

35. Angle and Miers's *Fire the Salute!* includes the contemporary accounts of Cincinnati's Murat Halstead.

36. Angle and Miers, *Fire the Salute!* 39.

37. Ibid., 40–41.

38. W. C. Harris, *Lincoln's Rise*, 209; Ecelbarger, *Great Comeback*, 221–31. Angle and Miers's *Fire the Salute!* lists the three ballots. 39–43.

39. Angle and Miers, *Fire the Salute!* 45; Duis, *Good Old Times in McLean County*, 280; Leonard Swett to William H. Herndon, August 29, 1887, item 67, *HI*, 709, 710.

40. W. C. Harris, *Lincoln's Rise*, 195; Goodwin, *Team of Rivals*, 258.

41. R. R. Wilson, *Intimate Memories of Lincoln*, 193; Burlingame, *Abraham Lincoln*, 1:615.

42. Thurlow Weed, quoted in Wakefield, *How Lincoln Became President*, 124, 125; R. R. Wilson, *Intimate Memories of Lincoln*, 194.

43. Leonard Swett to J. H. Drummond, May 27, 1860, in R. R. Wilson, *Intimate Memories of Lincoln*, 294.

44. *LDD*, 2:282–84.

45. King, *Lincoln's Manager*, 150–54; Green, *Lincoln and the Election of 1860*, 80–84.

46. Howells, *Life of Abraham Lincoln*, notes in margins throughout; "Endorsement: David Davis to John Wood Concerning Pardon of Thomas Patterson," August 14, 1860, *CW*, 4:93.

47. AL to William Fithian, August 18, 1860, *CW*, 4:95; Pavey, *O. F. Harmon*, 59; Lamon to AL, October 10, 1860, ALPLC.

48. R. C. White, *A. Lincoln*, 343.

49. Pratt, *Personal Finances*, 110, 111; Browne, *Abraham Lincoln*, 2:468.

50. Hamand, *Ward Hill Lamon*, 129, quoting Ward Hill Lamon to AL, October 10, 1860, ALPLC.

51. R. C. White, *A. Lincoln*, 347; Holzer, *Lincoln, President-Elect*, 173; Burlingame, *Abraham Lincoln*, 1:363.

52. Holzer, *Lincoln, President-Elect*, 173; Burlingame, *Abraham Lincoln*, 1:363.

53. Johannsen, *Stephen A. Douglas*, 749–73; R. C. White, *A. Lincoln*, 333; Andrews, "How We Got Lincoln," 1.

54. *New York Times*, June 2, 25, and 26, 1860, quoted in Green, *Lincoln and the Election of 1860*, 71.

55. AL to Simeon Francis, August 4, 1860, *CW*, 4:89, 90.

56. Guelzo, *Compilation of 1858 Election Returns*, flat file.

57. Allen and Lacey, *Illinois Elections*, 135–37, 144–47, 154–55; Moses, *Illinois Historical and Statistical*, 2:1208, 1209.

58. Ibid.

59. W. C. Harris, *Lincoln's Rise*, 87, 83.

60. Ibid., 201.

61. Johannsen, *Stephen A. Douglas*, 620, 733–40; R. C. White, *A. Lincoln*, 295.

14. We Saw Him No More

1. Holzer, *Lincoln, President-Elect*, 85; "Remarks at Lincoln, Bloomington, and Lexington, Illinois," November 21, 1860, *CW*, 4:143, 144; Ostendorf, *Lincoln's Photographs*, 67; AL to Whitney, November 26, 1860, *CW*, 4:146.

2. Goodwin, *Team of Rivals*, 287; Burlingame, *Abraham Lincoln*, 1:736, 740; King, *Lincoln's Manager*, 175; Holzer, *Lincoln, President-Elect*, 151, 169, 228.

3. Joseph Gillespie, recollections, in R. R. Wilson, *Intimate Memories of Lincoln*, 334.

4. *LDD*, 3:8.

5. *HL*, 290.

6. "Farewell Address at Springfield, Illinois," February 11, 1861, *CW*, 4:190, 191; *Clinton (IL) Central Transcript*, February 14, 1861, 2.

7. Tilton, *Lincoln's Last View*, 1, 4; Holzer, *Lincoln, President-Elect*, 305; Kyle, *Abraham Lincoln in Decatur*, 122, 123. Tilton includes the train's timetable.

8. "Remarks at Tolono, Illinois," February 11, 1861, *CW*, 4:191.

9. Richter, *Lincoln*, 273, 274; "Remarks at Danville, Illinois," February 11, 1861, *CW*, 4:191–92; Holzer, *Lincoln, President-Elect*, 306.

10. Holzer, *Lincoln, President-Elect*, 306; Burlingame, *Abraham Lincoln*, 2:36, 37.

11. Burlingame, *Abraham Lincoln*, 2:59; Garraty, Carnes, and Berwanger, *American National Biography*, 2:7, 8; Johannsen, *Stephen A. Douglas*, 843.

12. Duff, *A. Lincoln, Prairie Lawyer*, 168.

13. W. L. Miller, *President Lincoln*, 48–90.

14. Frank, *Lincoln as a Lawyer*, 141–67.

15. "First Inaugural Address—Final Text," March 4, 1861, *CW*, 4:262, 265; "Message to Congress in Special Session," July 4, 1861, *CW*, 4:421, 435–36.

16. Richard Hofstadter, quoted in Guelzo, *Lincoln's Emancipation Proclamation*, 2.

17. Guelzo, *Lincoln's Emancipation Proclamation*, 222–24.

18. *People v. Wyant*, L01676, LPAL; W. L. Miller, *President Lincoln*, 273–88.

19. Frank, *Lincoln as a Lawyer*, 153, 154.

20. Harper, *Lincoln and the Press*, 172–76, 221.

21. John Hay, quoted in Hamand, *Ward Hill Lamon*, 392.

22. Duff, *A. Lincoln, Prairie Lawyer*, 322–25.

23. Garraty, Carnes, and Berwanger, *American National Biography*, 19:838; AL to Simon Cameron, August 19, 1861, *CW*, 4:491, 492; James Shields to John G. Nicolay [February 1863], ALPLC.

24. Goodwin, *Team of Rivals*, 395, 396; Leonard Swett to AL, November 9, 1861, AL-PLC; Behrens, *From Salt Fork to Chickamauga*, 73.

25. Burlingame, *Oral History of Abraham Lincoln*, 58, 59; Wakefield, *How Lincoln Became President*, 131; Herbert Swett, diary.

26. Holzer, *Lincoln's White House Secretary*, 4, 5.

27. R. C. White, *Eloquent President*, 190–222; AL to James C. Conkling, August 26, 1863, *CW*, 406–10.

28. Burlingame, *Abraham Lincoln*, 2:83, 84; Berry, *House of Abraham*, 69.

29. Boslooper, *General Asahel Gridley*, 18, 19.

30. A. Hunt, *Kirby Benedict*, 158, 184, 224; *New Mexican* (Santa Fe, New Mexico), August 8, 15, and 22, 1863, with notes from Kirby Benedict to David Davis, McLean County Historical Library; Burlingame, *Abraham Lincoln*, 1:330.

31. Towne, "Such Conduct Must Be Put Down."

32. AL to Simon Cameron, March 21, 1861, *CW*, 4:297; AL to John P. Usher, April 3, 1863, *CW*, 6:161; AL to Alvin Truesdale, April 20, 1863, *CW*, 6:182; AL to Montgomery C. Meigs, May 4, 1863, *CW*, 6:196.

33. Usher Linder to AL, March 26, 1864, ALPLC.

34. AL to Gilman Marston, December 24, 1863, *CW*, 7:91; AL to Usher Linder, December 26, 1863, *CW*, 7:94; Linder, *Reminiscences*, 38, 395–98.

35. Ward Hill Lamon to Richard Yates, July 3, 1864, quoted in Burlingame, *Abraham Lincoln*, 2:86.

36. Jesse K. DuBois to AL, March 27, 1861, ALPLC.

37. Jesse K. DuBois to Henry Clay Whitney, April 6, 1865, item 513, *HI*, 620.

38. David Davis to William Orme, January 27, 1862, Orme Papers.

39. King, *Lincoln's Manager*, 191–96.

40. Clifton Moore to AL, January 29, 1862; Lawrence Weldon to AL, February 5, 1862; John Stewart (*sic*) to AL forwarded by Swett, January 25, 1862; Judge Samuel Treat to AL forwarded by Swett, February 13, 1862; Stephen T. Logan to AL, February 13, 1862; John M. Scott to AL, February 11, 1862; William Butler and Jesse K. DuBois to AL, September 7, 1862; Oliver Davis to AL, February 3; E. N. Powell to AL, February 21, 1862; Champaign County Bar to AL, January 30, 1862; Macon County Bar Association to AL, 1862, all in ALPLC; and AL to Jesse Fell, January 2, 1861, Papers of Jesse Fell.

41. Ward Hill Lamon to William Orme, February 10, 1862, Orme Papers; David Davis to William Orme, February 23, 1862, Orme Papers.

42. Leonard Swett to AL, August 15, 1861, ALPLC; King, *Lincoln's Manager*, 196; August 27, 1862, Basler, *Collected Works of Abraham Lincoln, Supplement*, 149.

43. William Orme to Leonard Swett, May 14, 1861, Orme Papers.

44. Leonard Swett to William H. Herndon, January 17, 1866, item 124, *HI*, 165.

45. William Orme to Leonard Swett, May 14, 1861, Orme Papers.

46. Plummer, *Lincoln's Rail-Splitter*, 127.

47. Moses, *Illinois Historical*, 2:1208, 1209.

48. "Anthony Thornton," Biography, Reference, *LPAL*.

49. Duff, *A. Lincoln, Prairie Lawyer*, 74, 75; Pratt, *Personal Finances*, 84; "Pass for Mrs. Harriett C. Bledsoe," January 16, 1865, *CW*, 4:218; Bledsoe, *War between the States*; Barnhart, *Albert Taylor Bledsoe*, 39, 167, 197–98.

50. B. F. Harris, *Harris,* 57, 58; *Memories of Abraham Lincoln,* 26, 27; Whitney, *Life on the Circuit,* 143.

51. Burlingame, *Abraham Lincoln,* 2:177, 178; AL to Ephraim D. and Phoebe Ellsworth, May 25, 1861, *CW,* 4:385.

52. Johannsen, *Stephen A. Douglas,* 872, 868; Robert T. Merrick to AL, June 3, 1861, ALPLC; "Memorandum: Advice to Mrs. Stephen A. Douglas," *CW,* 5:32; AL to James M. Cutts, October 26, 1863, *CW,* 6:538.

53. Burlingame, *Abraham Lincoln,* 2:199, 200, 81.

54. Baldwin, "Colonel Harvey Hogg," 307; Duis, *Good Old Times,* 201; AL to Fannie McCullough, December 23, 1862, *CW,* 6:16, 17.

55. Pavey, *O. F. Harmon,* 162.

56. Robert Latham to AL, March 4, 1865, ALPLC.

57. "Last Public Address," April 11, 1865, *CW,* 8:399–406, 403; AL to Michael Hahn, March 13, 1864, *CW,* 7:243; Burlingame, *Abraham Lincoln,* 803.

58. Hamand, *Ward Hill Lamon,* 380.

59. AL to William P. Dole, April 14, 1865, *CW,* 8:410; AL to James Speed, April 14, 1865, *CW,* 8:412.

60. Plummer, *Lincoln's Rail-Splitter,* 106–9.

61. King, *Lincoln's Manager,* 226.

62. *Daily Pantagraph* (Bloomington, Illinois), April 18, 1865, 2.

63. *Champaign (IL) Gazette,* April 21, 1865, 3.

64. *Daily Pantagraph* (Bloomington, Illinois), May 4, 1865, 1.

65. Stringer, *History of Logan County,* 230.

BIBLIOGRAPHY

Abraham Lincoln Memorial Highway Association. *Route Traveled by the Thomas Lincoln Family Coming from Indiana to Illinois in the Year 1830.* Greenup, IL: Abraham Lincoln Memorial Highway Association, 1929.

Abraham Lincoln Presidential Library and Museum, Springfield, Illinois.

Adams, Harold. *The History of Eureka College, 1855–1982.* Eureka, IL: Eureka College, 1982.

Alcorn, Richard A. "Leadership and Stability in Mid-Nineteenth Century America: A Case Study of an Illinois Town." *Journal of American History* 61, no. 3 (1974): 685–702.

Alexander, Milton. Biographical file. Edgar County Historical Society. Edgar County Historical Library, Paris, Illinois.

Allen, Howard W., and Vincent A. Lacey, eds. *Illinois Elections 1818–1990 Candidates and County Returns for President, Governor, Senate, and House of Representatives.* Carbondale: Southern Illinois University Press, 1992.

Allensworth, Ben C., Newton Bateman, and Paul Selby, eds. *Historical Encyclopedia of Illinois, History of Tazewell County.* 2 vols. Chicago: Munsell, 1905.

Andrews, Peter. "How We Got Lincoln." *American Heritage* 39, no. 7, November 1988, 1.

Angle, Paul M. "Abraham Lincoln: Circuit Lawyer." Lincoln Centennial Association Papers. Springfield, IL: Lincoln Centennial Association, 1928.

———. *Here I Have Lived: A History of Lincoln's Springfield 1821–1865.* Chicago: Abraham Lincoln Book Shop, 1971.

———. Introduction to *Life on the Circuit with Lincoln,* by Henry Clay Whitney, 19–30. Edited by Paul M. Angle. Caldwell, ID: Caxton, 1940.

———. *One Hundred Years of Law—An Account of the Law Office with John T. Stuart Founded in Springfield, Illinois a Century Ago.* Springfield, IL: Brown, Hay, and Stephens, 1928.

Angle, Paul M., and Earl Schenck Miers, eds. *Fire the Salute! Abe Lincoln Is Nominated, Murat Halstead Reports, the Republican National Convention in Chicago, May 16, 17, 18, 1860.* Kingsport, TN: Kingsport, 1960.

Baber, Adin, and Mary E. Lobb. "How a Railroader Saw Lincoln Leave Illinois in 1861." Clayton C. Daugherty files. Illinois History and Lincoln Collection, University of Illinois, Urbana.

Bader, William D., and Frank J. Williams. "David Davis: Lawyer, Judge, and Politician in the Age of Lincoln." *Roger Williams University Law Review* 14, no. 2 (2009): 163–214.

Bajuyo, F. Karmann. *John Milton Scott, Bloomington's Benefactor*. Bloomington, IL: Self-published, 1994.

Baker, Willis C., and Patrick L. Miller. *Commemorative History of Champaign County, Illinois, 1833–1983*. Champaign, IL: Heritage, 1984.

Baldwin, William M. "Colonel Harvey Hogg." McLean County History Society, *School Record* 302–9.

Bannister, Daniel W. *Lincoln and the Supreme Court*. Springfield: Self-published, 1994.

Banton, O. T., ed. *History of Macon County, 1976*. Decatur, IL: Macon County Historical Society, 1976.

Barnhart, Terry A. *Albert Taylor Bledsoe: Defender of the Old South and Architect of the Lost Cause*. Baton Rouge: Louisiana State University Press, 2011.

Barrett, Oliver. *Lincoln's Last Speech in Springfield in the Campaign of 1858*. Chicago: University of Chicago Press, 1925.

Barringer, Floyd S. *Tour of Historic Springfield*. Springfield, IL: Self-published, 1971.

Barringer, William E. *Lincoln's Rise to Power*. Boston: Little, Brown, 1937.

Barry, Peter J., Jr. *The Charleston Illinois Riot March 28, 1867*. Urbana, IL: Self-published, 2007.

Bartelt, William E. *"There I Grew Up": Remembering Abraham Lincoln's Indiana Youth*. Indianapolis: Indiana Historical Society, 2008.

Basler, Roy P., ed. *The Collected Works of Abraham Lincoln*. 9 vols. New Brunswick, NJ: Rutgers University Press, 1953.

———, ed. *The Collected Works of Abraham Lincoln, Supplement 1832–1865*. Westport, CT: Greenwood, 1974.

Basler, Roy P., and Christian O. Basler, eds. *The Collected Works of Abraham Lincoln, Second Supplement 1845–1865*. New Brunswick, NJ: Rutgers University Press, 1990.

Bateman, Newton, ed. *Historical Encyclopedia of Illinois and History of Livingston County*. 2 vols. Chicago: Munsell, 1906.

———. ed. *Historical Encyclopedia of Illinois and History of Shelby County*. 2 vols. Chicago: Munsell, 1910.

Beard, William D. "Dalby Revisited: A New Look at Lincoln's 'Most Far-Reaching Case' in the Illinois Supreme Court." *Journal of the Abraham Lincoln Association* 20, no. 2 (1999): 1–16.

Beaver, Paul J. *Abraham Lincoln in Logan County, Illinois 1834–1860*. Lincoln, IL: Self-published, 2010.

Beckwith, H. W. *History of Vermilion County*. Chicago: Hill, 1879.

———. "Lincoln Personal Recollections of Him, His Contemporaries, and Law Practice in Eastern Illinois." *Chicago Tribune*, December 29, 1895.

Beeson, Helen. *Places and People in Old Decatur*. Decatur, IL: Zonta Club of Decatur, 1975.

Behrens, Robert H. *From Salt Fork to Chickamauga: Champaign County Soldiers in the Civil War*. Urbana, IL: Urbana Free Library, 1988.

Benner, Martha L., and Cullom Davis, eds. *The Law Practice of Abraham Lincoln: Complete Documentary Edition*. DVD-ROM. Champaign: University of Illinois Press, 2000. http://www.lawpracticeofabrahamlincoln.org.

Bennett, James O'Donnell. *"Private Joe" Fifer, Memories of War and Peace Imparted in His Ninety-Sixth Year.* Bloomington, IL: Pantagraph Printing and Stationery, 1936.

Berlocher, Stewart H. "An Illinois Lincoln Site Rediscovered, the Ezekiel Boyden House in Urbana." *Journal of Illinois History* 13, no 3 (2010): 211–21.

Berry, Stephen. *House of Abraham.* Boston: Houghton Mifflin, 2007.

Beveridge, Albert J. *Abraham Lincoln 1809–1858.* 4 vols. Boston: Houghton Mifflin, 1928.

Billings, Roger, and Frank J. Williams, eds. *Abraham Lincoln, Esq.—The Legal Career of America's Greatest President.* Lexington: University Press of Kentucky, 2010.

Biographical Record of DeWitt County, Illinois. Chicago: Clarke, 1901.

Biographical Record of Logan County, Illinois. Chicago: Clarke, 1901.

Bledsoe, Albert T. *The War between the States, or Was Secession a Constitutional Right Previous to the War of 1861–65?* Lynchburg, VA: Bell, 1915.

Boas, Norman F. *Abraham Lincoln Chronology: The Prairie Years 1809–1861.* Mystic, CT: Seaport Autographs, 2007.

———. *Seaport Autographs—Catalogue 18.* Mystic, CT: Seaport Autographs, 2010.

Boslooper, Thomas. "General Asahel Gridley of Bloomington, Illinois, Compeer of Abraham Lincoln." Collection of McLean County Historical Society. 1994.

Bowman, Alexander. "Map of Urbana, Illinois." 1858.

Bradsby, Henry C. *History of Vigo County, Indiana.* Chicago: Nelson, 1891.

Bray, Robert. *Peter Cartwright: Legendary Frontier Preacher.* Urbana: University of Illinois Press, 2005.

———. *Reading with Lincoln.* Carbondale: Southern Illinois University Press, 2010.

Brokaw, Nancy Steele. "Metamora." *Bloomington Pantagraph,* November 29, 1999.

Browne, Robert Henry. *Abraham Lincoln and the Men of His Time: His Cause, His Character, and True Place in History, and the Men, Statesmen, Heroes, Patriots, Who Formed the Illustrious League about Him.* 4 vols. Chicago: Blakely-Oswald, 1907.

Bruce, Robert V. *Lincoln and the Tools of War.* Indianapolis: Bobbs-Merrill, 1956.

"Bryant Cottage, Bement, Illinois." Brochure. Illinois Historical Preservation Agency, Springfield, Illinois. 1994.

Bumstead, C. M., and Darrell Tippett, eds. *Centennial History Monticello, Illinois.* Monticello, IL: Piatt County Republican, 1937.

Burlingame, Michael. *Abraham Lincoln: A Life.* 2 vols. Baltimore: Johns Hopkins University Press, 2008.

———. Introduction to *Dispatches from Lincoln's White House: The Anonymous Civil War Journalism of Presidential Secretary William O. Stoddard,* by William O. Stoddard, xi–xxvi. Edited by Burlingame. Lincoln: University of Nebraska Press, 2002.

———, ed. *"Lincoln's Humor" and Other Essays,* by Benjamin P. Thomas. Urbana: University of Illinois Press, 2002.

———, ed. *An Oral History of Abraham Lincoln: John G. Nicolay's Interviews and Essays.* Carbondale: Southern Illinois University Press, 1996.

Calabro, Marian. *The Perilous Journey of the Donner Party.* New York: Clarion, 1999.

Callary, Edwards. *Place Names of Illinois*. Urbana: University of Illinois Press, 2009.

Capps, Elizabeth Lushbaugh. "Early Recollections of Abraham Lincoln." File number HH2, Vertical File. Lincoln Room, Abraham Lincoln Presidential Library and Museum.

Carlock, William B. *A Compilation of the Historical and Biographical Writings of William Carlock: Also of the Ceremonies Attending the Dedication of the Lincoln Trail Monument, on the Line between McLean and Woodford Counties*. Self-published, n.d. (ca. 1925).

Carpenter, F. B. *The Inner Life of Abraham Lincoln: Six Months at the White House*. Boston: Houghton Mifflin, 1883.

Cavanagh, Helen M. *Funk of Funk's Grove: Farmer, Legislator, and Cattle King of the Old Northwest, 1797–1865*. Bloomington, IL: Pantagraph Printing and Stationery, 1952.

Champaign County Historical Archives. Urbana Free Library, Urbana, Illinois.

Christian County Historical Society, Taylorville, Illinois.

Christian County Title Co., Taylorville, Illinois. Abstract of Title, Lots 3, 4, 5 in Block 3 in DeCamp's 1st Addition to Edinburg, County of Christian, State of Illinois.

Clayton, John. *Illinois Fact Book and Historical Almanac, 1673–1968*. Carbondale: Southern Illinois University Press, 1970.

Cole, Arthur Charles. *The Era of the Civil War 1848–1870*. Vol. 3. *Centennial History of Illinois*. Edited by Clarence Walworth Alford. Springfield, IL: Illinois Centennial Commission, 1919.

Coleman, Charles H. *Abraham Lincoln and Coles County, Illinois*. New Brunswick, NJ: Scarecrow, 1955.

Coleman, E. T. *History of Decatur and Macon County, Illinois*. Decatur, IL: Herald Review, 1924–29. Collection of the Macon County Historical Society, Decatur, Illinois.

Combined History of Shelby and Moultrie Counties, Illinois. Philadelphia: Brink, McDonough, 1881.

Conkling Family Papers. Abraham Lincoln Presidential Library and Museum, Springfield, Illinois.

Cooper, Homer H. "The Lincoln-Thornton Debate of 1856 at Shelbyville, Illinois." *Journal of the Illinois State Historical Society* 10, no. 1 (1917): 101–22.

Corliss, Carlton J. *Main Line of Mid America: The Story of the Illinois Central*. New York: Creative Age, 1950.

Crissey, Elwell. *Lincoln's Lost Speech; The Pivot of His Career*. New York: Hawthorne, 1967.

Cunningham, Joseph O. *History of Champaign County*. Salem, MA: Higginson, n.d. First published by Munsell, Chicago, 1905.

———. "Some Recollections of Abraham Lincoln." Address to the Fireland Pioneer Association, Norwalk, Ohio. July 4, 1907. Reprint, *Pioneer*, December, 1909. Archives, Champaign County Historical Archives, Urbana Free Library, Urbana, Illinois.

Daugherty, Clayton C. "Lincoln at Tolono, Illinois." Clayton C. Daugherty file. Illinois History and Lincoln Collection, University of Illinois Library.

Davis, David, Family. Papers. Manuscripts Division, Abraham Lincoln Presidential Library and Museum, Springfield, Illinois.

Davis, Edwin. "Lincoln and Macon County, Illinois, 1830–1831." *Journal of the Illinois State Historical Society* 25, nos. 1 and 2 (1932): 63–107.

Davis, James E. *Frontier Illinois.* Bloomington: Indiana University Press, 1998.

Davis, Rodney O., and Douglas L. Wilson, eds. *The Lincoln-Douglas Debates.* Urbana: Knox College Lincoln Study, and University of Illinois Press, 2008.

Day, Teddy. "Lincoln in Edgar County." *Museum Minutiae. A Collection of Columns in Edgar County History in the Paris Beacon News from July 2000 to July 2003.* Also published in the *Paris Beacon News,* February 6, 2002.

DeWitt County Museum, Clinton, Illinois.

Dickinson, Burrus, and Elmira Dickinson. *A History of Eureka College with Biographical Sketches and Reminisces.* Eureka, IL: Eureka College, 1985.

Dillow, Mark, and Robin Dillow. Deed copy, January 20, 1855, from David and Sarah Davis to Clifton Moore.

Dirck, Brian. *Lincoln the Lawyer.* Urbana: University of Illinois Press, 2007.

Dodge, Daniel Kelham. "Lincoln in Champaign County." *Illinois Magazine* 21, no. 4, January–February, 1921, 3–5.

Donald, David Herbert. *Lincoln.* New York: Simon and Schuster, 1995.

———. *Lincoln's Herndon.* New York: Knopf, 1948.

Dooley, Raymond, ed. *The Namesake Town: A Centennial History of Lincoln Illinois.* Lincoln, IL: Fogman's, 1953.

Douthit, Jasper. *Jasper Douthit's Story; An Autobiography of a Pioneer.* Shelbyville, IL: Shelby County Historical and Genealogical Society, 1996.

Drennan, Dorothy D., Thelma B. Gardner, and Helen B. Broverman, eds. *Illinois Sesquicentennial Edition of Christian County History, 1880.* Jacksonville, IL: Production, 1968. Reprint, *History of Christian County.* Philadelphia: Brink, McDonough, 1880.

Duff, John J. *A. Lincoln, Prairie Lawyer.* New York: Rinehart, 1960.

Duis, E. *The Good Old Times in McLean County.* Bloomington, IL: Leader, 1874.

Dunne, Edward Fitzgerald. *Illinois the Heart of the Nation.* Chicago: Lewis, 1933.

Early History of Washington, Illinois, and Vicinity. Washington, IL: Tazewell County Reporter, 1929. Reprint, Washington Historical Society, Washington, DC, 2000.

"Early Leaders of the Illinois State Bar Association." *Illinois Bar Journal* (September 1962): 52.

Ecelbarger, Gary. *The Great Comeback, How Abraham Lincoln Beat the Odds to Win the 1860 Republican Nomination.* New York: St. Martin's, 2008.

Eckley, Robert S. "Leonard Swett: Lincoln's Legacy to the Chicago Bar." *Journal of the Illinois State Historical Society* 92, no. 1 (1999): 30–45.

———. "Lincoln's Intimate Friend: Leonard Swett." *Journal of the Illinois State Historical Society* 92, no. 1 (1999): 30–45.

Edgar County Historical Society, Paris, Illinois.

Elghammer, W. R. "William Fithian, M.D." Stapp, *Footprints in the Sands* 19–20.

Evergreen Cemetery, Bloomington, IL. Grave site of Lawrence Weldon and family.

Ewing, James S. "An Address on Abraham Lincoln, February 12, 1909." *Short Addresses*, 5–22. Bloomington, IL: Self-published, 1912.

Faragher, John Mack. *Sugar Creek Life on the Illinois Prairie*. New Haven: Yale University Press, 1986.

Federal Writers Project. *Delavan, 1837–1937: A Chronicle of 100 Years*. Delavan, IL: City of Delavan, 1937.

Fehrenbacher, Don E. *Prelude to Greatness: Lincoln in the 1850's*. Stanford: Stanford University Press, 1962.

Fell, Jesse. Papers (copies). Ames Library, Illinois Wesleyan University, Bloomington, Illinois. (Original documents in Library of Congress.)

Felts, James K. "A. Lincoln in Piatt." In *The Good Life in Piatt County*, edited by Jesse Borror Morgan, 49–67. Monticello, IL: Board of Supervisors, Piatt County, Illinois, 1968.

Fenster, Julie M. *The Case of Abraham Lincoln: A Story of Adultery, Murder, and the Making of a Great President*. New York: Palgrave Macmillan, 2007.

Fifer, Joseph W. "Address to the Annual Meeting of the Illinois State Bar Association, May 29, 1930." [Unknown title.] Springfield, IL: Proceedings of the Illinois State Bar Association, 1930, 354–75. Vertical File, McLean County History Museum, Bloomington, IL.

Filby, William P. *A Biography of American County Histories*. Baltimore: Genealogical, 1985.

Findley, Paul. *A. Lincoln: The Crucible of Congress*. New York: Crown, 1979.

Foote, Shelby. *The Civil War: A Narrative—Fort Sumter to Perryville*. Vol. 1. New York: Random, 1958.

Ford, Thomas. *History of Illinois from Its Commencement as a State from 1818 to 1847*. 2 vols. Chicago: Lakeside, 1945–46.

Fowkes, John, ed. *History of Christian County*. 2 vols. Chicago: Munsell, 1918.

Fraker, Guy C. "The Real Lincoln Highway: The Forgotten Lincoln Circuit Markers." *Journal of the Abraham Lincoln Association* 25, no. 1 (2004): 76–97.

Frank, John P. *Lincoln as a Lawyer*. Urbana: University of Illinois Press, 1961.

Franklin, Noah. "Address to the Illinois Senate." February 12, 1935. Private collection.

Freeze, J. R. *Bloomington City Directory*. Bloomington, IL: Wolf, 1855.

Friedman, S. Morgan. "The Inflation Calculator." *The Inflation Calculator*. 2010. http://www.westegg.com/inflation/.

Furnas, J. C. *The Americans, a Social History of the United States, 1587–1914*. New York: Putnam's, 1969.

Garraty, John A., Mark C. Carnes, and Eugene H. Berwanger, eds. *American National Biography*. 24 vols. New York: Oxford University Press, 1999.

Gary, Ralph. *Following in Lincoln's Footsteps: A Complete Annotated Reference to Hundreds of Historical Sites Visited by Abraham Lincoln*. New York: Carroll and Graf, 2001.

Gates, Paul Wallace. *The Illinois Central Railroad Company and Its Colonization Work*. Cambridge, MA: Harvard University Press, 1934.

General Laws of the State of Illinois Passed by the Eighteenth General Assembly of the State of Illinois, June 3, 1853. Springfield, IL: Lanphier and Walker, 1853.

Gienapp, William E. *The Origins of the Republican Party 1852–1856*. New York: Oxford University Press, 1987.

Gillespie, Charles S. *The Gillespie Family in Madison County*. Edwardsville, IL: Madison County Historical Museum and Archival Library, 1926.

Gillespie, Joseph. Introduction to *Reminiscences of the Early Bench and Bar of Illinois*, by Usher F. Linder, 9–20. Chicago: Chicago Legal News, 1879.

———. Papers, 1835–61. Chicago History Museum.

Gillett Family Papers. Abraham Lincoln Presidential Library and Museum, Springfield, IL.

Glendinning, Gene V. *The Chicago & Alton Railroad, the Only Way*. DeKalb: Northern Illinois University Press, 2002.

Goodwin, Doris Kearns. *Team of Rivals, the Political Genius of Abraham Lincoln*. New York: Simon and Schuster, 2005.

Gordon, Beulah. *Here and There in Shelby County. Articles and Poems Covering Years 1818–1936*. Shelbyville, IL: Shelby County Historical and Genealogical Society, 1973.

Green, Michael S. *Lincoln and the Election of 1860*. Carbondale: Southern Illinois University Press, 2011.

Guelzo, Allen C. "Come Outer and Community Men, Abraham Lincoln and the Idea of Community in 19th Century America." *Journal of the Abraham Lincoln Association* 21, no. 1 (2000): 1–29.

———. "Compilation of 1858 Results—Illinois General Assembly." Elections—Illinois—Statistics, Vertical File, 2008. Illinois State Archives and Abraham Lincoln Presidential Library and Museum, Springfield, Illinois.

———. *Lincoln and Douglas—The Debates That Defined America*. New York: Simon and Schuster, 2008.

———. *Lincoln's Emancipation Proclamation: The End of Slavery in America*. New York: Simon and Schuster, 2004.

Hamand, Lavern Marshall. "Lincoln's Particular Friend." In *Essays in Illinois History*, edited by Donald F. Tingley, 18–36. Carbondale: Southern Illinois University Press, 1968.

———. "Ward Hill Lamon: Lincoln's "Particular Friend." PhD diss., University of Illinois, 1949. Illinois History and Lincoln Collection, University of Illinois Library, University of Illinois.

Harding, Jacob. "Harding's Tribute to Lincoln." *Paris (IL) Prairie Beacon*, June 29, 1860, 2. Reprinted in *Paris (IL) Daily Beacon*, March 26, 1923, 1. Biographical file. Edgar County Historical Society, Paris, Illinois.

Harmon, Elizabeth. *Mrs. Harmon's Reminiscences of Lincoln*. MS., 5 pages, Vermilion County Museum Society, Danville, Illinois, n.d.

Harper, Robert S. *Lincoln and the Press*. New York: McGraw-Hill, 1951.

Harris, Benjamin Franklin. *Harris, a Historical Account of His Life from Boyhood to Old Age*. Champaign, IL: Harris, 1899.

Harris, Gibson William. "My Recollections of Abraham Lincoln." *Woman's Home Companion*, January 1904.

Harris, William C. *Lincoln's Rise to the Presidency*. Lawrence: University Press of Kansas, 2007.

Hasbrouck, Jacob L. *History of McLean County*. 2 vols. Topeka: Historical, 1924.

Hendrick, Burton J. *Lincoln's War Cabinet*. Boston: Little, Brown, 1946.

Hendrick, Willene, and George Hendrick, eds. *On the Illinois Frontier Dr. Hiram Rutherford 1840–1848*. Carbondale: Southern Illinois University Press, 1981.

Herndon-Weik Collection of Lincolnania. Manuscript Division, Library of Congress, Washington, DC.

Herndon, William H., and Jesse W. Weik. *Herndon's Lincoln: The True Story of a Great Life . . . The History and Personal Recollections of Abraham Lincoln*. 1889. Edited by Douglas L. Wilson and Rodney O. Davis. Urbana: University of Illinois Press, 2006.

Hickey, James T. *The Collected Writings of James T. Hickey: From Publications of the Illinois State Historical Society*. Springfield: Illinois State Historical Society, 1990.

———. "Oglesby's Fence Rail Dealings and the 1860 Decatur Convention." *Journal of the Illinois State Historical Society* 54, no. 1 (1961): 5–25.

Hill, Frederick Trevor. *Lincoln the Lawyer*. New York: Century, 1906.

History of Champaign County, Illinois: With Illustrations Descriptive of Its Scenery, and Biographical Sketches of Some of Its Prominent Men and Pioneers. Philadelphia: Brink, McDonough, 1878.

History of DeWitt County, Illinois, 1839–1968. 2 vols. Clinton, IL: Sesquicentennial Committee, 1968.

History of DeWitt County Illinois: With Biographical Sketches of Prominent Representative Citizens of the County. Chicago: Pioneer, 1910.

History of DeWitt County, Illinois: With Illustrations Descriptive of Its Scenery, and Biographical Sketches of Some of Its Prominent Men and Pioneers. Philadelphia: Brink, 1882.

History of Edgar County Courthouse. Paris, IL: Edgar County Historical Society, 1981.

History of Edgar County, Illinois. Chicago: LeBaron, 1879.

History of Logan County, Illinois: Its Past and Present. Chicago: Donnelly Lloyd, 1878.

History of Tazewell County, Illinois. Chicago: Chapman Brothers, 1879.

Holder, William. "Saltonstalls in Tazewell County." Unpublished memorandum, 2004. Private collection.

Holzer, Harold, ed. *Lincoln as I Knew Him: Gossip, Tributes, and Revelations from His Best Friends and Worst Enemies*. Chapel Hill, NC: Algonquin, 1999.

———. *Lincoln at Cooper Union, the Speech That Made Abraham Lincoln President*. New York: Simon and Schuster, 2004.

———. *Lincoln, President-Elect: Abraham Lincoln and the Great Secession Winter 1860–1861*. New York: Simon and Schuster, 2008.

———, ed. *Lincoln's White House Secretary, The Adventurous Life of William O. Stoddard*. Carbondale: Southern Illinois University Press, 2007.

Horwitz, Morton J. *The Transformation of American Law 1780–1850: The Crisis of Legal Orthodoxy*. Cambridge, MA: Harvard University Press, 1977.

Howard, Robert P. *Illinois, a History of the Prairie State*. Grand Rapids, MI: Eerdmans, 1972.

Howard, Ruth. Collection. Vermilion County Historical Society, Danville, Illinois.

Howells, W. D. *Life of Abraham Lincoln*. Springfield, IL: Abraham Lincoln Association, 1938. Citations are to the reprint edition. First printed 1860 by Follett, Foster, Columbus, Ohio.

Hubbard, Gurdon Saltonstall. *Incidents and Events in the Life of Gurdon Saltonstall Hubbard*. Chicago: Rand McNally, 1888.

Hunt, Aurora. *Kirby Benedict, Frontier Federal Judge: An Account of Legal and Judicial Development in the Southwest, 1853–1874, with Special Reference to the Indian, Slavery, Social and Political Affairs, Journalism, and a Chapter on Circuit Riding with Abraham Lincoln in Illinois*. Glendale, CA: Clark, 1961.

Hunt, Eugenia Jones, *My Personal Recollections of Abraham and Mary Todd Lincoln*. Peoria, IL: Moser, 1966.

Iles, Elijah. *Sketches of Early Life and Times in Kentucky, Missouri, and Illinois*. Springfield, IL: Springfield, 1883.

Illinois History and Lincoln Collection. University of Illinois Library, Urbana, Illinois.

Illinois State Archives, Springfield, Illinois.

Illustrated Historical Atlas Map of Vermilion County. Chicago: Brink, 1875.

Jenison, Ned, ed. *Family Traditions, Celebrating Illinois Newspaper History*. Paris, IL: Paris Beacon News, 2002.

Johannsen, Robert W. *Stephen A. Douglas*. New York: Oxford University Press, 1973.

Johns, Jane Martin. *Personal Recollection of Early Decatur, Abraham Lincoln, Richard J. Oglesby and the Civil War*. Decatur, IL: Daughters of the American Revolution, Decatur Chapter, 1912.

Jones, Edgar DeWitt. *Lincoln and the Preachers*. New York: Harper, 1948.

Jones, Lottie E. *History of Vermillion County, Illinois: A Tale of Its Evolution, Settlement, and Progress for Nearly a Century*. Chicago: Pioneer, 1911.

Illinois. General Assembly. Senate. *Journal of the Senate for the Eleventh General Assembly of the State of Illinois*. Vandalia, IL: Whitten, 1838.

Illinois. General Assembly. Senate. *Journal of the Senate of the Twenty-First General Assembly of the State of Illinois*. Springfield, IL: Bailhache and Baker, 1859.

Journal of the House of Representatives of the Eleventh General Assembly, Springfield, Illinois, of the State of Illinois. Springfield, IL: Walters, 1839.

Journal of the House of Representative of the Thirteenth General Assembly of the State of Illinois. December 5, 1842. Springfield, IL: Walters, 1842.

King, Willard L. *Lincoln's Manager David Davis*. Cambridge, MA: Harvard University Press, 1960.

Krause, Susan. *From Log Cabins to Temples of Justice, Courthouses in Lincoln's Illinois: A Publication of the Lincoln Legal Papers*. Papers of Abraham Lincoln. Springfield, IL: Illinois Historic Preservation Agency, 2000.

———. *Judging Lincoln: The Bench in Lincoln's Illinois*. Papers of Abraham Lincoln. Springfield, IL: Illinois Preservation Agency, 2002.

Krause, Susan, Kelley A. Boston, and Daniel W. Stowell. *Now They Belong to the Ages, Abraham Lincoln and His Contemporaries in Oak Ridge Cemetery*. Papers of Abraham Lincoln. Springfield, IL: Illinois Historic Preservation Agency, 2005.

Kyle, Otto R. *Abraham Lincoln in Decatur*. New York: Vantage, 1957.

Lamon, Ward Hill. *The Life of Abraham Lincoln from His Birth to His Inauguration as President*. 1872. Reprint, Lincoln: University of Nebraska Press, 1999.

———. *Recollections of Abraham Lincoln, 1847–1865*. Chicago: McClurg, 1895.

Leroy, David H. *Mr. Lincoln's Book: Publishing the Lincoln Douglas Debates*. Chicago: Oak Knoll, 2009.

Lincoln, Abraham. *The Collected Works of Abraham Lincoln*. Edited by Roy P. Basler. 9 vols. New Brunswick, NJ: Rutgers University Press, 1953–55.

———. Collection. Abraham Lincoln Presidential Library and Museum, Springfield, Illinois.

———. Robert Todd Lincoln Collection of the Papers of Abraham Lincoln. Manuscript Division, Library of Congress, Washington, DC: American Memory Project, 2000–2001.

Lincoln Centennial Association. Abraham Lincoln Presidential Library and Museum, Springfield, Illinois.

Lincoln Heritage Museum, Lincoln College, Lincoln, Illinois.

Lincoln: Prelude to the Presidency. Prod. Alison Davis Wood. Dir. Tim Hartin. Urbana, IL: WILL-TV, 2009.

Linder, Usher F. *Reminiscences of the Early Bench and Bar of Illinois*. Chicago: Chicago Legal News, 1879.

Lloyd, Katherine. "William Williamson, First Sheriff of Shelby County." *Shelby County Ancestors* 28, no. 1, January 2006, 7.

Logan, Stephen T. "Stephen T. Logan Talks about Lincoln." *Bulletin of the Lincoln Centennial Association* 12 (1 September 1928): 1–5.

Lohman, Karl B. *Historical Map of Urbana, Illinois*. 1912.

Lothrop, J. S. *Champaign County Directory with History of the Same*. Chicago: Rand McNally, 1871. Reprint, Champaign, IL: Maxiprint, 1975. Citations are to the 1975 edition.

Macon County Historical Society, Decatur, Illinois. *The Lincolns, the Hanks, and Macon County, Illinois*. Decatur, IL: Macon County Historical Society, n.d.

Madison County Historical Museum and Archival Library, Edwardsville, Illinois.

Martin, Ivory John, and Robert Eden Martin, eds. *History of Moultrie County and Sullivan, Illinois*. Chicago: Martin, 1990.

Martin, John Barlow. *Adlai Stevenson of Illinois: The Life of Adlai E. Stevenson*. Garden City, NY: Doubleday, 1976.

Matheny, James H. "History of Springfield." *Springfield City Directory 1857–58*. 5–11. Reprint, Springfield: Sangamon County Genealogical Society, 1999.

Mathews, Milton W., and Lewis A. McLean. *Early History and Pioneers of Champaign County*. Urbana, IL: Champaign County Herald, 1886.

McCollum, Daniel. "Fort Clark/Bloomington Road." *Champaign County History Quarterly* 2, no. 1 (2002): 6–13.

McCormick, Mike. "Wabash Valley Resident William P. Dole Was Advisor to President Lincoln," *Terre Haute (IN) Tribune Star*, December 14, 2003, and "William P. Dole," *Terre Haute (IN) Tribune Star*, sec. D, William Dole file, Edgar County Historical Society, Paris, Illinois.

McDermott, Stacy Pratt. "Charles Wells in Lincoln's Springfield." Conference on Illinois History. Illinois Historic Preservation Agency, Springfield, Illinois. October 2002.

———. *"Spink v. Chiniquy." Lincoln Legal Briefs* 77, January–March 2006, 2–4.

McIntyre, Duncan T. "Lincoln and the Matson Slave Case." *Illinois Law Review* 1, no.6 (1907): 386–91.

McLean County Museum of History. Archives. Bloomington, Illinois.

McLean County Historical Society. *Meeting of the May 29, 1900, Commemorative of the Convention of May 29, 1856 That Organized the Republican Party in the State of Illinois*. Edited by Ezra M. Prince. Transactions of the McLean County Historical Society, Bloomington, Illinois. Bloomington, IL: Pantagraph Printing and Stationery, 1900.

———. *School Record of McLean County and Other Papers*. Vol. 2. Transactions of the McLean County Historical Society, Bloomington, Illinois. Bloomington, IL: Pantagraph Printing and Stationery, 1903.

———. *War Record McLean County and Other Papers*. Vol. 1. Transactions of the McLean County Historical Society, Bloomington, Illinois. Bloomington, IL: Pantagraph Printing and Stationery, 1903.

McPheeters, Addison. "Illinois Commentary, the Reminiscences of Addison McPheeters." *Journal of the Illinois State Historical Society* 63, no. 2 (1974): 212–26.

Memories of Abraham Lincoln in Edgar County, Illinois. Paris, IL: Edgar County Historical Society, 1925.

Memorials of the Life and Character of Stephen T. Logan. Springfield: Rokker, 1882.

Merriman, C. P. *History of McLean County, Illinois: Portraits of Early Settlers and Prominent Men*. Chicago: LeBaron, 1879.

Miers, Earl Schenk, ed.-in-chief. *Lincoln Day by Day a Chronology 1809–1865*. 3 vols. Washington, DC: Lincoln Sesquicentennial Commission, 1960.

Miller, R. D. *History of Menard and Mason Counties, Illinois*. Chicago: Baskin, 1879.

Miller, William Lee. *Lincoln's Virtues, an Ethical Biography*. New York: Knopf, 2002.

———. *President Lincoln: The Duty of a Statesman*. New York: Knopf, 2008.

Moore, Marion. "Lincoln in Tolono." Tolono Topics. Tolono, IL: Self-published, 1979.

———. "Visits by Train from Abraham Lincoln to Tolono, Illinois." Unpublished manuscript, ca. 1979. Archives, the Tolono Public Library, Tolono, Illinois.

Moore, Roy L. *History of Woodford County*. Eureka, IL: Woodford County Republican, 1910.

Morehouse, Frances Milton I. *The Life of Jesse W. Fell*. Illinois Studies in the Social Sciences, vol. 5, no. 2, 9–129. Urbana: University of Illinois, 1916. New York: Johnson, 1967.

Moses, John. *Illinois Historical and Statistical*. 2 vols. Chicago: Fergus, 1889.

Moultrie County Historical and Genealogical Society. *Lincoln's Footsteps*. Sullivan, IL: Moultrie County Historical and Genealogical Society, 1973.

———, Sullivan, Illinois.

Myers, Jean. *Justice Served, an Essay: Abraham Lincoln and the Melissa Goings Case*. Metamora, IL: Self-published, 2007.

Nelson, William E., ed. *City of Decatur and Macon County, Illinois*. 2 vols. Chicago: Pioneer, 1910.

Newman, Ralph G. *In This Sad World of Ours Sorrow Comes to All*. Springfield, IL: Illinois State Historical Society, 1965.

Nicolay, John G., and John Hay. "Abraham Lincoln: A History." *Century Illustrated Monthly Magazine*, 33 no. 11, November 1886–April 1887, 250–78.

Oakes, James. *The Radical and the Republican—Frederick Douglass, Abraham Lincoln, and the Triumph of Antislavery Politics*. New York: Norton, 2007.

Oakey, Charles Cochran. *Greater Terre Haute and Vigo County: Closing the First Century's History of City and County, Showing the Growth of their People, Industries and Wealth.* 2 vols. Chicago: Lewis, 1908.

O'Donnell, Dorothy Miller. *The Life of Judge Joseph O. Cunningham of Urbana, Illinois.* Urbana, IL: Self-published, 1963.

"Official Account of the Convention." McLean County Historical Society, *Meeting of the May 29, 1900, Commemorative* 148–64.

"Official Map of the Lincoln National Memorial Highway of the State of Illinois." State of Illinois, ca. 1930. Vertical File, Christian County Historical Society, Taylorville, Illinois.

Oldroyd, Osborne, H. *The Lincoln Memorial: Album—Immortelles: Original Life Pictures, with Autographs, from the Hands and Hearts of Eminent Americans and Europeans, Contemporaries of the Great Martyr to Liberty, Abraham Lincoln.* New York: Carleton, 1882.

Onstot, T. G. *Lincoln and Salem, Pioneers of Mason and Menard Counties: Made Up of Personal Reminiscences of an Early Life in Menard County, Which We Gathered in a Salem Life from 1830 to 1840, and a Petersburg Life from 1840–1850; Including Personal Reminiscences of Abraham Lincoln and Peter Cartright.* Forest City, IL: Self-published, 1902.

Orme, William W., Papers. Illinois History and Lincoln Collections. University of Illinois Library, Urbana, Illinois.

Ostendorf, Lloyd. *Lincoln's Photographs—A Complete Album.* Dayton, OH: Rockywood, 1998.

Palmer, John. *The Bench and Bar of Illinois, Historical and Reminiscent.* 2 vols. Chicago: Lewis, 1899.

Past and Present of the City of Decatur and Macon County, Illinois. Chicago: Clarke, 1903.

Past and Present of Vermilion County, Illinois, Illustrated. Chicago: Clarke, 1903.

Past and Present of Woodford County, Illinois, Illustrated. Chicago: LeBaron, 1878.

Patton, Charles H. *Glory to God and the Sucker Democracy, a Manuscript Collection of the Letters of Charles H. Lanphier.* 5 vols. Springfield: Self-published, 1973.

Pavey, Roger D. *O. F. Harmon, a Reluctant Hero.* Danville, IL: Vermilion County Museum Society, 1999.

Pearre, O. F. *History of Livingston County, Illinois.* Chicago: LeBaron, 1878.

Pease, Theodore Calvin, ed. *Frontier State 1818–1848.* Vol. 2. *Centennial History of Illinois.* Springfield, IL: Illinois Centennial Commission, 1918.

———. *Illinois Election Returns 1818–1848.* Springfield. IL: Trustees of the Illinois State Historical Society, 1923.

Peoria County Historical Society. Special Collection Center, Cullom-Davis Library, Bradley University, Peoria, Illinois.

Perrin, William Henry, ed. *History of Crawford and Clark Counties.* Chicago: Baskin, 1883.

Phillips, Isaac N., ed. *Abraham Lincoln by Some Men Who Knew Him: Being Personal Recollections of Judge Owen T. Reeves, Hon. James S. Ewing, Col. Richard P. Morgan, Judge Franklin Blades, John W. Bunn.* Bloomington, IL: Pantagraph Printing and Stationery Co., 1910.

Piatt County Historical and Genealogical Society, Monticello, Illinois.

Piatt, Emma C. *History of Piatt County, 1883: Together with a Brief History of Illinois from the Discovery of the Upper Mississippi to the Present Time.* Evansville, IN: Unigraphic, 1977. First published 1883 by Shepard and Johnston, Chicago.

Plummer, Mark A. *Lincoln's Rail-Splitter: Governor Richard J. Oglesby.* Urbana: University of Illinois Press, 2001.

Porter, Maurice Graham. "Portrait of a Prairie Lawyer, Clifton H. Moore." Unpublished thesis, University of Illinois, 1960. Vespasian Warner Library, Clinton, Illinois.

Portrait and Biographical Album of Coles County, Illinois. Chicago: Chapman, 1887.

Portrait and Biographical Album of Vermilion and Edgar Counties, Illinois. Chicago: Chapman, 1889.

Portrait and Biographical Album of Woodford County, Illinois. Chicago: Chapman, 1889.

Portrait and Biographical Record of Christian County, Illinois. Chicago: Lake City, 1893.

Portrait and Biographical Record of Macon County, Illinois. Chicago: Lake City, 1893.

Portrait and Biographical Record, Tazewell and Macon Counties. Chicago: Biographical, 1894.

Power, John Carroll. *History of the Early Settlers of Sangamon County.* Springfield, IL: Wilson, 1876.

Pratt, Harry E. "Abraham Lincoln in Bloomington, Illinois." *Journal of the Illinois State Historical Society* 29, no. 1 (1936): 42–69.

———. "A Beginner on the Old Eighth Judicial Circuit." *Journal of the Illinois State Historical Society* 44, no. 3 (1951): 241–48.

———, ed. *Concerning Mr. Lincoln: In Which Abraham Lincoln Is Pictured as He Appeared to Letter Writers of His Time.* Springfield, IL: Abraham Lincoln Association, 1944.

———, ed. *Illinois as Lincoln Knew It, a Boston Reporter's Record of a Trip in 1847.* Springfield, IL: Abraham Lincoln Association, 1938.

———. "In Defense of Mr. Justice Brown." *Bulletin of the Abraham Lincoln Association* 56 (June 1939): 1–8.

———. "Lincoln and Douglas as Counsel on the Same Side." *American Bar Association Journal* 26, no. 3 (1940): 214.

———. "Lincoln's 'Jump' from the Window." *Journal of the Illinois State Historical Society* 48, no. 4 (1955): 456–61.

———. *The Personal Finances of Abraham Lincoln.* Springfield, IL: Abraham Lincoln Association, 1943.

Price, Norma Adams, and Paul Adams. *Twelve Momentous Years in the Other Atlanta, 1853–1865: With Post Civil War Glimpses of Central Illinois.* Tempe, AZ: Beverly-Merriam, 2000.

Prince, Ezra M. "A Day with Abraham Lincoln." Paper (10 pages, ca. 1900), folder 17, box 3, Vertical File, Ezra Prince Collection. McLean County Historical Society, Bloomington, IL.

———. "Gen. William Ward Orme." McLean County Historical Society, *War Record* 421–25.

Prince, Ezra M., and John Burnham, eds. *Historical Encyclopedia of Illinois and History of McLean County.* 2 vols. Chicago: Munsell, 1908.

Proceedings of the First Three Republican Conventions of 1856, 1860, and 1864, Includ-ing Pittsburgh in February 1856. Minneapolis, MN: Johnson, 1893.

Proceedings of the Republican National Convention. Albany, NY: Weed, Parsons, 1860.

Proceedings of the Republican State Convention Held at Springfield, Illinois, June 16, 1858. Springfield, IL: Bailhache and Baker, 1858.

Radford, B. J. "Abraham Lincoln as Remembered." *Metamora (IL) Herald*, August 24, 1928, 6.

———. *History of Woodford County.* Peoria, IL: Dowdell, 1877.

———. "Woodford County's Early History, Lincoln and Woodford County." *Wood-ford County Journal*, October 9, 1924.

Ray, P. Orman. *The Convention That Nominated Lincoln: An Address Delivered before the Chicago Historical Society on May 18, 1916, the Fifty-Sixth Anniversary of Lin-coln's Nomination for the Presidency.* Chicago: University of Chicago Press, 1916.

Reinking, Donna. *Lincoln in Bloomington-Normal: A Historical Tour of Lincoln Sites in Bloomington and Normal, Illinois.* Bloomington, IL: McLean County Historical Society, 1998.

Rice, Allen Thorndike, ed. *Reminiscences of Abraham Lincoln by Distinguished Men of His Time.* New York: North American, 1886.

Rice, James Montgomery. *Peoria City and County Illinois: A Record of Settlement, Or-ganization, Progress and Achievement.* 2 vols. Chicago: Clarke, 1912.

Richardson, Elmo R., and Alan W. Farley. *John Palmer Usher: Lincoln's Secretary of the Interior.* Lawrence: University of Kansas Press, 1960.

Richardson, Robert Dale. *Abraham Lincoln's Autobiography, with an Account of Its Origin and Additional Autobiographical Material.* Boston: Beacon, 1947.

Richmond, Mabel E. *Centennial History of Decatur and Macon County.* Decatur, IL: Decatur Review, 1930.

Richter, Donald G. *Lincoln, Twenty Years on the Eastern Prairie.* Mattoon, IL: United Graphics, 1999.

Riddle, Donald W. *Congressman Abraham Lincoln.* Urbana: University of Illinois Press, 1957.

———. *Lincoln Runs for Congress: A Publication of the Abraham Lincoln Association, Springfield, Illinois.* New Brunswick, NJ: Rutgers University Press, 1948.

Rogers, George S. *Christian County History.* Millennium ed. Taylorville, IL: Chris-tian County Historical Society, 2000.

Ruggles, James M. "History of Mason County." *History of Menard and Mason Coun-ties, Illinois.* Chicago: Baskin, 1879. 391–686.

Sage, Harold K., Collection. Milner Library, Illinois State University, Normal, Il-linois.

Sandburg, Carl. *Abraham Lincoln—The Prairie Years.* 2 vols. New York: Harcourt Brace, 1926.

Sangamon Valley Collection. Springfield Municipal Lincoln Library, Springfield, Illinois.

Sancken, Barbara. "Abraham Lincoln Slept Here—Honest!" Paper presented at meet-ing of Pontiac Dialectic Society, Pontiac, Illinois. May 14, 2001.

Schlenker, Alice McCarty. "The Resurrection of General Asahel Gridley." *Illinois Magazine* 18, no. 6 (1979): 8–12, 39–44.

Schnell, Christopher A. *Stovepipe Hat and Quill Pen: The Artifacts of Abraham Lincoln's Law Practice*. Papers of Abraham Lincoln. Springfield, IL: Illinois Historical Preservation Agency, 2002.

Schwartz, Thomas F. "You Can Fool All of the People—Lincoln Never Said That." *For the People: Newsletter of the Abraham Lincoln Association* 5, no. 4 (2003): 1, 3, 6.

Schwartz, Vanette. "Compilation of Illinois Presidential Election Statistics, 1856, 1860, 1864." 2009. Compilation from *Illinois Election Returns from Archives Ledgers 1818–1964*. Milner Library, Illinois State University, Normal, Illinois.

Scott, Emma J. "Underground Railroad." Paper, monthly meeting, Woodford County Historical Society, August 30, 1934.

Scott, Franklin William. *Newspapers and Periodicals of Illinois 1814–1879*. Springfield, IL: Trustees of the Illinois State Historical Library. Chicago: Lakeside, Donnelley, 1910.

[Scott, John M.] "Lincoln on the Stump and at the Bar." Undated transcript, enclosed in Scott to Ida Tarbell, Bloomington, Illinois, August 14, 1895. Ida Tarbell Papers, Allegheny College, Meadville, Pennsylvania.

Sears, Stephen W. *George B. McClellan—The Young Napoleon*. New York: Da Capo, 1988.

Selby, Paul, ed. "The Editorial Convention, February 22, 1856." McLean County Historical Society. *Meeting of the May 29, 1900, Commemorative* 30–43.

———. *Historical Encyclopedia of Illinois History of Sangamon County*. 2 vols. Chicago: Munsell, 1912.

———. *Lincoln's Life—Stories and Speeches by Paul Selby*. Chicago: Thompson and Thompson, 1902.

Shaw, Elvis. Biographical file. Edgar County Historical Society, Paris, Illinois.

Shelby County Historical and Genealogical Society. *Abraham Lincoln in Shelby County, Illinois*. Shelbyville, IL: Self-published, 2005.

Shonkwiler, Frank P., ed. *Historical Encyclopedia of Illinois and History of Piatt County*. 2 vols. Chicago: Munsell, 1917.

Simon, Paul. *Lincoln's Preparation for Greatness—The Illinois Legislative Years*. Urbana: University of Illinois Press, 1971.

Simpson, A. W. Brian. Introduction. *Commentaries of the Laws of England*. Vol. 2 *Of the Rights of Things*. Chicago: University of Chicago Press, 1979.

Smalling, Donna. *St. Joseph, Illinois Centennial 1972*. St. Joseph, IL: St. Joseph Centennial, 1972.

Smith, Caleb B. Papers. Indiana Historical Society, Indianapolis, Indiana.

Smith, C. Henry. *Metamora*. Bluffton, OH: Bluffton College Bookstore, 1947.

Smith, D. C. "Lincoln—Thornton Debate, June 15, 1856 at Shelbyville, Illinois." *Journal of the Illinois State Historical Society* 10, no. 1 (1917): 97–101.

Smith, John W. *History of Macon County, Illinois, from Its Organization to 1876*. Springfield, IL: Rokker's, 1876.

Sparks, Edwin Erle, ed. "The Lincoln-Douglas Debates of 1858." Lincoln Series 1, 1908, Collection of the Illinois State Historical Library, Illinois State Historical Library, Springfield, Illinois.

Spears, Judge Ron. *The Courthouses of Christian County, Illinois*. Taylorville, IL: Kennedy, 2002.

Special Collection Center. Cullom-Davis Library, Bradley University, Peoria, Illinois.

Stapp, Katherine. *Footprints in the Sands, Founders and Builders of Vermilion County, Illinois*. Danville, IL: Interstate, 1975.

Starr, John W., Jr. *Lincoln and the Railroads: A Biographical Study*. New York: Dodd, Mead, 1927.

Steiner, Mark E. *An Honest Calling, the Law Practice of Abraham Lincoln*. DeKalb: Northern Illinois University Press, 2006.

Stevenson, Adlai E. *Something of Men I Have Known: With Some Papers of a General Nature, Political, Historical, and Retrospective*. Chicago: McClurg, 1909.

Stevenson, Lewis G., ed. *Blue Book of the State of Illinois 1915–1916*. Springfield: State of Illinois, 1916.

Stewart, J. R. *Standard History of Champaign County, Illinois: An Authentic Narrative of the Past, with Particular Attention to the Modern Era in the Commercial, Industrial, Civic, and Social Development: A Chronicle of the People, with Family Lineage and Memoirs*. Chicago: Lewis, 1918.

Stoddard, William O. "A Journalist Sees Lincoln." *Atlantic Monthly*, January–June 1925, 171–77.

Stone, Paul L., ed. *Preserving the Past for the Future*. Sullivan, IL: Moultrie County Courthouse Centennial Celebration, 2006.

———. ed. *Untitled Compilation of Newspaper Accounts and Reminiscences of the Sullivan Confrontation*. Sullivan, IL: Moultrie County Historical and Genealogical Society, 2000.

Stowell, Daniel W. "Abraham Lincoln and the Contest for the General Land Office in 1849." Illinois History Symposium. Illinois State Historical Society, Jacksonville, Illinois. February 2009.

———. "Almost a Father to Me." *Lincoln Legal Briefs* 84 (October–December 2007), 1.

———, ed. *In Tender Consideration: Women, Families, and the Law in Abraham Lincoln's Illinois*. Urbana: University of Illinois Press, 2000.

———. *The Papers of Abraham Lincoln, Legal Documents and Cases*. 4 vols. Charlottesville: University of Virginia Press, Illinois Historic Preservation Agency, 2008.

———. "Women's Encounters with the Law." Stowell, *In Tender Consideration* 7–45.

Strange, Alexander T., ed. *Historical Encyclopedia of Illinois and History of Montgomery County*. Chicago: Munsell, 1918.

Strevell, Charles N. "As I Recall Them." 11–25. Livingston County Historical Society, Pontiac, Illinois.

———. *The Story of the Strevell Museum—A Lifetime Hobby*. Salt Lake City, UT: Board of Education, 1940.

Striner, Richard. *Father Abraham: Lincoln's Relentless Struggle to End Slavery*. Oxford: Oxford University Press, 2006.

Stringer, Lawrence B. *History of Logan County, Illinois*. Chicago: Pioneer, 1911.

Swett, Herbert. Diary. Private collection.

Swett, Leonard. *David Davis, Address before the Bar Association of the State of Illinois*. Self-published, 1886.

———. Papers. Abraham Lincoln Presidential Library and Museum, Springfield, Illinois.

Taylor, Charles W. *Biographical Sketches and Reviews of the Bench and Bar of Illinois*. Indianapolis, IN: Bench and Bar, 1895.

Tazewell County Genealogical Society, Pekin, Illinois.

Tazewell County Historical Society, Pekin, Illinois.

Temple, Sunderine (Wilson), and Wayne C. Temple. *Abraham Lincoln and Illinois' Fifth Capitol*. 1988. Mahomet, IL: Mayhaven, 2006.

Temple, Wayne C. "Delegates to the Illinois State Republican Nominating Convention in 1860." *Journal of the Illinois State Historical Society* 22, no. 3 (1999): 289–99.

———. "New Documents: A. Lincoln Lobbyist." *Journal of the Abraham Lincoln Association* 21, no. 2 (2000): 35–43.

———. "Oglesby Fence Rail Dealing and the 1860 Decatur Convention." *Journal of the Illinois State Historical Society* 54, no. 1 (1961): 5–24.

Thomas, Benjamin P. *Abraham Lincoln a Biography*. New York: Knopf, 1952.

———. "Abraham Lincoln Country Lawyer." Burlingame, *"Lincoln's Humor"* 139–52.

———. "Lincoln and the Courts, 1854–1861." Burlingame, *"Lincoln's Humor"* 153–88.

———. *Lincoln's New Salem*. Springfield, IL: Abraham Lincoln Association, 1934.

Thomas, Richard, Jr. "Caleb Blood Smith: Whig Orator and Politician—Lincoln's Secretary of Interior." PhD diss., Indiana University, 1969.

Thompson, Jack. "George W. Minier Steward of Souls and Soil." Thesis, Lincoln Christian Seminary, 1971.

Tilton, Clinton Clay. "John W. Vance." Stapp, *Footprints in the Sands* 5–6.

———. "Lincoln and Lamon: Partners and Friends." *Transactions of the Illinois State Historical Society for the Year 1931*. Springfield, IL: Illinois State Historical Society, 1931.

———. *Lincoln's Last View of the Illinois Prairies*. Danville, IL: Interstate, 1937.

Tolono Public Library Archives, Tolono, Illinois.

Towne, Stephen E. "Such Conduct Must Be Put Down: The Constable Arrest on Civil War History." Conference on Illinois History, Springfield, Illinois, Illinois Historical Preservation Agency, October 2005. Paper.

Tremont Museum of History, Tremont, Illinois.

Turley Cemetery. Rural Elkhart, Illinois, grave site of A. L. Dalby.

University of Illinois Library, Urbana, Illinois.

U.S. Census. *Champaign County, Illinois, 1860*. Washington, DC.

U.S. Census. *DeWitt County, Illinois, 1860*. Washington, DC.

Usher, John Palmer. Papers. Kansas State Historical Society, Topeka, Kansas.

Usher, John P., and Nelson H. Loomis. *President Lincoln's Cabinet. Speech by Usher in Wyandotte, Kansas, June 20, 1887*. Omaha: Self-published, 1925.

Van Sellar, H. *Historical Encyclopedia of Illinois and History of Edgar County*. Chicago: Munsell, 1905.

Verduin, Paul H. "A New Lincoln Discovery: Rebecca Thomas, His 'Revolutionary War Widow.'" *Lincoln Herald* 98, no. 1, 1996, 3.

Wakefield, Sherman Day. *How Lincoln Became President: The Part Played by Bloomington, Illinois, and Certain of Its Citizens in Preparing Him for the Presidency and Securing His Nomination and Election*. New York: Wilson-Erickson, 1936.

Wallace, Lew. *Lew Wallace, an Autobiography*. New York: Harper Brothers, 1906.

Walsh, Mark. Interview with author, October 30, 2005. Abraham Lincoln registration at the Delavan House, Delavan, Illinois, September 12, 1843.

Warnick Family Papers. Private collection.

Webber, Thompson R. Journal, April 22, 1828–September 26, 1833. Private collection.

Weik, Jesse W. "Lincoln and the Matson Negroes." *Arena* 17, no. 89 (1897): 752–58.

Weldon, Lawrence. "Reminiscences of Lincoln as a Lawyer in Illinois." *Magazine of History* 50, no. 2, 93–107.

Wheeler, Samuel. "The Road to Illinois: The Early Life of Leonard Swett." Conference on Illinois History, Illinois Historic Preservation Agency, Springfield, Illinois. October 2002.

White, Jesse. *Origin and Evolution of Illinois Counties*. Springfield, IL: Secretary of State, State of Illinois, 2000.

White, Ronald C., Jr. *A. Lincoln, a Biography*. New York: Random, 2009.

———. *The Eloquent President, a Portrait of Lincoln through His Words*. New York: Random, 2005.

Whitney, Henry Clay. *Life on the Circuit with Lincoln*. Edited by Paul M. Angle. Caldwell, ID: Caxton, 1940.

———. *Lincoln the Citizen*. Vol. 1. *A Life of Lincoln*. Edited by Marion Mills Miller. New York: Baker and Taylor, 1908.

Williams, Jack Moore. *History of Vermilion County*. Topeka, KS: Historical, 1930.

Williams, T. Harry. *Lincoln and His Generals*. New York: Knopf, 1952.

Williams-Woodbury Collection. Illinois History and Lincoln Collections. University of Illinois Library, Urbana, Illinois.

Wills, Garry. *Lincoln at Gettysburg, the Words That Remade America*. New York: Simon and Schuster, 1992.

Wilson, Charles Edwards, ed. *Historical Encyclopedia of Illinois and History of Coles County*. Chicago: Munsell, 1906.

Wilson, Curtis M. *Cherishing the Past: A History of the Community United Church of Christ 1853–2003*. Champaign, IL: Community United Church of Christ, 2005.

Wilson, Douglas L., and Rodney O. Davis, eds., with the assistance of Terry Wilson. *Herndon's Informants: Letters, Interviews, and Statements about Abraham Lincoln*. Urbana: University of Illinois Press, 1998.

———. *Honor's Voice—The Transformation of Abraham Lincoln*. New York: Knopf, 1998.

Wilson, Rufus Rockwell, ed. *Intimate Memories of Lincoln*. Elmira, NY: Primavera, 1945.

Winkle, Kenneth J. "Abraham Lincoln: Self-Made Man." *Journal of the Abraham Lincoln Association* 21, no. 2 (2000): 1.

———. *The Young Eagle—The Rise of Abraham Lincoln*. Dallas: Taylor, 2001.

Woldman, Albert A. *Lawyer Lincoln*. 1936. New York: Carroll and Graf, 2001.

Wolfe, David, ed. "Metamora: In Lincoln's Path." *Metamora (IL) Woodford County Old Settlers Association* 1, no. 1, June 1964.

Woodford County Historical Society, Eureka, Illinois.

Wright, Bob. *Danville, a Pictorial History*. St. Louis: Bradley, 1987.

Zall, Paul M., ed. *Abe Lincoln Laughing: Humorous Anecdotes from Original Sources by and about Abraham Lincoln*. Berkeley: University of California Press, 1982.

Interviews of Descendants of Lincoln Contemporaries

Lincoln Contemporary	Descendant	Date of Interview
Baber, A. J.	Bruce Baber, collateral (Paris, IL)	12/04/08
Davis, David	Sarah Butler and Susan Sears (Bloomington, IL)	04/07/08
Fell, Jesse	Davis U. Merwin (Bloomington, IL)	12/02/03
Fifer, Joe	Florence Bloomer (Bloomington, IL)	11/06/04
Fletcher, Job	Myra K. Fleming (Bloomington, IL)	12/15/03
Franklin, John	Barbara Alsup (Bloomington, IL)	10/04/05
	John Franklin (Lexington, IL)	11/03/06
Gere, John	French Fraker Jr., Champaign, IL)	04/14/05
Gillett, John Dean	Gillette Ransom and Lisa Pasquesi, (Elkhart, IL)	12/02/03
Hall, Ira B.	Mark Walsh, (Delavan, IL)	10/30/05
Harris, Benjamin	Melissa Chambers, (Champaign, IL)	07/14/06
Harris, John	Sarah Butler and Susan Sears, (Bloomington, IL)	04/07/08
	Dan Holder (Bloomington, IL)	03/05/05
	William Holder (Cameno Island, WA)	08/07/06
Hoblit, John, and Hoblit, Samuel	Susan Hoblit (Atlanta, IL)	12/02/03
Kellogg, Benjamin	David Radley (Peoria, IL)	02/19/08
Lanphier Charles H.	James W. Patton III	07/15/11
Lemmon, Elvira	Nyra Lehman (Bloomington, IL)	08/04/10
Major, Ben	DeAnne Major Dillard (Elgin, IL)	10/17/04
McPheeters, Addison	Janet Roney (Lovington, IL)	07/15/07
Prettyman, Benjamin S.	Emily Watts (Champaign, IL)	06/16/08
Saltonstall, Samuel	Sarah Butler and Susan Sears (Bloomington, IL)	04/07/08
	Dan Holder (Bloomington, IL)	03/05/05
	William Holder (Bloomington, IL)	08/07/08
Spawr, Jacob	Barbara Alsup (Bloomington, IL)	10/04/05
	John Franklin (Lexington, IL)	11/03/06
Ward, William	French Fraker Jr., collateral (Champaign, IL)	04/14/05
	Robert Fraker (Lanesboro, MA)	06/14/07
Warnick, William	Nancy Chapman (Blue Mound Township, IL)	10/17/04
	Dean T. Austin, Canton, Illinois	11/13/04
Webber, Thompson R.	Richard Theis (husband of Marilyn Webber Theis) (Urbana, IL)	09/17/06
	Carl Webber (Urbana, IL)	12/28/08

INDEX

Page numbers in **bold** refer to photographs.

Coles County (IL), 14, 50, 153, 179
Columbus Insurance Company v. Peoria Bridge Company, 164
Conkling, James C., 18, 67, 77, 131, 177, 192; as Republican State Convention delegate (1856), 192; and Springfield reading of Lincoln's letter, 248–49
Constable, Charles, 50, 120–21, 143; argument with Lincoln, 148; treason arrest of, 249
Constitutional Convention. *See* Illinois Constitutional Convention (1847)
Cooper Union speech, 223
Crockett, Elliot, 126, 181
Cunningham, Joseph O., 104, **105**, 172, 176, 196, 199; on Lincoln, 44, 258
[Hezekiah] Cunningham v. [William] Fithian, 110–11

Daily Pantagraph (Bloomington), 158, 175, 183, 221, 258; on Douglas, 199; on Lincoln, 182, 183, 198–99, 213–14, 216, 223, 257–58; on "Lost Speech," 178
Dane County (IL), 34, 130; name change to Christian County, 34
Danville (IL), 108, 110–11, 112, 113, 114, 116, 117, 153, 217; Lincoln in, 30, 43, 106, 107–8, 109, 110, 114, 174, 176, 186, 204–5, 215, 244; settlement of, 119–11; as Vermilion County seat, 107, 109
Danville Illinois Citizen, 62, 63, 120
Danville Independent, 30
Davenport, William, 77, 144
Davis, David, 2, 6, 32, 33, 37, **38**, 44–45, 69, 79, 90, 109, 145, 147, 172, 181, 255, 257; appointment to Supreme Court, 251–52; Bloomington home of, **38**, 39, 81, 198, 265n4, 271n3; on David Campbell, 53; as Eighth Circuit judge, 1, 2, 26, 37, 39, 61, 73, 74, 76, 84, 85, 87, 91, 93, 98, 100, 106, 108, 111, 112, 113, 114, 117, 120, 122, 123, 124, 126, 131, 185; friendship with Lincoln, 39, 40, 83, 102–3, 105, 115; financial support of Lincoln's candidacy, 235;

girth of, 32, 39, 94, 262n1; as key to Lincoln's election, 229, 230, 234–35, 236; as landowner, 80–81, 94; letters to Sarah, 39, 45, 53, 61, 62, 72–73, 116, 121, 165, 265n5; on Lincoln, 45, 46, 148; as Lincoln political supporter, 90, 91, 173, 191, 197, 211, 230, 231, 236, 241; and "orgamathorial court," 55; and railroad litigation, 162–63, 165, 166; as Republican National Convention delegate (1860), 225, 227, 230, 231, 233; on slavery, 181, 197
Davis, Levi, 83
Davis, Oliver, 30, 53, 54, 112, 116, 174, 175, 191, 229, 230, 235; as Danville attorney, 112–13; and railroad litigation, 140, 167
Davis, Sarah Walker, 37, **38**, 39, 115–16; on Lincoln, 39
Decatur (IL), 1–2, 3, 128, 174, 178, 224, 226–27; courthouse in, 13, 127; description of early, 128; effect of railroads on, 152, 153, 160, 161; growth, 3, 127, 160; Lincoln's arrival in, 12; as Macon County seat, 3, 11, 127; newspaper editors' meeting in (1856), 5–6; settlement of, 12; as state convention site (*see under* Illinois Republican Party)
Decatur Convention (1860). *See* Illinois Republican Party, state convention (1860)
Delavan (IL), 70
Democratic Party, 17, 148; and convention system, 142; division in (1860), 189, 208; and Illinois Convention (1856), 189; and Illinois Convention (1860), 237
Democratic Register (Springfield), 179
Democratic State Central Committee (IL), 68
DeWitt (IL), 54, 98. *See also* Marion (IL)
DeWitt County (IL), 106, 185, 199, 238; effect of railroads on, 152, 153, 159, 165, 166; on Eighth Circuit, 92–97; settlement of, 92

Guy C. Fraker, is now retired after 52 years of practicing law in Bloomington, Illinois and counties that were once part of Lincoln's Eighth Circuit. He also wrote *Looking for Lincoln in Illinois: A Guide to Lincoln's Eighth Judicial Circuit*, published by Southern Illinois University Press. He has spoken frequently and written extensively about Lincoln. He was a consultant on the award-winning PBS documentary, *Lincoln, Prelude to the Presidency* and cocurated *Prologue to the Presidency*, an exhibit on display at the David Davis Mansion in Bloomington, a State Historic Site. He served as an adviser to the National Lincoln Bicentennial Commission. He served a number of years as the initial chair of the board of *Looking for Lincoln*, the action arm of the Lincoln National Heritage Area, created by congress in 2009.